SERGEI RACHMANINOFF

Sergei Rachmaninoff

A LIFETIME IN MUSIC

by
SERGEI BERTENSSON
and
JAY LEYDA

with the assistance of SOPHIA SATINA

NEW YORK UNIVERSITY PRESS
WASHINGTON SQUARE · NEW YORK
1956

Preface

WITH a persistence that increased with age, Sergei Rachmaninoff devoted time and energy to the concealment of his personal life from all but a few intimates. His daughter, Irina Wolkonsky, says of his later years:

Father could be sociable only within a circle of intimate friends, and here, too, his sociability had a clearly defined limit that he never—or rarely— passed. This limit was plainly visible in all reference to his compositions. As for his emotions and inner feelings, he seldom articulated these in words. In general he was very stingy with words. This may be why he disliked interviews so much, and did all he could to avoid them. I remember well how he once said to someone in my presence that words are useless for such a purpose—that all he felt and experienced was told far better, more clearly and truthfully in his compositions, and also found expression in his playing.

Those who love Rachmaninoff's music and respect his art may welcome our attempt to show his life as well as his career, even though this may seem to flout his wishes and habits. In view of Rachmaninoff's successful veiling of his private life, it may surprise the reader that there is so much to be said about it. His letters have been our chief source. We are lucky that so much of his private correspondence has been preserved; in the new Russian edition of his *Letters* there are nearly 500 letters through 1917, and the Rachmaninoff Archive in this country, to which many of his correspondents have contributed, contains almost as many letters from the second half of his life.

As for interviews and remembered conversations, is it necessary to remind ourselves that these are to be read with a grain of doubt? It might have been safer to discard all these as a source, but we hesitated to discard their grain of truth, too.

Dates in Part I of the book may present a problem to the reader who has grown up with only one calendar. Until 1918 Russians used the Julian calendar, which was twelve days behind our Gregorian calendar in the nineteenth century, and thirteen days behind in the twentieth century. Throughout Part I letters and events are dated only by the Russian calendar except when Rachmaninoff writes from abroad, when the foreign date (called "new style") is used. On a few occasions, when there is the threat of further confusion—as when Rachmaninoff leaves Europe in February and arrives in Russia in January!—we give both dates.

Nor should Russian names alarm the reader; the difference between the appearance of given name and nickname is actually no greater than that of Robert and Bobby. Sergei becomes Seryozha and, more intimately, Seryozhenka. Natalia becomes Natasha and, at the end of a diminishing series, Natashechka. Sophia becomes Sonia, Sonichka, etc. Alexander—Sasha. Fyodor—Fedya. Vladimir—Volodya. Yevgeni—Zhenichka. Irina—Irinochka. Tatiana—Tania, Tanyushka. Formal address (the equivalent of our "Mr. Rachmaninoff") is the given name and the patronymic together, thus: Sergei Vasilyevich; his sister would be addressed as Yelena Vasilyevna. There has been no effort to make the spelling of certain Russian names conform to correct English transliteration when they have become familiar to us in European forms, such as Rachmaninoff, Tchaikovsky, and Chaliapin.

To anticipate the wonder at encountering programs described as containing both orchestral and chamber music, it should be explained that, until the 1920's, Russian concerts maintained this older European custom.

Rachmaninoff never felt secure in the English language (a fact that must have contributed something to his natural "stinginess with words") and was always reluctant to write in it. All his letters in English were either dictated by him in Russian or copied from drafts prepared for him. In Part II we have tried to indicate whether he wrote a letter in German or in French, sometimes by retaining his salutation in its original language.

Quoted sources, either in manuscript or in print, are traced in the notes, beginning on page 387. One source requires explanation. The text will give the reasons for Rachmaninoff's dislike of Oskar von Riesemann's biography, misnamed *Rachmaninoff's Recollections* (published in 1934 and copyright by Allen & Unwin Ltd.). As most of its biographical information was furnished by Sophia Satina, and often expanded by the biographer for art's sake, we have condensed as well as corrected quotation from this work. We are aware that this is not orthodox procedure, but we feel that this book's accuracy has been thus increased in the least obtrusive way.

The title page contains an understatement. Sophia Satina did far more than assist us in writing this biography of her cousin and brother-in-law. Without her the book could literally not have been. With a person less sensitive to biographical problems or less conscientious on matters of fact, this account of Rachmaninoff's life could easily have taken on the superficial and dry form of an "official" biography, and if the reader finds something better than that, he has Miss Satina to thank. We, too, thank her, and through her we also thank the other helping members of her family: the late Mme. Natalia Rachmaninoff, who presented the Rachmaninoff Archive to the Library of Congress, and her daughters, Mme. Irina Wolkonsky and Mme. Tatiana Conus, whose permissions made possible our use of the Archive.

We have benefited by many other kindnesses: Alexander Aslanov, Nikolai Avierino, and Mrs. Dagmar Barclay gave us Rachmaninoff letters and reminiscences; Robert Russell Bennett and Mikhail Bukinik sent vivid memories to us; Mme. Maria Chaliapin allowed us to print her husband's correspondence with Rachmaninoff, as did Abram Chasins his correspondence; Henry Cowell and the late Olin Downes gave us tangible and moral assistance; Mme. Vera Fokina permitted us to use both sides of Michael Fokine's working exchange with Rachmaninoff; Charles Foley and his staff helped; Mrs. Ossip Gabrilowitsch, Harry Glantz, and Mme. Olga Glazunova gave us permissions; both Edwin Franko Goldman and his son Richard provided new materials; Alexander Greiner (of Steinway & Sons) and Arthur Hirst permitted use of their Rachmaninoff documents; Josef Hofmann allowed us to quote liberally from letters sent to and received from the composer whom he calls "the only Sergei"; Mme. Nina Koshetz unselfishly permitted our use of letters that she had planned to print for the first time in her forthcoming memoirs; Miss Estelle Liebling and Nikolai Mandrovsky gave us permission to use letters exchanged with Rachmaninoff; Mme. Anna Medtner, Dimitri Mitropoulos, Benno Moiseiwitsch, Lawrence Morton, and Eugene

Ormandy gave us various important permissions and assistance; Nikolai Rashevsky, Nadia Reisenberg, Joseph Reither (of the Rachmaninoff Society*), and Earl Robinson helped us; Nicolas Slonimsky, despite his reservations as to both subject and treatment of this biography, was extremely helpful; Mr. and Mrs. Eugene Somov not only allowed us the freedom of their long, privileged correspondence with Rachmaninoff, but also helped us in many less noticed ways; Michael Stillman added to our lists of works and records; Leopold Stokowski permitted quotation of his letters to Rachmaninoff, and Alfred J. Swan allowed our broad use of his invaluable reminiscences of the Rachmaninoff family, originally published in *The Musical Quarterly;* Mrs. E. Tillett, Basil Verkholantzeff, Dr. John F. Williamson, Lady Jessie Wood, and Joseph Yasser gave us necessary permissions, and Mr. Yasser also contributed a great deal of his time, patience, and wisdom, and gave particular attention to problems offered by the First Symphony.

Our basic library was, of course, the Library of Congress, depository of the Rachmaninoff Archive; Edward Waters and his colleagues in the Music Division made this use a pleasure. Other co-operating libraries include the Los Angeles and New York Public Libraries, the Libraries of the University of California at Los Angeles, Northwestern University, and the University of Minnesota, and the Library for Intercultural Studies, New York City.

The staff of New York University Press faced new problems bravely, and Wilson Follett gave us much sensitive advice. Philip L. Miller prepared the discography and William T. Morris, Jr. the index, with an authority that makes us proud of these valuable adjuncts to our book.

S. B.
J. L.

---

* Some passages of this biography have previously appeared in the notes published with the records issued by the Rachmaninoff Society.

Contents

Sergei Vasilyevich Rachmaninoff

Born March 20 (old calendar), April 2 (new calendar), 1873

A LANDSCAPE of the Russian north country stretching to a rugged horizon, threaded by the breadth of the Volkhov River; the odors of new-mown hay and the smoke of fishermen's bonfires; a great house near enough to ancient Novgorod to catch the echoes of its old bells; a family that filled the house with exciting, pleasant motion—an overkind and expansive father, a loving but strict mother, the noise and gallop of children and horses through the vast acreage, and, most vivid of all, a protective grandmother who defended all Seryozha's pranks and mischief from the punishment that was due him: these are the impressions that Sergei Rachmaninoff would always recall when he tried to recapture the lovely, sunny, blurred memory of his childhood on the estate of Oneg.

Little else survived of these days that were so soon to end. Rachmaninoff had to turn to other members of the family to add any detail to this idyllic picture. He could vaguely remember, perhaps because he was so often told about it, sitting at a piano with his grandfather, Arkady Alexandrovich, and playing four-hand pieces with this amateur pupil of John Field. The boy's clearest memory of this piano was of being punished by being placed under it, or of crouching in a corner while someone, usually his mother or father, played it. He certainly never recalled a scene that was supposed to have occurred during a duet with his grandfather: through the open French windows a peasant woman comes in, waits for the music to end before asking for a cartload of straw to mend the roof of her hut; Grandfather Rachmaninoff, recognizing her as Seryozha's wet nurse, replies, "You deserve far more—see what a grandson you nursed for me! You could look all over Russia and not find another like him!"*

* Notes on sources of matter cited in the text begin on page 387.

Arkady Alexandrovich Rachmaninoff had a temperament and love for music that little suited the army career forced upon him; and of Arkady's nine children, Vasili Rachmaninoff had not been allowed to deviate from the approved pattern: at sixteen, volunteering to fight in the Caucasus against the rebel Shamil—a few more years in a fashionable Guards regiment stationed at Warsaw—all the formal dissipations required of a wellborn officer—and then marriage to wealthy Lubov Petrovna Butakova and settling on one of her parents' estates, Oneg. Wealth did not increase the stability of Seryozha's father, and the six children did not make him more provident, nor did marriage put an end to his perpetual courtships of every woman in range. One of his sisters writes of him:

He would play the piano for hours—not familiar pieces, but God knows what they were. However, I could listen to him forever. He often told quite fantastic stories—and finally began to believe his own fantasies. (His mother did not like this trait, and was inclined to blame it on the family of his grandmother, the Bakhmetyevs.) He was kind and considerate of others. He couldn't bear tears and would give all the money in his pocket to stop the tears of a child on the street.

This was not the sort of husband to make a wife's life a happy one, especially when Lubov Petrovna saw the five estates of her dowry slipping through his fingers. Her firmest support came from her mother, Seryozha's *babushka* Butakova, whose long life as a general's wife must have rewarded her with tolerance and efficiency. Grandmother Butakova's sole weakness was Seryozha, whom she openly spoiled and preferred over his brothers and sisters. Though both Sergei and his oldest brother Vladimir (Volodya) were being prepared for the *Corps des Pages,* where places awaited them as grandsons of General Butakov, Sergei's apparent talent for music was considered worth cultivation—possibly as a future officer's pastime.

The part Sergei took in the choice of his own career was recalled to him, fifty-four years later, by the governess who had played a role in that important decision. While living in Switzerland, in 1934, Rachmaninoff received a letter from Mme. Defert, who was then an old lady asking for an inscribed photograph; but in 1880 she was a young Swiss girl looking after his sisters Yelena and Sophia, while the two boys were taught by a Russian tutor, Dembrovsky:

Let me prove to you that I was a witness to the discovery of your gift for music. . . . You will recall that Madame your mother enjoyed accompanying my songs at the piano, but do you remember the day when an excursion was arranged for some guests, and how you stayed home with the pretext of not feeling well, and I was obliged to stay too and take care of you? A few minutes after all had departed you came to me and in your most cajoling way asked if you could play the beautiful piano that was never to be touched without supervision. When I was finally persuaded to allow this, you surprised me by suggesting that I sing the song your mother liked to hear and that you would accompany me. I did not take you seriously, but you insisted and I agreed. And how astonished I was to hear your small hands play chords that may not have been complete, but were certainly without a single wrong note. You made me sing *three times* Schubert's "Plainte d'une jeune fille" and I had to promise not to tell your mother how we spent the afternoon. Unfortunately—or rather, fortunately, I did not keep my word and told your mother that evening. Next morning the news was sent to your grandfather [Butakov], who arrived on the next train and ordered your father to go to Petersburg and bring back a good piano teacher from the Conservatory.

That teacher was Anna Ornatzkaya, a piano graduate of the St. Petersburg Conservatory, who took over Sergei's training.

Sergei's dreaming father lost the four other estates brought him by his wife, and finally Oneg too was placed on auction in 1882, and the suddenly impoverished Rachmaninoffs moved away from the Volkhov River to an unattractive and crowded flat in St. Petersburg. Soon after their arrival, a married sister of Vasili Rachmaninoff offered to take one of the children until they were settled, and the choice fell on nine-year-old Sergei. Thus his first weeks in St. Petersburg were with the Trubnikovs, whose earliest recollection of the boy was his independence. Whenever one of the family moved to give him a hand with anything, he would push the hand aside with a half-whispered *"Ya sam"* (Myself). "Myself" became his nickname among the Trubnikovs.

On the social level to which the Rachmaninoffs had fallen the

Corps des Pages was, of course, out of the question. Volodya entered a military school, and Seryozha, with the recommendation of his piano teacher, Ornatzkaya, was enrolled in the St. Petersburg Conservatory with a scholarship providing that he would later become a pupil of Professor Cross after graduating from Demyansky's class. The Rachmaninoffs, not long after their arrival in St. Petersburg, found themselves in a diphtheria epidemic. The eldest sister, Yelena, escaped by being at boarding school, and the youngest was protected, but the two older boys and their sister Sophia caught the disease; Volodya and Seryozha recovered—Sophia died.

By this time the domestic scene was painful for all concerned. The case against Vasili Rachmaninoff was apparent to all, even to his children. It was easy to blame him for the genteel penury toward which Lubov Petrovna and the children were clearly headed. Husband and wife passed from disagreement to disagreement, giving little attention to their children, who, left to themselves and deprived of former care and comforts, did not know what to do with themselves. Their country amusements had vanished, and there seemed no place for them in the rumbling, alien city. In all this restlessness the parents' disagreements naturally broke into quarrels, and despite repeated reconciliations there was at last a complete rupture. Avoiding a formal separation, and with divorce within the church an impossibility, Vasili Rachmaninoff agreed to leave St. Petersburg, placing his children in his wife's care.

All suffered in this separation, and the effect on Seryozha was noticeable, for he was already lonely without the companionship of Volodya, who now lived at the Cadet Corps and came home only for Sundays. Yelena, almost six years his senior, had come home to help her mother, but had little time for him. All his mother's time was devoted, hopelessly, to the organization of the housekeeping. The only pleasure that Seryozha could count on was the annual winter visit from Grandmother Butakova. He awaited her arrival with impatience, for not only did he need her kindness and concentration on him, but now that he was familiar with the geography of St. Petersburg he could show her all the cathedrals and churches he knew she loved to visit. When he brought his grandmother home from one of their church visits he would sit at their small piano and play over the chants they had just heard, and he always got a coin from her for his performance.

His studies at the Conservatory were not so rewarded. Before the chaos created by the diphtheria epidemic and his father's departure, Seryozha did his homework conscientiously and attended all his classes, both musical and extramusical, regularly. Then the upset home gave him more freedom than was good for him, and he grew quite lazy, strolling aimlessly through the city rather than attend classes in subjects that did not interest him. Between his skating and his hopping on to the rear of the horse-drawn streetcars, he somehow found time for his music classes, for there he could shine with an absolute minimum of preparation. Even the Rubetz class in music theory was no burden, for this teacher so admired Seryozha's perfect ear and pitch that he did not bother him with tedious assignments. When term examinations came, Seryozha at the piano was fine, but the marks for his general subjects became so disgraceful that he altered his report card before showing it to his mother. She had too much on her mind to detect the fraud.

Babushka Butakova gave Seryozha a most precious gift: the sun and air of the Novgorod countryside; for his second vacation she bought a farm, Borisovo, near the familiar Oneg landscape, just to make Seryozha's vacations healthier and happier. When in 1885 he failed in all his general subjects in the last spring examinations, the only punishment he feared was to be forbidden his vacation with his grandmother. His report card fraud could not be kept up forever; Anna Ornatzkaya heard that the Council of the Conservatory might take away the Cross scholarship from the mischievous boy, and she came to his mother to give her all the details that had been so carefully hidden from her. His grandmother again interceded for him and begged his mother for another chance—and the summer at Borisovo was not forbidden.

Idling in Borisovo was more fun than on St. Petersburg's streets. Even the dangerous hopping from horsecars had a superior game here: the fishing canoe, called a "killer," with its space for only one person with a single oar, and its constant risk of turning over with any careless movement. The balance of this boat and the enjoyment of swimming to shore whenever it overturned was Seryozha's never-ending joy at Borisovo. His grandmother imposed very limited duties on him; when she had guests he would sit at the piano, announce works by Chopin or Beethoven, and play improvisations of his own. His other duty, equally pleasurable, was to drive his grandmother to nearby convents and churches to listen to the chimes and the choirs. How short were the three months of summer!

The winter of 1884 was again spent in the family of his aunt Maria Arkadyevna Trubnikova, in St. Petersburg. His cousin Olga recalls a normally spirited "Myself," lazy only when duty approached.

He was eleven and I was six. Every night, when we went to bed, he would frighten me terribly. I would always be curious to know what was going on, and would peep from my bed and as soon as he saw me do this, he would throw the sheet over his head and stalk towards me. I would hide beneath the pillows in my fear. Then I remember the Sundays when his older brother Volodya visited us from his military school, and such rows would start that my nurse Feofila almost went mad. Papa and mama would go out calling in the evenings. Then the boys would set up their "toboggan slide." They would take out all the extra boards used for the dining room table and run them from the tall sideboard to the table, and from the table to the floor, sliding down them and pushing me down them while the nurse screamed that they would break my neck. And I remember how Seryozha and I played store. He was always the salesman and I was the customer. I often heard that papa was angry with him for being such a lazybones.

When "lazybones" grew up he often spoke of how greatly influenced he had been by the musical tastes and accomplishments of his sister Yelena. As a child she had entertained her parents and friends with her musical ability, just as Seryozha now used his astonishing natural ability to slide through the Conservatory. At the age of sixteen she developed a beautiful voice—a contralto with a quite individual tone color. She sometimes allowed Seryozha to accompany her, and it was she who introduced him to Tchaikovsky's music, just then becoming popular. He was so proud to accompany her when she sang a song like "None But the Lonely Heart," and so entranced with the beauty of her voice, that he often grew too absorbed to realize that he was not following her very helpfully, and Yelena would dismiss her brother-accompanist angrily.

Yelena adored her father and maintained more regular communication with him than did any other member of the family. She spent her summers on the estate of Grandmother Rachmaninoff or with some other relative of her father's, where he could also come for a while. In 1885 she was invited to summer on the estate of his sister, Aunt Anna Pribitkova, in the state of Voronezh. On her way there she stopped off in Moscow with the idea of auditioning at the Bolshoi Opera, and her voice and talent made such an impression that she was at once engaged to join the company in the autumn, and an outstanding singer, Pryanishnikov, offered to coach her for her first roles. Public musical fame was about to come to a member of the Rachmaninoff family. At the end of summer, just as she was preparing to leave her aunt's estate to assume her position in Moscow, she fell ill and was soon dead, of pernicious anemia.

When Seryozha, in Borisovo for the last time, heard of his sister's death, it made his future even darker. He too was being sent to Moscow, and the thought that Yelena would also be working in Moscow had made the prospect of departure from his family less painful. But now . . .

His future had been decided in that spring of 1885 when the threat of dismissal from the Conservatory had become very real. His mother did not know what to do with him, and she was disturbed to realize that she was largely to blame for all that had happened. She had not watched over Seryozha carefully enough, and she doubted that she would do any better in the future; her talented son would waste his talents and drift away from his real vocation of music. She appealed to Alexander Siloti, who had recently returned to St. Petersburg in triumph as Liszt's favorite pupil. Here was Seryozha with his remarkable musical gifts and an equally remarkable gift for evading studies of any sort: what was to be done with him? He was Siloti's responsibility, too, for Siloti's mother was the sister of Sergei's father. Siloti listened to Sergei's playing, tested his ear and had a talk with him, and then gave his decision to Lubov Petrovna: the boy had great ability and must continue his musical studies—his laziness might be cured by separating him from his family and St. Petersburg. "I know only one man who can help him—my former teacher, Zverev. The boy must go to Moscow and submit completely to his discipline." So it was decided. At the end of this summer, he was to live at Nikolai Zverev's and take classes at the Moscow Conservatory. Everything that his cousin Siloti told him about Zverev and Zverev's discipline scared him thoroughly.

It was a very unhappy boy that Grandmother Butakova put on the Moscow train at Novgorod. No matter how painful this separation from her grandson was for her, she realized that the change would be best for him. That morning she had packed his linen, presented him with a gray jacket she had had made for him, and sewed a hundred rubles into the blessed amulet she placed around his neck. Then they drove to one of her favorite convents to attend a service she had ordered for the occasion. Finally they had to part. When she gave him her farewell blessing, and he boarded the train, he wept bitterly.

Zverev and His Cubs

It was in Moscow that Rachmaninoff the musician was born. Music as a game—the duets with his grandfather, the relaxed lessons with Anna Ornatzkaya, his grandmother's rewards—all that was past, and had little relation to the intense training that now filled every waking moment of his every day.

His first three days in Moscow were spent with his aunt, Siloti's mother, but after she delivered him into the care of his new master, Zverev, the boy saw little of her or of any other relatives living or visiting in Moscow. Nikolai Zverev was known as an excellent but severe piano teacher, trained by Dubuque and Henselt. He dictated his own terms to any pupil who wanted his lessons, and enough rich pupils accepted his terms to afford him a handsome living. When a needy pupil showed unusual gifts, Zverev's generosity matched his severity. This year Rachmaninoff was one of three pupils whom Zverev brought into his home, on the condition that he could supervise their lives and interests while they continued piano lessons with him at the Conservatory. Along with Leonid Maximov (known as Lyolya or Lo) and Matvei Pressman (known as Motya or Mo), Seryozha Rachmaninoff paid Zverev nothing for his board and clothes, in addition to which there was a steady stream of tickets for concerts, operas, plays that Zverev demanded his boys attend for cultural background. In exchange for all this the three boys had to obey his every command and recognize no other authority. Separation from their families was, of course, essential. These conditions must have seemed a fair price to pay for the color and richness that Nikolai Zverev attached to their lessons.

Moscow's musical life in the eighties was an emotional experience, and Zverev, in its center, made this the normal atmosphere breathed by his three "sons." In 1885, four of the Mighty Five of the Russian "national" group were still alive and active; only Musorgsky was gone—dead prematurely, in 1881. Balakirev, Rimsky-Korsakov, and Cui lived in St. Petersburg and saw little of Moscow; Borodin, with two more years to live, divided his life impartially between his Petersburg and Moscow friends. It was Tchaikovsky who was the acknowledged great man of Moscow music. His influence on audiences and musicians was tremendous; one use he made of his power this year was to seat the twenty-eight-year-old Taneyev in the Director's chair of the Moscow Conservatory. For Lyadov, teaching at the St. Petersburg Conservatory was an excuse for not composing. The infant prodigy Glazunov was growing up, warmed by successes abroad. Anton Rubinstein was going blind, but continued his dual career of composer and pianist. The musical worlds of both Russian capitals respected Zverev as teacher and enjoyed him as convivial companion. His house was headquarters for all musical travelers. And his pupils were always on show—"Listen to what *my* pupils can do!"

With the recommendation of Siloti the twelve-year-old Rachmaninoff came to Zverev, played some pieces (an *étude* by Reinecke made an especially favorable impression), and was accepted by the teacher on his usual conditions; the building of a musician had begun.

The three boys saw as much of Zverev's spinster sister as of Zverev, for when he left the house at eight each morning (for his classes at the Conservatory and for his numerous private lessons), she was in charge of house and boys, and she ran both with unforgettable discipline. Anna Sergeyevna sternly watched over their homework for the Conservatory and their daily practice of three hours each. "Motya" Pressman recalled:

This practice had to begin at 6 A.M., and we took turns in being the one to get up at that hour. No excuse was ever allowed—if a pupil had been at a play or concert the night before, or had not gotten to bed until 2 A.M.—nothing could change this schedule: he whose turn it was to begin at 6 would get up and crawl to that piano, no matter what. And woe to him if any sleepiness was betrayed in his playing—Zverev would storm in, a frightening figure in underwear, with a horrible shout and sometimes a hard smack. The sleepy pupil would instantly wake up, and play with new attention.

It was Maximov who got most of the smacks, from both Zverev and Anna Sergeyevna; he spent an enormous amount of ingenuity in trying to slice five minutes from either end of his practice period.

Zverev kept his pupils close to the piano, without letting them stray into the fields of theory and harmony, at least during their first year with him. Yet he did consider that the cultivation of musical taste was essential to their piano training, and for this purpose engaged an elderly musician, a Mme. Belopolskaya, to visit the house every week to play four-hand arrangements of the classical repertoire in chamber and symphonic music with each of the boys in turn. Zverev's own lessons with the boys were always awaited with great eagerness. The earliest of some fragmentary reminiscences (dictated by Rachmaninoff years later for an American journalist) concerns the greatest benefit of Zverev's teaching arrangement:

Zverev turned his home from what might have been a musical prison into a musical paradise. From a very strict teacher, he completely changed on Sundays. That afternoon and evening he always kept open house for the greatest figures in the Moscow world of music. Tchaikovsky, Taneyev, Arensky, Safonov, Siloti, as well as university professors, lawyers, actors, would drop in, and the hours passed in talk and music. For us boys the delightful feature of these Sundays was that Zverev would not permit any of the great musicians present to touch the piano, unless by way of some explanation or criticism. For we, not they, were the solo artists on these occasions. Our impromptu performances were Zverev's greatest joy. No matter what we played, his verdict was always "Fine! Well done! Excellent!" He let us play anything we felt like playing, and would call on his guests to bear him out in his opinion of us.

I cannot adequately describe what a spur to our ambition was this opportunity to play for the greatest musicians in Moscow, and to listen to their kindly criticism—nor what a stimulant it was to our enthusiasm.

As pianist and as teacher Zverev himself was something of a mystery. Leonid Sabaneyev, the music critic, who knew him a few years later, described him as tall, handsome, with a "Lisztian" head and the reputation of having wasted two fortunes. He was known to have been an intimate friend of Nikolai Rubinstein, and this credit was so potent that no one dared ask him to play the piano himself. In fact, no one could be found who had *ever* heard him play. But all acknowledged that "he had some sort of intuitive capacity for teaching a love of music."

Among the musical great who visited Moscow it was Anton Rubinstein who seems to have caused the most excitement among Zverev's
boys. He came in the fall of 1885 to conduct the hundredth performance of his opera *Demon* at the Bolshoi Theater. Taneyev, as
new director of the Conservatory, asked Rubinstein to honor the
institution by listening to a recital by some of its most gifted pupils.
On this occasion two girls sang, and two twelve-year-old piano students played—Joseph Lhévinne and Sergei Rachmaninoff (who
played Bach's English Suite in A minor). Rachmaninoff spoke of
this to his biographer, Oskar von Riesemann:

In the evening Zverev gave a dinner for Rubinstein at the house,
inviting about twenty people. As a reward for my "good playing" that
morning I was chosen to lead the guest of honor in, by the coat-tails, for
he was almost blind then. We three were seated far from him, so I do not
recall much that he said. Someone asked him about a young pianist (it
may have been Eugen d'Albert), inquiring how he liked his playing. He
thought a moment, and said, "Nowadays everybody plays well."

To show Europe how much better than "well" the piano could
be played Rubinstein was just then preparing his unprecedented
"historical concerts"—a series illustrating the history of piano literature from Bach and Couperin through Scarlatti, Mozart, Beethoven,
Chopin, to a grand finale of Liszt and Rubinstein's Russian contemporaries. Moving triumphantly from Berlin back to his native
country, he set up his concert schoolroom during January and February 1886, in St. Petersburg and Moscow simultaneously. For seven
weeks Rubinstein devoted the first half of each week to his Moscow
subscribers, shuttling to his Petersburg audiences for week-end concerts there. The Moscow concerts were given on Tuesday evenings
at the splendid Nobility Hall and were then repeated for nonpaying
student audiences on the following mornings at the plainer German
Club. Zverev and his three boys were present evenings and mornings,
without fail.

In this way I heard the program of these historical concerts twice, and
was able each Wednesday morning to re-examine my impressions of the
previous evening. It was less his magnificent technique that held one
spellbound than the profound, spiritually refined musicianship that

sounded from each work he played. I remember how deeply I was affected by his playing of Beethoven's *Appassionata,* and Chopin's Sonata in B-flat minor. Once he repeated the whole finale of the Chopin Sonata, perhaps because he had not succeeded in the short crescendo at the close as he would have wished. I could have listened to this passage over and over again.

One of Rubinstein's visits to Moscow is mentioned in Tchaikovsky's diary, for February 3, 1886, an entry that contains his earliest reference to Zverev's ménage. What a dazzling profusion of tipsy musical stars to be whirled past three pairs of enchanted young eyes!

At the Conservatory concert at 3 P.M. with Anton Rubinstein. Dinner at Zverev's. Madame Pabst and "the bottle." Whist. Arensky's foolishness and his excited condition.

Later in the year Tchaikovsky noted: "Appearance of Zverev and Co. Drunkenness."

At the end of May Zverev took his three charges with him to the Crimean estate of the Moscow millionaire Tokmakov, to whose children Zverev was giving expensive piano lessons. It was not to be any carefree vacation for his boys—that would not be consistent with his program. Taking a cottage near the millionaire's estate, Zverev placed the three in the care of Ladukhin, who taught theory and harmony at the Conservatory. Ladukhin's task was to cram a whole course in elementary theory and basic harmony into Zverev's prodigies, to prepare them for entry into Arensky's harmony course in the autumn term. This intense exposure to an exciting new world of music seems to have had an immediate effect on Rachmaninoff. Pressman recalls:

My sojourn in the Crimea remains in my memory largely because of Rachmaninoff; it was there that he began, for the first time, to compose. As if it were yesterday I remember how he grew quite pensive, even gloomy. He was after solitude, and I noticed that as he walked about, he lowered his head or fixed his eyes on some distant point, and at the same time whistled almost inaudibly and gestured as if he were conducting. This state lasted for several days. Finally, and mysteriously, choosing a moment when no one else was about, he beckoned me to the piano and began to play. When he finished, he asked me: "Do you know what that was?" "No," I replied, "I don't." "And how did you like this pedal point in the bass against the chromatics in the upper register?" he questioned me closely. Considering my answer satisfactory, he announced with a self-satisfied air: "I composed it myself, and I dedicate this piece to you."

Ladukhin apparently accomplished his mission with total success, for all three boys passed their fall entrance examinations in theory and were enrolled in Arensky's harmony class at the Moscow Conservatory. For the grand opening of the new school year Tchaikovsky arrived in Moscow, probably as bored as any of the students on September 1: "Dedication service at the Conservatory. Reading of the report. Kashkin's speech on Liszt was endless." Most of the students attending that occasion must have admired Tchaikovsky above all other living composers, and at least one of them—Rachmaninoff—idolized him. The younger composer never forgot the friendship that had begun at Zverev's:

To him I owe the first and possibly the deciding success in my life. It was my teacher Zverev who took me to him. Tchaikovsky at that time was already world-famous, and honored by everybody, but he remained unspoiled. He was one of the most charming artists and men I ever met. He had an unequaled delicacy of mind. He was modest, as all really great people are, and simple, as very few are. (I met only one other man who at all resembled him, and that was Chekhov.)

In the previous spring Erdmannsdörfer had introduced an important work by Tchaikovsky—the *Manfred* Symphony—at the concerts of the Imperial Russian Music Society. When the published score appeared, Rachmaninoff gave Zverev a pleasant surprise by producing a four-hand piano arrangement of Tchaikovsky's symphony. The new studies in theory and harmony had led the boy to learn, on his own, how to read an orchestral score. He applied his new knowledge to an ambitious project, in a gesture of homage to the composer he admired above all others, and Zverev gave him an opportunity to play it (with Pressman) for the composer. Tchaikovsky's diary for December 8 mentions an "Evening at Zverev's" that may have included the *Manfred* surprise, and his diary, two days

earlier, notes another musical and social occasion that brought all
together:

Von's [Erdmannsdörfer's] concert. King Stephen, Arma Senkrah,* Siloti
(superb performance of the sonata), Ninth Symphony. Excellent performance. Supper at Patri[keyev's] restaurant with the Huberts (he is
ill), Zverev, Siloti, Remezov, Safonov, and Zverev's pupils.

In years when Rachmaninoff enjoyed an international success comparable to Tchaikovsky's, the younger man recalled an incident:

When I was a boy of twelve, I happened to go to a Moscow restaurant with
Tchaikovsky and a friend of his. There was a good orchestra and the
leader, who had seen Tchaikovsky enter, had his men play one of his
pieces—I think it was a waltz from one of the ballets. Tchaikovsky, however, merely smiled and said: "When I was young it was the dream of my
life to think that some day my music would be so popular that I would
be able to hear it played in the restaurants." And then he added, with a
sigh, "Now I am quite indifferent."

    The earliest extant dated composition of Rachmaninoff's—possibly
homework for Arensky's class—was begun on February 5, 1887, a
Scherzo for orchestra, in F major. On the following day his virtuoso
cousin, Alexander Siloti, married Vera Tretyakova, daughter of the
wealthy art collector of Moscow, and Seryozha again met his musical
idol, for Tchaikovsky attended both wedding and wedding breakfast.
Two weeks later the newlyweds came to Zverev's for Sunday
luncheon with Tchaikovsky and his Conservatory friends. The day
before (February 21) Rachmaninoff had finished his Scherzo, and
the guests on Sunday may have been treated to a first hearing of the
new composition.
    Zverev's birthday, March 13, was always made an "occasion" by
his pupils. Pressman tells of Tchaikovsky's part in the celebration this
year:

We decided to prepare a birthday surprise for Zverev, playing piano
pieces that we had studied secretly. Rachmaninoff studied Tchaikovsky's
"Troika," and I worked on the "Snowdrop," both from Tchaikovsky's

---

* An American pianist who preferred her name, Harkness, to be spelt backwards.

Seasons, and Maximov prepared Borodin's Nocturne. After the morning coffee we led Zverev into the drawing room, where we played our birthday pieces to him. Nothing could have given him more pleasure. The formal birthday dinner, later, was attended by many guests, including Tchaikovsky. Before dinner Zverev boasted of the musical gifts he had received from us, and made us sit down at the piano to show the guests. Everyone was enormously pleased and Tchaikovsky kissed us all.

A violin student entering the Conservatory this September gives us a glimpse of the Zverev group; Nikolai Avierino was a genial soul who made friends with them at once:

When for the first time, in the fall of 1887, I ascended the staircase of the old Moscow Conservatory, in the former home of Count Vorontzov-Dashkov on the Bolshaya Nikitzkaya, I was on my way to the entrance examinations. On the landing of the second floor I saw a group engaged in a lively conversation, and I noticed that the five people were all of the same height—very tall. A passer-by remarked, "There is Zverev [literally: of the beast] and his *zveryata* [cubs]." Later in the day Tchaikovsky introduced me to Zverev and Siloti, and before the day was over I met the other three, the "cubs"—Zverev's pupils, Rachmaninoff, Maximov, and Pressman. I immediately became friends with these young people, and our friendship lasted "to the edge of the grave."

In a few days I was invited to lunch at Zverev's, and there I saw how my new friends lived. Those Sunday luncheons at Zverev's, presided over by a genial host and a great gourmet, were famous in Moscow, and I soon became an eager habitué of these occasions. I still recall them with joy. Who *wasn't* there! Rubinstein, Tchaikovsky, Arensky, Taneyev, Pabst—figures from Moscow society—wealthy men seeking protégés—everyone! And if one sought the unknowns who were to be the greats of the future, Zverev's was the place to look. . . . The rest of us led carefree students' lives, living at home and enjoying complete freedom—but the "cubs" were deprived of all freedom and their entire day was scheduled, hour by hour, under the guarding, severe eye of Zverev.

Among the "cubs," it was Leonid (Lyolya) Maximov with whom I was especially friendly. He had an enthusiastic, hot temperament, and was an incorrigible wrangler. Our nickname for him was "Don Quixote" and Tchaikovsky called him "impudent Lyolya." Another of the "cubs" had an entirely different character. Exactly the opposite of Maximov, Sergei Rachmaninoff was a balanced, quiet youth; he never argued or shouted, he laughed a great deal and loved our jokes and pranks, but rarely participated in them himself.

At the turn of the year Rachmaninoff composed three Nocturnes for piano and presented them to Zverev. Four other piano pieces may have been composed at this time—a Romance, a Prélude, a Melody, and a Gavotte. These are dated, in the hand of Goldenweiser (who was not, however, intimate with Rachmaninoff at this time), 1887; a later date is likely. Rachmaninoff planned to offer the four pieces (with two songs) as his Opus 1, but this number was saved for his first concerto, and the pieces remained unpublished until 1948.

At Easter of 1888 Sergei paid one of his rare visits, within the strict Zverev schedule, to his relatives, the Satins. One of his cousins, Natalia, who was also a music student, remembers their meeting:

I was eleven and he fifteen. This was the first time he had visited us. He was a rather tall boy, very well dressed. My older brother, Sasha, and I entertained our guest. Seryozha, learning that I played the piano, asked me, with a certain air of adolescent superiority, to play something. I agreed and played Vanya's aria from Glinka's *Life for the Tzar*.

This spring Zverev's three were moved into the senior section of the Conservatory, and Zverev tried to get them all into Siloti's piano class. He considered that Siloti, himself a Zverev disciple and fresh from his triumphs as Liszt's favored pupil, deserved only the best material—and his three were the best. Rachmaninoff would have preferred the piano class of Safonov (where Pressman went) to study with his own cousin, Siloti, but Zverev was in command.

At the end of this school year there was another choice to be made—once more, not *by* Rachmaninoff, but *for* him. In advancing into the senior section of the theory class, students were here divided into those who were to work in "general theory" or in "special theory," and it was clear to all that anyone recommended for the latter category was considered a potential composer. By the end of his junior course Rachmaninoff had made an excellent impression on his teacher Arensky with the harmonizing of simple melodies.

The Conservatory invited Tchaikovsky to serve as an honorary member of the examining board. He had only recently returned from several busy but satisfying months abroad, and had settled down at his country retreat to sketch his new—Fifth—symphony. But he still regarded the Conservatory as his duty, and came to Moscow when called. Rachmaninoff described the two-day examination to Riesemann:

At the last examination of the harmony course the pupils were separated and given two problems to be solved without the help of a piano. The first was to harmonize a melody in four parts (I think the theme was Haydn's, this time). The second was to write a prélude of sixteen to thirty bars, in a given key and with a specified modulation, to include pedal points on both the dominant and the tonic.

The examination began at nine o'clock in the morning. Tchaikovsky's presence gave the event a special character this year. When all candidates had turned in their work (each one bringing a frown to Arensky's face), I alone was left, for I had got entangled in a daring modulation of the prélude and could find no satisfactory solution. At last—by five o'clock— I had finished, and handed my two pages to Arensky. When he glanced at them he did not frown, and this gave me some hope.

On the following day the board was to hear us play our own work. When I had finished my turn, Arensky mentioned to Tchaikovsky that I had written some piano pieces in ternary song form for his class, and asked whether he would care to hear them. Tchaikovsky nodded his assent, and I sat down to play my pieces, for I knew them by heart. When I had finished I saw Tchaikovsky go over to the examination record and write something on it. It was only two weeks later that Arensky told me what was written there; he was probably afraid that I would become vain, and so had kept it a secret from me. The board had granted me a "5 plus," the highest rating, and Tchaikovsky had added *three* plus signs to this mark—over it, below it, and beside it.

It was decided that in the early autumn I should enter Taneyev's first-year counterpoint class, and thus my fate as a composer was, as it were, officially sealed.

Tchaikovsky's own report on the event appears in his letter to Mme. von Meck of June 1: "The conservatory examinations left in me the most pleasant of impressions. Thanks to Taneyev's energy, conscientiousness and love for work, all goes very well." Mme. Anatol Tchaikovsky also records a reaction to this meeting of master and disciple; speaking of the many hearings that Tchaikovsky gave young composers, she says:

One interview and audition led him to interrupt the solitude of his late afternoon to proclaim in our presence the great name of Rachmaninoff. "For him," he said, "I predict a great future."

Rachmaninoff divided his summer between work with Zverev in the Crimea and a visit to his family, and in September entered the Conservatory with a revised schedule and a revised future. He now had two majors, piano and special theory. His professors were Siloti (piano), Taneyev (counterpoint), and Arensky (harmony, a special class for prospective young composers)—and, hovering over his entire education, Zverev. He was to continue to live at Zverev's house, though no longer taking regular lessons with him. The classes with Taneyev were a special joy:

What a wonderful man he was. How he laughed! He would go into peals of laughter, like a happy child. He was incapable of the slightest insincerity. He was so upset by our laziness. There were four of us in the class, but I remember only Scriabin and myself. * We never did any work at all. Sergei Ivanovich reproached us, tried to make us ashamed of ourselves, but it was all of no avail. At last he appealed to Safonov, who called us in and tried to convince us that we must not hurt a man like Taneyev. But even this made no impression on us. Youth . . .

The only extant work by Rachmaninoff during this term is a group of fragments for an opera, *Esmeralda,* based on Hugo's *Notre Dame de Paris*—an introduction to Act I, an *entr'acte,* and portions of Act III; one of these is dated October 17, 1888.

Through the spring of 1889 Tchaikovsky continued to watch over the Conservatory and the Zverev group:

7 May. Arrival at Moscow. Conservatory performance at 1 P.M. at the Malyi Theater. *Waffenschmied* [by Lortzing]. Dinner at Zverev's. Evening at Safonov's.

* Rachmaninoff is here speaking to Alfred Swan, a friend of his American years. Somewhat earlier, in telling this to Riesemann, Rachmaninoff mentioned Lidack and the bassoon player Weinberg as the other two students—both *very* conscientious.

9 May. Dinner for the students at the Conservatory.
28 May. Dinner at Zverev's.

But Tchaikovsky's chief ambition for the Conservatory was not achieved. Taneyev, restive with all his stored-up ideas for musical works, resigned as director. He consented to continue his counterpoint class.

From the summer of 1889 Rachmaninoff brought back to Moscow a tremendous appetite for composition. It was inevitable that this would lead to conflict with Zverev, for the teacher had often made it clear that a good piano talent should not waste itself in composition—and Zverev considered Rachmaninoff the best of the young piano talents. Zverev's antagonism, passive thus far, was reinforced by a physical obstacle to Rachmaninoff's wish to compose: there was only one music room in the house, used by all of Zverev's boys; whenever Sergei heard something in his head that had to be composed or improvised, Mo or Lo would be at one of the two pianos. In the autumn Sergei approached Zverev with a request:

He finally summoned enough courage to ask Zverev for another piano and a room or some place in the house where there would be some degree of privacy for his work. According to Rachmaninoff, this request might easily have been granted by Zverev if it had been fully explained to him, and Rachmaninoff always felt chiefly responsible for what occurred because his approach to Zverev had been wrong or abrupt, and because he had not indicated the gratitude he felt for all that Zverev had already done for him. But his mingled pride, confusion and excitement during the interview somehow transformed a calm conversation into a stormy argument, and Zverev, losing control of himself, suddenly raised his hand against his pupil. Rachmaninoff was already a young man of sixteen, and would not tolerate such a gesture. He firmly declared to Zverev, "You don't dare hit me!" Whereupon Zverev's fury grew unmanageable, and the interview ended in a total break of relations.

Rachmaninoff continued to live in Zverev's house for another month, but the teacher did nothing to assist a reconciliation. Rachmaninoff often waited for him outside the Conservatory to ask his forgiveness, and would approach him, but Zverev would pass by, taking no notice of him. Once he turned to the boy and told him to meet him at a certain street corner that morning. When they met, they walked silently to Prechistenka where the Satins lived. A family council had been assembled, but Sergei was soon sent from the room to join the younger Satin children at cat's cradle. One of the daughters, Natalia, recalled being told by her mother, "Go talk to him—he is so unhappy." With his fate being decided in another room, the boy spent a miserable hour with the children, though he obviously wished to be alone. In the hourlong discussion his relatives could reach no agreement, and Zverev finally rose to go, summoning his "former" pupil to return to his house as wordlessly as they had come. This was Rachmaninoff's last night at Zverev's. In the morning he packed his things and moved in with a fellow student at the Conservatory, Mikhail Slonov, hoping that he could support himself with the monthly fifteen rubles he was then making with piano lessons.

After master and pupil had left, the family council continued: all but one there had not considered the matter any particular responsibility of theirs. One aunt alone, sister of Sergei's father—Varvara Arkadyevna Satina—had felt sorry for the boy and refused to side with Zverev, whose despotic nature was well known. She insisted that Seryozha must be helped, and she was the only one to offer him a family and a home.

Aunt Varvara gave him a room of his own where he could continue his studies undisturbed. Though Zverev's routine had precluded any intimacy with this branch of his family, the sixteen-year-old Rachmaninoff soon had a firm place in their circle. There were four children: Alexander (Sasha) was Seryozha's age, Natalia (Natasha) was 12, Sophia (Sonya) was 10, and Vladimir (Volodya) was 8. The sudden acquisition of four lively cousins and a home where he was loved must have been a milestone in the boy's emotional life. Hearing of the crisis with Zverev, his mother had invited him to come back to St. Petersburg and transfer to the Conservatory there, where Anton Rubinstein had resumed his piano classes and Rimsky-Korsakov taught composition, but Rachmaninoff excused himself from making the change.

The Satin household took Seryozha, disowned by fate and Zverev, to their hearts; and with them he found again the family that he had lost in childhood. It was not only his aunt and his young cousins who helped to change a strange house into a friendly home, but the three women who tended the Satins took on the "young gentleman" too as their lifetime responsibility: the nurse Feona, in charge of the house, was a former serf of the Rachmaninoffs, remaining with them after the emancipation in 1861; her sister was the cook, and the cook's daughter was Maria (or Masha), the maid.

Among the children Sergei spent most of his free time with the older ones, close to his own age, but he grew as attached as an older brother to the youngsters, romping with eight-year-old Volodya and carrying him on his back around the big yard and garden. After school and on Sundays schoolmates and friends of the Satin children made their yard the center of their fun. In the winter a great ice slide was constructed there for the neighborhood's entertainment, and in spring one of Sergei's favorite occupations was to lay out a great system of rivulets for the rain and melting snow. There were ball games in the autumn, and whenever the ball landed on the roof, Sergei was the first to climb there. To tease Natasha and the others, he would strike a posture as close to the edge as possible and sing an aria from Rubinstein's *Demon*—"Weep not, my child!" Sometimes the youthful composer would need an audience and invite the children to his room, where for the whole evening he would improvise at the piano and illustrate the playing with poetic or fantastic stories.

Rachmaninoff's mother with his
first teacher, Anna Ornatzkaya,
ca. 1882.

Nikolai Zverev with his pupils of 1886; seated: Scriabin (in the uniform of the
Moscow Cadet School), Zverev, Chernayev, Pressman; standing: Könemann,
Maximov, Rachmaninoff, Samuelson.

Anton Arensky with the three graduates in 1892 of his composition class at the Moscow Conservatory: Leo Conus, Nikita Morozov, and Sergei Rachmaninoff.

Sergei and Natalia Rachmaninoff with
their first daughter, Irina, Moscow, 1905.

Rachmaninoff with his second daughter,
Tatiana, on the Ivanovka estate, 1909.

Rachmaninoff's first automobile, "Lorelei," at Ivanovka, 1912.

A photograph taken in New York on Rachmaninoff's first American tour; the inscription is to Nahan Franko.

Rachmaninoff with Nikolai Struve
in Denmark, 1918.

In the Bohemian Club Grove,
California, June 28, 1919.

Photograph by Gabriel Moulin

Photograph by Fyodor Kapustin

Rachmaninoff at Locust Point, New Jersey.

Photograph by Yevgeni Somov

A Sunday at Locust Point, July 1923:
Chaliapin, Moskvin, Ramsh (standing), and Rachmaninoff

Photograph by Pach Brothers

At a reception given to Josef Hofmann by Frederick Steinway, on January 11, 1925: Coates, Stravinsky, Medtner, Furtwängler, Steinway, Kreisler, Rachmaninoff, Hofmann; at center, top, Siloti; at far right, Goldmark.

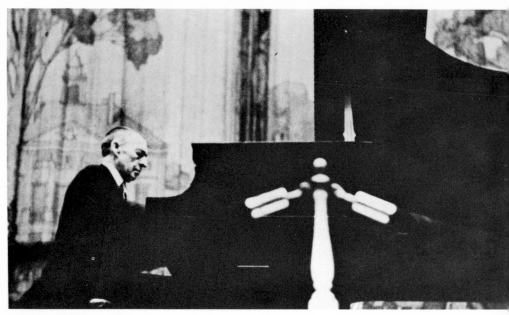

Rachmaninoff in recital at Washington, D.C., December 9, 1934; the photograph was taken by George Kalec, as Rachmaninoff played a Chopin Nocturne.

Rachmaninoff and Eugene Ormandy during rehearsals for the Rachmaninoff Cycle, 1939.

Photograph by Adrian Siegel.

Chapter 2

A New Family

AFTER the move from Zverev's house, Sergei Rachmaninoff's life at the Conservatory was little altered. When he passed Zverev on the steps or in the halls of the school, his salutations were never acknowledged by his former teacher.

The new class in fugue with Arensky, whose harmony class had been such a pleasure, was a bore for the students. They were frankly joyful when it was once announced that Arensky was too ill to teach; Taneyev took over the class meanwhile:

I remember how Taneyev once came to class and sat down, not at the teacher's desk, but on the bench with us, and said: "Do you know what a fugue is and how to write one?" The only thing we could say was, "No, Sergei Ivanovich, we do not know what a fugue is, and we do not know how to write one." He began to explain, and I suddenly saw light and understood it all in a few hours.

Unfortunately, Taneyev taught this class only twice before Arensky recovered.

In his own class in counterpoint Taneyev continued to struggle with the laziness of his two most talented pupils, Rachmaninoff and Scriabin.

At last Taneyev invented a new way of making us work. Pelageya Vasilyevna, his famous nurse, had a niece. This niece would suddenly appear in our kitchen with a sheet of manuscript paper. On it would be written a theme and a request to do a counterpoint exercise. "All right," I said. But she would not leave, because Sergei Ivanovich had instructed her to wait for the exercise and take it back with her. Once or twice I was caught, but the third time I told the family to say I was out, so she was obliged to leave the page of manuscript paper. She was sent in the same way to Scriabin's house.

At this time the lazy pupil was entering his first rich period of independent composition, in the freedom of a room of his own. There

are two sketched movements of an unfinished string quartet, inscribed "To Sasha [Siloti]"; and in the spring at least two songs were
tried, but put aside and left unpublished in his lifetime: "At the
Gate of the Holy Abode" (dated April 29, 1890), to a poem by
Lermontov, and dedicated to Mikhail Slonov; "I'll tell you nothing"
(May 1, 1890), to a poem by Afanasy Fet, whose melancholy verses
appealed to so many Russian composers, including Tchaikovsky.
There is another manuscript of this Conservatory year; for the examination in the special theory class (for graduation into the fugue
class), Rachmaninoff was assigned a six-part motet for mixed voices.
The result was successful enough to be performed by the Conservatory chorus, conducted by the composer, at a student concert the
following February. This may have been Rachmaninoff's debut as
conductor. The manuscript of the chorus, *Deus Meus,* is preserved
in the archives of the Moscow Conservatory.

This summer, one of Sergei's happiest, was to be spent with the
Satin family on their estate, Ivanovka, in the state of Tambov, five
hundred versts southeast of Moscow and even farther from the
familiar rugged northern landscape of his childhood. Another family
of cousins, the three Skalon sisters and their mother, were also to
live this summer at Ivanovka, and as they passed through Moscow
on their way from home in St. Petersburg to Ivanovka, they stopped
to see the Satins between trains; Varvara Satina introduced a new
relative to them:

"Let me at once introduce my nephew, Seryozha, a student at the
Moscow Conservatory. He will also be spending the summer with you.
Natasha! call Seryozha, tell him that my favorite nieces are here and
that I hope he will make friends with them."
Soon there entered a tall, thin youth, very pale, with disordered light
hair. We definitely did not like him—he was so morose, so uncommu-
nicative. "No," we all decided inwardly, "it will be hard to make friends
with him."

The endless steppe around Ivanovka had, at first, a rather oppressive effect on Rachmaninoff, used to the Novgorod forests. Even the
interesting dirt of Moscow, that overgrown village, seemed prefer-
able to this monotony of fields, unbroken by hill or stream. He found

himself regretting the break with Zverev, who had given him summers of Crimean cliffs and marble palaces. And then the peace and subtle beauties of the steppe began to work upon him:

I grew fond of this broad landscape and, away from it, would find myself longing for it, for Ivanovka offered the repose of surrounding that hard work requires—at least, for me. There were none of the beauties of nature that are usually thought of in this term—no mountain, precipice, or winding shore. This steppe was like an infinite sea where the waters are actually boundless fields of wheat, rye, oats, stretching from horizon to horizon. Sea air is often praised, but how much more do I love the air of the steppe, with its aroma of earth and all that grows and blossoms—and there's no rolling boat under you, either.

The estate of Ivanovka was well organized and managed. There were two ample houses, and a "park" in the English style planned and cultivated by Varvara Arkadyevna. The grounds near the houses contained two large orchards, a dairy farm, stables and stud, and offices, and all this was so far from town or city that the place was a busy self-contained community. Every summer its population was increased by numerous guests who brought their entire families and were housed separately in another building on the grounds.

There were two other families during the summer of 1890, the Silotis and the Skalons, in addition to the whole Satin family and Seryozha. New friendships began as mutual tastes were recognized. The three Skalon girls, Natalia, Ludmila, and Vera, were musical and personable, and Vera, the youngest, fifteen years old, made an immediate impression on the seventeen-year-old Seryozha. She was pretty, gay, and blonde, and the closest friend of Natasha Satina. Music bound all these young people together, and the evenings were full of music making and music talk, and from every group on the estate music poured constantly. Music poured also from the intimacy of Seryozha and Vera Skalon, and in August he dedicated to her a new Romance for cello and piano, as well as a song composed the year before, "In the silence of the secret night" (later revised for Op. 4), and there were also piano pieces for the six hands of the three Skalon sisters, including a valse with a theme by Natalia Skalon. A paying commission was given him by Jürgenson, Tchaikovsky's publisher, to arrange for piano duet the suite drawn from *The Sleeping Beauty* score as well as the entire ballet.*

It was a busy and happy summer, and its center for Seryozha was little Vera. He had a number of nicknames for her—"little white one," *Brykushka* [the little kicker], "little psychopath" (the youngsters were not interested in the meaning of the strange word—only in its modish sound). All the young people enjoyed sitting on a long bench in the dusk, and Vera and Seryozha used this opportunity to sit close together, holding hands—until Vera Siloti noticed this habit and reported it to the girl's horrified mother. Poor Verochka was scolded, and Seryozha was forbidden to write to her when he returned to Moscow at the end of August for the opening of the Conservatory; so that communication had to be maintained through her older sisters. Seryozha wrote the first of a long series of letters to her oldest sister Natalia:

My trip was not so fortunate: it seems I caught cold on my way to Burnak; at Griazi [a junction] I got a terrible headache and a chill; in Kozlov I stayed at my father's one day, and recovered somewhat, but from there I traveled second-class so I could lie down—which I did the whole way.

When I got to Moscow I surrendered myself to being pulled to pieces by our stupid but devoted Fedosia, who bombarded me with questions. Though I said NO over and over, this didn't help. So she forced me to tell her about everyone and everything. This took a good half hour. She finally released me, showing that in His mercy the Lord has not completely forsaken me. I went upstairs to my room, where I waited for lunch and rested from both Fedosia and the journey.

. . . Spent all of Tuesday and Wednesday on the ballet [*The Sleeping Beauty* transcription]. I finished the first act Thursday, and tomorrow I start the second. You ask, dear mentor, about the piano. I don't have it yet—it's to be delivered tomorrow, for sure—an absolutely new piano, direct from the factory. . . .

As I cannot write to the dear little psychopath [Vera], I ask you to tell her that I received her postscript with humility and reverence; I read it

---

* This commission was arranged by Siloti, who in 1889 had made the two-hand piano version of the ballet score. Now he asked Jürgenson to allow his pupil, Rachmaninoff, to prepare the four-hand version under his supervision, for 100 rubles. Both Jürgenson and Tchaikovsky agreed.

with astonishment and rapture; and I await the next postscript with tremendous impatience.

Please tell Natasha [Satina] that I like very much to be kissed via letters. . . .

[September 8, 1890]

There's absolutely nothing to write about myself: living has become so monotonous; I stay at home almost the whole time, going nowhere, and in general I merely "exist." I am burdened with work, but to tell you the truth, I do little, and scarcely practice the piano at all. I simply can't get down to work. My laziness is *gigantic*. . . .

[P.S.] I completely forgot. For Heaven's sake, look for my music. It's on the desk in the room where I slept, under uncle's papers, I believe. My songs and the quartet.

Nikolai Avierino gives us a portrait of Rachmaninoff at the beginning of this school year:

I believe I am not wrong in saying that at the age of seventeen or eighteen, Rachmaninoff had a completely formed character: he was self-centered but not arrogant, he held himself with dignity, behaving simply and nicely with us, but there was no one with whom he could be said to be "fraternal." When I was later told that he was "haughty and conceited," I could assure everyone that I had never detected a trace of hauteur or conceit in him. Such an appearance, strange as it may seem, must have derived from his shyness.

Another student, Mikhail Bukinik, who entered the Conservatory this fall to study the cello, shows us Rachmaninoff amid Conservatory society:

Between classes you could see the professors in the corridors. There was Nikolai Zverev, Rachmaninoff's [former] teacher, tall, slender, with carefully combed gray hair like Liszt, and unexpectedly black bushy eyebrows over a clean-shaven face. Peace and calm seemed to radiate from his kind, fatherly countenance. There is youthful Ferruccio Busoni with his pink lips and little blond beard. There is Alexander Siloti, also young, tall, lithe, animated, with a pleasant smile. There is Paul Pabst, huge, heavy, Teutonic, with the face of a bulldog (though his figure provoked fear, he was actually the kindliest of men!). There is the bulk of the near-sighted Sergei Taneyev. There is Anton Arensky, mobile, nervous, with a wry smile on his clever, half Tartar face, always joking or snarling. All feared his laughter and adored his talent. And there was the director Vasili Safonov, short, plump, stocky, with piercing eyes—professors and pupils alike felt that proprietary eye on them.

The numerous pupils crowded either into the clubroom on the second floor or downstairs in the coatroom, far from the eyes of the authorities. . . . I can still see the students: rosy Joseph Lhévinne with his bushy, curly hair, already performing in concerts as an accomplished pianist; the tiny, alert violinist Alexander Pechnikov, a conservatory celebrity who senses his own importance and pays attention to no one, but he is talented and we can't help admiring him; the puny and immaculate Alexander Scriabin, not deigning to converse or joke with anyone (when it snows he wears high galoshes and always dresses modishly); modest Alexander Goldenweiser, always by himself; Konstantin Igumnov, looking like a sexton, but he is studying at the Moscow University and commands our respect. Kolya Avierino loves to attend our gatherings—he is dark as a Negro and a great joker. Sometimes businesslike Modeste Altschuler comes, and Leonid Maximov, lanky and very sociable, loved by everybody, a true comrade—he is the center of various clusters, he talks a lot, loves jokes and dirty stories, and we crowd around him eagerly.

And in this throng there is Sergei Rachmaninoff. Tall and gaunt, his shoulders somehow seem hunched, giving him a rectangular appearance. His long face is very expressive, making him look Roman. His hair is unruly (not yet closely clipped). He doesn't avoid his comrades. Their jokes amuse him, even when they are boyishly cynical, and he holds himself simply, but with assurance. He smokes a lot, speaks in a bass voice, and though we know he is our age, he seems an adult to us. We all heard of his successes in Arensky's free composition class, we know his ability to grasp quickly the form of any composition, we know what an extraordinary sight reader he is, what a perfect ear he has, and we are infected by his love for Tchaikovsky. We are amazed by his keen analysis of each new composition by Tchaikovsky or Arensky. But as a pianist he made less of an impression on us.

I remember once being in a group of pupils who were standing around, talking about the fees they charged for lessons. At that time parents willingly engaged as music teachers for their children the students from advanced classes at the Conservatory. The fee was, of course, always small and usually amounted to no more than three rubles—more was charged only by professors. When one of the students boasted getting three rubles a lesson, Rachmaninoff calmly remarked that he would never accept less

than five rubles a lesson, "and if they won't give it, I wouldn't bother."
We knew he wasn't rich, but this young man had such quiet self-
assurance, setting him apart from us, that though we argued and grew
indignant, we were finally convinced that he was not boasting.

On the way back to St. Petersburg the Skalon family saw Sergei
again at the Satins', and the immediate effect of the visit was a renewed excitement in composition. He began a work (since destroyed
or lost) on the same *Manfred* theme that had fascinated so many
romantic composers before him.

It all turned out just as I expected [he reported to Natalia Skalon on
October 2]. After your departure, Manfred made extraordinary progress.
The first movement was composed in two nights, and during the next
two days was put on paper, and played on the third day—by myself, of
course. That's the sum of my life and doings for the last few days. As you
can see, plenty of variety. My quartet was not played—again I didn't go to
give a lesson at the Tretyakovs—haven't begun yet at the choral society.
I sent out letters to everyone about my illness. Since your departure I
haven't been able to do anything, except to compose Manfred. . . .

[October 10, 1890]

. . . I've had to write a fugue—an unpleasant circumstance, no matter
how you look at it. . . .

I began my work with the choral society* on Monday. All my pupils
are three times as old as I; even a college student managed to get in, though
what brought him there, only God and he know. When I entered the
class my exterior was quite calm, as it always must be on such occasions.
But actually, at heart I was a little embarrassed, for this was the first time
I found myself in such a situation. All the pupils stood up. Outside, my
face said nothing, but inside I laughed and swore at them, calling them
fools. At their age I'd never stand up for a man a third my age. I sat down,
and they sat down. I had to speak for almost the whole lesson. I spoke
badly, but what else could be expected of me now? Judge for yourself.
For instance, I said, "You future teachers of choral singing must know
this and that," and while I went on mumbling I was thinking of how
white the little psychopath looks, or how I was going to compose a certain
passage in the second movement of Manfred.

* This was a job arranged for Rachmaninoff by two friends of Arensky, A. P.
Chizhov and Klugen.

As letters addressed directly to the "little psychopath" were still banned, he wrote on October 21 to all three girls, though they were quite aware to whom he was speaking:

Now that everyone is on the way to bed, and you, too, are probably asleep already, I finally find time to write you and remind you of me. I say this without any set phrases—in such a situation I am no phrasemaker. Somehow it seems to me that all of you have grown much cooler towards me, that all your Petersburg barons have obliterated your memories of this poor wandering musician. Say what you will, this is quite natural, though very sad—that is, of course, sad for me, if not for you.

His birthday greetings to Natalia Skalon, on November 1, did not conceal his pique: "May the Lord, to please you, send your house as many barons as possible, and as few wandering musicians as possible."

[December 10, 1890]

My great wish was to go to Petersburg for *The Queen of Spades* [Tchaikovsky's opera, first performed on December 7] . . . . my own work* has done me an ill turn—it's to be performed at the Conservatory, conducted not by me, but by Safonov. Can't understand why they need me here. If I had known that for the sake of this piece I'd lose my holiday, I certainly would not have composed it. This composition isn't worth even one general's daughter.

Sergei did go to St. Petersburg to hear *The Queen of Spades* on December 26, staying at his mother's apartment. He spent as much of his vacation with the Skalons as their mother allowed him. Their first reaction was to his hair. During the summer they had complained about his unruly hair, and now he appeared before them clipped and grateful: "Thank you, little sisters, for cutting my hair."

[January 6, 1891]

I would have written you on the day of my return here, but when I feel depressed, I can't do a thing—I can only work. And after a whole day of work one feels a little easier. For these two and a half days I've been writing constantly; just finished orchestrating my suite. This is all good,

---

* The string quartet composed earlier in the year and orchestrated for a student performance.

except that after this work my right hand aches badly; nevertheless I sit down to write to the general's dear ladies.

This orchestral suite has not been identified and must be placed among the several lost works of Rachmaninoff's youth, along with the *Manfred* composition and the opera mentioned in the next letter to Natalia Skalon, on January 10:

It's not worth sending you the opera, for you wouldn't be able to examine anything in three days. I'd better give it to you in the Crimea—you can play it there. As for your suite I can say the same thing: it's not worth writing, especially because after my orchestral suite I began a piece for two pianos [Russian Rhapsody] which I want to play Monday or Tuesday with Sasha [Siloti].

No luck with the orchestral suite—it won't be played because it's written for a full symphony orchestra, and the instruments I need aren't to be found at our Conservatory. So this will be held until next year, when I want to arrange a concert of my own and play it there. Now I'll give it to Tchaikovsky for perusal; I trust him implicitly in everything. Arensky liked your valse very much. My choral piece will be performed in February at a student concert, and I'll conduct myself. To tell you the truth, I hate the idea of appearing with such trash—I don't like this piece. . . . Of course I'll be at the station to meet you. Write me once more from Petersburg and let me know whether you'll be staying for one more day at least in Moscow. . . . Among other things, you could tell me about *Brykushka*, then about the little psychopath, then about the little white one, and then about Vera Dmitriyevna.

Despite the tone of adolescent disdain, the young composer counted a great deal on the Conservatory concert of February 24. The orchestral suite had not been programed, and he was to conduct not his orchestrated quartet but a choral work (*Deus Meus*) that he disliked; these disappointments counted little beside his joy in a new work for two pianos that was to be played on February 24. This was the Russian Rhapsody, in E minor (dated January 12–14), whose origin may be hinted in a later letter from a Moscow friend, Vladimir Wilshaw:

. . . I recall a long, long distant episode from our past life. It was this: after some occasion, either some festival, or concert, or simply a *Vivat Bacchus*, a small group of us—you, I, the late Yuri Sergeyevich Sakhnovsky and

Ernst Eberg—somehow found ourselves late one night in the piano factory of Alexander Eberg, then on the Bolshaya Lubyanka. We were served coffee and then we tried out the instruments standing around the room. I remember how Sakhnovsky sat down at one piano and you at another. Sakhnovsky began to strum some Russian song, and at once you answered with a variation on it and then he played another variation, and you a third one, and so on and on, ever gayer and gayer. . . . Perhaps you don't recall this, but I do, and I want to point out to you that your love for the variation form dates from that incident.

The planned performance of the Rhapsody also ran into trouble, as its composer reported in a letter addressed to all three Skalon sisters in February:

No luck here, either with health, which the Lord doesn't grant me, or with matters at the Conservatory. Imagine, Tata, at the student concert I was supposed to play my two-piano rhapsody with Sasha's [Siloti's] pupil, Maximov, one of Zverev's inmates; we had rehearsed, we had matched our playing, everything was going on well, when suddenly Zverev, who of course remembers that incident with me, decided to create an unpleasantness for me, and meanly refused to allow Maximov to play with me. And Sasha also didn't go against Zverev, because he is terribly fond of him, and I was left with nothing but an enormous grief— how much I had wanted to play in this concert! For two days I grieved. Don't you find that this is written movingly and that the whole story is heartbreaking?

When Natalia Skalon wrote him a birthday greeting on March 20, Sergei had begun his most ambitious work to date. Nothing further is known of the boys' class he mentions:

March 26, 1891

Many thanks, dear Natalia Dmitriyevna, for the letter, for the remembrance, for the greetings, and for your good wishes. I would have answered you at once, but these days I've had to write a lot of music for Arensky.

You ask me in your letter what I am now composing. A piano concerto. Two movements are already written, the last movement is composed, but not yet written; I'll probably finish the whole concerto by late spring, and orchestrate it during the summer.

. . . It's now half past ten [of March 27]. Just got back from a lesson—

terribly upset. The boys nearly drove me out of my wits. I was simply in a rage. I can't remember myself in such a condition for a long while. I threw one boy out of the class, called another one an idiot, and left before the lesson was finished. I may be kicked out for this—I don't know. I only know that if I should give such lessons more often I would have perished long since. Truly, I'm unlucky to suffer so for the sake of five rubles, and knowing that in a few days, in a few weeks and months, it will be the same thing over again.

I am nervous, irritable, painfully impatient, and so it's harder for me to give lessons; if only the lessons would be given to you and your little white sisters, but no—I have to deal with these fools.

With more than a year left before Rachmaninoff's graduation as pianist, a change in policy at the Conservatory changed his plans as well. Safonov, who had replaced Taneyev as director, assumed at once a hostile attitude toward Siloti, and during this school year of 1890–1891 their quarrel came into the open. Finally Siloti asked to be relieved of his post, as he did not intend to return to Moscow in the autumn of 1891. Rather than face a last year of piano lessons under a new master who would certainly employ different methods, Rachmaninoff asked Safonov for permission to take his final examination in piano at the end of the current academic year. He was not surprised that Safonov granted this request, for Safonov had shown that he had no great hopes in him as a pianist. More than once he had told Rachmaninoff, "I know that your interest lies elsewhere"— by which he meant in composition.

Sergei's task for the piano examination was Beethoven's Sonata in C major (Op. 53, the *Waldstein*) and the first movement of Chopin's Sonata in B minor; Siloti was as surprised as he when the examination was passed with honors.

By mistake the examinations of Rachmaninoff in both piano and fugue were scheduled for the same day and hour, so his fugue examination was transferred to the following day, when he was to be examined alone, the rest of the class taking it on the regular day. On his way home from the piano examination he saw Arensky and Safonov in a lively discussion. As he came up to them, he heard that they were speaking of the theme for the general examination in fugue that day. Arensky stopped Rachmaninoff to tell him that he didn't want to come to the Conservatory next morning just to give him the theme, so he dictated the fugue problem to him right then. Safonov had stepped aside, and began to whistle the proper fugal treatment of the theme—and Rachmaninoff never knew whether this help was unintentional or deliberate. In any case, as Rachmaninoff later learned, none of the class had found the right answer. Only he, with this sidewalk coaching, passed the examination with a"5."

This summer the Skalons went abroad for the sake of frail Vera, and Ivanovka was a lonely place for the eighteen-year-old Sergei; even the Satins deserted him, accompanying their father to a Saratov estate that he was managing. Sergei wrote to the traveling Skalon sisters on May 31:

I haven't written you for a long while because of my examinations that ended about four days ago. Got through them all right. I believe someone has written you that Sasha and I are leaving the Conservatory. Sasha is positively leaving, but I can't say definitely about myself. Perhaps I'll leave, or perhaps I'll stay on, only with Arensky, and take lessons privately with Sasha. Perhaps Sasha and I will move to Petersburg (this would be pleasantest for me). In one way or another I'll graduate from the Conservatory in a year. My examinations ended May 27, and on May 29 Sasha and I moved to Ivanovka. . . .

Here, after the summer last year that was so pleasant for me in every way, it can't be very gay this time. Moreover, my first hours here were painful for me because I have not altered my relationship to you, sisters, and I still think of you as before. . . .

Don't forget the poor old musician.

Rachmaninoff

[June 11, 1891]

I didn't go to my family, although they asked me to come, because it seems to me that they don't like me (except my father, who doesn't live there). Though my family invited me, I think this was only to keep up appearances. . . .

You asked about Sasha and me and our relations with the Conservatory. Sasha has left the Conservatory. I stayed on. For my piano class I shall take private lessons with Sasha. I'll graduate in a year. Sasha's farewell to the Conservatory will be permanent if Safonov stays there. If Safonov should leave the director's post, Sasha will join the faculty and all will be as before.

The best of his Conservatory friends, Mikhail Slonov, a voice student who also composed, sent to Ivanovka a brief composition entitled "Yearning for Seryozha," to which Seryozha replied: "You contradict yourself. I do not see that you particularly yearn for me; actually your yearning is only two lines long, with a repetition of 14 bars. Very brief and very sad."

Proofs of the long-delayed four-hand piano transcription of *The Sleeping Beauty* score finally reached Tchaikovsky, and he exploded. To Jürgenson he wrote a controlled note on June 14 ("The proofs pained me, but I am glad that I saw in time what Rachmaninoff and Siloti have been doing"); but Tchaikovsky did not hide his irritation when he wrote to Siloti on the same day:

I have corrected the proofs of *The Sleeping Beauty* prologue, and this task gave me considerable pain. You may say that a first proofreading can be done superficially, while the vital corrections can be made in the second proof, but it is the *transcription itself that I do not like*. We made a great mistake in entrusting this work to a boy, no matter how talented. Not that he has done it carelessly; on the contrary, one can see that he has thought about every detail. But this transcription has two horrible deficiencies:

1) Lack of courage, skill, and initiative, too slavish a subordination to the composer's authority, depriving the work of force and brilliance.

2) It is too apparent that the four-hand transcription was made from the two-hand transcription rather than from the orchestra score. Many details necessarily omitted from the piano score, though quite convenient and possible for the four-hand transcription, are missing here, too.

These two faults cannot be corrected, alas. As you will see, I have added things here and there, and made some changes, but this helps little. You can see for yourself how closely Rachmaninoff has clung to your piano score. . . .

In general, inexperience and lack of boldness can be sensed at every step. For example, look how strangely he has done these harp arpeggios! . . . That's an exercise from the class in elementary theory!!! Yet in fairness it should be said that your cousin was conscientious, and some passages turned out well. . . .

I haven't had the courage to look through the first act yet, for these proofs have so upset me that I haven't been able to sleep—I feel a sickness approaching. . . .

I wanted this ballet to be done as thoroughly and seriously as a symphony transcription. But I can see now that this cannot be!

Siloti took both Rachmaninoff and the transcription in hand at once. He revised the first act and sent it to Tchaikovsky to calm him. It had that effect, but when Rachmaninoff wrote to Natalia Skalon on July 11, his nose was still at the grindstone:

You ask when will the ballet be off the press? It will be out by autumn. It could have appeared sooner, but Sasha and I are now changing it a little, because Tchaikovsky swears terribly at me for the transcription. And quite reasonably and justly.

Of all transcriptions mine is undoubtedly the worst. But now, as I've said, we're correcting this one, and it will look like something; it will look like a transcription.*

You also ask about my music. I am working a lot, is all I can say. My piano is good.

And you further ask me to send you a flower or a blade of grass. For your long silence I wanted to send you a branch of nettles.

To this letter Siloti added an irritated postscript: "While we correct Seryozha's four-hand transcription, I occasionally mention your name, but without kind feelings—for it's easy to see that he enjoyed making the transcription, that is, in your presence."

Meanwhile Rachmaninoff completed his first large-scale work, on which he reports to Slonov on July 20:

On July 6th I fully completed composing and scoring my piano concerto. I could have finished it much sooner, but after the first movement I idled for a long while and began to write the following movements only on July 3. Composed and scored the last two movements in two and a half days. You can imagine what a job that was. I wrote from five in the morning till eight in the evening, so after finishing the work I was terribly tired. Afterwards I rested for a few days. While working I never feel fatigue (on the contrary—pleasure). With me fatigue appears only when

* There is a note sent by Tchaikovsky from Klin to Mme. Hubert in February 1892: "It's very necessary that I see Seryozha Rachmaninoff, formerly or at present a student of the Conservatory. Don't you know his address? Please locate him and let me know immediately." This may relate to some final stage of the transcription's publication, or, more hopefully, to some work in connection with the suite that Tchaikovsky was then drawing from his *Nutcracker* ballet score.

I realize that a big labor is finished. I am pleased with the concerto. I can't say this of my last song. I consider that it turned out very unsuccessfully; at the most I think this piece, in quality, one of the least of my compositions. But I definitely don't wish to change it. For me this is always unpleasant and repugnant. It's bad—so to the Devil with it! Well, that's enough for my compositions. They are so weak, bad, and ugly, judging from my last piece, that they're definitely not worth writing two pages about. Believe me, dear Akimich, this song has made me slightly desperate.

[July 24, 1891]

After the song that I wrote you about in my last letter, I also wrote a prélude for piano [in F major]; after this prélude I have grown a little calmer and stronger in my weakened spirits. All is not as bad as the song.

Since he had so much to show for his first two summers at Ivanovka, it is not strange that he should always have looked back on this country place as the setting for his strongest desire to compose. He was to return often to it for revival and calm.

Before returning to Moscow for what he was determined should be his last year of school, he visited his grandmother Rachmaninoff at Znamenskoye, a ten-hour drive from Ivanovka. At his grandmother's the composing did not cease; he wrote Slonov from there on August 10: "In my head at present are our future living quarters, and a new symphony. . . ." And before the summer was ended he had written the first movement of this symphony and had completed the Romance for the six-hand piano work for the Skalons. The introductory theme of this Romance was to be used in the future Second Concerto.

It was well into September before Rachmaninoff left his grandmother's. As a gesture of farewell to the place he swam in the stream that ran through Znamenskoye; immediately afterwards he boarded the train for Moscow, and by the time he reached the city he had a severe chill. At the apartment that he and Slonov had rented together for this school year Rachmaninoff's illness grew worse, and Slonov grew panicky: the Satins had not yet returned to Moscow, and no other relatives were in Moscow at the time. Slonov appealed to a fellow student, Yuri Sakhnovsky, who lived comfortably with his well-to-do family, and the Sakhnovskys took in the patient, who appeared to be suffering from something more serious than malaria, which had been the first diagnosis of Rachmaninoff's nightly high fever and daily collapse. Now the friends around him were alarmed for his life. Siloti, who was back in Moscow, summoned Professor Mitropolsky and organized a nursing schedule. The doctor diagnosed brain fever (though malaria seems now more plausible) and with the help of Rachmaninoff's strong constitution arrested the progress of the disease. As Seryozha came out of his alternating coma and delirium he asked Slonov to write to Natalia Skalon:

I write you at the request of my friend and roommate, Sergei Vasilyevich Rachmaninoff, who asks me to apologize for his long silence. He has been ill for a month and a half, with recurrent fever. For three days he shakes, and then has two days of rest. Sergei Vasilyevich is astonished that you haven't written to him for so long and he says that a few lines written by you would give him great pleasure.

Chapter 3

Aleko and "Free Artist"

AFTER lying helpless at Sakhnovsky's for six weeks, Rachman-inoff would not agree to the long rest prescribed by Mitropol-sky after his convalescence, and plunged into work furiously to make up for his lost time. When he experienced some normal difficulty in his return to composition he decided at once that the brain fever had forever cost him "half" his facility in composing!

I've begun to recuperate [he wrote to Natalia Skalon on October 31]. Not long ago I was allowed to leave my bed—I was terribly bored there. Lots of things have waited a long while for my recovery. . . .

It may be my sickness that's responsible, but Moscow has grown re-pugnant to me—I wish I could break away from here and hide some-where and live for a long while in a new place. But this would be possible only with leisure, health, and money, and I have neither the first, nor the second, nor the third. And this isn't all.

Since birth I have always lived among my own people. Now that's all changed. I rent a room from people whom I know but slightly. There is every convenience, I am honored and respected, but I am not loved, and to tell you the truth I am used to that, and it is rather hard for me to live here. One sometimes feels so bad here, so uncomfortable, that one simply wants to hang oneself. Besides, this is a nasty time of year. I can't stand the winter. In my opinion winter exists only to ruin people's nerves. My secret wish is to leave Russia this spring at least for a month or so. I may have the possibility to leave then, and by all means alone, so there would be nobody to disturb my calm and rest after this long and hard path that I've been dragging along these ten Conservatory years. If this comes about, I'll make a complete recovery, or at least I feel that I can, and then I can start the propaganda for myself and my compositions with courage and freshness. I'm sure that cold water will be thrown over my first ap-pearance, but that means nothing; I can bear that, too. May the Lord only justify the hopes people have placed in me.

December 7, 1891

First of all let me thank you for the picture you sent me. My poor song (I say this sincerely, I don't like it) isn't worth your good photograph.

I was very pleased to receive it, very flattered and very touched. . . .

I feel much better now; apparently I've quite recovered. I am in a good mood, which for me is best of all. I believe that the frequent and long walks I've taken lately have contributed much to my sound condition. Sometimes I walk because I can't afford to ride, sometimes simply from a desire to walk. I very often visit Aunt [Satina] — this is now my most favorite house in Moscow. I stay there a long while and feel a blessed and irresponsible condition that makes me ready to romp, play tricks, fight, do mischief — and nobody can stifle me then.

After I finish this letter I shall immediately sit down at new work: I'll begin the orchestration of my recently completed piece that I am dedicating to my dear Professor A. S. Arensky. This will keep me busy until Christmas.

The "piece" was a poem for orchestra, _Prince Rostislav_, based on a work by Alexei Tolstoy. Rachmaninoff worked on it from December 9 to 15; he carried it to Arensky along with a request:

I informed him that I had no intention of staying in the Conservatory for another year, and that I wished to take my final examination in the spring. I asked for his help and he promised it, and actually succeeded in getting this permission for me, although it was against school rules.

When Scriabin heard about this request and its success, he asked for the same privilege, but Arensky, who could not abide Scriabin, replied, "On no account will I let you do it." Offended, Scriabin dropped the composition class altogether, and eventually left the Conservatory without a composer's diploma.

For my accelerated graduation, Arensky demanded several compositions — a symphony, some vocal recitatives, and an opera whose subject would be assigned in April. I began working on the symphony at once, but it came with difficulty; each bar had to be forced out, and the result was accordingly poor. I could see that Arensky was not pleased with the separate movements as I showed them to him. They satisfied me even less. Taneyev, too, whom Arensky asked to act as advisory expert, gave me some bitter criticism to swallow. I finally finished the work and handed in the required recitatives, as well.*

This last winter at the Conservatory was crammed with almost more new experiences than a young composer (presumably weakened

---

* Manuscript fragments exist—scenes for _Boris Godunov_ and _Masquerade_—that may relate to these "required recitatives."

by illness) might have been expected to endure. But the armor that was to protect Rachmaninoff's later private life and troubles, and which he would doff only at rare intervals, was already being forged. His many-sided activities of this winter were all under perfect control. Goldenweiser recalls the first performance of the Rhapsody on Russian Themes:

Someone had told him that nothing could be written on a certain Russian theme. He wrote a composition in E minor (in the form of variations). It was quite good music. I remember that at some benefit concert for our colleagues — we often arranged such concerts — Rachmaninoff and Lhévinne performed this piece on two pianos; it concluded with a variation in octaves, alternating from one pianist to the other, and on that occasion each increased the tempo, and everyone watched to see who would outplay whom. Each had a phenomenal wrist, but it was Rachmaninoff who won.

With his first formal concert scheduled for January, to be shared with the cellist Anatoli Brandukov, Rachmaninoff composed a prélude for cello and piano and a *Trio élégiaque* (the manuscript is dated January 18–21, 1892, Moscow).* The first public concert by the young pianist-composer was given at the Vostriakov Hall on January 30, 1892. No program of this concert was printed—too expensive!—but Goldenweiser wrote out the program that evening:

I.

Trio élégiaque	Rachmaninoff

played by the composer, D. A. Krein, and A. A. Brandukov

Etude in A-flat major ⎫ Etude in C minor ⎬	Chopin
Barcarole	Tchaikovsky
Etude	Liszt
Scherzo	Chopin

S. V. Rachmaninoff

[a group played by Brandukov]

* In 1893 Rachmaninoff had a second, more sorrowful occasion to use this title; it should be clear that Rachmaninoff wrote two works with the same title; this earlier trio is in the key of G minor; the later, more familiar trio (Op. 9) is in D minor.

II.

Prélude for violoncello and piano	Rachmaninoff

played by the composer and A. A. Brandukov

Etude	Tausig
Valse impromptu	Liszt

S. V. Rachmaninoff

[a group played by Brandukov]

En courant	Godard
Nocturne	Tchaikovsky
Valse [Kermess, from *Faust*]	Gounod-Liszt

S. V. Rachmaninoff

On February 18 he wrote to Natalia Skalon about this concert and his other activities:

Ever since I got back from Petersburg [where he had spent Christmas with the Skalons] I have been busy playing and taking part in concerts — six of them — and to top everything, I gave a concert of my own. You can't imagine what it means to give a concert of your own. It's a matter of begging at doors and antechambers of houses where you would otherwise never wish to go. This was extremely disagreeable, boring, and time-consuming.

This concert was given to help my poor financial condition. And, in this respect, the concert was not a success. I didn't even recover my expenses. So I still have creditors — this isn't very pleasant either. With the preparation and the sale of tickets for my concert I had little time to maintain my correspondence and good relations with some of my dear acquaintances. I wrote no letters to friends while this went on.

In three weeks I have to play one movement of my concerto, accompanied by orchestra, meaning Safonov. And this is not very pleasant. Then there are three invitations to play at concerts. And I'm pretty tired of it. But there are better things, too, in the offing: our Conservatory has set the day for examination of the graduating class in theory. This important day is April 15. So they will give us a subject for a one-act opera on March 15.

So you see that the composing, writing, and orchestrating has to be completed in one month. After April 15, following the example of the

Petersburg Conservatory, we shall prepare the graduation performance. The best one-act operas will be given at the end of May. If my opera is included among the best, then I'll have only one task after April 15: attending rehearsals of my future opera. If it's not included, I'll still graduate from the Conservatory and be freed on April 15 to go to the country. . . .

Now about my songs that I promised to send you. I'll positively send them, but my copyist has lately had a lot of work and hasn't done them yet.

Before this examination task another performance, a semipublic one, of the best pupils in all Conservatory classes, was given March 17 at the Small Salle of the Hall of Nobility. Bukinik observed that the boy had become a man who knew his own worth—and his own mind:

At this concert Rachmaninoff appeared, with the first movement of his first piano concerto. I played in the student orchestra, and I felt real boyish pride that my comrade was appearing as a pianist with his own composition. The melodic part of the concerto did not astonish me, but I was impressed by the freshness of its harmony, the free writing, and the easy mastery of its orchestration.

At rehearsals the eighteen-year-old Rachmaninoff showed the same stubbornly calm character that we knew from our comradely gatherings. Safonov, who ordinarily conducted the compositions of his students, would brutally and unceremoniously change anything he wished in these scores, cleaning them up and cutting parts to make them more playable. The student composers, happy to have their creative essays performed (these included Koreshchenko, Könemann and Morozov), did not dare contradict Safonov and readily agreed to his comments and alterations. But Safonov had a hard time with Rachmaninoff. This student not only refused categorically to accept alterations, but also had the audacity to stop Safonov (as conductor), pointing out his errors in tempi and nuance. This was obviously displeasing to Safonov, but being intelligent, he understood the rights of an author, though a beginner, to make his own interpretation, and he tried to take the edge off any awkwardness. Besides, Rachmaninoff's talent as a composer was so obvious, and his quiet self-assurance made such an impression on all, that even the omnipotent Safonov had to yield.

A.N.S., in *Dnevnik Artista*, reviewed this student concert, giving

his opinion of Rachmaninoff's work: ". . . there is of course no independence yet, but there is taste, a nervous quality, youthful sincerity, and definite knowledge—and this is already a promise." Rachmaninoff also accompanied Avierino in Vieuxtemps' violin concerto.

Behind the foreground of music Rachmaninoff's family life was
undergoing some revision. His father had moved to Moscow, and
with the help of Sakhnovsky's father work was found for him as a
horse specialist. He rented an apartment, to be shared with his son.

Toward the end of March three candidates for graduation from
Arensky's free composition class—Rachmaninoff, Leo Conus, Nikita
Morozov—were handed their assignment: a one-act opera libretto,
Aleko, adapted by Vladimir Nemirovich-Danchenko from Pushkin's
poem, *The Gypsies.* The single act was divided into two scenes.
Aleko, a stranger in the gypsy camp, has for two years been the lover
of Zemfira, but Zemfira grows tired of him and turns to a gayer com-
panion of her own tribe. Aleko finds them together and kills them.
He is driven from the gypsy camp to remain alone, again, on the
steppe.

The moment Rachmaninoff was given the long-anticipated
libretto, he took it home brimming with excitement and joy. As he
rushed home he thought of all he would do with this the instant he
reached his room. But his father had chosen that day to entertain
friends. This unexpected obstacle made such an impression on Rachmaninoff that he threw himself on his bed, sobbing in his frustration.
When his father looked in to see how he was, and heard what was
wrong, he asked his guests to leave so that his son could work.

I accepted the libretto as it stood, never dreaming that it might be improved. Slonov sat across from me at my desk, and as I wrote I passed the
completed pages over to him without even looking up, and the kindly
Slonov immediately made fair copies of them in his neat hand.

Rachmaninoff reminded Natalia Skalon of her responsibility:

You know of course that during this month I am writing an opera and
I'll be under a certain strain, so it would be very pleasant if people who
are well disposed toward me would not forget me during this time and
would encourage me with letters. . . .

The opera is entitled "Aleko." The libretto is done very well. Subject is wonderful. Don't know whether the music will be wonderful!

As the libretto had been given the candidates almost two weeks later than promised, Arensky expected to see little music when he called in the candidates in mid-April for an interim inspection of their progress. He interviewed the three, one at a time, while the other two waited in the garden. When Arensky asked Rachmaninoff what progress he was making, he replied that he had finished the opera.

"In the piano score?"
"No, in the orchestral score."
As he watched me take the whole score from my case, he remarked, "Well, if you continue at this rate, you could compose twenty-four acts in a year!" When I played the work for Arensky, he was pleased but he was also critical of some things in it. Though now, when it is too late, I feel all his criticisms were just, then I was too arrogant to admit I could be wrong, and I did not alter a single bar.

The interview with Arensky was long past when he sent news to Natalia Skalon on April 30:

We didn't have the examination on April 15, and couldn't have it, be-cause the libretto was not given to us until March 26. So I play my opera for the Conservatory Committee on May 7, after which, according to my promise, I'll notify you of my grade. . . .
I finished my opera on April 13. Since then I've been busy returning to my senses, doing nothing, celebrating the day of Saint Lazybones, drinking brandy, and finally attending to little corrections of my opera. But seriously speaking, my back aches terribly.

The final examination was held, attended by many officials and musicians, as well as by Taneyev and the whole Conservatory faculty. Rachmaninoff played his opera and he received his expected "5" with a plus, but there were more rewards to come. From among the group of Conservatory professors observing the examination, Zverev rose and came up to his former pupil. He led him out to the deserted corridor and there embraced him with many good wishes. He took out his gold watch and gave it to the composer whose educa-

tion he had formed. There were occasions later when Rachmaninoff
had to pawn this watch, but he always redeemed it and kept it to
his last hours.

To top all, the board unanimously recommended the highest honor
for him in the power of the Conservatory: the Great Gold Medal,
which had been awarded only twice before in the history of the institution, to Taneyev himself and to Koreshchenko. The name of
S. V. Rachmaninoff was added to the marble tablet of honor in the
lobby of the Great Salle, and the composer's schooling ended in an
almost dreamlike shower of blessings.

Zverev had an opportunity soon for a friendly gesture to the young
composer. News of a new talent and of an attractive new opera had
reached the publisher Gutheil, who approached Zverev to help him
persuade Rachmaninoff to listen to his offers. Zverev arranged an
elaborately flattering plan for all concerned: he invited Tchaikovsky
to his house to hear the new opera and to give its composer advice
about publication in general and about Gutheil in particular. The
plan worked: Tchaikovsky was enchanted with the opera (it showed
his influence clearly) and eager to give publication advice:

"You're fortunate, Seryozha—you were really born under a lucky
star! I was a great deal older than you before I found a publisher, and
even then I didn't receive a kopek for my first published composition.
I thought I was lucky not to have to pay the publisher for this
privilege. As Gutheil not only offers a fee, but asks you to name your
own terms, I suggest you go him one better—and insist that *he* make
the terms."

In addition to *Aleko* the works in negotiation were the two cello
pieces (Op. 2) and the songs of Op. 4. When Rachmaninoff asked
Gutheil to propose a price for these, and the sum of five hundred
rubles was offered, Rachmaninoff was speechless with astonishment,
and the deal was quickly closed.

At the graduation ceremonies on May 31, when all graduates were
awarded that noble term of "Free Artist," the musical program included the Intermezzo from *Aleko*. The reviewer of *Dnevnik Artista*
said it was "very powerfully written." Among the performers at the
graduation concert in the Hall of Nobility were Zverev's trio:
Seryozha, Mo, and Lo, as well as Scriabin and Altschuler. Zverev

arranged a supper after the concert for his old pupils, along with the Pabst and Arensky families. Avierino recalls: "Though the supper was officially in honor of all of us, as graduates, everyone sensed that the true occasion was Zverev's celebration of his reconciliation with Rachmaninoff."

For his first summer as a "Free Artist" Rachmaninoff was profitably but not very interestingly employed. He was engaged at the Konovalov estate in the state of Kostroma to give piano lessons to the Konovalovs' young son, Alexander. While there he had the excitement of correcting the first proofs of his opera from Gutheil and the pleasure of a visit from his mother. He wrote to Slonov on June 7:

My life here is monotonous and, I suppose, dull. At first I felt oppressed, uncomfortable, not quite myself. Now that I've grown accustomed to the people they've begun to bore me, and things have become dull and sad for me. But I found someone to offer my hand to — I wrote my mother to come here from Petersburg. She's been with me for the past week. Mother goes away on June 11, and then I'll again be left alone. . . .

Of course I'm not working as I planned. I'm not practicing at all, and during the past month it would have been hard to practice, for I've sat the whole time at my desk transcribing my opera for piano with the vocal parts. I was afraid to entrust this work to anyone else. . . . My cello pieces will appear soon, because today I shall be correcting the second proof. As for the opera and songs, they won't be published before the beginning of September.

On June 10 he reported to Natalia Skalon:

Just saw my mother off — she came at my request and stayed a week, going from here to Grandmother's. Too bad she couldn't stay longer; it would have done her good after Petersburg, and it would have meant a few more nice days for me. In general I felt better this week: I was happy and had a lot of fun and, what is quite rare with me lately, I played practical jokes. . . .

My opera, *Aleko,* has been accepted by the Bolshoi Theater in Moscow. Production is scheduled after Lent. For me the production of *Aleko* is both a pleasant and an unpleasant prospect. Pleasant — because it's good experience for me to see my opera on the stage and to check my theatrical mistakes. Unpleasant — because the opera is sure to fail. I say this quite sincerely. It's the way things are. All first operas by young composers usually fail, and for a good reason; they are full of defects that can't be corrected until we know the stage. . . .

Then your questions move from music to the Konovalovs and my life with them. There are three in the family: father, now living in the Caucasus, mother, and son, to whom I give an hour's lesson every day. These last two live here with me. They are very nice people. They take good care of me and there's no limit to their kindness. Yet I feel bored, bored. I'll stay until August 20, I suppose. My later plans are not known to anyone, least of all to myself.

August 2, 1892

I was indeed born under a lucky star, as Tchaikovsky recently told me. Imagine, dear Natalia Dmitriyevna, suddenly everyone begins to love me passionately. Everyone invites me, everyone asks me to stay at his place, everyone courts me, everyone wants to see me. After these lessons end I am invited to no fewer than five places. I simply lose my head and therefore delay all answers. What is this? Perhaps this is the fate of all bad composers? I have no answer to this, but this is how it is. All love me! I am happy—I never expected it. You see, Tata, of these five places, there is only one pleasant one—yours. . . .

If I do come to you, I shall set down certain conditions. Forgive, please, my rudeness! They invite me and I make the terms. First condition: I must practice the piano every day from two to four hours. Second condition: I am never to be asked to play, for this is now strictly forbidden. I'm even forbidden to think about anything. They forbid me to hear music, and of course I am not allowed to think of composing. I don't understand what they want me to do with my head.

On Rachmaninoff's return to Moscow he again moved in with Slonov. As only a part of Gutheil's fee had been paid in advance of publication, and as publication was postponed until later in the season,* Rachmaninoff was glad to accept an engagement (for fifty rubles) to play in one of the concerts at the Electrical Exposition in Moscow. On September 26 he performed the first movement of Rubinstein's D minor piano concerto, conducted by Vojtěch Hlaváč, as well as a group of solos. These were a Chopin Berceuse, Liszt's transcription of the Kermess in Gounod's *Faust*, and a little piano

* The publication of *Aleko* was passed by the censor on September 12, 1892.

piece he had just written (the ban on composition having been lifted), a prélude in C-sharp minor. *Artiste* reviewed the concert:

Exceptional interest was lent the concert by the participation of S. V. Rachmaninoff, who graduated this spring from the Moscow Conservatory in theory, and in the piano class of Prof. A. Siloti. His performance of the first movement of Rubinstein's concerto was beautiful both technically and musically. A group of solo numbers, including a Prélude of his own composition, also aroused enthusiasm.

And thus one of the world's most popular piano pieces began its long career, that was to bring its composer everything—fame and contempt, ease and embarrassment, money (indirectly) and annoyance aplenty. As for its inspiration, he later told an interviewer: "One day the Prélude simply came and I put it down. It came with such force that I could not shake it off even though I tried to do so. It had to be—so there it was." When he played it for Taneyev, who confined himself always to "formal" criticism, the only comment was: "This is very much like Schumann's *Novelletten*."

But Rachmaninoff's career, that had sped upwards so swiftly a few months ago, had slowed down to tortoise pace. He was depressed by the silence in regard to his opera, even though it was ready for publication. So far as the Imperial Opera Theaters were concerned, he had written no opera. Long afterwards he spoke to an interviewer, in a tone that sounds autobiographical, about a young composer's first obstacles:

A talented beginner, full of hope and confidence, may find actual success replaced by inward satisfaction, but real results can be obtained if he has not to struggle too much for his bread, if his nerve be not impaired by continually having to ask for support, and if he is not obliged to dissipate his time in trying to obtain a hearing for his works. Artists need help at the beginning of their career.

He described his dark mood first to Natalia Skalon:

Your letters made me feel good, but otherwise I am in a foul mood, for I'm definitely not well. This isn't the cause of my melancholy, the main thing being that I'm afraid to take to my bed completely. That would be quite untimely now. I've just started to be attracted to work, and suddenly all this has to be given up for some stupid reason—the lack of money to buy a winter coat. [The three sisters responded with the gift of a coat.] And besides, I hate to be ill away from home. A nuisance to oneself and a burden to others. For me there's nothing more unpleasant than that. I feel oppressed now. I can't move from here, for I'm unable to get a permit [to change residence]. Every office I go to feeds me "Tomorrow." They make me terribly angry. . . .

Recently I've been getting to bed late and getting up early, so my head is now heavy—after playing I get terribly tired, and my head gets heavier and heavier. A sort of apathy for everything is setting in. After playing I can't do anything, so the lecture I was planning has halted at the point where you heard about it.

The day before yesterday [he wrote to Ludmila Skalon on October 15] I wrote your older sister that I was not well, in a bad mood, and all this resulted in a bad letter. At present I feel wonderful, I am well, in good spirits, and I'm therefore capable of writing an agreeable letter. . . .

Here at the Satins' [who had moved to a smaller apartment] a very important event is about to take place: the departure of the great composer. Where to? I don't know, but nevertheless I leave here tomorrow, because I disturb everyone with my work and my work is disturbed by everyone. This means that we cannot go on living together. But if you should wish to write me, address me at the Satins', for I still hope to visit here and, of course, give great pleasure to all, because in general, you know, I am very nice and genial.

As for myself I can say that all day today everyone has afforded me pleasure, speaking as a musician. First, I learned that my opera will certainly be performed in March. Secondly, Safonov has promised to include the dances and other excerpts from the opera in a symphonic program [of the Russian Musical Society]. Thirdly, Gutheil is buying my piano concerto, which means some money to come. Fourthly, Gutheil tells me that the sale of my opera goes very well, especially in Kiev.

On December 14 he had another encouraging bit of news to send Slonov, then in Kharkov:

My coming [to Kharkov] depends on Orel, where they've asked me to play; the sooner my concert there takes place, the sooner I'll get to Kharkov. . . .

Altogether lately I've been afflicted by spleen. There's been only one happy thing happened to me since your departure, and this is what it was: A Petersburg critic came to Tchaikovsky (after the performance of *Iolanthe*) for an interview. And Tchaikovsky tells the critic that he is forced to give up composition to make way for young talents. To the question, Do these really exist? Tchaikovsky answered: "Yes," and named, in Petersburg, Glazunov, and in Moscow, myself and Arensky. This was a genuine joy for me. Thanks to the old man for not forgetting me. After reading this I sat down at the piano and composed a fifth piece. So now I'll publish five pieces.

These five pieces (to be published as Op. 3, and containing Elegy, *the* Prélude, Melody, Polichinelle,* and Serenade) were dedicated to Arensky, and were first performed as a group in the Kharkov concert of December 20, with works by Chopin, Liszt, Schumann, and Rubinstein and Pabst's fantasia on themes from Tchaikovsky's *Eugene Onegin*.

There was an urgent summons from Siloti's brother Sergei to come at once to St. Petersburg. A personable young navy officer (as well as amateur musician), Sergei Siloti knew influential members of Petersburg society and decided to apply all his energy to his cousin Rachmaninoff's problem. He arranged for an interview with the all-powerful Napravnik, conductor of the Imperial Opera. Nothing came of that. Sergei Siloti's ace, however, was farther removed from musical circles. This was the eccentric Mme. Yevgeniya Krivenko, whose husband was the Chief of the Chancery in the Ministry of the Imperial Court, as well as friend and first assistant of the Minister, Count Vorontzov-Dashkov. Another thread in the plot was furnished by Krivenko's influence being sought eagerly by Pogozhev, Chief of the Chancery of the Imperial Theaters. The setting for this comedy of intrigue was provided by the celebration of Mme. Krivenko's Saint's Day, December 24, at which all the characters in the tableau were assembled as close as possible to the hostess's chair. The plot got under way when Mme. Krivenko (prompted by Sergei Siloti) motioned Rachmaninoff to sit down at the piano and play something from his new opera. He obliged and played the Dances from *Aleko* ("No encores!" his cousin had instructed). Before the applause

---

* A title suggested by Slonov.

had died away, the hostess turned to His Excellency Pogozhev (so desperately eager to grant her any favor, to gain her good will in his own behalf) and said, "You *will* produce this brilliant work, of course, won't you?"

Rehearsals for *Aleko* were scheduled to begin at the Bolshoi Theater in Moscow early that spring, and Rachmaninoff's slowed career again picked up speed. Safonov's performance (on February 19, 1893) of the two dances from the opera produced a good impression, and in another concert the popular baritone, Leonid Yakovlev, gave the first professional performance of a Rachmaninoff song (from Op. 4)—"Oh, no, I beg you, don't forsake me." But Natalia Skalon was told, on February 7, that the composer was still not quite happy:

You were not mistaken in believing that my silence was caused by difficulties in my life. That is the genuine truth. Yes, my soul bears a large burden of grief. It's unnecessary to dwell on it, for this will not eliminate it but merely increase it, to talk about it, and analyze it.

Actually, all my relatives seem agreed on killing me and laying me in my coffin—not intentionally, of course, but simply through circumstances. My closest relatives console me in this way: my father lives a most senseless life; my mother is gravely ill; my older brother accumulates debts that God alone knows how he is to repay (in the present circumstances little hope can be placed on me); my younger brother is terribly lazy and is sure to be stuck for another year in his grade; my grandmother is at the point of death. . . .

You will tell me over and over: "Take treatments." But how can moral pain be treated? How can you change the whole nervous system which I've already tried to change with several nights of merrymaking and drunkenness? This didn't help—it only made me give up drinking for ever. . . . People often tell me, and you too in your last letter: throw off this melancholy— at your age and with your talent, it's a shame. But everyone forgets that besides being (perhaps) a talented musician, I am also a man, like everyone else, demanding from life the same things that others do. . . .

Destroy this letter after reading it, for otherwise someone may see it and read what I don't care for people to know about me, and then say, "What affectation," which would be as unpleasant for me as are truths spoken to a proud and egotistic man.

Goodbye. S. R.

Fortunately, Taneyev found an occupation for Rachmaninoff at this time. The Marinsky Theater planned to stage Taneyev's opera *Orestes* and needed a vocal score. Taneyev made his own piano reduction with the help of four copyists. He reported to Tchaikovsky, "Rachmaninoff spends four hours a day here, proofreading the copied pages, for which I have no time."

On February 27 Rachmaninoff was able to give his freshly printed piano pieces (Op. 3) to Tchaikovsky* when the older composer came to Moscow to conduct a concert for the Russian Musical Society. At this time Tchaikovsky rejected his brother Modeste's libretto for another try at the subject of *Undine,* and he suggested that Modeste submit it to Rachmaninoff:

Wouldn't you be satisfied just to send the scenario to Rachmaninoff, without writing the verses? Let someone else put the scenario into verse. Please, my dear, don't be angry and don't be hurt.

Tchaikovsky attended the last rehearsals of his protégé's *Aleko* and proposed that in the following season it be given on the same evening with his two-act opera, *Iolanthe.*

The mere fact of having a work performed at the Imperial Theater would have been enough to start my career; but Tchaikovsky did even more. Timidly and modestly, as if he were afraid I might refuse, he asked me if I would consent to have my work produced with one of his operas. To be on the poster with Tchaikovsky was about the greatest honor that could be paid to a composer, and I would not have dared to suggest such a thing. Tchaikovsky knew this. He wanted to help me, but was anxious also not to offend or humiliate me.

Tchaikovsky also helped him deal with Altani, conductor at the Bolshoi Opera:

We sat together in a corner of the darkened theater. Altani's ideas for some parts did not please me. I recall the following dialogue between Tchaikovsky and myself:
  "Do you like this tempo?" he asked.
  "No."

  * Tchaikovsky later wrote to Siloti that he liked the piano pieces very much, "especially the Prélude and the Melody."

"Then why don't you say so?"

"I'm afraid."

During a break in the rehearsal Tchaikovsky cleared his throat and spoke to Altani:

"Sergei Vasilyevich and I think that the tempo in that part might be taken a little faster."

The première of *Aleko* on April 27* was an event of first importance for several persons in the first-night audience. Rachmaninoff's father and his grandmother Rachmaninoff (who came specially from Tambov) occupied, emotionally, one loge. On Tchaikovsky's urging, Vsevolozhsky, Director of the Imperial Theaters, had come from St. Petersburg to hear the new work. In his loge sat Tchaikovsky, and another occupant of the loge, Julian Poplavsky, later reported his remarks before the curtain rose:

I recall his excited expectancy of "how the general public would receive the opera," and he said to me:

"We are finally seeing the day when a young Russian composer, Seryozha Rachmaninoff, can hear and see his 'first pancake' at an Imperial Theater, when not long ago, for example, I vainly tried to force my way into the Marinsky Theater, where they didn't even bother examining my first opera, *Undine*, and the manuscript was actually lost in the theater archives—probably unopened."

Tchaikovsky's applause at the end of the single act was not simply appreciation: he made a *point* of his applause by leaning far out over the ledge to show the whole audience that he, whom they admired so much, was showing them a new work to admire.** The youthful composer himself was brought before the curtain to face the audience's surprise and satisfaction.

In *Artiste* Semyon Kruglikov wrote a detailed review of the new opera, basing his judgments on both performance and published vocal score. The review concludes:

Rachmaninoff is a talented man with thorough knowledge and ex-

* In addition to *Aleko,* the program was completed with excerpts from *A Life for the Tzar* and *The Queen of Spades.* The singers of *Aleko* were: Deisha-Sionitzkaya, Korsov, Klementiev, Vlasov.

** His private reaction to *Aleko* is to be found in a letter (to I. I. Slatin, of May 3): "I like this lovely thing very much."

cellent taste. He can be a good composer of opera, for he has a feeling for the stage and an almost perfect understanding of the human voice, and he is endowed with the fortunate capacity for melody. . . . As the work of an eighteen-year-old composer, as the work of a student, *Aleko* is beyond all praise; as an opera designed for the stage of the Bolshoi Theater, it leaves a great deal to be desired.

For the composer also, the work left something to be desired. Later in his career he always dismissed it as unworthy, at one time saying, "It is written on the old-fashioned Italian model, which Russian composers, in most cases, have been accustomed to follow."

Chapter 4

Deaths and Failure

E ARLY in May Rachmaninoff left Moscow to visit his grandmother Butakova, who had not been able to attend the
première of *Aleko*. From her home he wrote to Modeste Tchaikovsky
about the *Undine* libretto, with a hint that he was aware that it had
not been written specially for his use (it had actually been offered
to Lyadov as well as to Pyotr Tchaikovsky):

May 13, 1893

Highly esteemed Modeste Ilyich,

First I must point out a slight matter. At the end of your scenario for
Undine there is a date, March 16, apparently the day on which you
completed it. But I did not receive *Undine* until the end of April. Since
then I have thought a great deal about the scenario, reread it many times,
and have decided there is nothing awkward in it. When I read it to Anton
Stepanovich [Arensky], he considered it awkward to have these two
episodes—Berthalda's recognition of her parents and Undine's death—in
the same scene. But I don't agree. Though this scene would be very
difficult to write, it is just here that these two personages of the poem
must be illuminated and contrasted, and if one is able to do this, it will
make a good impression. In the opinion of Anton Stepanovich, Undine's
death can't make its proper impression on the spectator coming right after
the episode with Berthalda, and at that moment the spectator's interest
will relax. However, I think Undine's death will be the climax of the
scene's interest. In general I must say that I am very pleased with it all,
and it is with delight that I begin to write the opera. Only one thing
troubles me: that if I write *Undine*, it may never reach the stage. It can't
be produced in a provincial theater because of the large production it
demands, and it can't be produced in the Imperial Theaters because the
director [Vsevolozhsky] doesn't care for the subject—he told me so himself
the other day; this would mean that my work, and a large work too, would
be all for nothing. If only you, highly esteemed Modeste Ilyich, could, on
your own initiative and at the proper moment, ask Vsevolozhsky.

Toward the end of May Rachmaninoff joined his friend Slonov

on the Kharkov estate of the merchant Lysikov, from where he wrote
to Natalia Skalon on June 5:

I couldn't stay on in Moscow. . . . I was feeling miserable and I had to
run away. So I ran away! I came here and began to lead a normal kind
of life. At your request I shall tell you how I spend the day. I get up at
eight and retire at eleven. I work on composition from 9 to 12. Then I
play for three hours. I forgot to tell you that I am very systematic about
my cure: cold sponges and four glasses of milk each day. I stop working
at 5 o'clock. . . .

At present I am busy with a fantasy for 2 pianos, representing a series
of musical pictures. I'll write you more fully about these in my next
letter, for by that time I believe this composition will be finished.

A fuller report on his hosts went to Ludmila Skalon on June 29:

Your questions about the Lysikovs—Who are they? What sort of people
are they? How did I run into them? What is their relation to me? and so
on.

The Lysikovs are two—husband and wife, both rather advanced in
years. . . . I met them in Kharkov, where they usually spend the winter;
on both my trips there I stayed at their home. . . .

Lysikov himself is a large-minded man, a man who knows a great deal,
a man interested in everything. A man who, although he calls himself a
"corn dealer," jokingly of course, is quite different from those merchants
that we may not think of so highly. He is a very kind man who will
sympathize with and aid every worthy enterprise with all his means. . . .

As for her—all fades away before her kindness, a tremendous, amazing
kindness. A rare person, you may even say unique. She had a son, an only
child, whom she worshiped. He died six years ago, but she can't forget
him, and all her life is attached to his memory. There's a woman living
here who was once the son's nurse—she's quite worthless, steals quite
openly, but never receives a word of rebuke, all because she had looked
after the boy for less than a year. . . . Once I began to read aloud a poem
that turned out to be a poem the son had read. The mother had
hysterics. . . .

Slonov tells me that I look a little like her son. This must be the reason
she looks after me as carefully as she does. . . . Once I mentioned that I
should like to work on my compositions in the garden. This was enough
for her to begin at once the construction of some sort of huge tower, with
monograms, stars, etc.

In general my position is such that even if I should like to leave, I couldn't. I would be ashamed to. . . . It's a wonderful, rare home, and a better person than I should live in it.

The letter that he wrote Natalia Skalon on August 25, just before leaving the Lysikovs', concluded with a rather bitter jest:

I'm terribly grateful for your invitation. I would accept it with delight, but the main thing is that I have no money for it, nor time. I am working extremely hard. Haven't yet finished the poem [*The Crag*]—four days more, I think. As for money, I have no right to spend any, and must, indeed, save what I have.

I must tell you that this fall I intend to get married. Fact! Irrefutable, indisputable. I've already listed for my fiancée all my real and movable estate. In the former category is a watch that has not been moved for a year from the pawnshop where it is lying, with other golden things. In this same category are my debts, though they may also be termed "movable," as they will probably move farther.

My plan, however, is for my wife to pay these. I have drawn up an inventory of my *movable* estate, beginning with neckties and ending with slippers and nightcap! There's one doubt: will anyone have me? But this is unimportant. I'm going to marry, and that's that! I invite you to my wedding!

The summer with the Lysikovs was productive. He brought back enough work for several summers, enough even to satisfy the super-productive Tchaikovsky: more than enough songs to complete Op. 4, including dedications to his cousin Natalia Satina and to Mme. Lysikova; a sacred concert, "O Mother of God, perpetually praying," for mixed choir; a Fantasia for two pianos (his first two-piano suite)* dedicated to Tchaikovsky; two pieces (Op. 6) for violin and piano (dedicated to Julius Conus); *The Crag* (Op. 7), a fantasia for orchestra.

Actually a symphonic poem, *The Crag* (sometimes referred to, in English, as "The Rock") is Rachmaninoff's most ambitious and

* The four parts of Op. 5: "Barcarole" (epigraph by Lermontov); "Oh night, Oh love" (epigraph by Byron); "Tears" (epigraph by Tiutchev); "Holy Day" (epigraph by Khomyakov). Of "Tears," he told Sophia Satina that it was inspired by the bells tolling during a funeral at the Novgorod Monastery.

interesting work of this summer. It has two programs: one for public consumption, the other its true and private program. There is this note on the published score:

This fantasy is written under the impression of Lermontov's poem, "The Crag." The composer has chosen, as epigraph for this composition, the opening lines of that poem:

> The little golden cloud spent the night
> On the chest of the giant crag.

Though we may never know why Rachmaninoff felt obliged to be secretive, the very precision of his statement can only be regarded as a careful concealment of the work's real program, for some years later he presented Chekhov with a copy of the printed score with this inscription:

To dear and highly esteemed Anton Pavlovich Chekhov, the author of the story "Along the Way," the contents of which, with the same epigraph, served as program for this musical composition.

S. Rachmaninoff

November 9, 1898.

It may have been because in 1893 he had not yet met Chekhov and hesitated to ask permission to use Chekhov's work in this way, or it may have been that his antipathy to publicly revealed programs was already formed.* In any case, the relation between Chekhov's "Along the Way" and Rachmaninoff's *Crag* is worth our attention. Chekhov's story is set in the travelers' room of a roadside inn on Christmas Eve, with a blizzard howling outside. Two travelers, traveling in opposite directions, are detained here: a gruff, passionate, middle-aged failure ("the giant crag") and a delicate and lovely young woman ("the golden cloud"). He tells her of his life and beliefs, the emotion in his voice drowning the storm's roar outside. In the brightness of Christmas morning she is overcome with pity for him, but has to continue on her way as he prepares himself for his next painful failure. To read the story as Rachmaninoff may have read

---

* When the work was first played, March 20, 1894, Nikolai Kashkin mentioned this "secret" program, but ever since it has been well hidden.

it makes us hear all the emotional musical imagery in it—the storm's angry whistle penetrating every crack, the bell sounds filtered through the driving snow, the "sweet, human music" of weeping, and the final picture that sounds as characteristic of Rachmaninoff as it does of Chekhov:

Snowflakes settled greedily on his hair, his beard, his shoulders . . . soon the imprint of the sleigh runners vanished, and he himself, covered with snow, gradually assumed the appearance of a white crag, but his eyes still sought something in the white clouds of the drifts.

Undine was soon to be put aside, and Rachmaninoff worked on no other opera subject this year, but in *The Crag* he composed a vivid wordless drama.

In mid-September Rachmaninoff introduced his friends to *The Crag* at one of Taneyev's evenings:

I well remember my last meeting with P. I. Tchaikovsky, to whom I showed "The Crag" and who said, with his gentle smile: "What hasn't Seryozha written this summer! A poem and a concerto and a suite, and Heaven knows what else. . . . And I wrote only one symphony."

The reason for this particular gathering was to hear the four-hand arrangement made by Leo Conus of Tchaikovsky's new symphony, not yet named the *Pathétique*. Conus and Taneyev played, and were constantly interrupted by the composer's corrections (not only of the arrangement, but of his full score). Ippolitov-Ivanov, who was also present, reports the atmosphere of the session:

Because of the many halts to correct some detail or for the cavilings of Pyotr Ilyich, who for some reason was especially nervous that evening, the symphony made no impression on us, and Pyotr Ilyich was gloomier than a storm cloud.

That evening I made the acquaintance of Sergei Vasilyevich Rachmaninoff, who had graduated from the Moscow Conservatory a year before my arrival in Moscow. . . . At the close of the evening he acquainted us with the newly completed symphonic poem, *The Crag*. . . . The poem pleased all very much, especially Pyotr Ilyich, who was enthusiastic over its colorfulness. The performance of *The Crag* and our discussion of it must have diverted Pyotr Ilyich, for his former good-hearted mood came back to him.

Tchaikovsky was so pleased with it, in fact, that he asked for it to play on his planned European tour this season. The new work that was dedicated to Tchaikovsky—the Fantasia for two pianos—Rachmaninoff did not wish to spoil by a hurried rendering on a single piano, and Tchaikovsky promised to come to Moscow to hear him play it with Pabst at the latter's concert, in the winter.

When Rachmaninoff visited St. Petersburg he was compelled to play his Fantasia for the Belayev circle:

When I was young I was completely under the spell of Tchaikovsky. I had a publisher who paid me more than Belayev. Belayev and his whole Petersburg circle were not worth a damn to me at that time. Once Belayev invited me to play for them. I had just written my Fantasy for two pianos. They put Felix [Blumenfeld] at the second piano, for only he could sight-read perfectly. I played from memory at the first piano. They were all there—Lyadov, Rimsky-Korsakov—and they listened very attentively and seemed to like it. Rimsky smiled the whole time. Then they praised me, and Rimsky said: "All is fine, except that at the end, when the chant of 'Christ is risen' is heard, it would be better to state it first alone, and only the second time with the bells."

I was silly and in love with myself in those days—I was only twenty— so I shrugged my shoulders and said: "And why? In reality it always comes together with the bells," and I never changed a note. Only later did I realize how just Rimsky-Korsakov's criticism had been. The true greatness of Rimsky-Korsakov dawned on me gradually, and I was very sorry that I never got to be his pupil.*

In September Rachmaninoff composed a new group of songs, to translations by Pleshcheyev of Ukrainian and German poems; these were published as Op. 8.

On September 30 Tchaikovsky and Rachmaninoff lost a friend in the death of Zverev, and both participated in the memorial ceremonies for him.

I am very sorry that I shan't be seeing you soon [Rachmaninoff wrote to the three Skalon sisters on October 3]. I leave for Kiev in mid-October,

* A happier moment in the relations between Rimsky-Korsakov and Rachmaninoff: In December 1894 Rimsky-Korsakov conducted the first Petersburg performance of the Dances from *Aleko,* and in gratitude the young composer dedicated to him the newly published *Crag.*

don't know the exact date, but I've been asked to go there to conduct the first two performances of Aleko. . . .

In January I shall conduct my opera in Odessa. In January too, if I can get there in time, I shall be in Petersburg, where Tchaikovsky is to conduct *The Crag*. So if we don't see each other now, then perhaps in January. . . .

Perhaps you've already heard of Zverev's death. We buried him yesterday. A very great pity. Each year the old Conservatory family shrinks and loses its "Mohicans." Meanwhile the world has one fine person less in it. Saddening and piteous. No one expected such a swift end, and he himself sensed death only 5 hours before it came, when he said to one of the persons sitting with him, "Farewell, brother. I am pouf-pouf!" Five minutes before he died he screamed through the apartment to have the shutters opened (he died at night)—to have the windows and doors opened—that he was suffocating, terribly suffocating. He threw himself about horribly. His old chef and the housekeeper (nobody else was there when he died) lifted him up, he inhaled some air—and never exhaled it. Pouf-pouf! just as he said.

The *Undine* project was finally shelved on October 14, with this letter to Modeste Tchaikovsky: "I want to ask you for the present to discontinue further writing or work on *Undine*, for I've decided nothing yet. Up to now I am terribly dubious about it, for besides having a great deal of traveling to do, I can't take up this work now."

Pyotr Tchaikovsky paid a hurried trip to Moscow to run through his new symphony with students of the orchestra class of the Conservatory, to make sure it was finished to his satisfaction before its first public performance in St. Petersburg. Rachmaninoff had accepted an invitation to conduct two performances of *Aleko* in Kiev, and Tchaikovsky waved a bantering farewell: "You see, Seryozha, we're famous composers now! One goes to Kiev to conduct his opera and the other to Petersburg to conduct his symphony!"

It was in Kiev, on October 25, that Rachmaninoff received word from St. Petersburg that Tchaikovsky had that morning died of cholera.

When the Fantasia for two pianos was played by the composer and Pabst in the latter's concert on November 30, Tchaikovsky, to whom it was dedicated, had been in his grave for a month, and

Rachmaninoff had begun a work in his memory, a *Trio élégiaque* for piano, violin, and cello. It was completed on December 15; he told Natalia Skalon of it two days later:

I've had only one reason for not writing you: I've been working hard, regularly, persistently. This work is a composition on the death of a great artist. It's now finished, so I can speak with you. While working on it, all my thoughts, feelings, powers belonged to it, to this song. . . . I trembled for every phrase, sometimes crossed out everything and started over again to think, think. Now that's over, and I can speak calmly. I wrote no one, not even the Skalons, whom I love sincerely. . . .

You ask how things go with me? These days things go well only with priests and pharmacists.

The trio was first performed as the opening work on the first concert (January 31, 1894) to be devoted exclusively to Rachmaninoff's compositions—all chamber works. In addition to the trio (played by the composer, Julius Conus, and Anatoli Brandukov), the Fantasia for two pianos was repeated by the composer and Pabst, Yelizaveta Lavrovskaya sang two songs (from Op. 4 and 8), Brandukov played the two cello pieces, and Rachmaninoff played his Op. 3 and his newly composed Op. 10 (dedicated to Pabst). Of these new piano pieces, the critic of *Artiste* commented:

Rachmaninoff is undoubtedly talented, yet it would do him no harm to show more modesty and more self-criticism.

For Rachmaninoff 1894 was a disturbed and restless year. No longer did he have the security of Tchaikovsky's presence and appreciation. For the first time he was trying to live alone; in the fall of 1893 he took a tiny furnished apartment in a house on Vozdvizhenka, called "America." He did not enjoy this lonely life, but stuck it out for a few months, spending the summer away from Moscow. Even though he wasn't fond of sprees and drinking, he needed more money than he could hope to receive from Gutheil. He was young, loved a certain amount of display—riding in "better" cabs, dressing well, tipping all, and enjoying the resulting smiles and bows. As his fees for compositions hurried out of his pockets faster than they entered, his dream of financial independence (never yet experienced) only increased in intensity. And his conscience bothered him when he caught himself writing compositions, such as the piano duets of Op. 11, just to balance his accounts.

The only steady income that could be counted on was from piano lessons, no matter how much he hated giving them. Though he received handsome fees for the lessons and even formed friendships in the families of his pupils, he felt a repulsion from teaching and did everything possible to avoid it: he would arrive late or not at all, or he would try to put off the lesson to another day. It is true that he was a poor teacher; merely to glance at him during a lesson was enough to destroy the pupil's last desire to become a pianist. When friends reproached him for his negative attitude to his pupils he would sigh and say that it was simply too boring to sit and listen to people picking at the piano rather than playing it, etc.

The family of one of his pupils again invited him for part of the summer. He spent the first half of the summer with the Konovalovs, playing cards a great deal of the time, and proofreading *The Crag* for Jürgenson (he had discerned the advantage in having two publishers). He began a symphonic poem inspired by Byron's *Don Juan,* "Two episodes à la Liszt," on June 20, and wrote to Slonov a month later:

I was terribly tormented, and even threw away part of what I had written; worst of all, I may throw away all that I now have. . . . Before June 20 I wrote one other thing (or rather, sketched one)—I'll write both of these after I get to the Satins'. This is a piece for orchestra alone, and will be called "Capriccio on gypsy themes." This composition is already completed in my head.

This *Capriccio on Gypsy Themes* (Op. 12) was finished in August, according to a letter to Slonov:

In about 4 days I shall finish this work. For the time being I think I shall write it for 4 hands, and orchestrate it later. I want to study some scores and think it over.

The work was dedicated to Pyotr Lodyzhensky, into whose family he had been introduced by Sakhnovsky. Lodyzhensky's wife, Anna Alexandrovna, was a gypsy by birth, and her kindness and loveliness greatly attracted Rachmaninoff. His visits to their house became a daily habit. A hopeless infatuation for Mme. Lodyzhenskaya had developed from these visits and talks; perhaps its hopelessness made it all the sweeter. This was an altogether different feeling from that he had for the pretty Vera Skalon, whose family had made the future of that relationship, too, as hopeless. Many projects but little music sprang immediately from the influence of Mme. Anna Lodyzhenskaya (Op. 4, No. 1, "Oh, no, I beg you, don't forsake me," was dedicated to her), but the next large work completed by Rachmaninoff was dedicated to "A. L."

The second half of this summer was spent at the Satin estate of Ivanovka, where the two older Skalon sisters were also summering; because of Vera's heart trouble, her mother had again taken her abroad, to Nauheim, for the summer. Unpromising reports continued to be sent to Slonov: "You're mistaken in thinking that I have a Symphony in existence. I am not writing a Symphony, though I have not given up the idea of Byron's *Don Juan.*" Ludmila Skalon recalls his efforts of this summer:

As usual he was extremely exhausted and felt weak. Nevertheless, he stuck to the piano and to his composing. When he was concentrating on a musical idea he usually went to his favorite avenue, paved with red brick, and we could see him there from afar—a tall figure in a Russian shirt, pacing with lowered head and drumming with his fingers on his chest and humming something. Naturally, at such moments, we kept out of sight, so as not to disturb his thoughts.

This winter [Rachmaninoff wrote to Slonov on September 3] ... I have nothing to live on. Nor do I have anything for sprees. And I cannot live, counting every kopek, considering and calculating every kopek. I absolutely must have an occasional moment when I can forget all in life that really disturbs me, that worries me, or perhaps even hurts me a little. Of course, calculating, considering, counting kopeks doesn't suit me at such times—doesn't fit me! Truly one should have some way of breaking away from this. But what am I saying! I won't even have enough for the most ordinary life. Even this is too costly for me. To cut this down materially is completely impossible. Something quite extraordinary will have to be invented.

Two things were invented to bring in some money. He found a

regular job as music teacher in the Marinsky School for Girls, and this was eventually followed by posts as music teacher and (six years later) music director at Yekaterininsky and Yelizavetinsky institutes. Classes of girls were less wearing than individual pupils. The principals of these institutes treated Rachmaninoff with the greatest consideration, and as time went on they did everything within the rules to shorten the torturous hours of Rachmaninoff's actual lessons.* That Rachmaninoff was sensitive to their kindness is shown by an undated letter from him found among the papers of the directress of the Marinsky School, Mme. Liventzova:

I left my class today before the end of the lesson because they had not studied their assignment. When I got home, I learned from the [Satin] sisters that this incident might reach your ears and that the entire class would be liable to punishment. This shocked me and I decided to ask a great favor of you: please forgive my class for this little misdemeanor and please do not punish them. I am in general a poor teacher and today, moreover, I was unpardonably malicious. If I had realized that my students would have to pay for my bad behavior, I would never have permitted myself this self-indulgence.

Another financial help is described by Sophia Satina:

We changed our living quarters in the fall of 1894 to a large house, and Rachmaninoff was invited to move in with us, which he did. A large room on the third floor was partitioned and made into a bedroom and studio for him. The advantage of this was its distance from the other rooms in the house; he could not hear the noise of living that went on on the first floor, and the second floor was occupied by the bedrooms of Volodya, who was away in school all day, and the three women servants, who spent their days on the floor below. There was a large yard, which the younger generation used in the winter for skating and for sliding down ice mountains. From this winter of 1894–95 Rachmaninoff lived with us every winter until his marriage.

Our only trouble was with thoughtless friends. We learned several

* "A pupil of Rachmaninoff" is a claim occasionally heard, but none of the claimants is old enough to have studied with him in the early years when lack of money forced him to take pupils; nor would the students at these girls' schools pretend to have received individual instruction. After adopting in 1918 the career of virtuoso pianist, Rachmaninoff taught no one.

polite ways to discourage his acquaintances from dropping in at all times
of day for a chat with him. Natasha, Volodya, and I had the help of
Lyolya Kreutzer, a pupil of Rachmaninoff, in preventing anyone from
getting upstairs while he was composing. There was one man who came
—and had to be outwitted—almost daily. He was a good man, but he
simply could not understand that his composer friend had something
better to do.

The other invention for making money was less successful: a national concert tour in the fall of 1895. The concert manager Lange-
witz engaged Rachmaninoff to tour Russia, sharing the program with
the Italian violinist Teresina Tua. Rachmaninoff reported to Slonov
from Belostok on November 9:

At the first concert, in Lodz, against my anticipation, I played pretty well.
I had a great success, but she—the Contessa Teresina Tua Franchi-
Verney della Valetta—had, of course, an even greater success. Incidentally,
she does not play particularly well; her technique is middling. But with
her eyes and smiles she plays magnificently for the public. As an artist she
is not serious, but she has talent. I can bear, without too much irritation,
her sweet smiles before the audience, her breaks on high notes, her
fermata (à la Mazzini). I've learned one thing about her: she is very
stingy. She is charming to me—very afraid that I'll scamper away.

Long before the conclusion of the three-month tour Rachmaninoff
did scamper away, excusing himself to impresario and virtuosa with
the pretext that the promised advance had not been paid. Content
to lose his fee as long as he didn't lose any more time playing accompaniments for uninteresting violin pieces and taking long trips under
the hard conditions usual for touring musicians then (such as a chilly
sixty-verst trip to Mogilev in an antique vehicle), he returned to
Moscow from Smolensk, admitting defeat. And Zverev's watch was
pawned once more.

Before leaving on the abortive tour Rachmaninoff had completed
his most ambitious work. Since January of 1895 all his energies and
hopes had been concentrated on a symphony based on traditional
chants of the Russian Orthodox Service. On September 2 there was
good news for Slonov: the symphony in D minor was completed.

Lately I have been working about ten hours a day. How could letters be fitted in! . . . On August 30 I finished orchestrating the Symphony. Nevertheless I'll spend two more days on it. I feel calm about the last three movements, though the first displeases me slightly, and I consider that there are several places that need changing. . . . The Symphony lasts 50 minutes. The Devil knows I'm afraid it will be tiresome.

The symphony was dedicated to "A.L.," the initials of Anna Lody-zhenskaya. The only hint of a program was contained in its epigraph, the same words of God that Tolstoy placed at the beginning of *Anna Karenina*: "Vengeance is mine; I will recompense."* But together symphony, dedication, and epigraph furnish fascinating material for speculation.. The "divine justice" theme of the epigraph gives point to the use of religious chants as base for the whole symphony. The temptation to hear in the slow third movement a "portrait" of the dedicatee is irresistible, for the melodic line is tender with a feminine grace, and its opening theme uses characteristics of the so-called "gypsy scale," with intervals of augmented seconds framed in semi-tones.

Belayev, Maecenas of Russian music, had not given up hopes of attracting the newest young composer to his publication and concert fold. He had financed a series of concerts exclusively for Russian music, and when he heard that Rachmaninoff had completed a symphony, he negotiated at once for its première. The new work was placed on the following season's schedule of the Russian Symphony Concerts of St. Petersburg, and its first performance was included in a concert to be conducted by Alexander Glazunov, who reported to Taneyev on November 23: "I have looked through Rachmaninoff's symphony, have found some slips of the pen, but on the whole I approve it, especially the orchestration. The parts are now being copied." Belayev also scheduled the first Petersburg performance of *The Crag;* this work and Ippolitov-Ivanov's *Caucasian Sketches,* on the same program of January 20, 1896, were accorded a friendly welcome by the Petersburg critics as "novelties from the young Russian school of Moscow." Though Cui wrote of *The Crag* that "the whole composition shows that this composer is more concerned about sound than about music," the tone of his review was well-wishing. Another

* *Deuteronomy* 32: 35, 41; *Romans* 12:19; *Hebrews* 10:30.

Belayev gesture: he commissioned Rachmaninoff to make a piano transcription of Glazunov's Sixth Symphony—200 rubles for two months' work.

Rachmaninoff had put so much of himself into his symphony that he could not settle down to further serious composition until it was heard; his future work was to be determined by the public's reaction to his symphony. In this period the advice and society of Taneyev was a blessing. Taneyev's diary shows this entry in March 1896: "Friday [22], in the evening, Rachmaninoff came. He is writing a quartet. We talked of quartet style and in particular of the C major quartet of Mozart." After a sketch for two movements this quartet, like the quartet for Siloti, was left unfinished. Another small work growing out of the evenings spent with Taneyev is an "improvisation," in a jesting group of improvisations by Arensky, Glazunov, Rachmaninoff, and Taneyev.

Sabaneyev tells of another "group project" at Taneyev's during the winter of 1896: a series of sessions to study the late compositions of Wagner. These sessions began at four in the afternoon, lasted until ten at night, and invariably concluded with a cabbage pie baked by Taneyev's famous nurse.

I also recall that present were: Igumnov, Goldenweiser, Rachmaninoff, Catoire, Scriabin, Conus, Pomerantzev, Metzel, my brother, and I. Goldenweiser and Igumnov were at the piano, sometimes helped by Taneyev. Of all only Catoire and I (I was fourteen) were familiar with Wagner's music—we were already "Wagnerites." The others were either hesitant in their praise, or open foes of Wagner and his principles. Rachmaninoff did not take part in the demonstrations; he sat in the corner in a rocking chair, with a huge orchestral score on his knees. From time to time we would hear, coming from his corner, some gloomy remark in his deep voice: "A thousand pages more." An hour later, and more gloomily: "Eight hundred and eighty pages to go."

In the fall of 1896 Rachmaninoff found his finances in so tattered a state that he "rushed into production," and by December 7, when he wrote to Alexander Zatayevich (a composer and folk song collector whom he had met on the Tua tour), he was exhausted:

I am using all my free time to write intensively and I hurry this work not just to be able to say to myself. "There—I've finished." No! I hurry in order to get money I need by a certain date. . . . This perpetual financial pressure is, on the one hand, quite beneficial—at least it makes me work on schedule; on the other hand, this motive keeps me from being especially "nice" in matters of taste.

Since October I have written in this way 12 songs,* 6 children's choruses [Op. 15] which, by the way, no children will ever be able to sing, and lastly, by the 20th of this month I have to write 6 piano pieces.**

The six pieces (*moments musicaux*) were written, dedicated to Zatayevich, and rushed into print by Jürgenson as Op. 16. This was to be Rachmaninoff's last composition for many darkened months.

He had taken his symphony to Taneyev, whose first reaction was not promising, according to Sabaneyev:

As was customary with him, he brought the symphony to Taneyev and I was present when he played it for him. I liked the somber originality of its harmonies, but Taneyev was not pleased.

"These melodies are flabby, colorless—there is nothing that can be done with them," said Taneyev in his high-pitched, "tearful" voice, as if he were complaining to the composer.

But Taneyev loyally sent Belayev nothing but encouraging news:

I've put off replying to your last letter until I saw Rachmaninoff again. He has made changes in his symphony, but has not yet incorporated the revisions in his score. This occupies him now and, as soon as it's done, he'll give the symphony to a cousin who is going to Petersburg, and you should have it by Wednesday so that it can be examined at the Committee meeting. . . . It is my sincere wish that the Committee be not oversevere about the several instances of harmonic pretentiousness in this work, which is unquestionably a talented one. A man with the rich musical gifts of Rachmaninoff will reach the right road all the sooner if he can hear his works performed. Such shortcomings as one encounters in his

* No. 11 in this Op. 14 is the well-known "Floods of Spring," dedicated to his first piano teacher, Anna Ornatzkaya.

** When Arkadi Kerzin asked Rachmaninoff in 1906 for details on all his works, the reply contained a more explicit motive for the composition of these pieces: "The fact that so soon after completing the [First] Symphony I wrote twenty short pieces can be explained by my need to pay a rather large sum of money that was stolen from me on a train, money that did not belong to me."

works are natural to our contemporary music, and it is quite understandable that a young composer should be attracted in that direction.

As soon as Taneyev heard that the Committee had approved the symphony's performance, he notified Rachmaninoff, who wrote him with thanks: "If it is performed, it will be only because of you, your intercession in my behalf, and your constantly kind attentions." Before he left for St. Petersburg to hear his symphony, generous Gutheil gave him five hundred rubles for the symphony without hearing or seeing it, engraving to begin on his return to Moscow.

In St. Petersburg the warnings were more specific. At the rehearsal Rimsky-Korsakov was more outspoken than Taneyev: "Forgive me, but I do not find this music at all agreeable." Even the program voiced a warning: included was a work, the *Fantasia Fatum*, that Tchaikovsky had considered a failure and had destroyed; this restoration had been made from the orchestral parts.

The night of March 15, 1897 was one that Rachmaninoff never forgot:*

Many years later he told us that during the performance of his symphony he could not bring himself to enter the auditorium, but hid on the stairs of the corridor that led to the balcony. He simply could not understand what had gone wrong; from time to time he pressed his fists against his ears to stop the sounds that were torturing him. At the end he ran out on the street, where he walked about trying to find the explanation for his mistake, and trying to calm down sufficiently to attend the supper that was being given later that night by Belayev, in Rachmaninoff's honor.

The Petersburg critics took full advantage of the fiasco of a work from Moscow—and "modernist trash" at that! The acid tongue of César Cui led the pack; in the *Novosti* he drafted Rachmaninoff's artistic death warrant. After reproaching the young composer for his "poverty of themes, his sickly perversity of harmony," and for the general gloom of the symphony, Cui dealt his *coup de grâce*:

If there's a Conservatory in Hell, and one of its gifted pupils should be given the problem of writing a programmatic symphony on the Seven

* Joseph Yasser points out: "By a strange coincidence . . . the fateful March 15 of the older calendar, which stood as a symbol of the most harrowing experience in Rachmaninoff's life, was also destined to become the date of his death"—March 28, 1943, by the new calendar, March 15 by the old.

Plagues of Egypt, and if he should write a symphony resembling Mr. Rachmaninoff's symphony—his problem would have been carried out brilliantly and he would enchant all the inmates of Hell.

Deep in this vitriol was something as close to a compliment as Cui could ever come: "Mr. Rachmaninoff does avoid banality, and he probably feels strongly and deeply, and tries to express these feelings in new forms," but Cui had done his work too well for anyone to notice this.* The more considered judgment of Findeisen, in the April issue of *Russkaya Muzykalnaya Gazeta,* appeared too late to salve the wounds dealt by Cui. Findeisen wrote:

The climax of the concert, Rachmaninoff's D minor symphony, was not very successfully interpreted, and was therefore largely misunderstood and underestimated by the audience. This work shows new impulses, tendencies toward new colors, new themes, new images, and yet it impresses one as something not fully said or solved. However, I shall refrain from expressing my final opinion, for it would be too easy to repeat the history of Tchaikovsky's Fifth Symphony, only recently (thanks to Nikisch) "discovered" by us, and which everyone now admires as a new, marvelous, and beautiful creation. To be sure, Rachmaninoff's first symphony may not be wholly beautiful, integrated, and definite, but some of its pages seem far from mediocre. The first movement, and especially the furious finale with its concluding Largo, contain much beauty, novelty, and even inspiration. . . .

Rachmaninoff's symphony is the product of a composer who has not yet fully found himself. At this point he could become either a musical crackpot or a Brahms.

Rachmaninoff's first escape from the catastrophe of his symphony was in the direction of Grandmother Butakova. From her estate he wrote on March 18 to Natalia Skalon, without a word on the symphony's fate:

I arrived here yesterday morning, dear Tatusha, and I leave tonight. I wasn't expected and so nobody came to meet me. I came out to Grand-

* Cui's deep-seated antipathy to the Moscow composers may be sensed in his letter of December 19, 1904 to M. S. Kerzina, placing them in the company of Richard Strauss, "whose absurd cacophony will not be music even in the 30th century," and other decadents: "I think that Moscow harbors more of these Scriabins and Rachmaninoffs, just as they have more houses there in *le style nouveau.*"

mother's at seven in the morning, and she was the only one who was awake (Volodya and his wife weren't up yet). I slept only about three hours on the train, so all day yesterday I was dozing off, but didn't go to bed, so I could be with my folks. My grandmother hasn't aged at all. She remains the same. . . .

Now I wish to thank you and your sisters for the money you gave me for the journey, as I was leaving you to go to Glazunov, and it suddenly occurred to me that I would have to ask him to lend me some money. The thought of this horrified me. I couldn't have asked him, even if I had not your money in my pocket. My tongue would have been tied.

In a letter to Zatayevich of May 6, Rachmaninoff tells him "of my impressions after the performance of my symphony . . . though it is difficult for me":

I'm not at all affected by its lack of success, nor am I disturbed by the newspapers' abuse; but I am deeply distressed and heavily depressed by the fact that my Symphony, though I loved it very much and love it now, did not please *me* at all after its first rehearsal. This means, you'll say, that it's poorly orchestrated. But I am convinced, I reply, that good music can shine through poor instrumentation, nor do I consider the instrumentation to be wholly unsuccessful. So two surmises remain. Either, like some composers, I am unduly partial to this composition, or this composition was poorly performed. And this is what really happened. I am amazed— how can a man with the high talent of Glazunov conduct so badly? I speak not merely of his conducting technique (there's no use asking this of him), but of his musicianship. He feels nothing when he conducts—as if he understands nothing! . . . So I assume that the performance may have been the cause of the failure (I do not assert—I assume). If the public were familiar with the symphony, they would blame the conductor (I continue to "assume"), but when a composition is both unknown and badly performed, the public is inclined to blame the composer. This view would seem plausible, particularly as this symphony, though not de-cadent, in the current sense of this term, is really slightly "new." This means that it must be played according to the most precise indications of the composer, who may thus somewhat make peace between the public and himself, and between the public and the composition (for the com-position would then be more intelligible to the public). . . . As you see, at present I'm inclined to blame the performance. Tomorrow, probably, this opinion, too, will change. In any case I will not reject this Symphony, and after leaving it alone for six months, I'll look at it, perhaps correct it, and perhaps publish it, but perhaps by than my partiality for it will have passed. Then I'll tear it up.

Though the First Symphony was not again performed in his life-time, and though the composer took back the manuscript from Gut-heil, Rachmaninoff did not "tear it up," nor did he "give up compos-ing." The symphony was put aside for some future revision, and in 1898 he did face its problems again, in making a four-hand piano arrangement. In April of 1917 he gave his final decision on it, in answering a query from Asafiev:

And now about my Symphony, Op. 13. What can I say about it?! It was composed in 1895. Performed in 1897. It was a failure, which, by the way, proves nothing. Over and over good things have failed, and even more often, bad things have pleased. Before the Symphony was played, I had an exaggeratedly high opinion of it. After I heard it for the first time, this opinion changed, radically. It now seems to me that a true estimate of it would be somewhere between these two extremes. It has some good music, but it also has much that is weak, childish, strained and bombastic. The Symphony was very badly orchestrated, and its per-formance was just as bad (Glazunov was the conductor).

After that Symphony I composed nothing for about 3 years. I felt like a man who had suffered a stroke and for a long time had lost the use of his head and hands. I won't show the Symphony to anyone, and I'll make sure of this when I write my will, too.

Chapter 5

Second Concerto

"IN THE most difficult and critical period of my life, when I thought all was lost and it was useless to worry any more, I met a man who took the trouble to talk to me. This man was Count Tolstoy. I was twenty-four years old when I was introduced to him . . ."

It was the Princess Alexandra Lieven, whose many charities had been assisted by Rachmaninoff's talents, who arranged this meeting. She sent a note to Tolstoy, asking him to see a young man who had lost faith in his powers. In later years Rachmaninoff gave two versions of his talk with Tolstoy. The earlier version is the more positive one:

"Young man," said he to me, "do you imagine that everything in my life goes smoothly? Do you suppose I have no troubles, never hesitate and lose confidence in myself? Do you really think faith is always equally strong? All of us have difficult moments; but this is life. Hold up your head, and keep on your appointed path."

Later, more privately, Rachmaninoff told Alfred Swan:

It all ended very unpleasantly. . . . When I visited him for the first time, he was playing chess with Goldenweiser. I then worshiped Tolstoy. When I approached him my knees trembled. He made me sit down beside him, and stroked my knees. He saw how nervous I was. And then, at the table, he said to me: "You must work. Do you think that I am pleased with myself? Work. I work every day," and similar stereotyped phrases.

Work—that was just what Rachmaninoff was unable to do. Immediately after the fiasco of his first symphony, he made and discarded sketches for a new symphony. Along with his creative resources, his financial resources were drifting away. Besides his personal expenses, he had, for some years, sent a monthly allowance to his mother. From time to time he appeared in concerts, but his depression did not leave him; and the concerts were too rare to distract him for any length of time from the conclusions he drew from the fate of his symphony. They were also too rare to be relied upon as a source of income. Piano lessons and the institute posts were the only supports of Rachmaninoff's existence during these difficult years.

A post at the Conservatory was out of the question; Safonov's feud with Siloti had been extended to his relatives as well, and in particular to Rachmaninoff. Partly responsible for this was Rachmaninoff's unbending attitude whenever he encountered Safonov. He was so terrified lest a smile be interpreted by Safonov, or by any other "powerful" person of the music world, as a courting of his favors, that his face turned unusually grim and unapproachable in such encounters. Safonov's enmity also prevented Rachmaninoff from being engaged as soloist for the concerts of the Russian Musical Society.

At home among the Satins the only music work he spoke about with any enthusiasm was conducting. He was attracted by the sounds and shadings that could be produced by a carefully prepared orchestra, and he enjoyed the thought of so many instruments bent to a single will. Surely he could better Glazunov! Except for the conducting of his own works at the Conservatory and of his own opera in Kiev, conducting was a profession foreign to him, and perhaps for that very reason the one musical topic that seemed to stir him. His most intimate friends explored the possibilities of finding a conducting post for him. Someone took his case to the millionaire Mamontov, and Rachmaninoff later described the next step in his career:

My life grew harder and harder. I gave a few piano lessons and sought (without much success) any sort of engagements as a pianist. It was really a quite desperate struggle for two or three years, when suddenly an extraordinary proposition came to me from a quite unexpected quarter. A rich man in Moscow, whose fortune had been made as a railway magnate, decided to organize a private opera company. This was Savva Mamontov. He approached me with the offer of the second conductor's post with his new opera company, and of course I accepted it immediately.

Mamontov was a conspicuous figure in the cultural life of Moscow. He was the friend and protector of arts and artists—in literature, in music, in painting—and the new opera enterprise was planned to absorb some of his talented friends, and considerable emphasis was placed on the originality and effectiveness of the settings and costumes to be designed for the repertoire.

When he offered me the conducting post with his company, Mamontov told me that he had engaged a young singer of infinite talent, with whom, he was sure, I would like to work. This young singer had not been overpraised, for his name was Fyodor Chaliapin.

The Mamontov enterprise was an exceptionally interesting one for an imaginative musician. Organized primarily to show what the Imperial Theaters *should* be doing in opera, Savva Mamontov's well-financed theater immediately became a center for the adventurous artists and young singers who were ignored by the complacent Imperial Theaters. Mamontov's good taste enlisted the best Russian painters to his cause—Serov, Korovin, Vrubel—and his ear for fresh dramatic voices gave a deserved setting to a talent such as Vrubel's wife, Nadezhda Zabela, and the yet unrecognized genius of Fyodor Chaliapin.

The orchestra, however, was run with efficiency but little inspiration. The opera's first conductor was the Italian Michele Esposito. Possibly knowing his own limitations better than did anyone else, he was not eager to aid a rival, especially a Russian with a reputation.

For his debut Rachmaninoff chose Glinka's *A Life for the Tzar;* he knew the opera well, and so did the orchestra and singers. This familiarity was essential to his choice, because Esposito allowed him only one rehearsal. As the morning rehearsal progressed Rachmaninoff was appalled to hear matters growing steadily worse. As long as the orchestra played alone, the sound seemed right to him, but everything went wrong with the singing. Rachmaninoff could not understand what caused the trouble, and did not dare ask the advice of Esposito, who was actually chuckling throughout the rehearsal. By the end of the morning it was obvious that Rachmaninoff could not conduct the opera that night, and Esposito, who said he needed no rehearsal, took over the performance. During the performance Rachmaninoff watched Esposito carefully, and suddenly realized why everything had gone wrong that morning: he had not known that it was necessary for the conductor to cue the singers!

Mamontov maintained his confidence in Rachmaninoff, however, and suggested that he try another opera. For the rehearsals of this opera, Saint-Saëns' *Samson et Dalila,* Rachmaninoff was more prepared.

With the performance of *Samson* on October 12, 1897 Rachmaninoff made his Moscow debut as an opera conductor. The mezzo-soprano

Chernenko was also to make her operatic debut as Delilah, and the young singer had less confidence and less talent than the young conductor. The double debut attracted a larger audience than usual to the Private Opera, and Mamontov felt that his confidence had been rewarded. The critic of the *Moskovskiye Vedomosti* reported:

Rachmaninoff is well known in Moscow as composer and pianist, but this was his first test as an opera conductor—and furthermore in an opera of many ensembles, where the orchestra plays an important and often independent role. . . . It is therefore understandable that the young debutant could not rid himself of a certain shyness, especially when he had to bring in the chorus. But when the first act was half over these uncertainties disappeared; Rachmaninoff firmly and commandingly took the reins of the orchestra and quickly showed what rich conducting capacities he has. . . . His chief merit, already apparent, is that he has been able to change the sound of the Private Opera's orchestra to so great a degree.

The *Russkoye Slovo* critic was less encouraging: "Though he showed considerable love for this work, he also showed very little experience, probably giving the singers more than one uneasy moment."

Rachmaninoff wrote to Natalia Skalon on October 19:

I am now a very busy man, old, slightly ailing, growing very tired from too much work, and missing you. . . . On Wednesday I conducted *Samson* for the second time. It went in the same mediocre way as the first time. My next opera is *Rogneda* [by Serov]. All the papers praised me. But I do not trust them! I'm on good terms with all at the theater, though I get pretty angry sometimes. I feel fine living with mama, as she does with me.

The personality at Mamontov's who made the greatest impression on Rachmaninoff was Chaliapin, and Chaliapin's memoirs show his admiration, too:

Destiny sent me a great many remarkable men in my artistic path. My meeting with Sergei Rachmaninoff is attached to the first emotional recollections of my youthful friendships in Moscow. It occurred during my first season with Mamontov. A very young man had joined the theater, and I was introduced to him. . . . I was considerably impressed by Rachmaninoff. A warm friendship began, and we often went to Tyestov's Restaurant to eat fish pies and to talk about the theater and music and all sorts of things.

At the single fatal rehearsal of the Glinka opera, in which the brilliant young singer had the role of Ivan Susanin, Chaliapin and Rachmaninoff had not had much opportunity to test or help each other, but in their second encounter they both touched their enormous potentialities in the field of conducting and singing opera. The work was Dargomizhsky's *Rusalka,* and Chaliapin was to sing the Miller. Together they created a role that was to be one of Chaliapin's prides and a production that was a revelation of Dargomizhsky's quality to Moscow critics.

Rachmaninoff's new employment absorbed every grain of his energy; it relieved his conscience of composing, and even of correspondence. He wrote to Zatayevich on November 4:

It's been very long since I've written you, dear friend, but, by God, it's no exaggeration to blame this on my new duties, where I am a novice, and to which I haven't quite adjusted myself, and that keep me busy 12 hours a day. I've been so tired, and I still get so tired that, believe me, I can think of nothing else.

After their satisfying triumph in *Rusalka,* even the brief portrait of Zuniga in *Carmen* was enjoyed by Chaliapin under Rachmaninoff's baton. In December they together prepared another of Chaliapin's best roles: the Mayor in Rimsky-Korsakov's lovely opera, *May Night.* Ivan Lipayev wrote in *Russkaya Muzykalnaya Gazeta* of Rachmaninoff's direction of *May Night:*

He leads that orchestra a hundred times better than does Esposito, the first conductor of the Private Opera. . . . If I were the manager, I could not dare give Russian operas to the ungifted Esposito when they have such a splendid musician as Rachmaninoff. However, one must hope that he will work more zealously on this, for him, new work. We need conductors with solid education and great talent.

Apparently Esposito had been justified in fearing the approach of Rachmaninoff. Esposito took some revenge by assigning to Rachmaninoff the task of conducting the Sunday matinees for children, and by giving the children such second-rate operas as Serov's *Rogneda* and *The Tomb of Askold* by Verstovsky. Finally the Mamontov season was over, and Rachmaninoff could catch his breath and sum up his experience:

Mamontov was a born theatrical director, and this perhaps explains why his chief attention was given to what took place on the stage. I have even heard him advise Chaliapin, usually with some brief phrase or casual remark, but always with such a sure sense of the theater that Chaliapin would be able to grasp his meaning immediately, and then develop and transform the suggestion with his own extraordinary gifts.

As for the strictly musical phase of his enterprise, that is, the orchestra and chorus, these were of less interest to Mamontov. In fact, he never had anything to say about our work, unless either the first conductor Esposito or I requested an extra rehearsal. He often refused such requests.

Even less attention was paid by Mamontov to the purely business aspect of his enterprise. Such things bored him, and as a result our opera theater always lacked capable and experienced business managers.

All these characteristics peculiar to Mamontov's attitude and interest were apparent at nearly every public performance: the stage settings were always very interesting, and they and the costumes were sure to show something fresh and original, while the orchestra was insufficiently re-hearsed and the chorus poorly trained. There were many smaller defects of management, such as delays in starting, overlong intermissions, etc. An example of the little thought given to details: when the scene was changed without a regular intermission, and the orchestra and audience remained in their places, the stage manager would announce to the con-ductor by violently slapping the curtain that the stage was ready for the next scene. The first time I was given this unusual signal I was shocked, but it took many days and many arguments before the stage manager would consent to signal me silently from the side of the stage. I was grate-ful for this concession, but whenever I happened to miss this signal, the curtain would again be pounded.

Whenever there was anything complicated in a production, the weak-ness of the management showed up in every way. I can still remember the troubles we had with the first performance of Sadko, which Rimsky-Korsakov had just completed. The settings, costumes, and make-up in the Mamontov production were excellent, but the orchestra was not very good and the chorus was worse. The singers of the chorus were so un-prepared that they were obliged to consult their printed parts constantly, at the same time attempting (unsuccessfully) to hide these pages in the wide sleeves of their costumes. The composer had to endure several other misfortunes in this first performance of his opera: a board thrown from Sadko's ship into the "sea" struck the stage floor with a tremendous non-watery crash; one of the monster fishes in the famous undersea scene crossed the stage with its wrong side to the audience. In spite of every-thing the success of Rimsky-Korsakov's new opera was enormous. Because of the composer's presence even small roles were given to the best singers, and Chaliapin in the role of the Viking Guest gave an unforgettable portrait.

Yes, Mamontov was a great man, with a decided influence on the de-velopment of Russian opera. In some respects Mamontov's influence was comparable to that of Stanislavsky in drama.

This was a judgment of later years. Rachmaninoff's estimate writ-ten at the time of these events was sent to Ludmila Skalon on No-vember 22:

In our theater chaos truly reigns. Nobody knows what is to happen the day after tomorrow, or tomorrow, or even today. There is no one to sing, not because we have no singers, but because in our large company of 30, about 25 should be fired for incompetence. There is also nothing to perform—the repertoire is huge, but everything is produced so badly, so sloppily (with the sole exception of *Khovanshchina*), that 95 percent of the repertoire should be discarded or completely restudied.

The theater achieves nothing, either artistically or commercially. For example, it has been decided that in the near future Verstovsky's *Tomb of Askold* and *Gromoboi* should be revived. . . . One trouble is that our chief executives are not very bright musically. It's too bad, too, that we are supervised not by one, but by ten, and everyone has something of his own to say that conflicts with all the others. But worst of all is that Mamontov himself is indecisive and yields to everybody's opinion. For example, I interested him so with the idea of producing [Schumann's] *Manfred* that he gave orders at once for its production. . . . Scarcely five minutes had passed before his friend Korovin, who understands nothing about music (but is a very nice and good person, as is Mamontov, too), had talked him out of it. I'll still try to persuade him. If only Chaliapin would agree to recite, he would be absolutely magnificent in *Manfred*. As for *Rogneda* and *The Snow Maiden*, turned over to me, I am trying to persuade them not to produce these, as they are splendidly presented at the Bolshoi Theater, and we have neither the time nor the means to present them, even tolerably. . . . Altogether, all goes so badly that I am afraid of falling again into a fit of black melancholy.

However, I am still employed at the theater and hope to endure this employment until the end of the season, though except for the financial side of this, the time spent here will afford me no benefit, because I have crossed the conductor's Rubicon and now need the total attention and compliance of the musicians, which as a *second* conductor I would never get from them. By the way, one of these gentlemen, in the presence of orchestra and full audience, slapped Esposito for some supposed abuse addressed to him by the conductor. . . . What if this should happen to me? May God prevent this! . . . Esposito continues to conduct!

By spring (April 18, 1898) Rachmaninoff had this report to give Zatayevich: "Your question, what have I been writing and doing, won't take long to answer—absolutely nothing. But I have plans." The only known plan of this time originated with Modeste Tchaikovsky, who suggested an opera based on Shakespeare's *Richard II*, but this was put aside when Rachmaninoff joined Chaliapin, with Mamontov and other singers and artists of his private opera, at the Yaroslavl villa of Mme. Tatyana Lubatovich, a well-to-do protégée of Mamontov's. Chaliapin recalls:

There with our conductor S. V. Rachmaninoff I was busy studying *Boris Godunov*. He was lively and companionable, a fine artist and magnificent musician. Though a disciple of Tchaikovsky, he woke my appreciation of Musorgsky and Rimsky-Korsakov. He introduced me to the fundamental laws of music, and even some harmony. Altogether he gave me a basic musical education. I enjoyed *Boris Godunov* so much that I studied all its roles, both male and female. This thorough study of the opera was so useful to me that I began to work on all operas in the same way.

Perhaps under the influence of this work with Musorgsky's tragic hero, Rachmaninoff renewed his interest in *Richard II*. He wrote to Modeste Tchaikovsky on July 28:

I've decided to put this question to you: Could you find the opportunity to write a libretto on that Shakespeare subject that you proposed to me last spring? I will add that your consent would make me very happy. If my affairs can be so arranged I would think of starting its composition in about two or three months. . . . If a scenario is not possible by then, would you be willing to do it a little later? I say "a little," for if I'm to write an opera, it will have to be written quickly.

In the meantime Modeste Tchaikovsky had made progress on another subject, suggested by Dante's *Inferno*: that of Francesca da

Rimini. His reply must have been accompanied by a sketched scenario of a full-length opera on this subject, for Rachmaninoff's letter of August 28 positively bubbles with enthusiasm and plans. He told Tchaikovsky that he liked the plan "very, very much," and went at once into detail on several scenes, chiefly the prologue:

I wish you would write about thirty more lines for an invisible chorus in the prologue. If not thirty, then at least enough for me to divide up and entrust to the several groups of a chorus. Besides this, I'd like to give the 7 stanzas now assigned to Vergil—beginning with the words, "My son"— to the chorus, changing the pronouns throughout, of course.

Chaliapin tells of a social and musical event of the summer:

. . . while we were at the villa, I married the ballerina Tornaghi in the tiny village church. After the wedding we had a sort of Turkish feast, sitting about the floor, and playing all kinds of childish pranks. . . .

At about six the next morning we heard an infernal noise under my window: my friends were playing us a concert on stove lids, iron oven doors, tin pails, and penny whistles. . . . The conductor of this mess was Rachmaninoff.

In September Rachmaninoff's physician sent him south, and Chaliapin went along to work with him and to give occasional concerts, with Rachmaninoff as accompanist. In the audience at their Yalta concert was Rachmaninoff's literary idol, Anton Chekhov. After the concert the enthusiastic audience crowded past the accompanist to reach Chaliapin. When Chekhov followed them into the greenroom, he headed straight for the accompanist with these words: "All this time I have been looking at you, young man. You have a wonderful face—you will be a great man." When Rachmaninoff later told this touching incident to Mme. Somova, he was deeply moved, and said, "Until I die I shall recall those words with pride and joy."

Rachmaninoff returned North, and wrote to Zatayevich on October 26:

I've moved into the country, where I plan to spend the winter, living and working quietly, just because this is impossible in Moscow. Besides, the doctor prescribed country life for me. I was recently ill, and even went to the Crimea to get a little better. Now I live in the country. I've begun to work a little and my health improves noticeably. I live quite alone. I have three big friends—huge St. Bernards. I talk with them and walk about these forests. I pay a weekly visit to my relatives in Moscow, to show myself and, incidentally, to give a few lessons. I've written nothing yet, but with God's help I hope to. As for *what* I'm writing—I'll let you know.

This autumn Siloti made a tour of Europe, England, and America that was to have a profound effect on Rachmaninoff's career. For one thing he played his cousin's Prélude in C-sharp minor and was astonished by the growth of its popularity, particularly in England and the United States; it overshadowed everything else, new and old, on his programs. English and American publishers issued several editions of it at once, and as no copyright for it had been taken out in these countries, nothing prevented these publishers from making handsome profits from its popularity, while its composer was in real need of money and unaware of the irony of his situation. Though Siloti could do nothing to rechannel these funds in Rachmaninoff's direction, he did arrange for Rachmaninoff to appear the following spring with the London Philharmonic Society as conductor and pianist.

It was only as conductor and pianist that he wrote to Zatayevich on March 3, 1899:

I am really quite busy now, because at the end of March I leave for London, where I am to play and conduct. . . . I've written nothing new, no more than you have.

But he was trying himself as composer again; he had written at least two piano pieces, a "Morceau de Fantaisie" on January 11, 1899 and a Fughetta on February 4.

Before leaving for England Rachmaninoff was asked a favor by Chaliapin. The Mamontov Opera had shown so much more interest in Rimsky-Korsakov's music than had the Imperial Theaters that Rimsky-Korsakov had given Mamontov not only his new opera *Sadko,* but also his revision of *Pskovitianka* and his new short opera on Pushkin's play of *Mozart and Salieri.* Chaliapin was to sing Ivan the Terrible in *Pskovitianka* and the brief but complex role of Salieri:

The more I performed Boris Godunov, Ivan the Terrible, Dosifei [in Musorgsky's *Khovanshchina*], the Viking Guest [in *Sadko*], and the Mayor in *May Night,* the more certain I was that in opera the singer must act his role as an actor in a drama. . . .

Just as this was growing clear to me I was asked to sing the role of Salieri, a more complicated and difficult problem than I had previously encountered, for the role was written in a continuous melodic recitative. I was attracted by this new task, and took it to Rachmaninoff, knowing that he could explain and ease every difficulty. What a wonderful artist he is!

Rimsky-Korsakov had indicated all tempi in the usual terms—Allegro, Moderato, Andante, etc.—but it was not always simple to follow these indications. When I would propose to Rachmaninoff that these indications be changed, he would tell me where change was possible and where impossible.

Without distorting the composer's conception we found a coloring for the performance that gave prominence to the tragic figure of Salieri.

In England Rachmaninoff was already known as the man who wrote The Prélude, and all newspaper notice and critical appraisal of him was built around that fact. Siloti may have warned him of this, but Rachmaninoff was quite unprepared to encounter his piano piece under guises that later adopted such titles as "The Burning of Moscow," "The Day of Judgment," and even "The Moscow Waltz."

At the Philharmonic Concert of April 19 Rachmaninoff conducted an aria from *Prince Igor* (unknown in England) sung by Mlle. Andray, and his own "Fantaisie in E major," otherwise *The Crag.* Before the concluding Fifth Symphony of Beethoven (conducted by Sir Alexander MacKenzie) Rachmaninoff played two numbers from his Opus 3, ending with the celebrated Prélude; this had to be repeated for the enthralled audience. *Musical Opinion* wondered:

How is it that some composers make a reputation so easily and so quickly? . . . I suppose there is a psychological moment for every man; and if what he has to say is just the thing for which the world at that moment is waiting, why then he becomes famous. . . .

Rachmaninoff certainly has a kind of genius. The Trio [Op. 9] is a work which has many beautiful movements, and is clever in workmanship; the hackneyed Prelude and some of his other pianoforte compositions have a decided individual charm, though one doubts if they would ever have found their way to paper if Chopin had not been there before; but in none of these works is there greatness either of mood or of invention, and especially is this the case with the Fantasia performed at the Philharmonic Society's concert.

The Monthly Musical Record was more than dubious about *The Crag:*

It was to be regretted that the orchestral work conducted by himself was not of a more solid value. It was a fantasia . . . suggested by a poem of Lermontov having the fantastic idea of a rock lamenting the departure of a cloud. We have frequently remarked on the impossibility of giving musical meaning to such ideas, and M. Rachmaninoff has not been more fortunate than other composers in his endeavors to give vitality to a subject so little suited for musical treatment.* . . . It cannot be denied that [its] movements contain some remarkably picturesque ideas embellished with orchestration revealing ample skill and inventive powers. The result left a vague impression upon the auditor . . . but a reception favourable enough to justify another appearance at the Philharmonic. . . . But it was unreasonable to suppose that all Russian composers would produce masterpieces like the "Pathetic Symphony."

The Musical Times approved *The Crag's* form and balance, but— "The themes are small and ill nourished. Nearly all creep about in apologetic half-tones."

The *Times* made its first of many pronouncements on Rachmaninoff's art:

We are all being seduced into the belief, willy-nilly, perhaps, that nothing but good can come out of Russia. Yet it would not necessitate a journey far beyond the four-mile radius from Charing Cross to find a musical composition at least as nearly "great" as the orchestral fantasie in E major. . . . Not that his work is not interesting. Even in a day like this, when the majority of composers can say their little nothings with beautiful musical phraseology, as it were, M. Rachmaninoff shines in virtue of his exceptional skill. . . . His orchestration, in a word, is superb and original. But

* Would the reviewer have accepted any more willingly the concealed Chekhov program?

that which he orchestrates is not always worth the orchestration. Now and then an idea occurred which came near being beautiful. . . . As a conductor the Russian musician showed to far greater advantage. His command was supreme; his method, quietness idealized. As a pianist, he plays like a conductor. . . . M. Rachmaninoff can certainly claim a success for his first appearance in England.

The Secretary of the Philharmonic Society, Francesco Berger, did invite Rachmaninoff to play for them in the following season. When the First Concerto was discussed Rachmaninoff promised to compose a second and better one for London.

Back in Russia by May for the St. Petersburg première of *Aleko,* Rachmaninoff found it still difficult to resume composition. When his cousin, Natalia Satina, reproached him for his idleness and dissipated life, he answered on May 17 with a "song-jest" to a poem by Prince Pyotr Viazemsky. On the manuscript is a note: "No! My muse has not died, dear Natasha. I dedicate to you my new song. I beg you, first, to read the text attentively."

The St. Petersburg production of *Aleko,* at the end of May, was made part of the Pushkin celebrations at the Taurida Palace. Chaliapin sang the role of Aleko, and press was kind; in *Teatr i Iskusstvo* Mikhail Ivanov tendered the "beginner" the accolade of "undoubted talent." Rachmaninoff sent Slonov his impressions (on July 18):

I wrote you nothing about the production of *Aleko,* but Gutheil must have given you a full account of it. For my part I can add only that from his first to his last note Aleko sang splendidly. Orchestra and chorus were splendid. Soloists were splendid—not to speak of Chaliapin, before whom they all, as do others, always fade. He's three heads above them all. By the way, I can still hear how he sobbed at the end of the opera. Such sobbing can only come from a great theatrical artist, or a man who has in his own life suffered as deeply as Aleko. . . .

My musical matters go very badly.

On the same day he wrote to Natalia Skalon:

Yes! You are right! Art never betrays, at least not those who love it, and I am the exception to prove this rule. There's been some misunderstanding between us, but I believe, God grant it, that Art may soon have mercy on me and again bestow those blessings which come from harmony with her.

The remainder of this summer was spent with the Kreutzers, who had often hoped that Rachmaninoff might find relaxation at their summer home. He did relax, but he did not compose.

An unproductive summer and autumn only served to deepen Rachmaninoff's depression. The projected work on *Francesca da Rimini* had been put aside. The promise to London of a Second Concerto could not be fulfilled. By the end of 1899 the only other work begun or thought worthy of preservation was a song composed for Chaliapin, "Fate," based on the two opening measures of Beethoven's Fifth Symphony. When the two musicians were invited to visit Tolstoy, who was then staying in Moscow, they took the new song along. This was Rachmaninoff's second meeting with the Great Man, and Chaliapin's first; it took place on January 9, 1900:

Tolstoy was then living with his family in Khamovniki district, in Moscow. Rachmaninoff and I received an invitation to visit him. We climbed the wooden staircase to the second floor of a very charming house, modest and intimate in character, built partially of wood, if I remember rightly. We were cordially welcomed by Sophia Andreyevna and her sons, Mikhail, Andrei, and, I think, Sergei. Tea was offered us, but I didn't feel like drinking tea. I was very excited. . . . Up till then I had seen only portraits of Tolstoy, and now he himself appeared. He stood by a small chess table and talked to young Goldenweiser. . . .

Sergei Rachmaninoff seemed braver than I, but he was also moved, and his hands were cold. "If I'm asked to play," he whispered to me, "I don't see how I can—my hands are absolutely ice-cold." The next moment Tolstoy asked him to play. I can't remember what he played. I was too agitated by the thought that it would be my turn next. My agitation was increased when Tolstoy addressed Rachmaninoff point-blank:

"Tell me, is such music needed by anybody?"

I was asked to sing. I remember that I sang "Fate," a song that Rachmaninoff had just composed. . . . Rachmaninoff accompanied me. We both did our utmost to present this work as well as possible, but we could not tell if it had pleased Tolstoy. He said nothing. Then, as before, he asked:

"What kind of music is most necessary to men—scholarly or folk music?"

Rachmaninoff's own recollection of this unsatisfactory evening was later told to Alfred Swan:

To describe how Fedya sang is impossible. He sang—the way Tolstoy wrote. We were both twenty-six years old. We performed my song "Fate." When we finished, we felt that all were delighted. Suddenly the enthusiastic applause was hushed and everyone was silent. Tolstoy sat in an armchair a little apart from the others, looking gloomy and cross. For the next hour I evaded him, but suddenly he came up to me and declared excitedly: "I must speak to you. I must tell you how I dislike it all!" And he went on and on: "Beethoven is nonsense, Pushkin and Lermontov also." It was awful. Sophia Andreyevna stood behind me; she touched my shoulder and whispered: "Never mind, never mind. Please don't contradict him. Lyovochka must not get excited. It's very bad for him." After a while Tolstoy came up to me again: "Please excuse me. I am an old man. I did not mean to hurt you." I replied: "How could I be hurt on my own account, if I was not hurt on Beethoven's?" But I never went back. Sophia Andreyevna invited me to Yasnaya Polyana every year, but I always declined. And just think, the first time I went to him, I went to him as to a god.

This second encounter, superficial as it may now seem, pushed Rachmaninoff to a new depth of despondency that made the Satin family far more anxious about his condition. He had become so severe in his self-criticism that completion and even initiation of any composition had become impossible. His cousins, his aunt, and their friend, Dr. Grigori Grauermann, thought it was time to take some positive step, and they agreed that he should be persuaded to see Dr. Nikolai Dahl.

Dr. Dahl has been a friend of Grauermann's at Moscow University, and had specialized in internal medicine. After graduation he became interested in the therapeutic values of hypnosis that were then being explored in France, and his first successes in the treatment made him devote his entire practice to this method. He was a great lover of music and played cello in an amateur quartet of his own organization. Hearing and playing music was his chief relaxation from the heavy emotional burdens of his patients. His treatment of friends of the Satins was so visibly helpful that they determined that Rachmaninoff should try it, too.

Rachmaninoff surprised his cousins by agreeing, without resistance, to see the doctor. He was desperate enough about his dark present and darker future to try anything suggested to him. Even his lack of money was no obstacle, for many of Dr. Dahl's patients were treated without charge, and any embarrassment felt by Rachmaninoff on this score was overcome. Dr. Dahl's apartment was only a few doors from the Satins' and Rachmaninoff visited the doctor daily. These sessions in Dr. Dahl's study, with Rachmaninoff seated in a deep, comfortable armchair, were concentrated on helping him to sleep soundly and peacefully every night, to brighten his daytime mood, to improve his appetite, and, above all, to reawaken his desire to compose. Actual hypnosis was supplemented by general conversation, and as Dahl was a cultured and musically intelligent man, these talks must have enhanced the salutary effects of the treatment. Soon after the treatments began in January, the Satin family noticed signs of improvement. Rachmaninoff later told Riesemann that the specific focus of these sessions was the concerto he had promised London.

Although it may sound incredible, this cure really helped me. By the beginning of summer I again began to compose. The material grew in bulk, and new musical ideas began to stir within me—more than enough for my concerto.

Rachmaninoff's post at the two girls' institutes was a godsend to his finances, if not to his morale. On their part the girls worshiped their music director. In later years one of the students at the Yekaterininsky Institute wrote of a semester examination:

The lessons after luncheon seem an eternity—the examination is to begin at 4.

I straighten the front bow of my apron, gather my music together, and run to the music room. The students to be examined are there already, sitting shyly on their stiff chairs. In the center of the room is a long table covered with a green cloth. Before the table, at an angle, is the piano.

The door opens. We stand. The principal, Mme. Krayevskaya, enters majestically, followed by the very tall Rachmaninoff, by Leo Conus, Goldenweiser, and the other music teachers of our Institute. They sit— and we sit.

They begin with Anileyeva—the most notorious prankster in the school. She'll surely do something improper. "Play the scale of C major." Anileyeva plays it—and then turns to Rachmaninoff: "May I play C minor?" Such questions during an examination just aren't supposed to be asked. The principal frowns, but Anileyeva is so spontaneous and so sweet that she seems to be a child who has not yet surrendered to the severe discipline of the Institute. Sergei Vasilyevich smiles and says, "Very well, play C minor."

A second pupil is introduced, and a third—and finally my turn has come. I concentrate my whole being on the figure of Sergei Vasilyevich. He has placed his great hands, with their long fingers, on the table; he leans slightly forward. From the list before him he reads my name aloud.

I rise, nearly staggering with excitement—the white keys of the piano spring toward me—my hands tremble. I play as if in a dream. A calm, even voice says, "Good." This "Good" encourages and kindles me. I am whirled away by the speed of an *étude* by Wollenhaupt, and the little *Tarantelle* by Leschetizky carries me gracefully to the happy end of the examination.

I get up, and the principal kindly nods her head. Again I see the reserved, but simple and unofficial smile of Sergei Vasilyevich. A deep curtsy and I rush madly out and downstairs to the classroom. My friends —Natasha, Marusya, Tania—surround me. "Well, did you pass? Did you play well?" I am in ecstasy—even Sergei Vasilyevich had said "Good." What joy! From my desk I take a post card—a photograph of Sergei Vasilyevich, whom we all adore—and I kiss it.

In April Rachmaninoff and Chaliapin again went south to the Crimea, and Rachmaninoff occupied a small house in Yalta on Prince Lieven's estate. They saw a great deal of Chekhov this summer, for the Art Theater had decided to take their theater to Chekhov, as long as he could not go north in the winter.

Another of the many victims of tuberculosis who sought cure in Yalta was Vasili Kalinnikov, and Rachmaninoff did all in his power to help him. His efforts were reported by Kalinnikov to his friend, the critic Kruglikov:

Rachmaninoff, who is staying with Lieven, has visited me. He gave me tremendous pleasure by playing for me—his playing always gives me the greatest delight. . . . He has promised to come again, and to *extract* 100 rubles from Jürgenson for my "Prayer" and two other songs. I felt so lightened and refreshed by his visit. His is a great talent.

[May 19, 1900]

The business with Jürgenson has turned out well. When Rachmaninoff heard the terms offered Jürgenson through Engel—my symphony *gratis,* plus three songs and two piano pieces—he was horrified and asked me to turn over this matter to him. I agreed and this is the result: Jürgenson has already sent me 120 rubles for the songs, and has also undertaken to publish the score, the orchestra parts, and a four-hand piano transcription of my Second Symphony, and asks to be my permanent publisher. And that's not all: Rachmaninoff has managed to extract 50 rubles from him for the four-hand transcription. . . . How do you like that! That's what Rachmaninoff's word means. I am so surprised and happy that all has turned out so well. And this isn't all. I have just received a request from Jürgenson to transfer the rights of the First Symphony to him. . . . Rachmaninoff has been kind in every way, visiting me, with pleasant conversation, and occasionally sitting down at the piano to introduce me to new works by Glazunov, Taneyev, Arensky, and others—which is especially welcome to me, after such a long musical starvation.

[June 20, 1900]

In a burst of generosity Jürgenson has paid me for the piano score of the First Symphony, and I am certainly indebted to Rachmaninoff for this latest act; before leaving for Italy he saw Jürgenson in Moscow, and set him rolling to my profit. . . . Thank God the symphonies will be brought into the world. Rachmaninoff came at the right moment.

A year later Kalinnikov was dead, at the age of thirty-four.

While in Yalta Chaliapin received an invitation from La Scala in Milan to sing the role of Mefistofele in Boito's opera of that name:

Joy and fear mingled in my breast. I began my study of the opera at once, and planned to spend the summer in Italy. Rachmaninoff was the first to hear my news and my feelings. He offered to go to Italy with me:

"Excellent in every way! I can work on my music, and help you work on the opera."

It seemed extremely significant to both of us that Italy, country of great singers, should invite a Russian for such a role.

Rachmaninoff was invited to live with the Chaliapins, and Chaliapin himself was to join him, after a necessary trip to Paris, in a house rented at Varazze, near Genoa, on the road to San Remo. Rachmaninoff sent news to Nikita Morozov, a fellow graduate from Arensky's composition class, now touring Europe between terms as teacher at the Conservatory:

June 14/27, 1900

I arrived here on the 11th, Nikita Semyonovich! I would have sat down at once to answer you if our house here hadn't been such a total mess. Today, though, I at least know my room, and I have paper and ink, and praise God for that! But they're still running about, fixing, cleaning, dusting—and the heat on top of everything else. I can't get accustomed to such disorder! . . . I have two things to tell you. First, that I profoundly regret coming here, instead of going with you. And second, that I shan't be going to Paris, for this trip has cost more than we planned. So again it all adds up only to anguish.

[June 22/July 5]

Since my first letter I've lived here for ten more days, and I'm still sorry I didn't go with you. The sort of domestic regime here is not for me, doesn't suit me at all. Even though I do have a separate room, there's sometimes such shrieking and noise alongside it as could happen only in a household like ours. "General Kheraskov" himself [Chaliapin] is not yet here. He got stuck in Paris, where he is powerfully occupied with, probably, the woman problem. In authoritative circles they say it's doubtful whether the "General" can settle this problem soon, in view of its complexity and, secondly, since in Paris interest in it dominates all other problems. He shoots occasional telegrams from there, in which he mentions his arrival here rather vaguely. Things will, of course, be jollier for me when he comes. . . . I've decided not to travel to you now. I want to go on working regularly.

"General Kheraskov" finally arrived, and the two got down to work. Chaliapin recalled: "We settled down to a very calm sort of life, getting up early, going to bed early, and giving up tobacco. . . . That summer I learned Boito's opera in the way that had become my habit, studying all roles." On July 9/22 Rachmaninoff wrote to Natalia Skalon:

I'm not to be here much longer—planning to leave here no later than the 20th. And I shall be leaving (I don't wish to conceal this) with great pleasure. I am bored without Russians and Russia. I have found it might be possible to travel abroad alone, but to live here alone without family or some substitute for family is hard. So, in about two weeks—Russia.

In mid-July Rachmaninoff broke up their summer workshop and wrote Morozov from Milan: "I leave here tomorrow for Russia—and for no other place. Life here has bored me to nausea, and working here has been impossible, for the heat alone. . . . I leave here enthusiastically and with the firm intent to work a lot when I get home." The summer had been more productive than one would guess from this message; an *a cappella* chorus, *Pantelei the Healer*, on a text by Alexei Tolstoy, had been composed in June and July; some work had been done on *Francesca;* ideas for the Second Concerto had been put in order; and sketches had been made that were later used in his second suite for two pianos. It was not a bad summer, and Dr. Dahl could justly feel pride in the evident improvement of his patient. Before the end of summer, while living with the Kreutzers at their summer place, Rachmaninoff composed the second and third movements of his Second Concerto.

The first results of the cure were to be displayed in Moscow on December 2, at a concert organized by Princess Lieven and Varvara Satina for the Ladies' Charity Prison Committee. It is easy to sympathize with the composer and his intimates, faced with this test of his cure. All those who had helped him through the crisis now placed all their hopes for him on this concert, at which he was to play the second and last movements of the new concerto. On the day before his appearance Rachmaninoff caught cold and, not admitting that he would prefer to cancel his appearance, willingly swallowed all remedies thrust at him by relatives and friends. One remedy was hot red wine with cinnamon and other spices, taken in such quantities that the patient nearly missed the concert altogether.

The success of the concert was so evident that all his well-wishers breathed more easily again. In *Russkaya Muzykalnaya Gazeta* Lipayev wrote:

Siloti, Chaliapin, Rachmaninoff could not complain of an indifferent public. It's been very long since I've seen such a huge audience at a concert—not since Rubinstein's Historical Concerts; and it's been long since the walls of the Nobility Hall reverberated with such enthusiastic, storming applause as on that evening. . . . Rachmaninoff appeared both as pianist and as composer. Most interesting were two movements from an unfinished Second Piano Concerto. This work contains much poetry, beauty, warmth, rich orchestration, healthy and buoyant creative power. Rachmaninoff's talent is evident throughout.

Dahl's treatment and the December success had the result that all wished:

Quickly and rather easily Rachmaninoff completed the concerto with the composition of its first movement, and finished the Suite for two pianos that he had sketched in Italy. Dahl's treatments had conquered his self-doubts, and now he wanted to work and create, but without thinking of money or of meeting deadlines. Who would trust him to return a loan in two or three years' time? After long discussions with the Satins and Lodyzhensky, he asked Siloti to lend him the money. Siloti agreed and paid the necessary amount to him in installments over the next two years. Rachmaninoff was able to repay him the whole sum within a year after the last installment.

Old doubts still arose, never to be permanently downed. On October 22 he wrote frantically to Morozov:

You are right, Nikita Semyonovich!
I've just played over the first movement of my concerto and only now it has become suddenly clear to me that the transition from the first theme to the second is not good, and that in this form the first theme is no more than an introduction—and that when I begin the second theme no fool would believe it to be a second theme. Everybody will think this the beginning of the concerto. I consider the whole movement ruined, and from this minute it has become positively hideous to me. I'm simply in despair! And why did you pester me with your analysis five days before the performance!

But the concerto, played for the first time in its entirety on October 27, at a concert of the Moscow Philharmonic Society conducted by

Siloti, was a notable success.* Further composition continued without break: a sonata for piano and cello (dedicated to Brandukov); a cantata for baritone, chorus, and orchestra, on a poem by Nekrasov, *Spring* (dedicated to Morozov); a piano prélude in G minor that was put aside for a full book of préludes; and eleven songs (to join "Fate"), composed at the beginning of April. The fee for the songs, three thousand rubles, was needed for a particular purpose—for a honeymoon.

* The Second Concerto was dedicated to Dr. Dahl. On at least one occasion his contribution to this work was publicly recognized. In 1928 he was playing viola in the orchestra of the American University of Beirut in Lebanon. After a performance of this concerto, with Arcadie Kougell as soloist and conductor, the audience, informed of the dedication and of Dr. Dahl's presence, would not be content until Dahl rose from his seat and bowed.

Chapter 6

Imperial Theater

THE Satins, especially the Satin children, had become Rachmaninoff's most intimate and trusted friends. His cousin Natalia Satina had continued her piano studies, first with Zverev and then to graduation from Igumnov's class at the Conservatory, and this must have given her an extra bond with Rachmaninoff; she doubtless saw him through many a musical and personal crisis. It was no surprise to their family when they announced their engagement. But the difficulties were formidable: first cousins were forbidden marriage within the Orthodox Church. Anna Trubnikova later described the reactions outside their immediate family:

To many the news of the engagement was like a bomb explosion. All of us were aware of the many obstacles to this marriage—family, civil, clerical—but somehow these were all overcome. In the first place, Sergei Vasilyevich was not a regular churchgoer and did not go to confession, and no priest would marry him without a certificate that he did both these things. And yet Sergei refused to attend confession. My mother came to the rescue with an acquaintance, Amfiteatrov, a priest of the Archangelsky Cathedral. He promised to take care of the matter if Sergei would come to see him.

In April 1902 Rachmaninoff on his way back to Moscow from a concert in St. Petersburg and a visit to his mother in Novgorod, sent the news to the Skalon sisters, writing to Natalia:

At the end of this month I shall have the carelessness to get married. I expect a gift from you, without fail—and a fine, expensive one, too, such as *only you* can afford. I do not expect you to come! For God's sake, I implore you, don't come. The fewer present, the better. I tell you this seriously. As for the gift, whatever you think up, it can be sent on the very day of the wedding. . . .

I am terribly tired, Tatusha! Not from today's journey, nor from this letter, but from the whole winter, and I don't know when I shall be allowed to rest. When I get to Moscow, several days will have to be spent squabbling with priests, and then I go off at once to the country in order to write at least 12 songs before the wedding, to make enough money to pay the priests and to go abroad. And even then there will be no rest, because throughout the summer I shall have to write, write, write like a fiend so as not to go broke. And as I've already told you, I am terribly exhausted and weakened and in pain. I don't know what is to happen.

Goodby, Tatusha! To sum up this letter: forgive me, send me a gift, and feel sorry for me.

Trubnikova writes: "The last and highest barrier was permission from the Tzar for first cousins to marry. The petition for this had to be sent *during* the marriage ceremony itself, for if the Tzar should refuse, no priest would agree to perform the marriage. But everything worked out." On April 29 Rachmaninoff brought an end to the Bohemian chapter of his life. With the spring rain pouring outside he married Natalia Satina in an army chapel of suburban Moscow, with Alexander Siloti and Anatoli Brandukov as best men.

Music naturally determined the range of the honeymoon journey —music to listen to and music to write. From Vienna to Venice, where they ran into Morozov on his way to Rome. Then to Lucerne, from where Rachmaninoff continued to persuade Morozov to visit them; he wrote on June 17:

If for a whole month one sees something every day, no matter what, no matter how interesting—city, cathedral, gallery, the dungeons in the palazzo of the doges (what particular interest did these have?)—all finally grows confused, insipid, boring, and then, of course, fatigue sets in (how is it you haven't succumbed?); not the sort of fatigue you mention, allowing you a good two weeks more to roam through various towns, but a genuine fatigue that drives you into some room and keeps you there for at least a week, so pleasant is it to look at bare walls, and any hint of a Madonna or a ruin would madden you. However, one must hope that you will soon be driven to this state. And so, I await you impatiently. Living here is not bad, the country is very beautiful, and the air is lovely. The only pity is that there's but *one* road for walks. But this is a lovely road: through a pine forest with beautiful views all the way. I walk this road twice a day and haven't yet grown bored with it, nor do I think I shall soon. We took two rooms in this pension: they are on the top floor (we chose this deliberately—there is a lift) and at the extreme end of the outside wall. We've turned the last room into a sort of salon. In Lucerne we rented an upright piano, absolutely new, for 50 francs the two months, and 18 francs for delivery. Quite inexpensive, in my opinion, and the piano is not at all bad. Little by little I've started working, and I'm still holding on to the songs [Op. 21]: they were much too hastily written, and therefore are quite unfinished and quite unbeautiful. . . . But they'll have to be left almost in this state—I don't have time to fuss with them. It would be nice to get rid of all this dirty work (the songs and the cantata) by the first of July, so I could get to work on something new. I'll try. . . .

Good-by. For God's sake, hurry up and get tired—and come here. Incidentally I've postponed our excursion on Lake Lucerne until your arrival. In a week we plan to climb the Rigi. Or should we wait for you on this, too?

After Morozov's arrival, and before he was due back in his Conservatory classes, the little Russian party went up to Bayreuth for the Wagner Festival (the tickets were Siloti's wedding gift), where they heard the *Ring, The Flying Dutchman,* and *Parsifal.* Back in Ivanovka the young couple joined Siloti, who lived there that summer, and Rachmaninoff began his Variations on the theme of Chopin's Prélude in C minor. Other compositions were made ready for printing, the most important of these being the cantata, *Spring:*

September 11, 1902, Ivanovka

Dear friend, Nikita Semyonovich, do me the favor of writing the German text into the score.* The main thing is to get this done in one day (forgive my impudence) and take it to Gutheil for printing. It has made me so late that my dream that we talked about when we last met will hardly be realized. How I regret that! . . .

I have worked only since the departure of Siloti, that is, since August 30th. I can find nothing comforting to write of myself. So I just meander. I plan to get to Moscow no later than the first of October.

In October the couple went to Moscow and took a small apartment on the third floor of the same building in which Rachmaninoff's lonely "America" was located. The busy year's work was displayed in

---

* The Nekrasov text for *Spring* was translated into German by Vladimir Chumikov. The manuscript score shows that Morozov did this favor.

a concert given February 10, 1903 for the Ladies' Charity Prison Committee. Yuli Engel wrote of Rachmaninoff and his new piano works:

Of his new compositions the most congenial impression was made by three of the préludes, distinct in character—F-sharp minor, D major, and G-flat major. It would be difficult, however, to predict for these that European popularity enjoyed by the earlier Prélude in C-sharp minor. . . . Much less interesting, at least on first acquaintance, seemed the larger work, *Variations on a Theme by Chopin.* The variations, though significant, are not always worthy of the beautiful theme that inspired them.

The public reception was more encouraging; Siloti's financial help had accomplished its purpose. With new and "old" works Rachmaninoff played in St. Petersburg and other Russian cities, and made a successful debut in Vienna this spring, playing the new Second Concerto with the Vienna Philharmonic.

This Vienna engagement precipitated a family crisis, for along with Rachmaninoff, the Vienna Philharmonic had also invited Safonov—by now traditional enemy of the Siloti-Rachmaninoff clan—to conduct the concert. Rachmaninoff was torn between his loyalty to Siloti and his need for the large fee promised, and, as was usual in such crises, he appealed to Taneyev's judgment. Taneyev wrote in his diary, "I calmed him "—and Rachmaninoff played in Vienna.

This spring heard the revival of an early Rachmaninoff work that had palled on its composer: his *Trio élégiaque* (Op. 9). The Moscow Trio had announced a performance of this trio in their last concert of the season, so that when Rachmaninoff met David Schor (the pianist of the trio, with Krein and Ehrlich) on the street, the composer complained bitterly: "What a nuisance! Why do you insist on playing a work that I don't like?" Schor defended it and invited him to their final rehearsals; a quarter of a century later Schor reminded Rachmaninoff of the incident:

I remember the rehearsal of that morning. I still have the copy where we noted your cuts and changes, and there are even five bars written in by you (an introduction after the third variation—not usually played). I recall our conversation about the changes which you thought of making in the third edition, and how flattered we felt that some of the shadings of our interpretation were to be incorporated in the new edition.

Rachmaninoff promised to attend the performance, but an hour after he left Schor's house, Schor received a note from him that he could not come, but that his wife would attend in his place. Her report must have been satisfactory, for when the Moscow Trio repeated the work at a Tchaikovsky memorial concert, Rachmaninoff came to hear. Afterwards he came to the artists' room and told the musicians: "You have made me love my Trio. Now I will play it."

The Rachmaninoffs' first child was born on May 14—a daughter, christened Irina; and the augmented family spent the summer of 1903 at Ivanovka, but not very happily. On August 18 Rachmaninoff wrote to Morozov:

It's been long since I've had as bad a summer as this one, and if I should describe it for you, there would be nothing to tell you but illnesses. I was ill for almost half the summer, my wife was very sick until July 15, and, finally, my little girl has also been sick up to two or three weeks ago. It has been possible to work only the past couple of weeks, but then I fell ill with angina, which kept me in bed all last week. You will, of course, understand that the whole question of my working was in other hands— I have done nothing, and my only hope now is to be able to work peacefully for at least the six remaining weeks. That's how things have been! ... Even writing about all this is unpleasant, for as soon as I realize that nothing has been accomplished—anguish overcomes me! . . . You, too, must have spent none too gay a summer, if you've both decided to cut it short. Was it really so bad where you were that even Moscow at this season is better? What could be worse than Moscow in the summer? At least you got some work done, you lucky one! Every place can seem good to you, for your soul is satisfied—everything and everybody around one seems better when completed work lies on the table.

This year Rachmaninoff worked on an opera, but not on *Francesca da Rimini*. That libretto was again put aside, to give place to Pushkin's "dramatic scenes." From these short plays Dargomizhsky had previously taken *The Stone Guest*, Rimsky-Korsakov *Mozart and Salieri*, and Cui *The Feast During the Plague*. Rachmaninoff fixed his attention on *The Miserly Knight*, Pushkin's disguised attack on his own selfish father. Rachmaninoff, like his predecessors, took Pushkin's text as his libretto without alteration or addition. The three short scenes are set in a vaguely medieval period, and no country is specified. A miserly baron regards his son Albert as a squanderer, and refuses to touch his treasure for his son's frivolities. Albert asks the help of a usurer, but throws him out when he suggests a way to end Albert's troubles—a few drops of poison in his father's cup. While the miserly knight counts his fortune beneath his castle, Albert approaches the reigning Duke, asking an audience in the presence of his father. When father and son face each other before the Duke, their argument becomes so violent that father challenges son to a duel; but the baron, horrified by his own act and by the scorn of the Duke, dies of a heart attack.

In the spring of 1904, for a variety of reasons, all employed most persuasively by Telyakovsky, director of the Imperial Theaters, Rachmaninoff signed a contract to conduct at the Bolshoi Theater not for years, as was customary, but for five months, without superseding Altani, the old Italian conductor at the Bolshoi. The news of even so brief a contract for Rachmaninoff aroused speculation, anxiety, eagerness, and antagonism in various quarters. Conservatory circles, headed by Ippolitov-Ivanov, expressed their displeasure in "diplomatic" ways, spreading gossip that no one could work peacefully with Rachmaninoff, that he was too demanding, too severe, too inflexible. The musician critic, Ivan Lipayev, wrote that Rachmaninoff was burning his candle at three ends.

One of these burning ends was as an opera composer. *The Miserly Knight* had been completed in February (and taken at once to Taneyev for his approval), and his plan was to add to this another short opera, finish this before beginning work at the Bolshoi Theater, and produce the two together there by the end of the year. The revised libretto of *Francesca da Rimini* was still far from satisfactory to the composer, and he now wrote Modeste Tchaikovsky (on March 26), asking him to rewrite the libretto drastically, omitting the first two scenes and the scene with the Cardinal completely, to provide a long monologue for Gian Ciotto, and "to allow more space for the love duet." The prologue and epilogue were left unchanged, and these, framing a two-scene narrative of the tragedy, formed the final version of the libretto on which Rachmaninoff set to work, as he wrote to Modeste Tchaikovsky on June 8, 1904:

I began to work only a week ago. I've received your corrections of the libretto and am, so far, pleased with them. There's only one thing more I must ask you: that should I need some extra words or phrases, here and there, you would not refuse my request. This, obviously, will appear only as I proceed with my work.

The nearer the approach of autumn, the greater obstacle seemed the "theater question" to Rachmaninoff. The following letter was written to Morozov on the letterhead of the Musical Section of the Students' Society of Arts and Belles-Lettres (*another* activity) on July 2:

Nikita Semyonovich, first of all let me ask you a favor. I've just sent to Moscow the third scene of the *Miserly Knight* and I must ask you to look over and correct the [German] translation, which has been done with an amazing ignorance of such matters. Look especially at the places I've marked. You may add notes wherever you wish, as long as the accent falls on the strong beat of the measure, and too, there should be no rests between two syllables of a single word, such as "oh⌢ne." . . . You won't have to alter more than ten phrases, and then please send the manuscript to Gutheil, who will ship it abroad for printing. For God's sake, do this. Now this is what's happening to us. . . . The last doctor explains Irina's rising temperature as a result of influenza. We've heard from several sources of similar cases of children's illnesses, which has calmed me. . . . I'm working a great deal now. About ten days ago I sent off a scene of *Francesca* for [German] translation. As for the work at the theater, I stubbornly refuse to think of it, and this fact tends to wake in my soul a tiny fear. It is two or three weeks before I must turn my attention to this theater question. Altogether, work piles up, and I don't see how there will be time enough for everything. I'd like to offer a reward of 2000 rubles to anyone who will release me from service in the theater. I want to insert a notice in the newspapers: "Thanks to a signed contract, I have lost all peace of mind this spring. There is so-and-so-much reward to anyone who brings it back to this address." Though I doubt if one could find it now!

A choice eventually had to be made between completing *Francesca* and studying the scores of the season's operas. He wrote to Morozov (on July 21) to thank him for his chore on the translation, to report that Irina was again ill and being taken to Moscow, and that *Francesca* neared completion:

Only one scene and the epilogue remain for me to do. As I want to finish *Francesca* now, I shan't have enough time to prepare for the theater, and this begins to worry me, to torment me. On the other hand, if I begin now to cram the opera scores, I'll never finish *Francesca*. I've decided to finish my opera first. On the whole, I am terribly tired and eager for a rest. But this is a wish not to be realized, for I see before me, not less work, but more. Besides, my little girl worries me, and I don't see how this will end. I must say that it is very difficult and painful to be, at one and the same time, a father, a composer, and a conductor.

A report to Modeste Tchaikovsky on August 3:

A couple of days ago I finished *Francesca*. I took the liberty of making some minor corrections in your text, and in one place—forgive me—I have even written two lines for which I blush. But these two lines were indispensable, and, having no others, I couldn't be too particular. . . . Now that I'm finished, I can tell you that while working I suffered mostly through lack of sufficient text. This shortage was chiefly felt in the second scene, in the approach to the love duet; there is a conclusion for the love duet, but no duet itself. Another reason for feeling a shortage of words is that I won't allow myself to repeat words. But in *Francesca* I had to allow it. There were just too few words. The whole opera lasts only a little over an hour.

On the following day he wrote a franker letter to Morozov; *Francesca* was not yet finished, and he was not forced to be polite:

I come to Moscow either on the 16th or on the 17th of August. Natasha and my little girl have returned to me and, praise God, her health was restored in your city. I'll be finished with *Francesca* in a few days. In this opera, as in *The Miserly Knight,* the last scene seems cut short. Though Tchaikovsky added words for me (and very banal ones, by the way), they turned out to be insufficient. He probably hoped that I would repeat words, and that then perhaps there would be enough. Now I have an approach to the love duet and a conclusion for it—but there's no real duet. . . .
     Till we meet soon, and I plunge into *Life for the Tzar*.

A *Life for the Tzar* was not to be the first opera conducted at the Bolshoi by Rachmaninoff, but it was to be one of the most important events of the opera season. In sixty years of performances this Glinka

opera had gone through many changes, some even becoming hal-
lowed by repetition and transformed into "tradition," though they
violated some of the composer's ideas. Early in 1904 a special commission had been formed to supervise the Bolshoi Theater's revival
of the opera on the occasion of the centenary of Glinka's birth.
Balakirev was suggested for musical director of this anniversary performance, as the greatest living authority on Glinka's work, but there
was more interest in the potentialities of Rachmaninoff's first season
with the Imperial Theaters, and he was appointed to the post. At the
beginning of his term he was allowed only two rehearsals for a repertory opera, but for this revival (with its new sets and costumes) he
was allowed seven rehearsals. By the time of the performance he
had established a common language with singers and musicians, and
of great importance in this new work was his long-standing friendship with Chaliapin. It was a friendship that could weather incidents
disastrous to any less firm relationship.

Years later, Rachmaninoff was speaking with Chaliapin's son Fyodor of opera singers who didn't bother to learn their roles:

"Your papa alone always knew his roles.—Yes, he always knew his roles,
but was always late for rehearsals. . . . Only once did I have a misunderstanding with your papa. He was singing Susanin, and there's one point
where he had to begin and I was to follow with the orchestra. But that
Fedya of mine was so carried away by his acting and took such a long
pause that I couldn't bear it any longer and said loudly, 'It's about time
to start, Fyodor Ivanovich!'" And Sergei Vasilyevich covered his eyes with
his hand and laughed his silent laugh.
"What about the audience? What happened then?" I asked.
"There was no audience—only the musicians and singers; it was the
dress rehearsal."
"And how did papa react?"
"He said nothing—he just gave me his lion look."

The opera chosen to introduce Rachmaninoff to the Bolshoi audience was Dargomizhsky's *Rusalka*, one of the Rachmaninoff-Chalia-
pin successes at the Mamontov Opera seven years before. The role
of the mad miller had become a cornerstone of the singer's fame.
The great surprise, however, for the audience on the evening of
September 3 was to see that the conductor's chair had been moved

from its old familiar place between stage and orchestra pit, with the conductor's back to the musicians. For the first time in an Imperial Russian opera house, the conductor faced both orchestra and singers —an innovation first shown Russia by that radical, Wagner. The new position soon became an established custom in Imperial opera after Rachmaninoff's gesture, but old Altani always had the chair moved back to its "proper" place for the few more performances that he conducted before his death. Rachmaninoff introduced changes of more significance during his tenure, such as insisting that young people be trained as apprentice conductors and that the conductor study roles with individual soloists, but Russian history remembers best that novelty of the conductor's chair.

His second opera to conduct was Tchaikovsky's *Eugene Onegin*, and during the day of his first performance of it (September 10) he had occasion to complain again to the late composer's brother, Modeste. At the last minute before publication of the libretto of *Francesca* Modeste Tchaikovsky had made a great many changes, regardless of the fact that Rachmaninoff was unable to rewrite the music for all these changes. The unexpected move provoked this letter from Rachmaninoff:

I should have preferred to make these corrections myself, to facilitate the synchronization of text and music, but I always try to treat the text with care. I changed but little, and all these changes are yours. . . . The arioso that you've inserted I should like to put into the duet, rather than at the beginning. My duet is too short. Perhaps you would write some words for the duet.

Despite the difficulties with *Francesca*, the candle end of opera conducting had to burn on schedule, and rehearsals of the third opera, Borodin's *Prince Igor*, proceeded. The soprano Salina has left recollections of her first rehearsal with Rachmaninoff that would indicate that the Conservatory gossips had done their work well backstage: "The encounter was a particularly exciting one, because there were such disturbing rumors circulating through the dressing rooms: Rachmaninoff scolds everyone—he grows furious with everyone—he claims no one knows how to sing, and so on." But when he heard Salina go through Yaroslavna's aria he showed complete confidence in her and in the artist's understanding of her task. At the orchestra rehearsal he pointedly commented on the excellent work of the singer and thanked her. Apparently he was taking extra pains to offset the ogreish behavior expected of him. Working for the Imperial Theaters was no simple matter:

The enormous company of dancers, musicians, chorus singers, and soloists at the Bolshoi Opera was under the management of the Directorate of the Imperial Theaters, whose Moscow offices occupied an entire building not far from the theater. Frankly speaking, this office gave me little pleasure in my dealings with it—too much red tape and endless official written communications were required. Even a minor request involved one in a huge apparatus of reports. When I was rehearsing *A Life for the Tzar* I wished to play one of the dances in the Polish scene *pianissimo*, but as all the male dancers in the scene wore spurs, the clanking of these sixty pairs of spurs drowned out the orchestra entirely. I stopped the orchestra and asked the stage manager to spare me that disturbing noise. He replied that he could do nothing about it, because all Polish officers were supposed to wear spurs. I insisted. Finally, after an exchange of several written reports on the subject between stage manager and Directorate, the latter passed a resolution: During this particular number the Polish officers would be permitted to remove their spurs.

However, I must state that in other respects the Directorate was very generous and did not spare funds, though sometimes very substantial ones were needed to produce an opera in the most imposing manner. And everything, to the smallest detail, was well organized and prepared. Nothing like the incidents common at the Mamontov Opera ever occurred while I conducted there.

On September 21 the Glinka anniversary performance of *A Life for the Tzar* was given—the 478th performance of the opera in Moscow. In *Russkiye Vedomosti* Engel wrote:

If not an ideal *Life for the Tzar*, it was such as Moscow has not heard for long. There were new sets, new costumes, but the main thing was a talented new conductor with fresh ardor, Mr. Rachmaninoff, who gave new power to all performers, from soloists to chorus and orchestra. There was a new wish to be firm, to heighten, to give one's best. And the audience that filled the theater sensed this.

Early this autumn Rachmaninoff and Chaliapin gave an enthusi-

astic nonprofessional performance in Nikolai Teleshov's house that
was vividly recorded in the host's recollections:

I remember one remarkable evening in the autumn of 1904 . . . It was
to be a big day; Gorky* had arrived in Moscow and was coming, Chaliapin was going to sing. . . .

And indeed the place was packed. And Chaliapin, the minute he got
in, said joyfully: "Brothers!—I want to sing!"

He telephoned Rachmaninoff and said: "Seryozha, I'm just dying to
sing. Take a cab and hop around quick. We'll sing all night!"

Rachmaninoff was soon there. Chaliapin did not even give him time
for tea. He sat him down at the piano, and something very wonderful
began. This was at the height of Chaliapin's fame and powers; he was
in an exceptionally fine mood and sang literally without pause. There
was no reading *that* evening, nor could there be. He was inspired. Never
anywhere at any time was he so magical as he was that night. He himself
said, several times: "This is where you should hear me—not at the
Bolshoi!"

Chaliapin fired Rachmaninoff, and Rachmaninoff set Chaliapin on
fire; and these two, urging each other on, achieved miracles. This was not
music or singing as anyone had ever known it: it was the inspired ecstasy
of two great artists.

I still see that great room, lit by a single hanging lamp above them,
all eyes looking one way, at the piano where Rachmaninoff sat, at his
black-coated back and the nape of his neck and his clipped hair. His
elbows move swiftly, his long thin fingers strike the keys; and against
the wall, facing us, a tall, fine figure of a man, Chaliapin. He is in high
boots and light black Russian coat of a fine woven material; one hand
rests lightly on the piano, his face tense, not a glimmer left now of the
just uttered jest: he waits for the moment of his first notes, he is transformed into the character whose soul he is to open before us, to let us
feel the things it feels, know the things it knows.

Of equal importance with his work on *A Life for the Tzar* was
Rachmaninoff's study this autumn of Tchaikovsky's three finest

* From the publication of Maxim Gorky's first book he, Rachmaninoff, and
Chaliapin were fast friends. Asafiev tells of an occasion when he was asked by
Stasov to play Rachmaninoff's music for Gorky and Repin, at Repin's Finnish home,
"The Penates." Asafiev played the new préludes of Op. 23 and some songs. Gorky's
comment: "How well he listens to silence!"

operas. To *Eugene Onegin* was added *Oprichnik,* and in the last
week of October, in honor of the 100th performance of *The Queen
of Spades,* Rachmaninoff conducted a newly studied production of
this opera in an entire week devoted to Tchaikovsky. The three ballets, *Swan Lake, The Sleeping Beauty,* and *The Nutcracker,* were
also performed this week, though not conducted by Rachmaninoff. It
was his production of *The Queen of Spades* that roused the greatest
enthusiasm; in *Moskovskiye Vedomosti* Kashkin praised Rachmaninoff's careful conception of the whole, in which the orchestra had
"a continuous life, reflecting the development of the drama."

The other two operas that he conducted for the first time this
season were Musorgsky's *Boris Godunov* (in Rimsky-Korsakov's first
revision) in January 1905, and Rubinstein's *Demon.* Both were
triumphs for Chaliapin. On February 2, 1905 the performance of
Aleko, along with scenes from *Eugene Onegin* and *Boris Godunov,*
was of special interest because Chaliapin sang three roles that evening: Aleko, Onegin (for the only time in his career), and Varlaam.

Two other events of more personal importance for Rachmaninoff
this season: The first Glinka Awards, founded according to the will
of Belayev and administered by Rimsky-Korsakov, Glazunov, and
Lyadov, were announced; Rachmaninoff received the five-hundred-
rubles prize for the popular Second Concerto. Arensky's trio and
Scriabin's symphony also took prizes in these first awards. On January
8, 1905 Rachmaninoff's cantata *Spring* was performed by Siloti, with
Chaliapin singing the bass solo. *Russkaya Muzykalnaya Gazeta*
wrote, in part: "Glorious talent! Here are inspiration, living warmth
of emotion, exquisite taste, and winged flight of free imagination."

The end of Rachmaninoff's season at the Bolshoi Theater was not
the end of his season's musical activities. He conducted for the Kerzin
concerts, giving an interpretation of Tchaikovsky's Fifth Symphony
that Medtner could recall in 1933:

It is sad that such a conductor can only be *remembered,* and that there
are but few of this generation with whom one can share such recollections. I shall never forget Rachmaninoff's interpretation of Tchaikovsky's
Fifth Symphony. Before he conducted it, we heard it only in the version
of Nikisch and his imitators. True, Nikisch had saved this symphony
from a complete fiasco (as conducted by its composer), but then his

pathetic slowing of the tempi became the law for performing Tchaikovsky, enforced by conductors who followed him blindly. Suddenly, under
Rachmaninoff, all this imitative tradition fell away from the composition,
and we heard it as if for the first time; especially astonishing was the
cataclysmic impetuosity of the finale, an antithesis to the pathos of
Nikisch, that had always harmed this movement.

Even more unexpected [in a later season] was the impression of Mozart's G minor Symphony, which had long been labeled dull—a thing in
rococo style. I shall never forget this symphony as conducted by Rachmaninoff; it suddenly came towards us, pulsating with life and urgency.

On March 18 Rachmaninoff conducted a program consisting of
Glazunov's *Spring*, Borodin's Second Symphony, Balakirev's Over-
ture on Three Russian Themes, and Musorgsky's *Night on Bald
Mountain*. Engel wrote:

Here were the basic qualities of Rachmaninoff as conductor: a conscious
definition of aims and a firmness in their execution. In general, in this
realm of the symphony, the young conductor of the Bolshoi showed an
equally great talent. This is a conductor by God's grace.

To win a conductor meant to lose—temporarily—a composer. In later
years Rachmaninoff summed up his career:

The whole time of my musical activity thus far—some twenty-four years
—might be divided, roughly, into three periods of approximately eight
years each, of composing, concert work, and conducting. When I am con-
certizing I cannot compose . . . when I feel like writing music, I have to
concentrate on that—I cannot touch the piano. When I am conducting
I can neither compose nor play concerts. Other musicians may be more
fortunate in this respect; but I have to concentrate to such a degree on
any one thing I am doing that it does not seem to allow me to take up
anything else.

Russian musicians added to the early rumblings of political change
in 1905. On February 2 thirty-two musicians, including Rimsky-
Korsakov, Chaliapin, Taneyev, Rachmaninoff, Gretchaninoff, and
Siloti, signed and published a declaration:

When life is in shackles, art cannot be free. . . . When there is no freedom of thought, no freedom of religion, no freedom of expression, and no freedom of the press, all living artistic ideas of the nation are constrained, and creative art withers. The title of "Free Artist" then becomes a bitter mockery. We are not free artists, but victims of the present abnormal conditions, deprived of civil rights as much as the rest of Russia's citizens. . . . There is but one way out of this impasse: Russia must at long last enter the path of basic reforms.

Chapter 7

Operas and Projects

RACHMANINOFF's chief musical duty this summer at Ivanovka was the scoring of *Francesca,* for his two short operas were now scheduled for the coming season. He wrote to Morozov on July 6, 1905:

It's as usual with us. Every day I work a lot (though less than before, from 9:30 to 3:30 with a dinnertime rest). I don't let myself work more than this, and we have a general battle of tennis every day. This is the state of *Francesca's* instrumentation: I began the scoring on June 9 and have already finished the prologue and epilogue, and tomorrow the first scene will be finished. Such swift traveling is possible because my daily chore is no longer three pages, but four. As you can see, this is not too strenuous, for I am practicing less than before. As for the quality of the work, it is the same as ever with me in any work—in the midst of it one thinks it well done, sometimes even very good, but as soon as a little time passes, you see how almost completely unsuitable it really is and how it would be better to change everything, even though I don't know how to do it any better.

Now there's only the instrumentation of the second scene to be done—42 pages in 10½ days. A day of rest tomorrow, though it should all be finished by July 20. In general the orchestration of "Hell" pleases me more than that of the first scene. I've read recently in *Russkiye Vedomosti* [of June 26] that the performance of my operas has been advanced to October. That means all the more rush to be in time with the copying....
Your compliments to Ivanovka do not leave me indifferent, they touch me very deeply. I feel so good here that I have already begun counting with anguish the days between now and my departure, and at every evening's tea I subtract one more, with a sigh, from the remainder. Tonight the number will be "42." This is too little, too little, and will pass too quickly, and then—Moscow (half misfortune) and the theater (total misfortune). Not to mention the fact that my family and Irochka will stay on here.

The time to leave for Moscow and the Bolshoi Theater did at last come. His first important job this season was to conduct not his own operas, but Rimsky-Korsakov's new opera, *Pan Voyevoda,* a work that Rachmaninoff did not wholly admire:

The music is poor, but the instrumentation is stupendous. At that time Rimsky orchestrated without writing a score. In his workroom he had many stands, and he used to move from one stand to another, filling in the part of each instrument—so marvelous was his ear. I said to him, "Leave me alone up to the last rehearsal and, if something in my interpretation doesn't suit you, I'll have another rehearsal on the day of the performance and make changes according to your wish."

Rachmaninoff's letter to Rimsky-Korsakov on this occasion had a somewhat different tone; it was sent September 17, 1905:

Highly esteemed Nikolai Andreyevich,
    The première of your opera, *Pan Voyevoda,* is scheduled for September 27; dress rehearsal Saturday, September 24. I do not know if the administration has informed you of these dates. I have often asked them, without getting a definite answer. Therefore I take the liberty to ask you personally, will you come? There is no need to tell you how happy I would be if you would come and show me my mistakes. It would be fine if you could come on the morning of the 23rd. There is to be a piano rehearsal that day, followed next day by the dress rehearsal. September 26 would be kept in reserve to correct as much as possible anything that doesn't please you. (This rehearsal can be with orchestra.)
                                    With sincere and profound respect for you,
                                                    S. Rachmaninoff

Rimsky-Korsakov wrote of this première in his memoirs:

I was called to Moscow to attend the production of *Pan Voyevoda* at the Bolshoi Theater. The talented Rachmaninoff conducted. The opera proved to have been well rehearsed, but some of the artists were rather weak. . . . Orchestra and choruses went splendidly. I was pleased with the way the opera sounded, both vocally and orchestrally. . . . The whole orchestration had hit the mark squarely, and the voices sounded beautiful. . . .
    The time in Moscow was tumultuous. A few days before the first performance a strike of printing shops broke out. . . . The ever-growing frequency of the strikes, the political disturbances, and finally the De-

cember uprising in Moscow led to the disappearance of my opera from the repertory after several performances. Telyakovsky was present at the first performance. On learning from Rachmaninoff that I had completed *The Legend of the Invisible City of Kitezh,* he expressed a desire to produce it in St. Petersburg the following season. I told him that henceforth I did not intend to submit my operas to the Directorate; let the Directorate itself select whichever it wished of my published operas.

Rachmaninoff's association with Rimsky-Korsakov gave him a totally new outlook on the importance of this composer, whom Moscow-trained musicians tended to underestimate:

His mastery of the technique of composition, especially his skill in instrumentation and his sensitive control of tone color, filled me with admiration. I grew really fond of him, and this feeling deepened from day to day. To this day [1933] my appreciation of his music has not reached its limits. My association with Rimsky-Korsakov taught me a great deal. I was given more than one opportunity of verifying his incredibly fine ear for orchestral detail. One evening after a rehearsal we went to the Solodovnikov Opera to hear *May Night.* . . . Just as Levko began his aria I saw Rimsky-Korsakov frown, as if he were in great pain. "They are using B-flat clarinets!" he groaned, and gripped my knee. Later I verified from the score that A clarinets were indicated.

If *Kitezh* were to be produced by the Bolshoi, Rimsky-Korsakov hoped that Rachmaninoff would be its conductor, but to the latter's deep regret, he had by then left the service of the Imperial Theaters.

On Rachmaninoff's return to Moscow from Ivanovka with his completed operas, Chaliapin planned to work on the roles of Malatesta in *Francesca* and the Baron in *The Miserly Knight.* It was the prospect of this latter characterization by him that had inspired this use of the Pushkin play; Rachmaninoff even said, "I composed the opera for him." But Chaliapin delayed starting the work for so long that Rachmaninoff, extremely disappointed, was forced to look elsewhere for his central singer. In this emergency Altani recommended to Rachmaninoff a young baritone, Georgi Baklanov, to whom the composer gave both the Chaliapin roles. Working closely with Rachmaninoff and the actor Lensky (on the dramatic aspects of the roles),

Baklanov began a substantial career on the night of January 11, 1906, in the première of *The Miserly Knight* and *Francesca da Rimini*.

The career of Baklanov lasted longer than that of the two operas. Though *Francesca's* music had a more popular appeal, its literary structure was too weak to command respect. The critics agreed with Rachmaninoff's private preference for the *Knight;* of it Engel wrote in *Russkiye Vedomosti:*

As in the drama the most interesting scene in the opera is the second, the monologue of the covetous baron. Here are individual moments of great power. The composer's talent shows throughout *The Miserly Knight,* in harmonic richness and orchestral color as well as in the supple precision of its musical declamation, fused with the text. And yet this opera is not for the large audience; this is, perhaps, a *Kabinettstück* for those who can appreciate the subtle filigree work of its exquisite composition.

Hard upon the pressures of the première came other pressures, personified in V. A. Telyakovsky, director of the Imperial Theaters, come to Moscow to guard the theaters against the political unrest already seeping through their thick walls. In his memoirs Telyakovsky tells of his conversations with Rachmaninoff—and of the "'information" he received about him:

While in Moscow I ran into some complications caused among the company of the Bolshoi Theater by the prevailing political atmosphere. I speak of the bitter dissatisfaction openly expressed not only by Rachmaninoff, its conductor, but also by the double-bass player in that orchestra, Sergei Koussevitzky. Both these musicians presented an extremely harsh appraisal of the situation within the Bolshoi Theater as well as an obvious desire to slam the door noisily as they departed. Their characterizations of the situation, quite divergent, threw less illumination on the position of the theater than on their own natures.

Rachmaninoff came to notify me that it was doubtful whether he would remain as conductor at the Bolshoi for the next season. He said that his most immediate reason for this decision was his coming concert tour in America. I regretted this and tried to persuade him to stay, even offering him the post of musical director of the Bolshoi Theater. At first he received this proposal in silence, but, growing more frank, he pointed to several circumstances that made my proposition unacceptable.

According to Rachmaninoff, the trends of the time had had a most disturbing effect on the members of the Bolshoi orchestra. Discipline, so high in the time of Altani, the now aged musical director, was falling lower and lower, and after the recent events of the winter, it seemed to have disappeared entirely. In his opinion it had become unbearable to work with such an orchestral ensemble, for it was absolutely impossible to obtain a realization of the conductor's demands. If the harmful and improper element could not be eliminated from the orchestra immediately, the orchestra would be uncontrollable, for most of the time would be occupied not with art, but with all sorts of incidents and petty tales grounded in personal envy, intrigue, etc.

When I argued that the Directorate could not dismiss the musicians that he indicated as unsuitable, for among them were some who had served seventeen or eighteen years, with only two or three years left before their retirement with pensions, Rachmaninoff replied that this was no concern of his as conductor. He wished to state merely that certain musicians not only do not fit into this orchestra, but actually injure it, and that they must be replaced if the Directorate wants an orchestra equal to the demands of the Opera. Let the government give such musicians their pensions ahead of time, for their earlier merits, but to keep on the unfit just to wait for their pensions was absurd. He said much the same thing about the singers. . . .

Of course it was difficult for me to come to terms with Rachmaninoff on this basis. As an artist he was right, but in practice, within a government institution, it was impossible to act on such a principle. . . . It was clear that Rachmaninoff would not remain as a permanent conductor. He agreed with pleasure to appear occasionally as a guest conductor with an opera that interested him. A final decision was postponed till the end of the season, and with that we parted. That evening Rachmaninoff conducted a splendid performance of his two new operas. . . .

My next trip to Moscow took place at the end of February. During this visit I had a typical conversation with Kazansky, chief staff physician of the Moscow Imperial Theaters. Everything always looked black to him, and he was as frightened of political events as of fire. The incidents in Moscow had had an extremely depressing effect on him, and everywhere he now saw rebellion and danger. . . . Among his many warnings the most curious was in regard to Rachmaninoff. Some of the singers had already warned me that Rachmaninoff was particularly untrustworthy. Now here was a second warning, but Kazansky's distrust of him was based on another suspicion. He saw in Rachmaninoff a dangerous rival for my post of director of the Theaters. I told him that it was unthinkable even to speak of trusting or distrusting Rachmaninoff, and that I simply consider him a fine conductor, not only useful to the theater and opera, but indispensable.

Kazansky answered, "That's just it: the more outstanding a conductor he becomes, the more success and authority he has, the more dangerous he'll be, and the more careful of him one must be. Take my word for this—I know the theater and these artists well. Why, even Chaliapin is afraid of Rachmaninoff!"

Kazansky was especially distressed when I told him I was so satisfied with Rachmaninoff that my wish was to place him in charge of the Opera, creating for him the same position in Moscow that I offered Napravnik in Petersburg. . . . When finally Kazansky told me that many feared the production of *Sadko* because Rachmaninoff was sure to stage this opera unusually well and would thereby acquire greater authority, I pacified him by revealing that Rachmaninoff not only cared nothing for his position in the Opera, but had already categorically announced to me his decision not to stay in the service of the theater, even if he should be showered with gold and appointed director of the Opera. Yes, he was attracted by glory—but of a different sort: that of composition, of concert activity, of freedom and independence. But Kazansky persisted: "I still advise you to be more cautious with him."

It seems scarcely surprising that before the end of the season Rachmaninoff carried out his threat to end his contract with the Imperial Theaters for good and to get far away at once from the political heat and noise of 1906. It was Italy, the hospitable refuge of harried Russian composers, that received the Rachmaninoff family in March. But it was a vacation that would be looked back on with little pleasure.

Six days after arriving in Florence Rachmaninoff sent Morozov a larger request than usual. Flaubert's *Salammbô* had snared another composer, and Rachmaninoff hoped that his literary responsibility could be shared between his friend Morozov and the poet, M. P. Svobodin. Rachmaninoff's full sketch for the scenario gives us an insight into his music drama methods:

Now for my request . . . be so good as to see Svobodin, and talk over with him my scenario that I attach herewith. Have a look at it yourself beforehand and let me hear about anything you don't agree with. I haven't yet received your scenario and I am very eager to know how you approach this work. So—I begin.

Scene I. Terrace of Salammbô's palace. According to the novel "her tones were plaintive, as if she called someone," and with this she greets the goddess, queen of the earth. She turns toward the moon and rapturous speech pours from her lips.

> Address to the moon } just as in the novel.
> Address to Tanit

Talk with Taanach (playing of the "nebel" to be cut). Hamilcar is mentioned. Entrance of Schahabarim. Continue exactly as in novel. Legend told by Schahabarim: creation of the world. Salammbô's request about Tanit. Refusal. Scene ends with news that the barbarian army is returning to Carthage. ("Suddenly the priest perceived on the horizon behind Tunis what at first appeared to be a light mist floating over the ground. . .," etc.) End of scene.

Scene II. Beneath the walls of Carthage. In Mâtho's camp. Mâtho should not relate the whole scene of his encounter with Salammbô, which Salammbô herself will tell in a subsequent scene. He must begin by saying only that the thought of Salammbô, whom he saw in Carthage, would not leave him in peace. This is a brief introduction. Enter Spendius. The following scene should be built from several chapters. In order to make this more understandable, I'll write out almost all the words, except for the monologues.

Enter Spendius. "Begone!" Mâtho shouts at him. "No," he replies, "you delivered me from prison, and I am entirely yours! You are my master." Mâtho is silent. "Listen," says Spendius, "do not despise me for my weakness. I have lived so long in Carthage (not in the *palace,* as in Flaubert) that I can crawl like a viper between its walls."—"Well, what is that to me?" says Mâtho. Spendius continues. "What wealth, what treasures." Here follows a monologue: "Do you comprehend me, soldier! . . . We shall go about arrayed," etc., to the words: "Carthage is ours, let us fall upon it!"—"No," Mâtho stops him.—"There is a curse hanging over me." He looks around and says: "Where is she?"—"You are in pain?" the slave asks quietly. "Can I not in some way help you? Tell me. Master! Master!" Finally Mâtho tells him: "Listen, it is the wrath of the gods! The daughter of Hamilcar pursues me, I fear her, Spendius! Speak to me! See, I am ill. I wish to cure myself, I have tried everything," etc., to the words: "Ah, the stones must thrill under her sandals, and the stars themselves bend down to gaze at her." Then Spendius says: "Master, if your heart is brave, I will conduct you to Carthage." "How?"—"Swear to execute my orders . . ."—"I swear by Tanit." "I will fulfill my promise," Spendius says. "You remember, just at sunrise on the terrace of Sa- lammbô's palace I pointed out Carthage to you. We were strong that day, but you would not listen to me. Master," he continues, "there is in the sanctuary of Tanit a mysterious veil, fallen from Heaven, that covers the goddess."—"I know that!"—"If you wish, I shall take you there to steal it," and so on, to the cry of Mâtho, "Let us go," on which the scene ends. I like this scene very much, though it will be just as dull as the first scene of *The Miserly Knight*. Yes, and I should like Mâtho to open this scene with an exclamàtion "Salammbô!" in a very exalted tone. It may be good if at the beginning he would tell the audience how Salammbô during the feast had offered him a gold cup and said "Drink"—this might be included.

Scene III. Temple of the goddess Tanit. Here the Zaimph is stolen. Flaubert provides few words for this, but with his outline one can some- what broaden the scene. . . .

After the rites all leave, there is silence, and our heroes enter. Let the mute priest come in, let them kill him and go through the door by which he entered. Let the author of the libretto invent some way for them to get into the temple.

Scene IV, in Salammbô's room. As in Flaubert let the couch be sus- pended, with a stool beside it, serving as a step. As in Flaubert let a corner of red mattress be seen, and the tip of a little bare foot, unless the foot of the prima donna should make this unwise. Entrance of Mâtho. Women, servants, slaves rush in. Turmoil. Spendius shouts: "Save your- self!"—then runs out. Salammbô's curses and Mâtho's exit. End of 4th Scene. I see this as two acts, thus far, with two scenes in each.

Scene V. A whole act. Temple of Moloch. Stage full of people (Elders). This is, so to say, a session of parliament. At the beginning the Elders should announce to the audience that in the war with the barbarians things are going badly, and that their sole hope rests in Hamilcar, whom they await. By the way, this Hamilcar will be an interesting person for music. His arrival must be prepared at the start of the preceding scene. He's been mentioned in the first two scenes.

Scene VI. In Salammbô's apartments. She is alone. She should have a scene, possibly filled with recollections of her sight of the Zaimph, of the face of her father when he came to her after the assembly of the Elders, and a general description of her spiritual condition. Schahabarim enters, tells her that her father has been surrounded by the three armies of Mâtho, and that the preservation of the republic and of her father de-

pends on her alone, and so on, as in the novel. End on Schahabarim
forcing her to kneel and swear. After priest leaves, preparations for departure are begun at once, dressing, short talks between pauses with
Taanach. She leaves. Taanach weeps.

Scene VII. In Mâtho's camp. All exactly as in novel; i.e., Mâtho enters
his tent with Salammbô and begins the scene with the words, "Who are
you?" and to the end as in novel. Now for an important question. Hearken
to me. Do we have to go on from here? Couldn't the opera end on this
scene?—"By the bedside a dagger glistened; the sight of this shining blade
inflamed her with murderous desire. She heard voices that whispered
sorrowful words to her. She drew near and seized the weapon. At the
rustle of her robe Mâtho awoke; he moved his lips over her hands, and
the dagger dropped." Shouts burst out, and the tent is lit with a frightful
light. The Libyan camp is in flames. Screams: "Mâtho!" Hamilcar approaches. "We are beaten," etc. Mâtho rushes out, and Salammbô is
left alone; she moves toward the Zaimph, takes it down and "remained
melancholy before her ardent dream." Couldn't it end here, without the
superfluous scene of Salammbô's death? As for Mâtho's death, it can be
assumed from the shouts of the attacking Hamilcar, who had set the
camp on fire. Think about this. I fixed my attention on Salammbô: I began
with her, ended with her, and gave her name to the opera. I completely
discard Narr' Havas. In my opinion he's quite superfluous. Only a few
concluding words need be invented for Salammbô. Perhaps she could be
forced to die, falling, as at the end of the novel.

If you like this scenario, go to Svobodin, explain that what you need
is not an opera libretto, but a drama, and commission him to send me
any one scene quickly. Tell him that *all words should be taken literally
from Flaubert,* but arranged in verse. That all settings should come from
Flaubert. Tell him not to be afraid of lengthy dialogues. They can always be shortened. If you should find my scenario unsuitable, tell me so.
But let Svobodin send me at least one scene, and then we can discuss
it all.

April 10, 1906

Dear friend Nikita Semyonovich, I received your letter about five days
ago—the day after I sent you the scenario. I couldn't answer you at once,
for I had to remove from my soul a burden in the form of the *Miserly
Knight* score. Today I finally finished the proofreading, made a great
many changes, and sent off the score to Leipzig. I feel easier, for now I am
faced only by the corrections of *Francesca.* Then I'll be free for other
work. I haven't entered a single gallery. I've only been to look at some

cathedrals and all the gardens and parks I see during my walks. I'm delighted with everything, especially the Boboli gardens and the Michelangelo square. . . . *Francesca* will take about ten more days. If I need a piano after that, Madame Lucchesi offers me (without extra payment, I believe, but this remains to be clarified) a room at her place, in the basement, where there is an upright piano that her brother plays. There I would be allowed to play from 9 to 1, and from 3 to 6. . . . Now about *Salammbô*. I was sorry to hear that you don't like this subject. Sorry mostly because you now won't look carefully into what I wrote in my last letter, and as long as you don't do that, you won't be able to point out its faults. That's what is worst of all. Altogether I like the subject. There's much that's "musical" in it. I am dissatisfied only with the conclusion of my first scene. Couldn't something be devised for this—some chorus at least? Maybe Taanach could be given something to sing and play, as in Flaubert. . . . I long to hear objections to my scenario, and then corrections, and, finally, at least one scene of text [from Svobodin], so I can start doing something—as long as I shan't be criticized to death. Evidently all goes well in Moscow. But won't the victory of the Kadet party provoke troubles?

When Rachmaninoff next wrote to Morozov, they agreed that it was easier to forget Svobodin than to wait for him to make up his mind. Rachmaninoff suggested (with no enthusiasm) applying again to Modeste Tchaikovsky, "or I'll even ask Slonov." In the meantime Morozov had taken pity on his waiting friend and himself prepared a scene of *Salammbô* for him to try. Rachmaninoff replied on April 27:

I received your sketched verses, and find only two things wrong with them. For one thing, there's not enough for a complete scene, in my opinion, and, as I've said before, the end of this scene doesn't satisfy me. All that choral shouting off stage never "convinces" the audience. Even on stage a chorus is too unconvincing and too insufficiently understood an element to *make* it carry the *thread of the action*, so I am inclined to hold on to my first variant, making Schahabarim (as in the novel) tell the audience "with orchestra" that the cloud again approaches. And into his music I can always throw exclamations from the chorus (this sometimes works well), which would in this case not play a chief role, which is what I'm against, but a subsidiary one. That is all, dear friend. I like everything else very much and I thank you from the bottom of my heart for your work. I finished correcting the *Francesca* score only the day before yesterday. As usual I made a mass of changes, which took up a lot of time. Yesterday we found a villa. It is in "Marina di Pisa," about ten versts from Pisa, on the seashore. The little villa is very nice and, above all, clean. In my opinion cleanliness in Italian homes is as rare as, for example, clarity in the compositions of all musical innovators. *Pardon!* There are five rooms in the villa, which is one more than we need, and this gives me the occasion to invite you both to visit us. . . .

Now, Nikita Semyonovich, listen to me attentively. For next season I have: a contract, unsigned, with the theater for five months from September 1st to February 1st. Fee, 8000 rubles. I have a proposal (also unsigned) for 10 symphonic concerts. Fee, 4500 rubles. I have 3 Russian concerts* for 900 rubles and two charity concerts for nothing. To this I must add that after September 1st I shan't have a kopek of savings. I add this to be absolutely clear. Then I *shall have,* according to a telegram I received yesterday, a contract for America next season at terms that I've insisted upon from the start of negotiations with the impresario, and then I have some slight hope of composing something in the future. I never have a big hope. Now for the question. Weigh all I have and all that I *may* have and tell me quite frankly: Should I send to the devil all that I have (bird in hand) and keep only what I *may* have (birds in bush)? Please think about this and write me. You, being a decisive person, can't imagine what torments I go through when I realize that it's I who must decide this question and cut it. The chief trouble is that I can't cut anything. My hands tremble! Think it over and write me quickly. This can be decided *only this year*—that is, right away. If I choose the "two birds in the bush," I can live abroad, but only if I can control my longing for Russia. On this question mark I end my letter.

Your S. Rachmaninoff

P.S. Give your wife this opinion from an experienced and tested parent. All first children, until they adjust themselves to their parents, and until (and this is the main thing) the parents are adjusted to the first children, all are difficult at the beginning. Later everything straightens itself out, and children soon begin to bring you nothing but consolation.

Console her for me, please!

Just this minute received a contract to be signed, from the Moscow office of the Imperial Theaters.

"Fate knocks at the window! Tap! Tap! Dear friend, cease striving for happiness!"**

* The Circle of Lovers of Russian Music, organized by Kerzin.
** Rachmaninoff's song "Fate."

Rachmaninoff's letter of May 4/17 touched all the things on his mind—the *Salammbô* libretto, the opera contract, the American offer, the political rumblings in Russia:

... I want you only to warn Slonov not to be stingy with the text. There's nothing more annoying than to find oneself short of text. It's always easier to abridge it than to lengthen it. We live quietly and pleasantly. So far I like it here, though I'm afraid of the beginning of the season, when everything here will fill up and silence will vanish. As for my head, it's still empty, and now I can rely only on a text to pull something out of this head of mine. A few days ago I wrote to the Directorate of the Imperial Theaters asking them to let me delay my definite answer for another month; as it is quite possible that by that time I may not be able to sign after all, I've asked them to have a substitute in mind. I've sent a similar letter to your Directorate, regarding the symphonic concerts. . . . After such a long interval it is painful to compose—and I must say that all this is very disturbing: both for my personal feelings and in respect to my future plans. It seems that nothing will work out with America. I think they want to squeeze me. I've sent them an ultimatum with a month's deadline. Incidentally, I absolutely need America if I give up the Moscow offers. Without one or the other I can't exist. Which should I hold on to? I cling to America, not only because it would bring in a good amount of money, but mostly because it demands only two months. But suppose I am cheated there and I compose nothing? Thus my perpetual refrain. . . .

I receive two papers here: *Novoye Vremya* and *Russkiye Vedomosti,* and every time the doorbell rings I rush to the door myself, thinking that it's the mail. So far I know only about the solemn opening of the Duma. The speech of Petrunkevich* seemed to me unsuccessful. The first speech at the first session at the opening of the first Russian parliament—and a speech on such a theme, moreover—should have been more complete, more illuminating in every respect, and therefore more convincing. And how did the members of the Duma respond to it? They merely applauded.

A few days later Rachmaninoff wrote to his new librettist, Slonov:

Dear friend Mikhail Akimovich!

I'll start by saying that I am very glad to be working with you and

* Reported in *Russkiye Vedomosti,* April 28, 1906.

that I entrust the composition of the libretto to you. I must ask you only not to refuse to make corrections and alterations, and not to be offended with me if I shouldn't like some of the verses, which I'll tell you without ceremony. I see no offense in this.

We've undertaken to write an opera together. If it is painful and unpleasant for you to change something you've written, it's just as painful and unpleasant for me to compose music to a text that doesn't suit me. You must therefore prepare yourself to hear me make many changes. I am completely confident that you can write good verses, especially with Flaubert's help. . . .

Before analyzing the text you've sent, I want you to familiarize me with the plan of your whole scenario. I've written one of my own that I hold on to until I have a better one. Besides, I'm sure it is not perfect, so I'll be glad to hear it criticized with suggestions for its improvement. So criticize, please! . . .

Now for the song of Taanach [taken from Chapter VII]. I don't really like it, except for the idea itself, which is satisfactory. The first thing that strikes me is that this song is not in Hamilcar's honor. Of its 22 lines of text only three are devoted to him. Then it contains too many characters. I'd omit the she eagle and leave the eagle alone with the lamb, giving a little more emphasis to the struggle itself. With the boy clutching the eagle, the eagle trying to lift itself and fighting with the boy, and finally losing its strength and falling dead to earth. *Make the meter of these verses much shorter,* more energetic. Short and powerful phrases! . . .

I warn you: I'll be displeased if you don't follow Flaubert closely. I have indicated all the parts of the novel to be used. For the hundredth and last time I beg you: the more closely you follow Flaubert the better it will be.

Slonov did move ahead, but Rachmaninoff did not gain confidence:

May 16/29, 1906

Dear friend Mikhail Akimovich!

Yesterday I sent off to you an analysis of the 2nd scene, and yesterday I tried to adapt myself to it. But I had no success—something in your verses kept irritating me. Finally I realized that your rhymes made my obstacle. Dear friend, I don't need them! They nauseate me—I can find no way to fit them naturally to music, and I keep wanting to smooth and redeem and hide this monotonous ending. That's why I like the introduction of Mâtho—unrhymed. And even in it there is still one line that doesn't satisfy me; I beg you to transpose, somehow, the words: "there you stand before me, in all your living beau-*ty* . . ." For this, too, I can find no music.

This may also explain why I like the words of Spendius so much: "Remember, master," etc. No rhymes there. And I like the rest of his words much less, just because there are rhymes. Rhymes are so disgusting when you write declamatory music.

But whenever you see some resemblance to an aria or a set number, let's have rhymes. Otherwise, no! Unnecessary. Write only such verses as I've mentioned to you, such as, for example, the introduction to Salammbô's first scene, which I like in verse, but in which I've asked you to change the content to be closer to Flaubert. Or, in the same way, the legend of Schahabarim, which I like. This is all I wanted to tell you—don't seek rhymes, but seek more natural arrangements and words.

A week later Rachmaninoff sent Slonov his last word on the *Salammbô* project: "I've composed nothing of *Salammbô* as yet. I just measure and examine." And we hear no more of Carthage in his correspondence.

At the beginning of summer, the Rachmaninoffs in Florence had a visitor from Moscow: their cousin, Anna Trubnikova, who later wrote of the birth of a popular piano work:

The days were sultry; the Venetian blinds remained lowered on windows and doors. The streets were empty. Whenever the heat relaxed a little, the first to appear on the street were a young man, poorly dressed but with a silk top hat and a cane, and a woman in a brightly colored dress. A tiny donkey with very long ears pulled an upright mechanical piano on wheels, and a crib with a baby in it was attached to the piano. The young man sang popular ballads and the woman cranked the piano. They were itinerant musicians. Our favorite number in their repertory was a simple but quite melodious polka. Many years later, when I heard Rachmaninoff's *Polka Italienne,* I knew where it had first entered his consciousness.

May and June had changed the Russian household at Marina di Pisa from workshop to hospital: Natalia Alexandrovna became ill on May 14, and then little Irina also became dangerously ill.

When Rachmaninoff next wrote to Morozov (June 18), he had unraveled some of his knots:

. . . I am *not* going to America. I've *rejected* the theater—and *accepted* the symphony concerts. By the way, will you make up a program for the concerts for me? When I get back, I'll send you my choice and you send me yours. We'll agree on something, God willing. I want to start working. I feel bad. Terribly tired, mostly from not sleeping well for so long a time.

[July 3/16, 1906]

I'll describe our life in a few words. I can't remember as bad a summer as this one has been! (That's the introduction—then the first theme begins): Natasha has been ill since May 14th and only on June 16th did she leave her bed for the first time since then. (Second theme): Irinochka fell ill on May 26th. (Now the development): Natasha's illness was neither painful nor dangerous; Irinochka's illness was very painful and we were very frightened. Pisan doctors are rotten! Natasha's is so-so. But Irinochka's was good for nothing. Had to call one from Florence. Though very expensive, he at least showed the blunders in treatment, and told us what the *actual* illness was, instead of the *imaginary* one treated by the rotten Pisan doctor.

It was hell in our house. Poor Irinochka screamed nearly the whole day. Natasha suffered the more for being sick herself and thus tied to bed. I was alone with them. Marina [Ivanova] arrived at the beginning of June to help. (Recapitulation): Natasha has now recovered. Though I wrote you in my last letter that Irinochka was on the road to recovery, that was premature. Every other day she has fever. Unable to summon the Florentine doctor again, Natasha, Irina, and the nurse went to live there two days ago. (Now for a brilliant finale.) In a week we leave for Russia. Finale constructed on the following themes: Irina is completely exhausted and weakened. . . . Fearing complications from such a condition, and without a doctor at hand (even the Florentine leaves in a week for abroad, fortunately or unfortunately for us), we can't consider staying here. Just to look at Irina now is to realize what she has gone through. That, dear friend, is the story. Of myself I don't write. I've been well, but this has led to nothing good. So in response to the description in your sad letter, I can answer in the same way. Remember how Maria speaks to Andrei (in Tchaikovsky's *Mazeppa*)? It's so beautiful:

We'll arrive in Moscow, probably, on the 12th or 13th. It's not yet certain how we'll get there. Yesterday I read that disturbances have begun on the Warsaw-Vienna railroad. What an affair! Impossible to stay, impossible to go. Nothing possible remains. Shall we see each other in Moscow? How far outside the city are you living? Two acts written?— I don't even have two measures.

The phrase as recalled by Rachmaninoff (from Act I of *Mazeppa*) had been composed by Tchaikovsky with a slightly different harmonic treatment:

Ivanovka was good medicine for all:

July 23, 1906, Ivanovka

Dear friend Nikita Semyonovich, it's now a week that we have been living here. All here is calm and quiet. Everyone is well! I can't tell you how well I feel here. At last I am settled in the right place. All around me is familiar, congenial; and inwardly I feel a repose that I haven't had for some months. How happy I should be if I could live here longer....

To greet Rachmaninoff in Ivanovka the Kerzins sent him a volume of verses that seemed to them suitable for his use as songs—too suitable, perhaps, as his response to Mme. Kerzina would indicate: "All the words of this book demand the minor key. Would it be impossible to find a few verses slightly more major in key? Otherwise I shall sink completely into apathy."

At the end of August he again wrote Morozov:

Ivanovka, as ever, pleases me and mine, and I still feel sorry that I lost so much time in Italy. My work—not so good now. After arriving here on July 16 and idling for about a week, I tried to begin work, but invariably discovered what a deplorable condition my head was in. After dawdling in this manner for about a week, I decided to sacrifice the entire month of August to some insignificant things, working on them regardless of their merits. And that's what I did. Now I compose trifles, and already feel that my head makes some slow progress. We intend to move to Moscow around September 15th and till then I want to go on working on this sort of composition, and then later I'll tackle something else. . . . Now for more news.

I begin with a *secret*. Jürgenson wrote me, describing the deplorable circumstances of the Musical Society, and went on to say that "the concert question this season is up in the air," which he considers it his duty to warn me about! I answered that after such a statement I have the right not to feel bound by my promise, and that I withdraw my consent to conduct the concerts. Now events begin to move at breakneck speed, but don't be scared. Before sending this rejection to Jürgenson, I turned in my resignation at the two Institutes. Now I have only to refuse the Russian Symphonic concerts—and then I'll have nothing left, either for soul or for pocket, and the pocket itself is clean as a picked bone. There's only one way out of such a situation: to compose. As long as I'm not sure I can compose and work in Moscow this season, then—go abroad for the entire winter, perhaps? I've talked this over with the family. We've decided we could manage to live, for example, in Leipzig or Dresden. We can pay for this with the trifles that I'm busy with now. True, I get bored abroad; but Leipzig is a good town for music, and, secondly, living in Moscow without being sure I can work there is not so good. Therefore we have, thus far, decided to leave. . . .

The "insignificant things" written in the last weeks before leaving Ivanovka in mid-September were his fifth group of songs, Op. 26, including two of the most loved: "To the Children" and "All things pass."* The group is dedicated to Mr. and Mrs. Kerzin—possibly balm enough for their disappointment in not having him conduct their Russian concerts this season.

There was one more letter from Ivanovka to Morozov before the friends met in Moscow to say good-by for the winter:

Dear friend Nikita Semyonovich, only a few words: I received your letter yesterday and I am very grateful to you for it. It bolstered me and strengthened me. What can I do if my indecision requires my wishes to be encouraged by the people around me whom I love and trust? People like me are never able to do anything alone, and love to be pushed. So I am very grateful for your push. Now I can tell you openly that I have

* No. 3, "Let us rest," is taken from Act IV of Chekhov's *Uncle Vanya*, once mentioned to friends as a possible opera subject.

refused everything that bound me to Moscow, and that I go abroad for the whole winter. I am very glad that you approve my plan.

As usual I work a lot and as usual everything comes to me in an extremely hard way. . . .

Rachmaninoff had to move to Dresden. So long as he spent the winter in Russia he would be forced to do the one thing that hindered his composition most: work on the music of others. Nothing else was so great an obstacle, not even the hectic social life of a Moscow winter, with its inevitable turmoils and wastes. Taking his wife and daughter to Dresden was not a move away from responsibility, but a move toward work.

Chapter 8

Dresden

O NE of the first to be told of the Rachmaninoffs' new home in
Dresden was Morozov:

November 9, 1906, Dresden

Dear friend Nikita Semyonovich, today we finally moved into our
apartment. First let me tell you that this apartment or, as they call it here,
Garten-Villa, is simply charming! No apartment has ever pleased me as
this does. The house stands in the middle of a garden. There are six rooms:
three below, three above (all on the sunny side). Such an arrangement
of rooms helps me work. The bedrooms are upstairs, and downstairs are
my study and the dining room. Downstairs I am alone and can live like
a real lord. This means that the most important thing for me has been
settled splendidly. The villa rents for only 2200 marks. The other details
and adventures have been far less pleasant. . . . I like the city itself very
much, but the people are quite antipathetic and rude, with nothing but
crooks all around, or perhaps it's just my luck to bump into such people.
. . . Living here is very expensive. Don't believe them when they tell you
it's cheap to live here. I'll give you a few examples. A pound of soup meat
costs 1 mark. One pound of ham, 2 marks. A chicken or duck, 3 marks.
I tried shopping for a goose and he, the devil, cost 7 marks. Six candles,
75 pf. Bottle of milk, 22 pf., etc. Music here is expensive, too. A poor seat
in a second tier box costs 6 marks. By the way, I've heard the opera
Salome by Richard Strauss, and was completely delighted by it. Most of
all with the orchestra, of course, but there were many things in the music
itself I liked, whenever it didn't sound too discordant. Yet Strauss is a very
talented man. And his instrumentation is amazing. As I sat there in the
theater, after hearing *Salome,* I suddenly imagined, if an opera of mine
should be played here, how awkward and ashamed I should feel. A feeling
exactly as if I had appeared undressed before the audience. That Strauss
certainly knows how to dress up. . . .

Today the piano was delivered, too. Tomorrow I begin work. I have to
stop writing to you, for I am being chased from my room by workmen
who want to hang the curtains.

He had three works in mind, all to be kept secret: a symphony that would wipe away the stain of his first; a piano sonata with an unstated *Faust* program; and a doubly secret project about which he wrote to Slonov a week before settling into the Sidonienstrasse villa. The dramatic situation in the last scene of his discarded *Salammbô* was to be revived, with changed period, costumes, and author:

Dear friend Mikhail Akimovich, *not a single soul must know* what I write to you now.

Be so kind as to open Maeterlinck's *Monna Vanna* (in the translation by Mattern and Vorotnikov) at page 27 (entrance of Vanna) and try to do this scene for me down to the end of the act, six pages, without omitting anything, in verse. Rhymes not necessary. The line should not be long, and all attention should be given to making the speech flow naturally, as in prose. I wished to do this myself, but nothing came of it. If you have any free time, do this for me, quickly. I'll be very, very grateful to you. It is possible that I may accomplish something with this. If anything should be achieved, the rest will come by itself, otherwise it will stop by itself. But it's most important that you *do not speak of this to a single soul,* or this news would get around with surprising speed. Meanwhile, this is no more than a trial, so there's really nothing to talk about. Perhaps nothing will come of it. . . .

By November 21, Rachmaninoff had received the test scene from Slonov:

I am quite pleased and satisfied with your work. What will come of this I can't say definitely, but if you go on with what you've started, I beg you now to be very *swift and secretive,* for which I'll be very much obliged to you. Two conditions only!

We live here like real hermits: we see no one, we know no one, and we go nowhere. I work a great deal and feel very well. Such a life for my old age pleases me greatly, and suits me exactly now. I strive towards nothing, there's nothing more that I want, and I envy nobody. All I want is for everyone to be healthy and for my work to move ahead successfully. This latter hasn't happened yet, but who will stop me from hoping!

Morozov, who received all other confidences from Rachmaninoff, is *not* told on December 5 of the *Monna Vanna* project:

. . . you write that if you could be alone for a few days you would recover your peace of mind. . . . I am very dubious about this. I recall how once

I wanted to get away for a while from all these squabbles, to be left alone to think about my personal affairs and work; but absolutely nothing came of all this, for instead of work, I went on thinking of the same squabbles I had run from, but which remained precious and interesting to me, and the consequences of which still worry me.

. . . I continue to be satisfied with my life. I work a lot and I can boast about the *quantity of labor*. Unfortunately there is neither quantity nor quality in the work itself, but for this I always have at hand this consolation in my soul, *"Alles vergeht mit der Zeit."* I feel well and peaceful here, and only rarely, when a whole day passes without my moving a step forward, do I feel bitter and oppressed. But this is inevitable.

I shall be very glad and grateful for an idea for an orchestral Fantasy. It will not disturb me at all to have some work at hand for the future. And if you should come upon a good text for a cantata, don't forget to note it for me.

In Russia Rachmaninoff's cantata, *Spring*, had just brought him, for the second time, a Glinka award. In Moscow, too, the Kerzins had programed his Op. 26 in one of their Russian Concerts, and Rachmaninoff wrote to Mme. Kerzina to ask Sobinov to sing four of the songs:

. . . none of these is especially ingratiating, yet I earnestly ask him not to refuse to sing them. Particularly the song, "The night is mournful" [No. 12], in which it is not he who must sing, but the piano. In spite of this I beg him sincerely not to refuse to sing it. . . . Now for the accompanist; I must say that in these songs his part is more difficult than that of the singers. Who will it be? Personally I should be very glad if you would ask Goldenweiser to do this, for when he came here to see me, he offered to accompany these songs. I was very much pleased by his offer. . . .

All as usual with me. I work the whole day. Natasha is bored the whole day, and Irina behaves like a bandit the whole day, singing songs. All her songs are wild, desperate, piercing—just as if she were performing in Strauss's *Salome*.

In asking Morozov's help with the knotty sonata (nearly transformed into a symphony at this time), Rachmaninoff tells him no more about the sonata than is absolutely necessary.

December 10, 1906, Dresden

Dear friend Nikita Semyonovich, please solve this problem for me, or help me solve it myself. It's this: Imagine Theme I, which I call the principal one. Then Theme II, not long, which returns to the principal one, in its original tonality, but stated in a more compressed way. This theme is concluded in the same chief tonality again. Theme III, developed in detail, is something integral and complete, beginning and ending in the same tonality. After this comes a sort of *elaboration* or *development of the principal theme,* and this leads again to the principal theme. It's begun as a recapitulation. Again Theme I, then Theme II (of course in another tonality than at first) and a return again to the principal tonality and the principal theme. Now for my question. What must I do next? What sort of form is this that I'm writing? Is there such a form? Must I really, after all I've said, go into a Coda? This doesn't seem to satisfy me. Must there be some further 3rd Theme? Of course this is one of those accursed Rondo forms, and I don't know a single one of them. Be kind and write me an answer at once to this question. And I beg you to show me *all five* of the accursed Rondo forms in Beethoven's piano sonatas. I'll buy them here and collate them. Do that quickly, for this troubles me and impedes me.

Morozov must have been fully aware of Rachmaninoff's good reasons for his caution. He sent a full lesson on the rondo form, and Rachmaninoff was grateful without relaxing his secrecy:

. . . I received both your letters, and I doubly thank you. Your second letter, on the Rondo forms, I shall save and treasure. It can be useful to me in the future, when I again run into something incomprehensible; and I'll treasure this letter as a souvenir of my *first* lesson in form, that I was taught only in my old age. With the help of the Beethoven sonatas it clarified a question that hampered me.

As before I continue to work a lot, and thus far have lost only a week. Two days of this week were taken up with sick Irina, who is now, thank God, well. One day was spent in Leipzig, where I went to a dress rehearsal at the Gewandhaus.

Incidentally, I am not in raptures. In Leipzig I like Klinger's sculpture of Beethoven more than the Nikisch performance of Max Reger's bad serenade and Carreño's playing of a bad piano concerto by somebody named Dowell,* but the most annoying thing was the audience that applauded everything frantically. It was all this together, probably, that made me ill, sneezing and coughing for three days without pause. These were the empty days. Now about a program for the orchestral fantasy.

* Edward MacDowell's second piano concerto was played on this occasion, conducted by Arthur Nikisch, with Teresa Carreño as soloist.

No, not "In the Wild North," nor "Pine and Palm" [a Heine subject], nor North and South. I like this, but not very much.

When Slonov, eager to know the chances of his work as librettist being used, asked a direct question about *Monna Vanna,* Rachmaninoff gave him a full answer on January 4, 1907:

Now, Mikhail Akimovich, you ask me whether I shall compose *M.V.* Though I understand quite well that if anyone is to know about this first, it will be you, of course—yet I beg you to let me answer this question later and, as before, don't speak of this to anyone, just as I have spoken to no one else about it. You see, I am in general very distrustful of myself while composing, and particularly in selecting a subject. Only while I see my-self making great progress do I become almost convinced of the final result, and only then do I definitely and almost imperceptibly acknowl-edge my aim. And sometimes both subject and music bore me to the limit, and I cast everything to the Devil. Therefore do hold off asking me about this. I myself will write you first—but only when it seems possible. Mean-while I beg you to work into the *second* half of this second act, while sending me before and *speedily* the changes requested in the *first* act.

To Morozov Rachmaninoff sent a fuller report on his work, yet with no word to him of *Monna Vanna* or the sonata:

February 11, 1907, Dresden

Dear friend Nikita Semyonovich, I've long intended to write you, but various matters, mostly proofreading, have overwhelmed me. For the last 12 days I've been checking the vocal parts of my operas. This had to be done anyhow, but I had to get it done in this brief time for the sake of Siloti, who is performing them in concert form (2 scenes).* Before this I had to correct the trio [Op. 9, revised] and the songs [of Op. 26]. I should also tell you that my eyes are quite ruined ("In his old age the monkey's eyes grew weak" [from a Krylov fable]). In doing any strenuous

---

* The first St. Petersburg performance of two scenes from Rachmaninoff's short operas, *The Miserly Knight* and *Francesca da Rimini,* was given under Siloti's direction at the Hall of Nobility on February 3, 1907; the soloists were Chaliapin and Ivanova, and the composer considered it "a fiasco." At the end of the month he wrote Morozov, "As yet I've had no private news from the performers, which makes me suspect even a more total failure. Someone from the audience wrote me." Chaliapin's first performance of the Baron had been at Rimsky-Korsakov's house, along with a historic reading of the one finished act of Musorgsky's *Marriage.*

writing or reading the eyes go misty and the head aches badly. I don't recall if I wrote you that I already wear glasses on a doctor's advice. I've seen him three times and shall go again. I begin to fall to pieces. This aches and that aches. Most of the time I sleep badly, too. Because of this proofreading, for two weeks I haven't attended to my own work at all. Perhaps this is just as well, for two weeks ago I fell into a certain frame of mind—something that often happens to me while working; a mood of anguish, apathy, and disgust at what I've been doing in my work, and this means disgust at everything else, as well. Tomorrow I get back to work, but so far I do not relish this thought. I'll see what happens.

Recently heard from Slonov that he read in some paper that I had finished a symphony. As you also may have heard something about this, I want to say a few words on the subject. A month ago, or more, I really did finish a symphony, but to this must be added the phrase "in draft." I have not announced it to "the world," because I want first to complete its final writing.

While I was planning to put in it "clean" form, it became terribly boring and repulsive to me. So I threw it aside and took up something else. Thus "the world" would not have known, yet, about my work—if it hadn't been for Siloti, who came here and pulled out of me everything I have and everything that I am going to have. I told him that "I will have" a Symphony. That's how I've already received an invitation to conduct it next season!—and news of the Symphony has flown everywhere. I can tell you privately that I am displeased with it, but that it really "will be," though not before autumn, as I shall not begin its orchestration until summer. . . .

Now for our domestic affairs. We've decided, if Russia is to be calm, to spend the entire summer in Ivanovka. Even the date of our departure is set. Natasha leaves here on May 10 (new style) for Moscow, and I for Paris, presumably, where I give one concert that I don't look forward to. On this—later. This will hold me there for about ten days, and then I also go to Moscow and Ivanovka. This year our summer will not be so calm as usual. Natasha's confinement is expected in June. . . . I am very glad to have another child, but only if this accursed process goes off well and speedily. . . .

Lately I was in Leipzig (for the second time). In the morning I attended the Nikisch conductors' class at the Conservatory. It was very boring, but the lesson interested me very much. Watched three pupil conductors. Poor Nikisch! In my opinion all three deserve to be sent to Stolypin's gallows for their criminal thoughts about conducting.

In the afternoon I went to Breitkopf's printing plant and saw the whole process of music printing from beginning to end. Spent two hours there. Very interesting. But the climax of all was the Gewandhaus concert in the evening. Nikisch was in extraordinary form. The program consisted of two symphonies without a soloist. The First of Brahms, the Sixth of Tchaikovsky. In the full sense of the word it was a work of *genius*. One can't go beyond this. The audience gave him a wild ovation. They say such a reception hasn't been heard for years. By the way, when Nikisch first came out, only *one* person applauded, and that was I.

More news to Morozov on April 13:

My only consolation is that when I don't write you because of work, you don't get angry with me. During the last couple of weeks my working time has been cut down. First, because for two weeks I've gone daily to an eye doctor. By the way, I changed doctors because the first one completely ruined my eyes. I like this second one, and he has already helped me in this short time. He ordered the glasses off altogether and started massage treatment instead. Secondly, I am not allowed to work or read or write by artificial light. This is a great loss. Thirdly, I am forced to play the piano [in preparation for the Paris concert], not for an hour as before, but for two hours. As you can see, these make for great losses of time. In this way, for example, today I worked only from 9 A.M. to 12:30. Then lunch, and now I write you instead of working. I have one free hour and then an hour's walk. Then 2 hours' practice, and then I retire with the chickens. Thus I have only about 4 hours a day for composition. Too little! Now for compositions. I've worked here for five months and five days. In this time I've done a lot but, unfortunately, I finished nothing— nothing is in final shape. This is very disturbing, and in the month left me before going to Paris, I want to bring everything into as much order as possible. I have three works started. The third, on which I'm working now, I want to finish trimming completely—that is, *a large portion* of it— in a few days. So far, enough! I'll take up the second work [the sonata] after this, and I wish to complete trimming it *all* in two weeks. Then there's the Symphony to be trimmed, which I've written to you about, that only its *draft* is complete. Of course I'd like to put this in order, too, so that only the orchestration would remain to be done. But this won't work out! Not enough time, and besides, to tell you the truth, I'm tired. As for the quality of all these things, I must say that the worst of all is the Symphony. When I get it written and then correct my *first* Symphony, I give my solemn word—no more symphonies. Curse them! I don't know how to write them, but mainly, I don't want to. My second work is slightly better than the Symphony, but still is dubious in quality. I am fully satisfied only with my third work [*Monna Vanna*]. This is my whole consolation. Otherwise I'd be completely crushed. But this one is farthest away from completion. Therefore, what I am to do with it is still a remote question. There's a hazy report for you!

I've recently heard many interesting works here. I'll list them: 4 oratorios. Beethoven's *Missa Solemnis.* Händel's *Samson.* Bach's *Hohe Messe* in B minor, and *St. Paul* by Mendelssohn. Then I've seen *Tristan* and *Meistersinger.* The best of these was Beethoven's *Mass.* Performed excellently. I was quite enthralled—it was so good that nothing more can be said. *Meistersinger* is given here wonderfully. Unfortunately they seldom perform it, for some reason, otherwise I should go again without fail. Then—Händel's *Samson.* If you have it, look at the 4th number (aria for tenor) and then at the finale of No. 7, Largo *"Nur Trauer-töne sing ich nun."* Both one and the other are works of "genius." To tell the truth: they write well nowadays, but they wrote even better in the past. I also saw an operetta, [Lehar's] *Die lustige Witwe.* Though written now, it too is a work of genius. I laughed like a fool. Absolutely wonderful. That's all I've seen—and in this order. Such is my spiritual food! . . .

I'll write you again if I have time to finish my second work. Now all my thoughts are on Paris, and they are most unpleasant. I can't tell you how I hate to go there. But I must go, if only for the sake of money—for our resources are coming to an end.

Monna Vanna, the only work that "fully satisfied" the composer, was never finished.

The Paris invitation was not a merely musical affair. The *Saison Russe* there was essential to Franco-Russian relations, as well as to the ambitions of its organizer, Sergei Diaghilev. For this first of his huge show windows of Russian art abroad, Diaghilev had assembled the greatest representatives of Russian music—a galaxy studded with such stars as Rimsky-Korsakov (under protest), Rachmaninoff, Glazunov, Scriabin, and Chaliapin. This high-powered display was not a soothing prospect for Rachmaninoff, no matter how well it paid. Before leaving for Paris early in May he wrote once more to Morozov:

. . . I work all day long and burn with fire. . . . I am terribly behind in my work. As you were displeased with my last vague account, I want to correct this now, for I now have put many things in order. My next to last work is an opera. I've finished, that is, composed one act.* (Some changes still necessary.) When I finished it, it unfortunately began to seem less satisfactory to me. *This work is a secret.* Now I'm completing a piano sonata. Yesterday I finished writing the second movement. Only the last movement is left to do, but I don't know if I can finish it before going to Paris. Probably not. This work is *not* a secret. . . . Two days ago I played the sonata for Riesemann, and he *doesn't* seem to like it. Generally I've begun to notice that no matter what I write lately—nobody likes it. And I myself often wonder; maybe it *is* all nonsense. The sonata is certainly wild and interminable. I think it takes about 45 minutes. I was lured into this length by its guiding idea. This is—three contrasting types from a literary work [*Faust*]. Of course no program will be indicated, though I begin to think that the sonata would be clearer if the program were revealed. Nobody will ever play this composition, it's too difficult and long and possibly—and this is the most important—too dubious musically. At one time I wanted to make a symphony of this sonata, but this seemed impossible because of the purely pianistic style in which it is written. I hope you'll now be satisfied with my lack of vagueness. I miss you a great deal and want to see you soon. I'll telegraph from Warsaw when I know the day of my arrival.

When Diaghilev had insisted that Rimsky-Korsakov conduct his music at Paris, the old composer replied, "If we must go, we must, as the parrot said when the cat pulled him out of his cage!" and the habitually shy Rachmaninoff seems to have been no happier with his Paris duty. His concert was made up of the cantata *Spring,* with Chaliapin as soloist, and the Second Concerto, which he played with Chevillard conducting. When Rimsky-Korsakov came backstage afterwards, he had a comment on *Spring* that its composer had to agree with: "The music is good, but what a pity that there's no Spring in the orchestra!" The presence of the old master in Paris was a source of the greatest pleasure to Rachmaninoff. Later he told his friends the Swans:

. . . the three of us were once sitting at the Café de la Paix: Scriabin, Rimsky, and I. Rimsky, speaking into his beard, explained to us the whole of the *Coq d'Or!* As he expounded this fairy tale, he saw some-

---

* The manuscript of *Monna Vanna's* Act I (100 pages) is dated "Dresden, 15 April 1907."

thing very profound in it. At that time he had finished the first act. He said: "I will now tackle the third act." "Why the third," we wondered, "not the second?" "No, I will write the third before the second." What untold riches there are in the *Coq d'Or!* The beginning alone—how novel. And then the chromaticism. This is where the source of all the wretched modernism lies hidden. But with Rimsky it is in the hands of a genius. I don't know what impression this conversation made on Scriabin, but I was deeply stirred.

Scriabin made, however, an impression on Rimsky-Korsakov when he listened in Paris, along with Rachmaninoff, Glazunov, Blumenfeld, and Hofmann, to Scriabin playing his *Poem of Ecstasy*. Rimsky-Korsakov remarked, only half jokingly: "Isn't he losing his mind, perhaps?"

Rachmaninoff, the moment his Paris task was completed at the end of May, hurried back to Russia to join his family. Stopping in Moscow on the way to the Ivanovka estate, he tried out one of the Dresden works on his most trusted friends. Catoire, Conus, Medtner, and Igumnov were invited to Wilshaw's apartment to hear Rachmaninoff play his piano sonata in D minor, less than a month old. The impression made on Igumnov was such that, as he says, "I was afterwards impelled to write to its author, asking whether it was being printed and how soon one could expect it to be available. In reply I received my first letter [dated June 15, 1907] from Sergei Vasilyevich, from Ivanovka":

My esteemed Konstantin Nikolayevich,

I received your letter of June 8 last evening, and I hasten to reply. My new piano sonata is not yet printed, nor can I tell you definitely when it will be. The fact is that I want to make some changes in it and, mainly, to shorten it—it's unbearably long. I've already tried this, but nothing came of it. I now wish to put this off for a while, and I've therefore begun another work. As soon as this has taken shape, even in draft, I'll get to the sonata again. So it will be *approximately* by August 1 that I'll send the sonata to the printer, which means that proof won't be ready before September 1. This will probably be too late for you. In any case I should be the first to regret it if you aren't able to play it this season.

Morozov asked for news on all pending matters—*Monna Vanna,* the symphony, and the "future son." Rachmaninoff answered him on June 16:

I'll begin by saying that my Natasha, thank God, is well and from day to day awaits my future son. . . . when it's all over—we'll be glad. Only recently I've begun to work. I was resting, or—actually—loafing for three whole weeks. I've done only five days' work, so when you suppose that I've finished the second act, you are very much mistaken.

Incidentally, about that act. Slonov has just sent it to me, and I was horrified at its dimensions. About a thousand lines. (The entire *Miserly Knight*, by comparison, had about 450.) I am now mainly occupied in cutting down the text. So far it seems very difficult to bring order to it. It's a pity, but, with few exceptions, very little can be discarded. That's why I am very late. And I still have before me the many entr'actes to be done. I am not yet "in the mood," but may soon be. . . .

I returned in time to catch the lilacs blooming. (Remember the driveway at Ivanovka?) Now the roses are blooming. Aunt Varvara has planted roses all along the drive by the lilacs. You can imagine how beautiful it is. There's such an abundance of them this year.

When the son came, on June 21, he turned out to be a daughter.

[June 24, 1907]

The little girl has behaved rather decently for the first three days of her life. She sleeps far more than Irina did at the beginning, and cries less—but when she does cry, she does so in a voice of thunder. In general my daughters have powerful voices. Natasha now feels perfectly well. We're naming the little girl Tatiana.

A month later (July 27) he brought Slonov up to date: *Monna Vanna* was about to be shelved.

It was wrong of me not to answer you as soon as I received the 2nd act. To begin with, just after my arrival here, and the libretto from you not having been received, my enforced idleness saddened me; but with each passing day I was drawn more into this kind of life, and several weeks later, after the rest period should have ended, and the libretto had arrived, I had recognized the beauty of "doing nothing." Not only did I not work, but I didn't care to write to anyone.

What shoved me out of my rut was the birth of my second daughter. Then I began to think about working. I thought about it for almost ten days, after which I began, finally, to work. . . . Now, regretfully, I cannot work on the opera, for I must devote myself to the orchestration of the symphony, with which, of course, I'll be late. There you have my entire "Odyssey."

Excuse me for not writing sooner, and don't be cross with me. I like the libretto, but it must be shortened—it's already too long. Now it won't be before autumn in Dresden that I can attend to it. . . .

Apologies also to Morozov, on August 2:

I hope you'll forgive me—and I know that to win your forgiveness all I have to do is work. And I am working, and that is the only reason I haven't answered your first letter. I received your second letter last evening, and this shamed me so that this morning I set myself to letter writing. However, I can't write much. I was heartily glad to learn that the Sonata pleased you, though inwardly I think that you were more pleased than it deserves. Keep the sonata—I don't need it now. When I get to Moscow (in the middle of September), I'll take it from you. For two weeks now I have been busy with the orchestration of the Symphony. The work proceeds very laboriously and sluggishly. It's slow not only because of the instrumentation, which ordinarily comes to me with difficulty, but also because I left it in draft, and some movements are yet to be worked out. It's a shame to realize that in these two weeks I have done only the introduction and the first theme with development; that is, 25 pages. If I don't speed up (which I hope I can), the Symphony won't be completed in less than six months. I work a lot. Everything at home is all right. Tania is six weeks old today.

The Second Symphony was completed, but *Monna Vanna* never was, though Rachmaninoff always remained interested in his first act.* During the following year, 1908, he considered resuming work on the opera and requested Stanislavsky to ask Maeterlinck to grant him the operatic rights to *Monna Vanna,* for Russia and Germany. Maeterlinck's contracts precluded this, and thus the matter of Rachmaninoff's last opera ended. But this first act, along with sketches for the second act, Rachmaninoff kept near him to the end of his life. Though this was his last operatic effort, he often spoke of other subjects for operas. He particularly wanted one set in his beloved land-

---

* Years after putting *Monna Vanna* aside, Rachmaninoff gave an enthusiastic reading of this act for his friend, Alexander Goedicke.

scape of a Russian country estate, and spoke of Turgenev's *Spring Floods, The Lull,* and *A Song of Triumphant Love* as possible libretti. Even Chekhov's *Uncle Vanya* was seriously considered—a plan that can be dated by the song based on a passage from Act IV of that play, in Op. 26 (No. 3 is dated August 14, 1906). Other operatic projects mentioned in the press, without confirmation by the composer, were *The Minstrel,* with a scenario by Chaliapin based on a poem by Maikov, and a one-act opera, also suggested by Chaliapin, *The Mysterious Island.*

Chapter 9

Europe

BEFORE leaving Rùssia again this fall, Rachmaninoff sent a manuscript copy of his piano sonata to Igumnov,

asking me, after becoming acquainted with it, to send him in Dresden my opinion of it, particularly as to its suitability to the piano. This request was flattering, but in some degree it did leave me at a loss. Under the direct impression of its music I didn't feel I could be objective enough to give a detailed analysis, and therefore I called on Leonid Nikolayev to examine the sonata with me; with his co-operation a series of comments was composed, accompanying my reply. . . . For a long while I had no word from Rachmaninoff, and I began to be afraid that the comments had been somewhat tactless.

But Igumnov need not have worried. Rachmaninoff was busy with concerts in Europe and with relatives in Dresden. From Warsaw he sent a post card to Morozov, on November 20, 1907:

Arrived yesterday. Tonight, after the concert, I leave for home. I'm still tired after yesterday, and of course I scarcely slept last night, just as in your Russia. The conductor accompanies me so-so, or rather, badly. The orchestra is not bad, and the auditorium is very good. I ran into Buyukli here. You remember him. He's creating a furor here. He plays here tomorrow, and my friend Zatayevich grieves that Buyukli will attract a full house, and that my concert (announced, for some reason, on the street pillars as "extraordinary") cannot. To tell the truth, I don't care, so long as I get my money and leave here pretty soon, for it's boring here. I work a lot in Dresden, and now the work moves a little faster. As always, I am very pleased with life there.

His New Year's Eve message to Morozov, from Dresden, showed good spirits:

For four days now I've done nothing. Uncle, Aunt Varvara, Volodya, and Grauermann are visiting us. They leave the day after tomorrow, and happy as I am to have them here, I'll be glad to get back to work if the

Symphony is to be finished in time. I was stopped in about the middle of the 4th movement. I have 12 more days to complete the rewriting. This is the absolute limit, and time is short. It was written in approximately these periods: 1st movement—three months; 2nd movement—3½ weeks; 3rd movement—2 weeks; Finale—about 4 weeks. This means 2 months for the last three movements and three months for the first. I should add, too, that the first movement was written in Russia. Now I have to play some more—soon I play in Berlin. And at the end of our January I go to Warsaw, Petersburg, and Moscow, where I'll arrive on your January 29.

The Berlin concert, on January 23, 1908, was Koussevitzky's debut as conductor; it was an all-Russian program, and Rachmaninoff played his Second Concerto. In St. Petersburg Rachmaninoff conducted one of the Siloti concerts on January 26 (old style), with Siloti playing the Grieg Concerto. For Rachmaninoff this concert's greatest importance was that it included the first performance of his new symphony—his Second. His Moscow duties began on February 2, when he conducted the Second Symphony with the Philharmonic Society at the Nobility Hall and played the Second Concerto (with Brandukov conducting). Yuli Engel wrote:

After a year-and-a-half stay abroad Rachmaninoff again appears before the Moscow public as composer, conductor, and pianist. . . And Rachmaninoff is worth an entire concert devoted to his works. Despite his thirty-four years he is one of the most significant figures in the contemporary music world, a worthy successor to Tchaikovsky, if not in the dimensions of his talent (of which it is too early to speak), then certainly in its concentration, sincerity, and subjective delicacy. Successor, and not imitator, for he has already his own individuality.

This was confirmed most impressively by the new E minor Symphony by Rachmaninoff. . . . After listening with unflagging attention to its four movements, one notes with surprise that the hands of the watch have moved sixty-five minutes forward. This may be slightly overlong for the general audience, but how fresh, how beautiful it is!

On the way back to Dresden Rachmaninoff performed his Suite (with Mikhailovsky) in Warsaw and conducted his Second Symphony. Back in Dresden, he wrote to Morozov on April 12:

. . . only today I finally got around to answering your letter of March 8. You ask, what have I done during this time? However sad to confess, it must be said that I have done nothing, or nearly nothing. Soon it will be two months since I left Moscow—and this is how this time was spent: 2 weeks ill with influenza, a week in Warsaw, a week taken by the young Satins visiting us in Dresden. The Symphony has taken about ten days, with a thousand silly corrections. The Sonata has taken about eight days. That's about all. Only last night did I finish correcting the Sonata, and tomorrow I send it to the printer. Today, according to schedule, I must write 11 letters—no more, no fewer. Already wrote six. Now I plan to take my 1st concerto in hand tomorrow, look it over, and then decide how much time and work will be required for its new version, and whether it's worth doing anyway. There are so many requests for this concerto, and it's so terrible in its present form, that I should like to work at it and, if possible, get it into decent shape. Of course, it will have to be written all over again, for its orchestration is worse than its music. So tomorrow I decide this question, and I should like to decide it in the affirmative.

I have three pieces that frighten me: the first concerto, the Capriccio, and the first Symphony. How I should like to see all of these in a corrected, decent form!

You ask me what my attitude is towards my 2nd symphony. Coming from you this is a quite natural question, and not at all "impudent," but I want to put off answering it until we meet. I've not yet given the symphony to the printer, for I've been waiting for the bowing marks from Conus, which I've not yet received. That's all in regard to my music.

At first we intended to come to Moscow for Easter. Now plans have been slightly changed. Natasha and the children will probably arrive in Russia about May 12–13 (new style). And I'll stay here alone (poor me) till the 22d, when I go to London, where I must play my concerto on May 26 (again with Koussevitzky). . . .

P.S. Last night I heard a beautiful performance of Beethoven's Ninth Symphony. Nobody will ever write anything better than this Symphony.

Another of the eleven letters was a long-delayed reply to Igumnov:

My greatly esteemed Konstantin Nikolayevich,

Yesterday I finished correcting my piano sonata and tomorrow I send it to the printer. Only now can I answer your letter of November 12, 1907.

When you see the music you will, of course, notice all in which I agreed with you and all in which I didn't. The only thing left for me is to thank you heartily for your comments.

I'll order the first proof sent to you at once.

In reviewing Koussevitzky's all-Russian concert at Queen's Hall, London, the *Times* wrote of Rachmaninoff's Second Concerto:

The direct expression of the work, the extraordinary precision and exactitude of his playing, and even the strict economy of movement of arms and hands which M. Rachmaninov exercises, all contributed to the impression of completeness of performance. The slow movement was played by soloist and orchestra with deep feeling, and the brilliant effect of the finale could scarcely have been surpassed, and yet the freedom from extravagance of any kind was the most remarkable feature.

By the end of May the Rachmaninoffs' Russian summer was under way at Ivanovka, but Rachmaninoff himself was not encouraged by the work in hand, as he wrote to Morozov on June 21:

In this whole month I have worked only one week *for myself*. The other three were spent on proofs of the Symphony. This goes very slowly, even though I do it diligently—so far I have examined the full score and the string parts. This amounts to about 400 pages. I'm still behind with all the wind instrument parts, which haven't yet arrived, but will—perhaps today.

[June 29, 1908]

. . . yesterday, after a whole week's penal servitude, I completed proof-reading the Symphony. Tomorrow I send everything to Moscow. I want to talk with you about the four-hand piano transcription. You write that you could do it yourself. I am perfectly aware, of course, that you could do a splendid transcription, and my only objection to your doing it is based on the same arguments you yourself advanced—chiefly, that you would have to tear yourself away from your own work. Incidentally, it seems to me that this Symphony will require more than two months. When I transcribed Glazunov's 6th Symph., I sat at it for 2 months, and my Symphony is longer. . . . Terms—200 rubles. That's the fee I received for the Glazunov symphony. . . .

Now I too can get back to my work. As usual with my head, I cannot yet find anything in it fit for composition. Therefore I again face a difficult period, getting back onto the composer's tracks. Again the tortures begin! . . .

For five days we've had no rain. . . . Now the barometer—and the heavens—are falling! My children are well. On June 21 Tania was a year old. As before, she doesn't walk, she doesn't crawl, she doesn't talk. Only "boo" in all keys.

This was too arduous a summer for new work. Before returning to Dresden he started his friend Wilshaw to work on the four-hand piano reduction of the symphony.

Except for one important composition Dresden this winter was little more than a base for Rachmaninoff's European appearances as pianist and conductor. But before this hectic schedule began he wrote one of his most playful compositions: a musical letter to Stanislavsky on the occasion of the Moscow Art Theater's tenth birthday. This theater was acknowledged as a permanent fixture in Russian life, and some of the productions of its first ten years, such as the Chekhov plays and Maeterlinck's *Blue Bird,* were to remain in the repertory for more than five decades. At the birthday celebration on October 14, in the midst of deputations and tributes, Chaliapin asked permission to sing a message to Stanislavsky from Dresden:

Very dear Konstantin Sergeyevich, I congratulate you sincerely, with all my heart! For these ten years you have moved forward, forward, and forward, and somewhere on this road you have found the *Blue Bird!* It is your greatest victory!

I must tell you how sorry I am that I'm not in Moscow; that I'm not able, with all the others, to honor you, to applaud, to call out in all the keys, Bravo, bravo, bravo—and to wish you very many years, very many years, very, very many years.

I beg you to give the whole fine company my greetings, my warm and hearty greetings.

Yours,
Sergei Rachmaninoff.

Dresden, on the fourteenth of this October, year nineteen hundred and eight *anno domini.*
Postscriptum. My wife seconds me in this.

The deputations halted and forced Chaliapin to repeat the whole half sung, half spoken message. And four hours later, at the close of the celebration, Stanislavsky thus expressed his gratitude to everyone present: "One would have to be, at the very least, Rachmaninoff and Chaliapin fused together to give appropriate thanks to all of you assembled here."

LETTER TO KONSTANTIN STANISLAVSKY FROM SERGEI RACHMANINOFF,
IN DRESDEN, OCTOBER 14, 1908

рёд, впе-рёд и впе-рёд, и на э-том пу-ти Вы на-шли „Си-ню-ю пти-цу!" О-на Ва-ша луч-ша-я по-бе-да!

Те-перь я о-чень со-жа-ле-ю, что я не в Мо-скве; что я не мо-гу, вме-сте со все-ми, Вас чест-во-вать, Вам хло-пать, кри-

*) Полька и „Синей птице," музыка И. Саца.

_чать Вам на все ла_ды бра_во, бра_во, бра_во... И же_

замедляя   **Оживленно. Бодро** (♩.=♩)
В темпе

_лать Вам мно_га_я ле_та, мно_га_я ле_та,

Пер_

мно_га_я, мно_га_я ле_та.   Про_

воначальное движение

_шу Вас пе_редать всей труп_пе мой при_вет, мой душевный при_вет.

Ваш Сер_гей Рах_ма_ни_нов.   Дрез_ден. Че_тырнадцато_

_е Октяб_ря ты_ся_ча де_вять_сот восьма_го го_да.

Post scriptum.   Же_на мо_я мне вторит.

Довольно скоро

Величественно

When Igumnov compared the proof of the sonata with the manuscript copy of the first version "it was apparent that the most essential
part of my comments had been taken into consideration by the
author. A considerable part of the recapitulation in the first movement had been recomposed, shortening it by more than 50 bars; some
cuts had been made in the finale, mostly in the recapitulation, about
60 bars. Changes of treatment were made only in the finale. The
second movement was unchanged. The sonata was played publicly
for the first time in my concert of Rachmaninoff works, in Moscow
on October 17, 1908." This concert naturally occasioned critical sum-
maries of Rachmaninoff as composer more than of Igumnov as
pianist. To Engel in the powerful *Russkiye Vedomosti,* the new work
was *not* a peak in Rachmaninoff's career:

Rimsky-Korsakov is dead, and Russian music has been orphaned. In
the realm of opera a great void has been left by the death of *The Snow-
Maiden's* composer. . . . The symphonic and chamber music of Russia is
more fortunate. Its future is in strong, trustworthy hands. Here Rachmaninoff is in the front rank. It is sufficient to recall his last three important works to convince oneself of this—the second symphony, the
second piano concerto, and the cello sonata. Each was an event in its
field, each evidenced the growth of Rachmaninoff's talent, and each
broadened the circle of this talent's admirers.

So it was not astonishing that the pianist Igumnov should devote an
entire program to Rachmaninoff's works. The Small Hall of Nobility was
filled to overflowing. The "peak" of the concert was a new piano composition of Rachmaninoff, performed for the first time on this occasion.
This new sonata is musically complex and quite intricate in its pianism.
Merely to read it for oneself at the piano, unraveling this tangle of
passages, rhythms, harmonies, polyphonic twistings, is no easy matter,
even for an accomplished pianist. The more credit to Mr. Igumnov for his
energetic, thoughtful performance, in which he presented the sonata to
the audience in clean lines and as a well-rounded, vital unit. But even
with this performance it was difficult for the listener to free himself from
an impression of dryness, generated by a first encounter with the sonata.
The new sonata appeals with its mastery of form, its abundance of
interesting details, just as, for example, do the piano concerto and the
cello sonata, but it does not have their freshness of fantasy, nor comparable thematic inspiration. Besides, in it Rachmaninoff can occasion-

ally be heard repeating himself—which would be no calamity if these repetitions were "in a finer edition," but this one cannot say. The variations played by Mr. Igumnov on the theme of Chopin's well-known C minor prélude also do not belong to Rachmaninoff's best compositions. Some variations are excellent, but on the whole the piece in no way rises to the heights of the prélude that inspired it.

At the beginning of November, Igumnov played the sonata on two other occasions, in his concerts at Berlin and Leipzig.

I had hoped that Rachmaninoff would be able to hear the Leipzig concert, but he wrote me on November 5 that he was obliged to leave that day for Antwerp, instead. His letter had this characteristic postscript: "I have read in the *Russkiye Vedomosti* about your successes in Moscow, spoiled somewhat by my intrusion. I fear that in Leipzig I'll again be a hindrance to you." When, after the Leipzig concert, I stopped in Dresden to see the Rachmaninoffs, I learned from him that when he composed this Sonata he had had Goethe's *Faust* in mind, and that the first movement corresponds to Faust, the second to Gretchen, and the third, to the flight to Brocken, and Mephistopheles [in the exact order of Liszt's "Faust" Symphony].

In respect to the programs of his compositions, Rachmaninoff often seems as dependent on extramusical sources and as unwilling to reveal them as Weber was.

From Antwerp, where he was to conduct and play in a Russian program, Rachmaninoff sent Morozov his reaction to Engel's review:

The rehearsal has just ended and I have come back to my room in great anguish. The orchestra is large, the attitude of the players is fine, but—the orchestra is bad. Something like the one in Warsaw, only in worse tune. The program is big, there are three rehearsals, but only *two hours* for each. Today, for example, I didn't even have time to finish my symphony. Besides the symphony, there is Musorgsky's *Night* [*on Bald Mountain*] and 2 concertos: mine and the violin concerto of Glazunov—Mischa Elman is to play this, with my accompaniment. A real calamity! . . . Day before yesterday in Dresden I read in the *Russkiye Vedomosti* that they again abused me for the Igumnov concert. What a run of luck. I'll stay here three more days before leaving. Can hardly wait to get home.

December 2, 1908, Berlin

Dear friend Nikita Semyonovich, I'm sitting in Berlin, where in two hours I play my trio with members of the Czech quartet. Tonight after the concert I leave for home. . . .

Yesterday I heard the Philharmonic concert, at which Nikisch conducted the Brahms Second Symphony wonderfully. And what a beautiful Symphony! At the same concert Casals and his wife played (they'll be playing soon in Moscow, too). They both play really marvelously, and they are very well worth hearing. Also here, tomorrow (just received an invitation and a program) Lamond plays my cello Sonata. That's how important we are! For two whole days we occupy "all Berlin."

Now for you. I did not like your last letter at all, dear friend, and I get the impression from it that you do not attend too *many* concerts, but too few! I have a feeling that you are giving too many lessons this year, that they tire you too much, and that you feel unwell. So you really should come to Dresden for, say, at least two weeks; to stroll about, *to go to concerts,* and to think of nothing. Or go visit your people in the South—to change your environment, and to forget for a while that there is a Conservatory there, lessons, teachers—forget that you are employed at that Conservatory, etc., etc. Or, stay in Moscow, but to go to *more* concerts and theaters. Or are you and I really growing so old that we don't need this?! and aren't interested any longer?! Then things will surely get boring. Now, have you seen *The Blue Bird?* Did you go to *Stockmann* [Ibsen's *Enemy of the People*]? No. Why not? Be sure to go!

Be well, and don't feel blue!

[December 11, 1908, Amsterdam]

. . . I've been here in Holland since the 7th. So far am playing three concerts; yesterday here, in Amsterdam. Tomorrow in The Hague, and the following day I repeat my concert in Amsterdam in the afternoon, and in the evening—home. Everywhere here I play my second concerto. It's always the same orchestra, on tour—and a splendid orchestra, too. Mengelberg conducts it everywhere (it is he who conducts at Frankfurt am/M. and with whom I am to play my concerto next week in Frankfurt). He accompanies perfectly! It's such a pleasure to play! In spite of this "such a pleasure," I am terribly tired. Today, finally, I sit alone in my room. It's now 7:30 in the evening. I'll write letters, have tea, and go to bed. After all I don't fit into these "tours" and I begin to wonder whether I shouldn't refuse altogether the American trip, which I probably shouldn't be able to endure? And only 10 days ago I again sent America my new terms, in which I agree to come for 25 concerts, but *"mit Privilegium auf mehr,"* that is, 1000 rubles a concert. So now I'm afraid that they might agree! Though the earnings could be big, which would "console" me to a certain extent, it will be very hard to endure this penal servitude, if even these tiny European tours torture me. So now I hope to be home on Monday the 14th. . . . Well, and how is it with you? Did you go to hear *Carmen* with Nikisch? Most likely, you didn't! That's not good. And do you know that Nikisch took my Symphony off his two programs (Berlin and Leipzig), though it had been announced there? Explanation: probably because he saw on the Symphony my dedication to Taneyev, and not to himself. He had asked me in May, in London, *"Was macht meine Symphonie?"* I answered that "it was being printed." He buys it and sees that it says, "To Taneyev." That's probably the reason, for now in Berlin he didn't even care to see me.

In answer to a letter from Alexander Goedicke, telling of the first performance of Goedicke's Second Symphony and complaining of the critical reaction, Rachmaninoff wrote:

Put yourself in the position of a critic who hears a large work for the first time. The "inner circles" will label him an ignoramus if he can find no faults to mention; on the other hand, the poor critic is obliged to find *new merits* at every later hearing of the work. Don't forget the "defects" that the critics heard in the first performance of Tchaikovsky's Sixth Symphony. And you complain that one critic "did not hear the trumpet" in your last movement!!

The Glinka Award announcement in December brought the news to Dresden that Rachmaninoff's Second Symphony had won the symphonic prize of a thousand rubles. But this seems to have increased the composer's anguish over his inactivity, and it showed in each letter he wrote. When he wrote to Slonov on New Year's Day, this sometimes depressing holiday had unusually severe effects on him: "I've aged terribly. I am very tired and terribly afraid that I'll soon go to the Devil."

Yet, considering the work Rachmaninoff was to do in the next three months, this depression may have been a symptom that something was stirring. From January through March he composed the orchestral poem whose subject he had sought for two years: *The Isle of the Dead*. It was not Morozov, but Rachmaninoff's new Dresden friend, Nikolai Struve, who first suggested the Böcklin painting as the subject for a symphonic poem; and Rachmaninoff's first acquaintance with the painting, through a reproduction seen in Paris in the summer of 1907, made a stronger impression on him than did any of the several versions of the painting that he later saw in Berlin and Leipzig: "I was not much moved by the color of the painting. If I had seen the original first, I might not have composed my *Isle of the Dead*. I like the picture best in black and white."

Fortunately, Rachmaninoff was less secretive about this source for his symphonic poem than he was for other works that came into being from outside strictly musical sources. He once said of the *Isle*, "There must be something definite before my mind to convey a definite impression, or the ideas refuse to appear." And he gave another glimpse of his method when he said, on another occasion:

When composing, I find it of great help to have in mind a book just recently read, or a beautiful picture, or a poem. Sometimes a definite story is kept in mind, which I try to convert into tones without disclosing the source of my inspiration.

He also warned, "If there is nothing within, nothing from outside will help." In one interview he was unusually explicit about the process of composing the *Isle*:

My composing goes slowly. I go for a long walk in the country. My eye catches the sharp sparks of light on fresh foliage after showers; my ears the rustling undernote of the woods. Or I watch the pale tints of the sky over the horizon after sundown, and they come: all voices at once. Not a bit here, a bit there. All. The whole grows. So *The Isle of the Dead*. It was all done in April and May. When it came, how it began—how can I say? It came up within me, was entertained, written down.

Rachmaninoff continued to polish *The Isle of the Dead*, one of the most perfectly shaped of his works, not only after his return to Russia this year (the completion date on the manuscript score is April 17, 1909), but even twenty years later, in America.

The American tour still hovered in the offing. To Morozov he reported on the negotiations (March 21 [n.s.], 1909) from Dresden:

I am working a lot and I intend to do much more in this last month before leaving for Moscow. My opinion of the new compositions remains the same—they still come the hard way and I am perpetually dissatisfied with myself. Nothing but continuous torture.

Imagine—America still hangs in the air. I tell this to *you* alone, as I've decided to say nothing to the others. I've already talked of this American tour so much to no purpose that it's become disgraceful to go on repeating oneself. But what is one to do, if these negotiations drag on and on? for I've had a contract for a long while, and now we mark time on trifles. The whole trouble lies in one clause, and now we've agreed even on that, so that I sent him [Wolfsohn] the contract to have this clause altered. He promised to do this. Unfortunately, this correspondence drags out this long because of the distance. Twenty days must elapse before the contract is returned. Yet I don't believe they will send it back, because six months for publicity is too little for them. . . .

You ask about Berlin. I turned down a concert there till next year. I'm sick of it all.

The family left Dresden in April, and it was many years before they found themselves again in that quiet city. Moscow put the composer to work at once, as a conductor. Nikisch had been invited to conduct the Moscow Philharmonic, but when Nikisch heard rumors of a cholera epidemic in Moscow, he declined the engagement, and Rachmaninoff was asked to conduct the concerts—the first, on April 15, including Strauss, Wagner, and Scriabin's First Symphony. On April 18 he conducted the first performance of *The Isle of the Dead.*

While in St. Petersburg he received a new honor and a new responsibility. The Princess Helene of Saxe-Altenburg had been appointed President of the Imperial Russian Musical Society, and in her turn she appointed Rachmaninoff as a vice-president to examine and correct the purely musical interests of the Society, including provincial colleges maintained by Society funds. Rachmaninoff accepted this post on the condition that his tasks should be real and not honorary.

In Ivanovka Rachmaninoff began a new work—a concerto that in spite of his postponed American tour was to have its première in New York. With his usual secretiveness he hinted of the new work to Morozov on June 6:

I arrived here exactly a month ago. Till the 20th I did nothing—nothing more than treatments, walking, and sleeping. I began to feel stronger. Then I decided to start work, but as soon as I began I could see that I had too little strength and that after an hour or so my back would begin to ache, I'd feel weak and yearn to lie down on a couch. You see, my friend, after 36 years I realize that my health, or rather, my strength, has clearly begun to decline. . . . At the most I have about 2–3 hours a day when I feel strong. These are a couple of hours in the morning and, for some reason, from 8 to 9 in the evening. And I must practice, too, in these hours. Recently I began practicing an hour a day. After this hour in the afternoon I get so tired that I go to sleep at once on the couch. . . . Now, about work. In these two weeks I've had time only to correct *The Isle of the Dead* for the printer. I made a great many corrections in it. Rewrote almost half. Changes mainly in the orchestration, though I also changed the exposition itself; and in one place, for the sake of the modulation scheme, I even made a transposition. Yesterday, at last, I sent it off to be printed. I'm afraid to guarantee it, but it seems to me that now this composition will gain something and sound better. In any case I now feel that at no point would I be "ill at ease" if I should again perform it.

Now I've taken up a new work. And I again add *for the first time,* that if *health* doesn't hinder me and take up a lot of time, I shall work steadily on it.

There's something else—*a secret.* It is possible that this time, too, I shall *not* get to America. About ten days ago I received a cable about the death of my impresario. It said that the widow of the deceased along with some other people will take over my management. I wished to tempt fate once more, so I sent back my contract at once with a request for all these people, including the wife, to endorse the contract, which, I added, I would consider a sufficient guarantee.

Now I suppose they who receive this contract over there will rejoice at disposing so easily of at least one of the artists remaining on their hands, and will destroy my contract. To the Devil with it! I'll be inexpressibly happy! Incidentally a week ago I received notice from a New York bank that Wolfsohn had deposited there in my name, according to the contract, 2500 dollars, for the last five concerts. So he made it! Maybe he died of chagrin.

In a letter to Joseph Yasser, written in 1935, Rachmaninoff told something of the birth of the new concerto's first theme: "[It] is borrowed *neither* from folk song forms nor from church sources. It simply 'wrote itself'! . . . If I had any plan in composing this theme,

I was thinking only of sound. I wanted to 'sing' the melody on the piano, as a singer would sing it—and to find a suitable orchestral accompaniment, or rather one that would not muffle this singing." And he went on to explain that his treatment showed no wish to impart a liturgical character to the theme.*

By July 15 it seemed possible that American audiences would be the first to hear the new work, dedicated to Josef Hofmann. Rachmaninoff wrote to Morozov:

. . . it wouldn't be a bad idea for me to have a secretary, if only the salary would correspond with the amount of business correspondence I get. But before that, I'd like to buy an automobile. I can't tell you how much I want one! That's all I lack now—an automobile and a secretary!

Otherwise everything suffices. Today I canceled part of my work to write letters. So you see I am working a lot. You, of course, would like to know with what result, but so far I have no answer to this except that "I haven't finished," that little time is left, that this worries me very much, that what I've done doesn't particularly please me, that composing is still hard, etc., etc. The usual story. I can also add that I am *not* idling. The only consolation! . . .

What is *not* consoling is that I'm going to America after all. Devil take it! I think I'd even give up the secretary if I could get out of going there. That's how much I don't want to go. But then, perhaps, after America I'll be able to buy myself that automobile. So it may not be so bad!

I intend to be with you soon. They plan to open the "shop" of the Imperial Russian Publishers on August 8. I'm coming to this ceremony to drink champagne. . . .

"Imperial" was an irony, not a slip: this was the newest enterprise of the wealthy Koussevitzkys. This wealth had established a fund to aid young and needy Russian composers, and Rachmaninoff had been added to the advisory committee, possibly as the most objective and distinguished Russian composer whom Koussevitzky could name. He was also the only composer who had appeared with Koussevitzky in his first conducting season. In his support of Russian music Koussevitzky took his next step in the spring of 1909.

Since Belayev's death in 1904 Russian composers had no philanthropist to support and publish their work, and Koussevitzky proposed

* The full text of this letter appears on pages 311–12.

to fill this gap with a new house called Russian Music Publishers, or Editions Russes de Musique, or (since its copyright headquarters were established in Berlin) Russischer Musikverlag, with Nikolai Struve as director. As Rachmaninoff was still under contract to Gutheil, he agreed to serve on an advisory board, to choose compositions and composers. Scriabin, too, served on this board; and the new house became his publisher.

When Koussevitzky returned to Russia to arrange his crucial first Russian season as a conductor, he gave a gala opening for the Moscow office of the new firm. It was not long after this gala that Rachmaninoff left for his first American tour; he practiced the piano part of the new work on the way, using for the first time a silent piano on board ship.

Chapter 10

First American Tour

THE American tour, in pressure and haste, was all that Rachman-inoff dreaded it would be. When Modeste Altschuler met him at the pier, it was a depressed Rachmaninoff that asked, "When is the first rehearsal?" In addition to the few recitals for the Wolfsohn Bureau, arrangements were made for him to appear as soloist with the Boston Symphony, with the New York Symphony Orchestra (for the première of the Third Concerto under Walter Damrosch), with the Philadelphia Orchestra, and with the New York Philharmonic under Gustav Mahler. Some additional appearances were fitted in as the tour progressed and as his name gathered commercial weight.

Rachmaninoff's recital program was usually composed of his first sonata, pieces from Op. 3 and 10, and a group of préludes, including the obligatory C-sharp minor, of which a typical press release of the period boasted, "In academic Berlin, it has been said, if one strolls through the lodging house quarters on a summer evening the tremen-dous chords of the Rachmaninoff prelude can be heard pealing forth from every open window."

In the American manner his recital was "opened out of town," in Northampton on November 4, and on November 8 he gave his first American performance with orchestra, playing his Second Concerto with the Boston Symphony and Max Fiedler at the Philadelphia Academy of Music. In a short tour with the Boston orchestra, he played this concerto in Baltimore and, on November 13, in New York. Richard Aldrich, of *The New York Times*, reviewed Sergei Rachmaninoff's first New York concert:

Mr. Rachmaninoff, who is perhaps the tallest known pianist, is one of the youngest of the modern Russian school of composers, though he lives now in Dresden. . . . his second concerto has been given in New York in the last few years a number of times, somewhat out of proportion with its intrinsic merits. But with the assistance of the orchestra, which counts for a great deal in this composition, he made it sound more interesting than it ever has before here.

He is a pianist of highly developed technique, as who must be that plays this concerto, and he has ample resources of expression upon the instrument, though a beautiful and varied tone is not conspicuous among them.

The Second Concerto seems to have made a bad start in America. All critics dismissed it, following the lead of Philip Hale who wrote in his program note for the Boston Symphony's first performance of the work: "The concerto is of uneven worth. The first movement is labored and has little marked character. It might have been written by any German, technically well trained, who was acquainted with the music of Tchaikovsky."

Before leaving New York on November 14 Rachmaninoff was visited by an interviewer from *The Delineator,* who plied him with questions about the Prélude. Granting that its fame had made it possible for him to come to America, Rachmaninoff went on to say:

Under the circumstances I should be thankful, I suppose, that I wrote the composition. But I am undecided whether my oversight in neglecting to secure international copyright for it was altogether fortunate for me. Had I copyrighted it, I might have had wealth as well as fame from it. And again, I might have achieved neither. . . . I took the precaution to have [the ten Préludes of Op. 23] copyrighted by a German publisher. I think them far better music than my first Prélude, but the public has shown no disposition to share my belief. I can not tell whether my judgment is at fault or whether the existence of that copyright has acted as a blight on their popularity. Consequently it will always be an open question with me whether intrinsic merit or absence of copyright is responsible for the success of my earlier work.

Before giving, on request, a detailed analysis of the piece and how it should be played, he said:

Since my arrival in this country I have discovered some peculiar notions current regarding this Prélude and the circumstances of its creation. I may as well take this opportunity to tell the exact truth about it.

When I graduated from the Moscow Conservatory I was a boy of eighteen. Music is not a lucrative profession, even for those who have achieved fame, and for a beginner it is usually desperate. After a year I found myself out of pocket. I needed money, and I wrote this Prélude and sold it to a publisher for what he would give. I realized, all told, forty rubles out of it—that is about twenty dollars in your money—very little compensation, you will admit, considering the sums the piece has earned for publishers. But in this case the law of compensation has worked out nicely, and I have no reason to complain.

In Hartford and Boston he played the Second Concerto with Fiedler and the Boston Symphony; this concerto was played in Toronto on November 18, and on November 20 New York heard his recital. The *Times* was somewhat overcome by the Rachmaninovian melancholy: "A plaintive Russian note wandered through all this music. In fact, towards the end of the program many of the listeners began to feel as if they were prisoners bound for Siberia."

In Philadelphia Rachmaninoff made his American conducting debut with the Philadelphia Orchestra, in Musorgsky's *Night on Bald Mountain* and his own Second Symphony. On Sunday afternoon, November 28, in New York's New Theater, he gave the first performance anywhere of the Third Concerto, under Walter Damrosch, in a program of Mozart, Lalo, and Chabrier. This concert was repeated on the evening of November 30. The critic of the *Sun* wrote of the new concerto: "Sound, reasonable music this, though not a great nor memorable proclamation."

In December he conducted the revised *Isle of the Dead* with Chicago's Theodore Thomas Orchestra. There was a Pittsburgh recital on December 9, and then Boston, Cincinnati (under Stokowski), and Buffalo heard him play the Second Concerto. On January 9, 1910 he gave a recital at the Metropolitan Opera, assisted by Anna Meitschik and Adamo Didur singing a group of his songs.

Rachmaninoff must have sent many unhappy letters home from his American tour, but few have been preserved; one of these is to his young cousin, Zoya Pribitkova, written at the Hotel Netherland in New York on December 12, 1909:

My dear Zoyechka,

You were very kind to write to me. Your letter made me very happy. You know, in this accursed country, where you're surrounded by nothing but Americans and the "business," "business," they are forever doing, clutching you from all sides and driving you on—it is terribly pleasant to receive a letter from a Russian girl, and from such a sweet Russian girl as you. Thank you. But I couldn't manage an immediate reply. I am very busy and very tired. Here is my perpetual prayer: God give me strength and patience. Everyone treats me nicely and kindly, but I am horribly bored with it all, and I feel that my character has been quite spoiled here. Sometimes I even grow angry as the devil. And I have two more months here.

Rehearsals began for the performance that Rachmaninoff had most anticipated: the New York Philharmonic's performance on January 16 of the new concerto under Gustav Mahler. Rachmaninoff later told Riesemann:

At that time Mahler was the only conductor whom I considered worthy to be classed with Nikisch. He devoted himself to the concerto until the accompaniment, which is rather complicated, had been practiced to the point of perfection, although he had already gone through another long rehearsal. According to Mahler, every detail of the score was important—an attitude too rare amongst conductors.

After a rehearsal of the Berlioz *Symphonie Fantastique* that dazzled Rachmaninoff with Mahler's conducting power, his concerto was rehearsed:

Though the rehearsal was scheduled to end at 12:30, we played and played, far beyond this hour, and when Mahler announced that the first movement would be rehearsed again, I expected some protest or scene from the musicians, but I did not notice a single sign of annoyance. The orchestra played the first movement with a keen or perhaps even closer application than the previous time.

A last-minute arrangement was made for a concert on January 27 with Modeste Altschuler's Russian Symphony Society, the program including both *The Isle of the Dead* (conducted by the composer) and the Second Concerto. Aldrich, of the *Times,* thus bade farewell to the visiting composer:

Russian music in general, and Rachmaninoff's music in particular, is weighted down with a melancholy, which seems to be racial in its insistence. It is but natural that this composer should turn with a sort of gruesome delight to so congenial a subject for his inspiration [*The Isle of the Dead*]. . . .

The melodic outline is scarcely apparent, and there are neither strange harmonic combinations nor instrumental effects of sufficient interest to divert the ear. It was possibly the composer's intention to show that death is as empty as life. Under the inspiration of the composer's baton the band developed qualities of sonority and precision which it has hitherto given little evidence of possessing.

The programme ended with a performance of Rachmaninoff's second pianoforte concerto, which he played himself. This is a work which is not worth such frequent performances as it has received this season, and not in any way comparable to Rachmaninoff's third concerto.

Before his departure the Boston Symphony offered him the post of Fiedler's successor, but the prospect of such a long absence from Moscow "with or without my family" struck him as absurd. Contracts were offered him to return to America in the following season, but he declined all proposals. His reasons appear in an interview he gave to a Russian magazine on his return:

America was a strain. Imagine giving an almost daily concert for three whole months. I played only my own works. The success was great. They forced me to play as many as seven encores, which is quite a lot for that audience. The audiences are astonishingly cold, spoiled by the tours of first-class artists and forever looking for novelty, for something they've never had before. Local papers are obliged to note the number of times you are recalled to the stage, and the public regards this as a yardstick of your talent.

Immediately on his return to Russia he participated in one of Siloti's Petersburg concerts, on February 6, playing his Second Concerto* and his Second Suite for two pianos with Siloti at the other piano.

When Siloti conducted the Second Concerto in Moscow, both rehearsal and performance were mentioned by the Countess Tolstoy in her diary, for February 13; she also recorded a more important occasion on April 4: "Went to the Philharmonic rehearsal at 8:30 a.m. —a Rachmaninoff concert in which he himself is taking part, and which consists entirely of his own works. One cannot appraise it at

---

* It was the new concerto that had been scheduled, but the parts went astray in transit from America and did not arrive in time for this or the Moscow concert.

once, but it is interesting." This concert, under Eugene Plotnikov, consisted entirely of recent works, including the first Russian performance of the Third Concerto as well as *The Isle of the Dead* and the Second Symphony. Grigori Prokofiev, of *Russkiye Vedomosti*, was satisfied:

The new concerto mirrored the best sides of his creative power—sincerity, simplicity, and clarity of musical thought. . . . it has a freshness of inspiration that doesn't aspire to the discovery of new paths, it has a sharp and laconic form as well as simple and brilliant orchestration—qualities that will secure both outer success and enduring love by musicians and public alike for this new composition.

Rachmaninoff entered, briefly, a new field of music at the time that his *Polka Italienne* was in popular circulation; while he was in Petersburg his cousin Sergei Siloti asked him to allow the leader of the Imperial Marine Guard Band to arrange the polka for his band. He agreed; his own participation is described in a later letter to Edwin Franko Goldman: "To his score of this Polka I added only some Fanfares, and when the Imperial Marine Guard Band performed the 'Italian Polka,' I liked it very much and found that the Fanfares were especially effective. The whole performance had a great success with the audience."

It was about the time of his return from America that the mysterious activities of the "white lilacs lady" began. Rachmaninoff could give no concert or recital without a bouquet of white lilacs among the floral tributes. Bouquets of white lilacs were also delivered on every birthday, every saint's day; and if he happened to be abroad on these dates, the white lilacs would just as surely arrive at his hotel or the compartment of his train. The notes accompanying this tribute were always brief and tender, congratulating him on his birthday or wishing him success in the concert, and the only signature was the Russian initials of "White Lilacs"; the song "Lilacs" in Op. 21 appears to have inspired this extraordinary labor of love. Rachmaninoff appreciated the lady's incognito as deeply as the simple, warm words of her notes, though sometimes the gift was a little flamboyant—especially when the everlasting white lilacs arrived on schedule in the depth of winter. Not only did bouquets, wreaths, and other ornamental florist's designs arrive with these flowers, but the gift took other forms, such as an ebony conductor's baton engraved with a design of white lilacs and Rachmaninoff's initials. The giver's identity remained hidden from the composer and all members of his family.*

In 1910 the estate of Ivanovka became mine. And from then on I became passionately interested in its management. During the winter I would work very hard, give recitals, earn money—and in the summer most of my earnings would be invested in the land, in livestock, in machinery, mostly of American manufacture.

One of Rachmaninoff's chief interests in Ivanovka was his love of horses, a love inherited from his father and cultivated in his years of acquaintance with the Sakhnovskys. Each of his landowning neighbors near Ivanovka took pride in his stud of race horses, and one of Rachmaninoff's keenest enjoyments was in training young thoroughbreds for racing. Even before he took over the management of Ivanovka, its former owner, Alexander Satin, gave him charge of all horses being prepared for sale or for personal use. Rachmaninoff himself was an excellent rider. Escape to Ivanovka had a special proprietary flavor this year; he wrote to Morozov on June 4:

I was *not* surprised that the Riga shore doesn't suit you. In summer nothing pleases you but your regular room on Granatni Lane in the Rittich house, with your estimable old upright and the score of *Götterdämmerung*. That's the way you're created. . . .

I've been here in Ivanovka for a month now. Began to work yesterday, but didn't do a thing up till then. I drink mare's milk (another unpleasant occupation, when you have to drink 8 bottles of it daily) and take arsenic injections. By the end of the treatment I expect tremendous blessings.

---

* It was not until 1918, after the Rachmaninoffs had gone abroad, that "White Lilacs" was identified. Sophia Satina tells of this: "As I walked to my laboratory one day I heard a horse galloping behind me: I turned and saw a cabman whipping the horse frantically, with an elderly woman standing in the lurching cab, clinging to him with one hand and waving to me with the other. When they came up to me, this woman, breathless and agitated, said, 'Thank God! How happy I am to find you! I am White Lilacs—my name is Rousseau.—Where is Rachmaninoff? Is he alive?' She was overjoyed to hear that he was well and working abroad. When Sergei Vasilyevich heard about Mme. Rousseau, he offered to help her to leave Russia, but she preferred to stay in Moscow with her daughter."

Up till now the whole month has been spent dillydallying. I often fish, and plant willows. The latter occupation was and still is fascinating. For it I bought a bore, with which I bore holes two feet deep, and then plant willow cuttings that stand five feet above the earth. I've set out 120 of these. I watered and continue to water them with an accuracy and patience and persistence worthy of a better cause. But how great is my rapture when I see a fresh bud of a young green leaf. I keep a strict account of the trees that take root. There are now 43 of these. Congratulate me!

When the last willow was planted he got down to work on his summer composition. This was his first large religious work consisting of twenty numbers for a four-part chorus, the *Liturgy of Saint John Chrysostom*. It went more easily than he expected:

You ask me [he wrote Morozov on July 31] what I have written. . . . I am working a very great deal, but finished things are few—very few.

I have finished the Liturgy (this probably surprises you). Long ago I thought about the Liturgy, and long ago I aimed towards it. I set about it somehow unexpectedly and was at once carried away by it. And then I finished it very soon. I haven't composed anything for a long while (since the time of *Monna Vanna*) with such pleasure. That is all. Beyond this, all is wishes and good intentions. Worst of all goes the business of the little piano pieces. I don't like this occupation and it's always difficult for me. Neither beauty, nor joy.

During August and September he finished the "little piano pieces," thirteen préludes for Op. 32, and departed on his European concert tour.

While Rachmaninoff was in Vienna, where he was having a tremendous success both as composer and as pianist, a correspondent for one of the less dignified Moscow newspapers, the *Utro Rossii*, visited him to talk about the recent difficulties in the Bolshoi Theater, and particularly about the trouble into which his friend Chaliapin had gotten himself there. At the time of this interview there was talk in the Vienna Opera of engaging Mahler and others as guest conductors. Rachmaninoff expressed the opinion that something similar would be a help at the Bolshoi, too. The correspondent, knowing that Telyakovsky had often approached the composer with such a proposal without success, asked him the same question, to which Rachmaninoff replied (or was so recorded as saying):

I will never return to the Bolshoi Theater, even if they offer me big money. They don't need a man like me. Now everyone blames Fedya, yelling "Chaliapin is a brawler." This is true, Fyodor is a brawler. They are scared there of his very spirit. He shouts suddenly or even hits someone! And Fedya's fist is powerful. . . . He can take care of himself. And how else should one behave? Backstage at our theater it's just like a saloon. They shout, they drink, they swear in the foulest language. How can there be creative work there, or even the possibility of such work? They need a brawler like Chaliapin, from whom all have to hide in corners to avoid trouble. But this isn't work, only a perpetual irritation and antagonism between subordinates and their chief. Under such conditions nothing can be created. Meanwhile, there is so much that one could do.

The publication in Moscow of this interview added fresh fuel to the flaming temperaments at the Bolshoi. A delegation went so far as to demand that Telyakovsky go to Vienna and investigate the accuracy of these statements, a demand that the director indignantly rejected. When the article and its repercussions reached Rachmaninoff, then in Berlin after playing in Frankfurt-am-Main with Mengelberg, he felt compelled to deny, explain—anything that would calm the noise that had been raised. To the editor of *Russkiye Vedomosti* he wrote this letter, for publication:

[November 8/21, 1910]

There has been printed in the newspaper *Utro Rossii* an article entitled "Rachmaninoff in Vienna and His Remarks about Moscow." I received this yesterday on my way through Berlin, where my mail had been held for me. My first reaction on reading the article was to ignore it. Not, however, because it was either satisfactory or true, but because my experience has been that few readers pay any attention to such interviews, and those who do believe them rarely believe more than a tenth part of them. . . . A certain amount of fantasy is permitted the interviewer, who is guided only by the main line of your conversation, which he proceeds to communicate in *his* and not in *your* words. Therefore, on reading interviews, one is often amazed: on the one hand, there is the impression that you really said this; on the other, an impression that you are hearing these words for the first time.

And in the letters which I received with the article there was this same doubt, "Did you really say this?" Happily I thought, "This means they don't believe it either!" But when this was followed by advice to print a denial, as this "had made a most depressing effect on the Bolshoi Theater and on Chaliapin," I realized that they had believed some part of it. . . .

I should be willing to forgive the printing of the interview without my permission if it were only myself described therein. Even described as here, with no approximation to truth and, actually, a contradiction of truth. . . . All my oratory, for example, about a supposed new opera of mine, or my statements that I am supposedly "happy only when I play in Moscow," and that "I will never enter the Bolshoi Theater" (even the edi-tor of *Utro Rossii* had his doubts about the probability of these words, as can be seen in his footnote), "even if they offer me big money." Or, finally, such interesting details as that at some point in the conversation "my lower lip trembled with excitement" and so on. True or not, none of this would concern me, for such things are quite unimportant and concern, in general, only myself. . . .

But this is what is very bad: The article *publishes* without *my knowl-edge* words of mine about the Bolshoi Theater and Chaliapin. The tragic element in this is that *here and only here* happens to be the "tenth part" of the truth. Before refuting this, I wish to point out a few more facts that testify to my complete ignorance that this conversation was intended for print.

Even assuming that *all* these abuses addressed to the *entire* Bolshoi Theater (in the conversation attributed to me I always supposedly spoke in the plural: "they shout," "they drink," "they swear in the foulest lan-guage," "they don't need anyone like me," etc.) had actually been uttered by me and were intended to be published with my consent, in the best of lights this would mean that I don't possess the slightest grain of good sense. . . . I don't speak of decency, which is apparently denied me by those who believed in the reality of my words in this conversation. . . .

And now I return to the "tenth part of the truth" which I would not have allowed printed if the correspondent of *Utro Rossii* had asked my permission, but which I am now forced to declare.

1. I said that we often have regrettable confusion backstage at the Bolshoi Theater. There is no quiet, nor is there that which so impresses one abroad, everyone assisting the common cause to the best of his ability; and if one must speak during a performance, one whispers, and if one

must walk, one tiptoes. There really is confusion backstage at the Bolshoi Theater, and while I conducted there this attitude caused me considerable pain. 2. I also said that I had heard rumors that since Chaliapin had been appointed *régisseur* of those operas in which he sings, there is more quiet backstage.

This is *all* that I said. . . .

S. Rachmaninoff.

Rachmaninoff was back in Moscow in time to hear the first public performance of the *Liturgy,* sung by the Choir of the Synod School under Danilin's direction, on November 25. Rachmaninoff had a double reason for recalling this performance:

The Choir sang beautifully. For one number of the *Liturgy,* "We sing Thy praise, O Lord," the whole Choir supplies a humming accompaniment for the solo of a boy soprano. At that performance the voice rang out in such crystalline, ethereal beauty against the rich, deep harmonies of the choral background, that I experienced a moment of sheer delight. After the performance I asked to see the boy soloist. A shy, blushing lad was presented to me, and I patted him on the shoulder and thanked him for his exquisite singing. Years later, after a Berlin concert of the Don Cossacks, its very able conductor, Sergei Jaroff, was introduced to me and he said at once that he had already met me. I have a good memory for faces, but I could not recall him. "Where was it we met?" I asked, and he told me that he was the boy who had sung the soprano solo in the *Liturgy.*

Then there was the Jubilee concert of the Russian Musical Society conducted by Emil Cooper and dedicated to three great graduates of the Moscow Conservatory: Taneyev, Rachmaninoff, and Scriabin. Rachmaninoff played his Third Concerto. The concert was notable chiefly for the opportunity given critics to compare Rachmaninoff and Scriabin (represented by his Third Symphony); they attached Rachmaninoff to Tchaikovsky, and Scriabin to Chopin and Wagner. On January 15, 1911, before leaving Moscow, Rachmaninoff conducted his *Spring* cantata in a concert of the Moscow Philharmonic and played his Second Concerto (conducted by Pomerantzev).

After conducting a concert of his symphonic works in Kiev on January 21, he visited Rostov in connection with his duties as in-

specting vice-president of the Russian Musical Society before returning to Kiev for a recital on the 27th. His schoolmate, Nikolai Avierino,
who was then director of the Rostov Music School, tells of Rachmaninoff's unexpectedly official behavior in Rostov:

I awaited his arrival impatiently, for I could hardly wait to boast of my
achievements here to my old friend. When visiting Rostov he always
stayed in my apartment, and as usual I went to meet his train, but to my
surprise he told me he could not stay with me, for he had come in the
capacity of an inspector—it didn't seem appropriate to stay with the
director of the institution he was inspecting. . . .
    On the following morning he came to the Conservatory for the in-
spection. General excitement in the office, among teachers and students.
The inspection began. Sergei Vasilyevich was very conscientious: he
inspected the accounts, making our lady bookkeeper terribly uneasy with
queries on various items. Then, after examining a complete inventory,
he attended the classes, sometimes remaining in the classroom of each
teacher for as much as half an hour, his presence considerably unnerving
both teachers and students. Finally, on the third day, his visit ended with
a concert by the students, with chorus and orchestra conducted by me. . . .
This went very well. At the end of the program Rachmaninoff approached
the platform, extended his hand, and said rather loudly (not habitual
with him): "Thank you, Nikolai Konstantinovich. All that I've seen and
heard here, in respect both to order and discipline, exceeded all my
expectations!" I was in seventh heaven. When, afterwards, Rachmaninoff
and I were left to ourselves, he told me, "You know—I was afraid to inspect
your school. It's hard to inspect an old friend, and I wasn't sure of you.
I thought to myself, What sort of director can Avierino be? God knows
what may be going on there! I was seriously considering, perhaps it would
be better not to go to Rostov at all!"

    Rachmaninoff returned to St. Petersburg for a sad occasion, the
memorial concert for the young actress Vera Kommissarzhevskaya on
February 10. On February 12 there was a Siloti concert devoted to
Rachmaninoff's works (Second Symphony, *Isle of the Dead*, Third
Concerto), and on March 10 the Synodical Choir brought the new
Liturgy to St. Petersburg. The memorable performance of the
Liturgy, however, was that given at a Siloti matinee concert of March
25, in which the composer conducted the chorus of the Marinsky
Opera.

As applause is not permitted in concert performances of Russian ortho-dox church music, it is difficult to say which of the twelve numbers sung made the greatest impression on the audience. . . .

In the praise heard afterwards there were many remarks as to the music not being "churchlike," that it contained apparent operatic nuances and symphonic refinements. Our impression is that the *Liturgy,* first of all, is written highly musically, and stands apart from the stylistic con-ditions of "ecclesiastic formulas." Obviously the composer never intended to fit his music into this formula. We leave it to the experts in church music to try him for not accomplishing what he didn't set out to do.

At Ivanovka the Muse did not arrive until mid-August, and there-upon Rachmaninoff wrote nine *études-tableaux* for the piano. Before turning them over to the printer he removed three, two of which he put away in his desk. When Boris Asafiev submitted a list of Rach-maninoff's compositions for him to check, the composer crossed out these two, in C minor and D minor, and wrote determinedly in the margin: "The deleted ones lie in my desk. They will not be pub-lished."*

Rachmaninoff might have put away more of these pieces if he could have seen the politely damning review in the London *Times* of two song albums published in Rosa Newmarch's translation by Breitkopf & Härtel, from two "diametrically opposed attitudes of mind," Rachmaninoff's and Musorgsky's:

Rachmaninov's compositions are the work of a man who, as an excep-tionally brilliant public performer, has travelled and mixed much with many minds and imbibed a cosmopolitan view of his art. All the exigencies of the executive side of it are met by sure instinct which requires little or no conscious mental effort. Technique in composing, as in playing, is a part of his nature; and consequently his work has that apparent facility which is constantly characteristic of the music of great executants, whether they are writing for their own instrument or not. It is both a gain and a loss to them; a gain because they experience little of that difficulty in expressing themselves which often tortures men whose whole life is devoted to creative work, a loss because that very difficulty some-

* A third, in A minor, was also discarded, but later revised for inclusion in the nine *études-tableaux* of Op. 39 (No. 6).

times leads to deeper and more enduring results than a man with a glib tongue or a ready pen can reach.

Rachmaninoff came to London this autumn, again with his own compositions. Following a recital at the London Ballad Concerts, he gave London its first hearing of his Third Concerto, conducted by Mengelberg, on which the *Times* commented:

It is more than usually difficult to judge of the actual value of this remarkable work from a first hearing, because it is almost impossible to dissociate the music from the extraordinary glamour cast upon it by the magical piano playing of the composer. He is one of the very few pianists, and probably the chief among them, who have succeeded in adding types of effect to the resources of the piano which are not the natural outcome of Liszt and his school. The whole of this Concerto illustrates these contributions in a striking way. The climaxes are built with wonderful power, but the musical ideas from which they spring are also distinctive.

Returning from a recital tour of southern cities, Rachmaninoff gave his St. Petersburg recital, an event added to the Siloti series. Before this date he played at the Conservatory for students and faculty. One of the professors, Vladimir Drozdov, tells of that pleasant afternoon:

I remember one day at the St. Petersburg Conservatory full of excited joy. . . . A day or two before, our bulletin board had displayed a notice from the office that Sergei Vasilyevich Rachmaninoff had expressed a desire to play for the students and faculty.

The overflowing auditorium held an atmosphere of tense expectancy. . . . While the students held their breath, watching and listening with their whole being, Rachmaninoff played a long program of his compositions. . . . He was in good spirits, talking and joking between the numbers. "Now I'll play my last *études-tableaux* for you, but that doesn't mean I'll play no more—just that these were composed recently." While Sergei Vasilyevich was saying this, addressing the audience, one of the Conservatory ushers tiptoed out onto the stage and placed on a second piano on the stage a pot of white lilacs. When Rachmaninoff turned to play and saw this, he was obviously touched.

When, at the end, we showed no signs of leaving the auditorium, Sergei Vasilyevich said humorously, "I don't know whether it's a good or a bad thing, but a custom seems to have been established that a request for my polka is a signal given to me that the audience has had enough. So I'll conclude with it."

Glazunov, director of the Conservatory, came to the stage and thanked Rachmaninoff for the pleasure he had given all of us, and then suggested to the faculty and students that no further work be done that day, because "this is a day to be marked no less than a day when the school is visited by a member of the Imperial family."

The first Moscow concert of the season confounded the critics who enjoyed pitting Rachmaninoff and Scriabin against each other. As conductor for a group of the Philharmonic Society's concerts Rachmaninoff engaged Scriabin as soloist for his first concert on December 10. The program included Tchaikovsky's Fourth Symphony, *Don Juan* by Strauss, and Scriabin's Piano Concerto, and the single-purposed performance of the concerto by pianist and orchestra downed forever the rumor of "rivalry."

Rachmaninoff's piano recital of December 13 introduced Moscow to the new *études-tableaux* and the préludes of Op. 32, of which Yuli Engel wrote:

Rachmaninoff's préludes differ from Chopin's in that they generally incline towards a solid and often polyphonic treatment, a broad structure, or towards clear contrasts of musically independent sections; in a word, they approach Chopin's exceptions to his own rule, as in the famous D-flat major prélude. Instead of Chopin's two-page or even half-page works, Rachmaninoff's préludes grow into 4, 6, or even 8 pages. This is a growth to be welcomed when it derives from the natural tendency of a musical idea to reveal itself as fully as possible, as, for example, the beautiful Prélude-March in G minor, Op. 23. But when a thematic embryo, whose chief interest is as a brief sketch, insists on expansion, as in the long B minor prélude, then one is sorry both for the piece and the composer.

Two days later Rachmaninoff participated in Baklanov's concert for the benefit of needy students, conducting the monologue from *The Miserly Knight* and Grieg's first *Peer Gynt* Suite, a performance that to Engel seemed a revelation of this familiar music. This full week ended on December 18 with Rachmaninoff playing Tchaikovsky's First Piano Concerto under Siloti's direction, with solo encores and accompaniments for Rachmaninoff songs sung by Zbruyeva.

Chapter 11

"Re" and *The Bells*

IN FEBRUARY 1912 Rachmaninoff entered into one of those strangely remote friendships that seem so characteristically Russian. Though the twenty-three-year-old poet, Marietta Shaginyan, had never met the composer, she had the precedent of Marie Bashkirtzeva's postal bombardment of Maupassant, and on his part Rachmaninoff had the precedent of his beloved Tchaikovsky, who had faithfully responded to Madame von Meck's epistolary compliments and suggestions. Shaginyan began the correspondence à la Bashkirtzeva, concealing her identity:

One February night I wrote a letter to Sergei Vasilyevich Rachmaninoff, whom I had never met, and sent the letter to St. Petersburg, where he had gone to give a concert. I concealed my name, signing the letter with the musical note *Re,* and thereafter, throughout our entire personal contact—from February 1912 till our last meeting in July 1917—I remained *Re* to him: he never addressed me otherwise.

That year Rachmaninoff was at the peak of his glory and outward success; his concerts were greeted by terrific ovations. . . . But it was in these very years of wide recognition and good fortune that Rachmaninoff was seriously ill with doubt, doubt in himself, and the youth of Moscow knew this.

Rachmaninoff's first replies sound almost as if he were writing to a very young child:

Dear *Re,*

Thank you for your nice letter, which I received yesterday. I am quite willing to talk with you—but I am so busy, I have so much to do, so many trips to make, and I get so tired, that it's rarely that I do any talking. This time I'll do my best to give you a precise answer, in view of your ultimatum at the end of your letter. Write me here (where I'll be till the end of next week). Is there anything wrong?—are you ill?—why does a certain sad impression emanate from your letter?

S. Rachmaninoff

March 15, 1912

Dear *Re,* would you be angry with me for asking you to do something? And if this request won't require too much work of you, will you do it? Here is how you can help me: I need texts for songs. Couldn't you suggest some that you consider suitable? It seems to me that *"Re"* knows a great deal in this field, nearly everything—perhaps even everything. Authors may be living or dead—makes no difference!—only the things must be original, not translations, and not more than 8 to 12 lines, at most 16. And another thing; the mood should be rather more sad than gay. I'm not so lucky with bright tones! I await your answer. . . .

P.S. I write you nothing about myself: I don't know how and I don't like to. It was the truth (and by no means a lie) when someone told you that I'm a most ordinary and uninteresting sort of person.

March 29, 1912

Dear *Re,* I received your letter and the books. . . . I am very grateful to you for everything! I've read all that you copied. The only one that fits is Baratynsky's lovely "Spring." The "Eastern Melodies" are good, but they're all unsuitable for songs, as you yourself quite fairly pointed out. I haven't yet had time to look over everything in the little book that you marked with a cross that looks like a *dièse* [sharp]—*"Re dièse."* All those you mention or recommend I'll force myself to copy before summer, as soon as I can think about starting this work.

As for the content of your letter, I'll answer your questions in a "businesslike" way. A few introductory words on your injustice. In that last letter of yours you weren't entirely fair to me, dear *Re.* Here's an example:—your merciless criticism of Galina's "doggerel." Not without poison you say that I "willingly used" this doggerel. Actually it was only on two or three occasions* out of a possible fifty-one that I made use of these. . . . You also warn me that I shouldn't seek "a cheap music hall success" for my songs! This is even worse! Do you really think you have to tell me this, dear *Re?* . . . And furthermore—about Sakhnovsky: I'll not protest the characteristics you attribute to him and to his writings. But why should you suspect me of treating all this writing as some command, not only to be noted, but to be put into action, as well?! According to you, as soon as Sakhnovsky says somewhere that I am "a singer of horror and tragedy," then I immediately change my course and declare to you

---

* He used Galina's verses for three songs, "How nice it is here," "How painful for me," and "Before my window" (Op. 21; Nos. 7 and 12; Op. 26, No. 10).

that "I'm not so lucky with bright tones," and you adjure me not to believe in Sakhnovsky. . . .

As a matter of fact I don't read Sakhnovsky's articles (I know they are
complimentary) any more than I read others (which, I know, are mostly
uncomplimentary). I don't read them; somehow none of this is very convincing to me. I must say, from the depth of my soul, that I am more
inclined to trust and heed the latter than the former, because there is in
the whole world no critic more doubtful of me than I am of myself. . . .
From this "unbusinesslike" wandering I'll return to my answers. I write
so little (or not at all) about myself, for I know you so slightly, or not at
all, dear *Re!* You must let my eyes or, rather, my ears, get more accustomed
to you. . . .

You also ask about my children? You say it will give you pleasure to
have me tell you something about them. Very well! I have two girls:
8 and 4 years old. These two are disobedient, unmanageable, and ill-
mannered—but the most charming and interesting girls. I love them
terribly! They are the dearest things in my life! and the brightest! (And
there is in such "brightness" such calm and joy! How right you are about
that, dear *Re!*) And the girls love me very much, too. Not long ago it
happened that I grew angry at the younger one and told her that I would
stop loving her—at which she pouted, left the room, and told me that if
I stopped loving her, she would go "into the forest"! I would probably say
the same thing to them. Lately both the girls and I were ill. All of us had
influenza with more or less serious complications. But we're all nearly well
now. On the evening of March 24, when your roses were brought to me,
I had just returned to my room after a consultation beside my daughter's
bed—the one who wanted to go "into the forest."

April 28, 1912

Dear *Re,* I had no time in Moscow to write you and I want to do it here
in Tambov, where I have a short wait for the train that is to carry me
farther into the country. I want to write you at least a few lines: a few
words of gratitude for your nice, amusing letter and for the little book
of poems, that you copied out with such patience and valor. . . . I'm going
alone into the country. My family follows in about a week. . . .

What, dear *Re,* made you think that I love conservatory and philharmonic girls? One rarely meets people so self-satisfied—outside, and so
wretched—inside. What could be worse? You ask what else I love, beside
my children, my music, and my flowers!? All that you would wish,

dear *Re!* For instance, crayfish soup!—only, please, none of our musical ladies. . . .

This spring Rachmaninoff had a more fundamental disagreement with the "musical ladies" and other heads of the Musical Society— and on a matter of basic principle to him. He took his work as vice-president of the I.R.M.S. seriously, and for Rachmaninoff "seriously" meant with moral as well as artistic seriousness: these were really fused in him. When, as vice-president, he heard that a very good musician in an administrative post in one of the Society's schools was to be dismissed on the ground that the musician was Jewish, Rachmaninoff promptly submitted his own resignation. If the artistic affairs of the Society were to be conditioned by any political attitude, he would assume no further responsibility within the Society.

From the peace of Ivanovka Rachmaninoff continued to write his unseen correspondent. On May 8:

Beside my children and music and flowers, I love you, dear *Re,* and I love your letters. I love you because you're clever and interesting and because you're not extreme (one of the categorical conditions for me to "be attracted" by anyone); and I love your letters because every word in them breathes faith, hope, and love: that balm to heal my wounds. Though there may yet be some timidity and uncertainty, you describe me amazingly and you know me well. How? I never tire of being astonished. . . . One thing only isn't good! . . . You look to me for something that isn't there, and you wish to see me as the sort of person I'll never be. My "criminally sincere humility" (*Re's* letter) I am sorry to say does exist—and my "ruin by philistinism" I imagine, as you do, to be in the not very distant future. This is all true! and it is true because I have no faith in myself. Teach me to have faith in myself, dear *Re!* Even half as much faith as you have in me. If there was ever a time when I had faith in myself, that was long ago—long, long ago—in my youth! . . . Isn't it significant that I have had almost no other doctor, for these past twenty years, than the hypnotist Dahl, and my two first cousins (one of whom I married ten years ago, and whom I also love and wish to add to my list). All these persons, or rather, doctors, taught me one thing: to take courage and have faith. Sometimes I have succeeded in this. But the illness hangs on to me tenaciously and with the passing years digs in ever more deeply, I fear. No wonder if I should, after a while, make up my mind to abandon composition altogether and become, instead, a professional pianist, or a conductor, or a farmer, or even, perhaps, an automobilist. . . . It occurred to me yesterday that all you wished to see in me you can find right at hand, face to face, in another: Medtner. . . . I have no prejudice against him. On the contrary! I love him very much, I respect him very much, and, to be perfectly frank (as always with you), I consider him the most talented of all the modern composers. He is—as musician and as man— one of those rare beings who gain in stature the more closely you approach them. That is the fate of very few! and may this bring him much good. But that is Medtner: young, healthy, bold, strong, armed—a lyre in his hands. And I am soul-sick, dear *Re,* and I regard myself as disarmed, and aging, as well. If there's any good in me, I'm not sure that any of it is in the future. . . .

To conclude with a few words of another kind. Ever attentive to your wishes, I am writing this letter on a "drowsy spring evening." This "drowsy evening" may be the reason for such an unforgivable letter, which I ask you to forget quickly. . . . The windows are closed. It's cold, dear *Re!* But then the lamp, according to your program, stands lit on the table. Thanks to the cold, those beetles that you love, but which I can't stand and which scare me, are, thank God, not yet born. We have on our windows great wooden shutters, which can be locked with iron bolts. This makes me calmer—in the evening, and at night. And here too, of course, I am just as criminally "timid and cowardly." I'm afraid of everything: mice, rats, beetles, bulls, robbers; I'm afraid when the wind blows and howls in the chimney, when the raindrops hammer on the window; I'm afraid of the dark, and so on. I don't like old attics and I'm even ready to believe that goblins exist (all this must interest you!), for otherwise it would be difficult to understand what I am afraid of, even in the daytime, when I am left alone in the house. . . . "Ivanovka" is an old estate that belongs to my wife. I think of it as mine, as my home—for I have lived here 23 years. It was here, long ago, when I was quite young, that I could work well. . . . However, this is an "old tune."

Together, the peace of Ivanovka and the enthusiasm of Marietta Shaginyan helped to bring Op. 34 into being. In sending the young poet his good news Rachmaninoff could not resist teasing her for her severe disapproval of his earlier use of Galina's poems; and he hinted of his recent accidental discovery that "Re" was Marietta Shaginyan:

June 19, 1912

Dear *Re,* a few days ago I finished my new songs. Almost half of them were written on poems from your notebooks. I'll list them, if it's of any interest to you.

Pushkin—"The Storm," "Arion," and "The Muse" (this last I dedicate to you).
Tiutchev—"You know him well," "I remember that day."
Fet—"With holy banner firmly held," "What happiness."
Polonsky—"Music," "Dissonance."
Khomyakov—"The Raising of Lazarus."
Maikov—"It cannot be." *
Korinfsky—"In the soul of each of us."
Balmont—"The migrant wind." . . .

Unfortunately, I could make no use of Galina's words. They didn't happen to be at hand.

I can say that in general I am satisfied and infinitely happy with all these songs, for they came to me so easily, with no great pain. Please God that I may continue to work this way. . . .

I received the "Anthology" ** that you sent. There are few poems in it that I like! and those not very much! I'm horrified by most of them. Occasionally I come across marginal notes by *Re:* "This is good" or "All of this is good." And I struggle long to understand, what did *Re* find that was good in this?!

I recalled a remark by M. Shaginyan, from another book I received: "It is sometimes very difficult to explain to someone else the meaning of a line of poetry." This remark applies exactly to the "Anthology."

Back in Moscow's hectic world of music Rachmaninoff made his conducting debut for the season with the Moscow Philharmonic, conducting the Berlioz *Symphonie Fantastique* on October 6. His next concert was on October 20, with Josef Hofmann as soloist, playing the Tchaikovsky and Liszt concertos. Though Engel compared Hofmann's performance of the Tchaikovsky unfavorably with Rachmaninoff's own performance of the preceding season, he did *not* like Rachmaninoff's interpretation in this same concert of Mozart's G minor Symphony. Two days later, however, in reviewing a Grieg program conducted by Rachmaninoff on the fifth anniversary of

* The first version of this song, dated March 7, 1910, was written on receiving the news of Vera Kommissarzhevskaya's death.
** The *Anthology* was a collection of modern Russian poems; the authors included, among others, Belyi, Briusov, Gorodetzky, and Soloviov.

Grieg's death, Engel was overwhelmed: "Rachmaninoff is a truly 'God-given' conductor who stirs both audience and orchestra. He may be the only great Russian conductor whom we can compare with such figures in the West as Nikisch, Colonne, Mahler." Comparing the impression of this concert with the Moscow Art Theater's new production of *Peer Gynt,* Engel wrote: "For Anitra's Dance alone, as conducted by Rachmaninoff, we would trade the whole Art Theater's production of Ibsen's play."

Rachmaninoff received further criticism, praise, complaint from his young poet admirer, who finally confessed her identity as Marietta Shaginyan. In his reply of November 12:

Thank you for your article.* There's a great deal in it that is interesting and to the point: and what is especially to the point you have already said to me in your letters. However, in the result, you are proved wrong: in summing up the content of the article, my "weight" seems exaggerated. My weight is actually far lighter (and it grows less each day). Now for the reproaches: you always have some. For example, dear *Re,* why should I be to blame for the fact that reporters concoct all sorts of tales about me in the press? And, "thinking" of me as a musician, is it possible that you can't guess that I am a person far removed from newspaper noise, and one who hates the sort of passages beloved by "tenors"!

Your reproaches in reference to Berlioz and Liszt convince me that you regard these composers negatively. I can only regret that we do not think alike of these composers. . . .

I don't have tuberculosis or anything of the sort. I'm just tired—very tired! and I exist on my last morsels of strength. (Yesterday, at a concert, for the first time in my life, during a *fermata,* I forgot what was to follow, and to the agony of the orchestra, I pondered for a painfully long time before I could recall *what* and *how* to continue conducting.) I pray God to get away from here soon. My songs will come out in about a month. "The Muse" is dedicated to *RE.* . . .

I impatiently await the book promised by *you.* Can't you point out to me something Russian that is new and interesting? (Only please nothing like the "Anthology"!) You've revealed your name to me. I must tell you that I've known it for a long while. I found out by chance.

All distinguished visitors to Moscow were eager for a private glimpse of Rachmaninoff. Busoni wrote to his wife (on November

* "S. V. Rachmaninoff," *Trudi i Dni,* July–October 1912.

19): "In the last days in Moscow I was visited by Josef Hofmann and Rachmaninoff—both of them musical darlings of Russia." Harold Bauer recorded his youthful encounter in his memoirs:

I met a number of distinguished musicians at Koussevitzky's home in Moscow. The man who interested me most was Rachmaninoff. During dinner we spoke of music in France, and Rachmaninoff, who had recently [in 1907] played his second concerto there with immense success, expressed his surprise at the prevailing catholicism in French musical taste. "They like everything," he said, "even their own moderns." I asked him if he played Debussy's piano pieces, and he said no, he did not care for that music. Koussevitzky, after dinner, asked me to play some Debussy, which I did. Rachmaninoff sat silent for a few moments, and then suddenly started up and began haranguing Koussevitzky. "Speak French or German," said the latter. Rachmaninoff turned to me and attempted to explain exactly why Debussy's music displeased him, but he was too excited and lapsed into his native tongue again, so I never found out.

The source of Rachmaninoff's irritation was neither Debussy nor Bauer. His composer's conscience was bothering him again; looking back at his work, he saw too little accomplished since 1910. To break away again from familiar demands and surroundings he decided to take his wife and children abroad. Before leaving, a meeting was finally arranged with the elusive "Re," an event as joyful for her as the coincident publication of her first book of poems, Orientalia (dedicated to Rachmaninoff). On December 5 the Rachmaninoffs departed for Berlin, Switzerland, and points South. The goal was Rome. Rachmaninoff told Riesemann:

In Rome I was able to take the same flat on the Piazza di Spagna that Modeste Tchaikovsky had used for a long time and which had served his brother as a temporary retreat from his numerous friends. It consisted of a few quiet, shady rooms belonging to an honest tailor. I lived, with my wife and children, at a pension, and went to the flat every morning to compose, remaining at work there till evening.

Nothing helps me so much as solitude. For me, it is possible to compose only when I am alone and nothing from the outside hinders the flow of ideas. These conditions were ideal in the flat on the Piazza di Spagna. All day long I spent at the piano or the writing desk, and not until the pines on the Monte Pincio were gilded by the setting sun did I put away my pen. Here I worked on my Second Piano Sonata, and the Choral Symphony, *The Bells. The Bells* had an unusual source. During the previous summer I had sketched a plan for a symphony, and then one day I received an anonymous letter, begging me to read Balmont's wonderful translation of Poe's poem, saying that the verses would be ideal for music and that they should appeal particularly to me. I read the enclosed poem, and decided at once to use it for a Choral Symphony in four movements. The necessary funereal finale had the precedent of Tchaikovsky, and need not be a strange conclusion for a symphony. I worked on this composition with feverish ardor, and it remains, of all my work, the one I like best. . . .

In his dictated reminiscences Rachmaninoff wrote:

The sound of church bells dominated all the cities of the Russia I used to know—Novgorod, Kiev, Moscow. They accompanied every Russian from childhood to the grave, and no composer could escape their influence.

One day at an estate of a friend—Chekhov loved fishing, for fishermen are not supposed to talk lest they frighten off the fish, and Chekhov was sparing of words—when the sound of church bells ringing at vespertide had died away, Chekhov turned to a friend and said, "I love to hear the bells. It is all that religion has left me." Faith and hope had fled, but the beauty of bell song still woke an echo in his soul.

All my life I have taken pleasure in the differing moods and music of gladly chiming and mournfully tolling bells. This love for bells is inherent in every Russian. One of my fondest childhood recollections is associated with the four notes of the great bells in the St. Sophia Cathedral of Novgorod, which I often heard when my grandmother took me to town on church festival days. The bellringers were artists. The four notes were a theme that recurred again and again, four silvery weeping notes, veiled in an everchanging accompaniment woven around them. I always associated the idea of tears with them. Many years later I composed a Suite for two pianos, in four movements, each developing a poetic motto. For the third movement, prefaced by Tiutchev's poem, "Tears," I knew at once the ideal theme—and the cathedral bells of Novgorod sang again. In my opera, *The Miserly Knight,* I used the same theme to express the tearful entreaties of the unfortunate widow who pleaded with the baron to spare her and her child. If I have been at all successful in making bells vibrate with human emotion in my works, it is largely due to the fact that most of my life was lived amid vibrations of the bells of Moscow. . . . In the drowsy quiet of a Roman afternoon, with Poe's verses before me, I heard the bell voices, and tried to set down on paper their lovely tones that seemed to express the varying shades of human experience. And there was the added stimulus of working in the room where Tchaikovsky had worked, of writing on the table on which he had written.

From the Piazza di Spagna Rachmaninoff wrote to "Dear *Re*" on March 23, 1913:

A few words about myself. . . . I was much better during my month in Switzerland, but I've lost all the good that did me, during my six weeks here. But I've been working a lot and I'm still working. It's too bad that I've again begun to get very tired, to sleep poorly, and to feel weak. By the way, this is why I haven't answered your letter for such an unpardonably long time. . . .

We'll stay here for about a month longer and we hope to get back to Moscow by Easter. Before that I have many, many things to do.

The "many, many things" were abruptly interrupted by the two girls' illness. It was typhoid fever, and the family rushed to Berlin, away from the Italian doctors Rachmaninoff never trusted. By the time the girls improved a return to Rome was out of the question.

When they returned to Ivanovka Rachmaninoff took on the estate's responsibilities with enthusiasm, developing a taste for farming that remained with him for the rest of his life. There were at that time very few automobiles in Russia outside the big cities, and Rachmaninoff's new automobile was the wonder of the countryside as well as his most pleasing recreation. He would visit friends 200 versts away— for the joy of driving for hours and hours over the black earth steppe. From Ivanovka he wrote to Marietta Shaginyan (then in the Tyrol) on July 29:

My children are now, thank God, quite well. As for myself, I have been able to work the whole day for the last two months. Whenever this work is too much for me, I get into my car and fly about 50 versts from here to the open air of the highway. I breathe the air and bless freedom and the blue sky. After such an air bath I feel bolder and stronger.

I finished a work not long ago.* A poem for orchestra, chorus, and solo voices. The text is Edgar Poe's *Bells*. Translation by Balmont.

---

* The score is dated July 27, 1913. Rachmaninoff later wrote, "I composed *The Bells* at Rome in 1913, and I orchestrated it and finished it in Russia, on my own estate."

There's one more work I must finish before leaving here. And from October on—concerts and tours, tours and concerts.

When he played his Second Concerto in Warsaw on October 17 a reviewer pointed to a fact that Rachmaninoff himself was already painfully aware of: that "it is a pity that Rachmaninoff doesn't refresh his repertoire; this is the fourth time he has played his Second Concerto here." There was a successful piano recital in Tiflis on November 9 before he went to St. Petersburg (via concerts at Voronezh and Saratov), where his recital, as usual, was hailed by the public. Vyacheslav Karatygin, reviewing the recital in *Rech*, was not impressed; in this critic's energetic campaign for the music of Musorgsky and the moderns (Reger, Debussy, Scriabin, and Stravinsky), it was necessary to oppose the Tchaikovsky-Rachmaninoff "tendency."

The public worships Rachmaninoff because he has hit the very center of average philistine musical taste. One need be neither joyous nor distressed to hear this fact. What is distressing is that the unusual musical gifts of Rachmaninoff always take a line tangent to art, brushing its sphere, never penetrating it. . . . Elegance of externals and insignificance of content are found together in most of Rachmaninoff's piano works. They are terribly "sincere." In them one hears an "experience" of some highly emotional feelings.

But these experiences are coarse, petty, affected. What a strange psychological riddle: Scriabin is very much inclined to affectation—it often seems that he not so much experiences certain musically artistic emotions as, with a terrific effort of will, excites himself to an illusory experience of them—and yet this affectation gives an impression of tremendous sincerity and power; whereas Rachmaninoff's music, saturated with "soul," lofty emotion, and the most sincere "experiences" in spite of them appears so full of pretension and affectation that one must put its "sincerity" in quotation marks.

Comparatively speaking, the most successful numbers on the program were a clever piano arrangement of his song "Lilacs" (though quite hackneyed, the original song must be considered the best composition that Rachmaninoff has yet written, and more poetic than its piano transcription) and his new sonata. The latter has no interesting or profound ideas, and exterior pianistic virtuosity dominates its musical potential, but it has some fresh and, for Rachmaninoff, rather unusual harmonies

and counterpoint. In certain passages of the central movement the composer shows an excellent inventive capacity for variations. It was interesting to note that this sonata, with musical aims far higher than all of this
composer's elegies, barcaroles, and préludes, was received by his public
with considerable reservation.

In the capital, rehearsals were begun on *The Bells,* and the newspaper announcement had a peculiar effect on one girl. Rachmaninoff's friend the cellist Bukinik recalls:

I had a cello pupil, a Miss Danilova, who once came to her lesson in
great agitation; while she played, she seemed very excited and eager to
tell me something. She finally revealed that Balmont's translation of
Poe's poem, *The Bells,* had once made a great impression on her—she
could think of it only as music—and who could write it as music but her
adored Rachmaninoff! That he must do this became her *idée fixe,* and she
wrote anonymously to her idol, suggesting that he read the poem and
compose it as music. She excitedly sent off this letter; summer passed, and
then in the autumn she came back to Moscow for her studies. What had
now happened was that she read a newspaper item that Rachmaninoff
had composed an outstanding choral symphony based on Poe's *Bells*
and that it was soon to be performed. Danilova was mad with joy. But
someone had to be told her secret—and that's how all her emotions were
unloaded during my lesson. She told me the whole story. I was astounded
to think that our reserved and quite unsentimental Rachmaninoff could
have been capable of being inspired by someone else's advice—to create
so important a work! I kept my pupil's secret till Rachmaninoff's death.

The first performance of *The Bells* on November 30, in a Siloti
concert conducted by the composer, was given as warm a reception
as any composer could wish for a new work. In *Russkaya Muzykalnaya Gazeta* Tyuneyev wrote:

Sincerity and spontaneity have always been close to Rachmaninoff's
muse, but against this tragic, sorrowing background, the concentrated
shades of hopeless anguish and despair that first appeared in *The Isle of
the Dead* reveal themselves with unusual clarity in *The Bells.* In Rachmaninoff's new poem are heard with special force the pessimistic passion
and sublime tragedy characteristic of a great artist and a noble heart.

Moscow's introduction to *The Bells* was greeted with the usual floral tribute from "White Lilacs," but it was something exceptional this time: bells of all sizes hanging from a crossbeam attached to a table. These bells were made of solid masses of white lilac blossoms—and it was February. The Lady of the Lilacs was probably present, enjoying not only the music, but also the surprise of composer and audience when the huge object was carried in. This first Moscow performance of *The Bells* was not given until February 8, 1914. Rachmaninoff returned from a concert visit to England in January, during which arrangements were made for the first English performance of *The Bells,* in Sheffield, in the autumn of 1914.

A post card brought this word from the composer at Ivanovka to Marietta Shaginyan at the end of April:

Today I heard from a committee arranging the celebration of Shakespeare's 350th anniversary, asking me to write a scene from *King Lear*—the scene on the moor. Tell me, is there a new translation of *Lear*? If not, which of the old ones is the best? Could I beg you to send me a copy at once? Though I possess neither envelopes nor Shakespeare, I do have a *conscience,* so I swear I'll refund you the cost of the book in stamps, along with my sincerest gratitude. How is your health? I am farming!!

There is no record of any composition at Ivanovka this year—and no further word of the *Lear* project.

Before autumn war brought down the barriers around Russia. Years passed before Russian musicians could travel abroad again. It was over twenty years before Sheffield heard *The Bells.*

Chapter 12

War and *Night Vigil*

THE farm at Ivanovka was a relaxation and a pleasure for Rachmaninoff; even the tasks of its maintenance that would have burdened a farmer were joyfully assumed by the composer. In the years away from Russia, Rachmaninoff always looked back on the springs and summers spent at Ivanovka as a blessing, and he was to make repeated efforts to find such a blessing again, on foreign soil. Years later, in dictating some autobiographical notes, he said:

In the spring of 1914 I almost realized my oldest dream for Ivanovka— the purchase of a good American tractor. This was being arranged through our Ministry of Agriculture, but not without some difficulties. I went to St. Petersburg to call on one of the directors at that Ministry whom I happened to know, and explained my wish to him. He spent considerable time and effort in dissuading me from this notion, pointing out that with all the horses I had (about a hundred, by that time) I did not need a tractor.

He finally asked me, rather excitedly, "But if you did get it, what would you do with it!?"

"I'll drive it myself," I replied.

He consented to put through my order, no doubt thinking that every man loses his mind in his own way. The tractor would be delivered in the fall. But I never saw it, for in August the war began.

Rachmaninoff's first concert of the season was devoted to the music of Anatoli Lyadov, who had died in August. The memorial concert, conducted by Rachmaninoff, included Lyadov's six symphonic "miniatures," some having their first performances on this occasion. Rachmaninoff's next several appearances were as soloist in a series of Russian programs arranged with Koussevitzky, for the benefit of soldiers' aid, in Kharkov, Kiev, and Moscow. Koussevitzky's fourth Moscow concert was a Rachmaninoff program: the Second Symphony, the Second Concerto, and *The Isle of the Dead*.

Restless to compose again, if possible in an unfamiliar medium, Rachmaninoff applied to Siloti on November 1:

My dear Sasha, I have a favor to ask you. If it should be unpleasant for you—forget it! I promise to bear no grudge. This is what's on my mind: I'd like to find a subject for a ballet. Do you happen to know Fokine or anyone among the Petrograd dancers, and would you ask about among them? Fokine would be best of all. At this end I will ask among the Moscow dancers, though I am acquainted with none of them, and for some reason I fear them!

Since the beginning of the war my work has been at a standstill. Nothing works out, and everything seems as repulsive as can be. Suddenly a few days ago I had this ballet idea. I believe that if someone now gives me a good and interesting theme, I could start composing at once.

I must also tell you that last spring a new ballet director at the Marinsky Theater—Andrianov?—approached me to accept a commission for a ballet to be done this season, mentioning three subjects. I spoke of a large fee and he promised to think it over, and is still thinking it over—and I now regret that I can't resume those negotiations, but I think you had best leave him in peace. Perhaps Telyakovsky knows something about this? In any case a dancer is needed, who will determine the number of bars and indicate all tempi.

Naturally everyone must be warned that a given subject might not suit me, or that a subject that pleases me might not suit the purpose. For if any nonsense should be handed to me,—I would refuse, and they would be offended!! Please think this over, Sasha—but not for as long as that director is thinking over my fee.

This project came to nothing,* and the inspiration for Rachmaninoff's next composition had a very different source.

In less than two weeks during January and February of 1915 Rachmaninoff composed his most important and most beloved liturgical work, a masterpiece in the repertory of Russian religious music. Usually referred to as his "Vespers," the *Night Vigil* is a service for the nightlong vigil in monasteries, and is sung in the Russian Orthodox Church on the eve of holydays. According to the rules of the Church, certain parts of this service must be written on traditional

---

* The choreographer Goleizovsky has said that in 1915 Rachmaninoff completed the major part of a ballet, *The Scythians*.

chants from the ritual, but six of the individual numbers could be treated more freely, and in these a composer was allowed to employ original melodies. In a letter to Joseph Yasser on the subject of "folk themes" (the full text is given on page 311), Rachmaninoff later explained that his approach to these six numbers was "a conscious counterfeit of the ritual—for example: 'Blessed is He,' and 'Mother of God.'" The *Night Vigil* was dedicated to the memory of Stepan Vasilyevich Smolensky, the kindly bespectacled authority on ancient church music who had introduced Rachmaninoff to the wealth of old Russian manuscript music.

Immediately on completion of the *Night Vigil*, Rachmaninoff played it for Kastalsky and Danilin, director and conductor of the Moscow Synodical Choir. In speaking to his first biographer, Rachmaninoff recalled this audition:

My favorite number in the work, which I love as I do *The Bells*, is the fifth canticle, "Lord, now lettest Thou Thy servant depart in peace" [Luke 2:29]. I should like this sung at my funeral. Towards the end there is a passage sung by the basses—a scale descending to the lowest B-flat in a very slow pianissimo. After I played this passage Danilin shook his head, saying, "Now where on earth are we to find such basses? They are as rare as asparagus at Christmas!" Nevertheless, he did find them. I knew the voices of my countrymen, and I well knew what demands I could make upon Russian basses!

Kastalsky announced the first performance of the new work (*Russkoye Slovo*, March 7), showing a pride in it that was especially generous, for he was himself Russia's most productive composer of church music:

Rachmaninoff's new composition, *Night Vigil*, is undoubtedly a contribution of great importance to our church's musical literature . . . one must hear for oneself how simple, artless chants can be transformed in the hands of a great artist. . . .

Of unusual value is this artist's loving and conscientious attitude towards our church chants, for in this lies the promise of a splendid future for our liturgical music.

The *Vigil* was first sung, for the benefit of war relief, on March 10 in Moscow, and this first performance gave its composer "an hour of the most complete satisfaction," so magnificent were the choir singers. Audience, musicians, and critics were enthusiastic; even Grigori Prokofiev, often Rachmaninoff's harshest critic, wrote that it was a great step forward from his *Liturgy* and remarked that "its miracle is in its fusion of the simple and the sincere." Over the next month the Choir gave five performances of the *Night Vigil*.

Of all reactions to the *Vigil,* none gave its composer more joy than that from his teacher Taneyev, always a severe critic of contrapuntal forms. As Rachmaninoff had employed counterpoint in most of the *Vigil's* fifteen numbers, he must have been particularly eager for Taneyev's praise of it. The praise came, warmer than ever—and the last that the student was to receive from his teacher; within three months Taneyev was dead.

Russia's musical losses in the first year of war were almost as stunning to the people as the losses at the front. On April 14, at the age of forty-three, Alexander Scriabin died of blood poisoning, the tragic result of a trivial accident. Years later Rachmaninoff recalled the most minute details of Scriabin's funeral—the rain, the crowd, the rain pouring down on the coffin and on the fresh grave—and his decision that day to devote his recitals and tour of the coming season to Scriabin's piano works. Full of this plan, he left for Khalila in Finland, near Siloti's home there, to study and prepare these unfamiliar works. Another who stood in the rain to watch the burial of Scriabin was Taneyev, and a cold that he caught that day worsened and developed into a fatal illness.

On June 6 Taneyev died, and among the sorrowing messages was one telegraphed from his student at Khalila: "Bright and dear to me the memory of him will be carefully guarded till the last day of my life." This was not all that Rachmaninoff wished to say of his great teacher. He addressed this letter to the Editor of *Russkiye Vedomosti:*

Sergei Ivanovich Taneyev is gone—composer, teacher, the most scholarly musician of his time, a man of rare originality, of rare spiritual quality, Moscow's musical leader, maintaining this high position with unwavering authority until the end of his days. For those of us who knew him and sought him out, he was the best of all judges, wise, righteous, affable, and direct. He was a model in everything, for everything he did was done well. Through personal example he taught us how to live, how to work, even how to speak, for he spoke in a peculiarly "Taneyev way:" concisely, to the point, wittily. Only necessary words came from his mouth. . . . All of us valued his advice and counsel—because we trusted it, because it was always good. To me he always seemed the personification of that "truth on earth" rejected by Salieri [in Pushkin's *Mozart and Salieri*]. . . . "All say there isn't truth on earth. But none is higher either . . ."

His apartment, his little house, attracted the most varied people, persons of all degree, people who seemed to have little in common—from novices to the musical great of all Russia. Here all felt at ease, all felt it a kind of home, all were treated tenderly, all were refreshed with new courage, and I would say that all lived and worked better after a visit to "Taneyev's little house." . . .

Taneyev wrote two cantatas that seem to bound his life as a composer; the first cantata was his first composition, the second was his last. The first was written in his "early spring"—the second, at sunset. In the first he sang in the words of John of Damascus: "I walk the unknown road"; in the words of the Lord he sang in the second, "Was it not I who mounted flames upon your heads?" Linking with these two phrases the farthest points of his creative activity, I should like to say that Sergei Ivanovich did not walk that "unknown road" long; with the powers of his mind, his heart, and his talent, he soon found his soul, and it showed him the road to the final height, where the lamp lit by God's flame shone so brightly.

And this lamp burned throughout his life with a steady, quiet flame, never flickering, never smoldering, lighting the path for others who ventured onto the strange "unknown" road. And if that lamp has now been extinguished, it is only because his life has also been extinguished.

S. Rachmaninoff

16th June 1915

Did Rachmaninoff also pay a musical tribute to Taneyev's memory? On September 21 he composed the pure singing line of his *Vocalise;* and in this year Jürgenson published for war relief an album contributed by various writers, artists, and composers, including Rachmaninoff, whose song, "From the Gospel of St. John," had for its text: "Greater love hath no man than this, that a man lay down his life for his friends."

Early in August Rachmaninoff sought in Moscow a more suitable atmosphere for work, and reported his summer troubles to Golden-weiser:

Up to June 15th I managed to do some work, but everything always dragged, and brought no satisfaction, and by the 15th I was at a point where I could no longer control either my work or myself, so I gave up trying. Whenever dissatisfaction drags on for so long, I always reach this point. After that my days were spent in nothing more than reading, walking, and sinking further into anguish. Then I visited Sasha Siloti, and enjoyed myself for a whole week. I led this sensible life until July 15th, when I again tried to work. This time things seemed to go better, but the atmosphere grew heavier and unhappier. Bad news from the front, anxieties about our ill-advised residence [in Finland], a new draft summons to give me another medical examination, etc.—all this made it absolutely impossible to concentrate on work. So I escaped to Moscow, trusting to a better fate here. . . .

Day before yesterday, when the war news seemed particularly discouraging, I was dragged to a symphony concert, to which I didn't at all care to go, but the compositions I heard there* by Tchaikovsky, Korsakov, and Glazunov breathed new life into me. My "funereal features" brightened and I saw with new clarity that my nature is principally a musical one, and that the best prescription for it is always "musical rays."

In a few days I leave for Tambov to take a new examination. If I'm drafted, I am almost assured the choice of leading a bishop's choir or conducting a park orchestra in Tambov. Not so bad.

With his first appearance of the season, Rachmaninoff began the fulfillment of his pledge over Scriabin's grave: he played Scriabin's F-sharp minor Concerto in Siloti's Petrograd concert of September 26. When Koussevitzky opened his season with a memorial cycle of Scriabin concerts, for the benefit of Scriabin's family, the first of these (on October 11) included both the First Symphony and the Third with Rachmaninoff again playing the Concerto. After a tour through the southern provinces with two recital programs, one of his own works, the other of Scriabin's piano works, Rachmaninoff gave his first Moscow recital of the season, with his own program. In the

* The program included Tchaikovsky's First Symphony, Glazunov's *Spring*, and Rimsky-Korsakov's *Capriccio Espagnole*.

intermission of this recital Marietta Shaginyan saw him in one of his blackest moods:

...the reception of Rachmaninoff was so tempestuous that it was difficult for us to push our way through the crowd. We finally reached the artists' room, where we saw at once from the expression on Rachmaninoff's face that he was in an awful state: he was biting his lip furiously, his complexion was yellow. As we opened our mouths to congratulate him he exploded in complaint—he must be losing his mind, he's growing decrepit, better discard him altogether, prepare his obituary; once there was a musician, but that's all over now, he could never forgive himself, and so on. "Didn't you notice that I missed the point? Don't you understand—I let the point slip!" On a later occasion he explained that each piece he plays is shaped around its culminating point: the whole mass of sounds must be so measured, the depth and power of each sound must be given with such purity and gradation that this peak point is achieved with an appearance of the greatest naturalness, though actually its accomplishment is the highest art. This moment must arrive with the sound and sparkle of a ribbon snapped at the end of a race—it must seem a liberation from the last material obstacle, the last barrier between truth and its expression. The composition itself determines this culmination; the point may come at its end or in the middle, it may be loud or soft, yet the musician must always be able to approach it with sure calculation, absolute exactitude, for if it slips by the whole structure crumbles, the work goes soft and fuzzy, and cannot convey to the listener what must be conveyed. Rachmaninoff added, "I am not the only one who experiences this—Chaliapin, too. At one of his concerts while the audience was wild with enthusiasm, he was backstage tearing his hair because the point had slipped."

When Shaginyan, at his request, told him stories during a practice period, and complained about the eternal polishing of a single phrase, Rachmaninoff explained, half-jokingly, "You have to peer into every corner, take every screw apart, so that you can then easily put the whole together again."

Rachmaninoff's November 18 program was of Scriabin's piano works, and the recital aroused a storm of protest and anger from Scriabin's Moscow admirers. In this audience was a young composer, Sergei Prokofiev, who had met the older composer earlier this year:

... among other works he played the 5th Sonata. Now when Scriabin played this sonata it all somehow took wings, but with Rachmaninoff all its notes stood very clearly and firmly on the ground. Among the Scriabinites in the audience there was a disturbance—someone was holding Alchevsky, the tenor, by the tails of his coat, while he shouted: "Wait, I'll go and have it out with him!" I tried to suggest an objective point of view: though we were accustomed to the composer's interpretation, perhaps there are other ways of playing this work. Entering the artists' room, I continued my thought as I spoke to Rachmaninoff: "And yet, Sergei Vasilyevich, you played very well." Rachmaninoff smiled acidly—"And you probably thought I'd play badly?" and he turned away to someone else. This put an end to our good relations. Some part in this was certainly contributed by Rachmaninoff's rejection of my music, and the irritation it provoked in him.*

The entire press had been transformed by Scriabin's death from his denunciators to his eulogists, and Rachmaninoff offered himself as their sacrificial goat. In *Russkaya Muzykalnaya Gazeta* Grigori Prokofiev wrote:

... the audience was generous in its appreciation, though it distinctly sensed that something was wrong. Rachmaninoff played with his usual technical perfection and the musical quality natural to him, but in his approach to Scriabin's works, he did not (or did not wish to) grasp the basic nature of this music—the unprecedented emotional saturation of Scriabin's creative power. ... As if seeking a logic in Scriabin's harmonic structure, Rachmaninoff artificially condensed the tempi. This showed the harmonic line with extraordinary clarity, but—the vital spirit was gone! ... You should have seen the disappointment with which the admirers of Scriabin's later piano works looked at each other as they heard the innocuous and prosaic interpretation of the *Satanic Poem*, or the academically chilled treatment of the Second and Fifth sonatas.

Rachmaninoff went to Petrograd to play his Second Concerto at a Siloti concert, to play a recital of his piano works, and to repeat his controversial Scriabin program, and there were similar reactions from the Petrograd critics.

* In 1945, speaking to Alexander Werth of his musical tastes, Prokofiev said, "Rachmaninoff—well, I'd rather say nothing about him. The truth is we hated each other's guts!"

Rachmaninoff is a composer [wrote Glinsky] of clearly and frankly expressed tendency towards musical ideas of the past. He organically developed along his somewhat outmoded lines, and his place now among
contemporary musicians is as the last of the musical Mohicans of the past
century, stubbornly ignoring new trends in music. His musical personality is based on formulae borrowed from neoclassicism. Controlled by
those technical means that Tchaikovsky bestowed on Russian music,
Rachmaninoff seasoned this old style with originality and spontaneity. . . .
His own artistic individuality imposed on another composer's work in-
evitably changes that work, giving it the character of its executant. This
was obvious in his interpretation of Scriabin's works. . . . That super-
sensual melody of Scriabin was brought back to earth, saturated in Rachmaninoff's own melodic style.

Joseph Yasser, who attended Rachmaninoff's Scriabin concerts, has
another explanation for the Scriabinites' disappointment:

One of Rachmaninoff's corrections of established attitudes can be seen
in his interpretation of Scriabin who at one time used to be viewed as a
musical descendant of Chopin, Liszt, Wagner and even, partly, of
Debussy. To the dismay of Scriabin's numerous disciples, Rachmaninoff
transformed him, with justice, into a fundamentally Russian composer
with all the characteristics of the Moscow school trained in the tradition
of Tchaikovsky.

For both Rachmaninoff and Siloti the "Scriabin issue" brought
their war with the critics into the open; Siloti announced that free
tickets to his concerts would no longer be sent to critics, and Rachmaninoff answered a questionnaire sent him by the Moscow magazine, *Teatr:*

I can only say that a critic must be a man of knowledge who is honest,
clever, and sensitively responsive. Without these qualities, a critic is no
critic, and does not deserve the public's attention. Through his lack of
fundamental knowledge such a writer leads the public astray—thus
hindering art, not helping it.

During the past summer Koussevitzky had purchased the Gutheil
music publishing firm, thus making himself Rachmaninoff's sole publisher and copyright holder. He stepped into the controversy, on
Rachmaninoff's side, by giving an ambitious program of his works

in Moscow on November 30; this included the two cantatas, *Spring* and *The Bells,* with the composer playing his Third Concerto. At another Koussevitzky concert, on January 24, 1916, Nezhdanova sang a group of Rachmaninoff's songs to his accompaniment. This group ended with the new *Vocalise* (dedicated to Nezhdanova), which was received so warmly that Nikolai Struve suggested that Rachmaninoff orchestrate it for a later concert. The composer's Moscow season ended with his participation in a concert of his chamber works.

During the war Rachmaninoff had retreated farther into his antisocial shell—so far, indeed, that when his old friend Avierino came to Moscow to be married, he hesitated to invite Rachmaninoff to a stag supper before the wedding.

I knew his fear of crowds, so I went personally to invite him, swearing to take him home no later than midnight. He promised to come, and came. There was a fine supper and a fine mood; throughout supper there were jolly toasts, with Chaliapin making especially witty ones. What with the noise and gaiety I forgot all about my promise to Sergei Vasilyevich, and it was 2 A.M. before I remembered to look for him. There was a burst of laughter—Moskvin and Chaliapin were dancing an indescribable polka, while Könemann played the piano, and there behind him, hidden by the piano, sat Sergei Vasilyevich, literally weeping with laughter.

"Well, Seryozha," I said when I finally reached him, "time to go home. I promised to deliver you by midnight—and look at the time now!"

"Oh no, brother—I'm not going now. . . ."

A less successful attempt to draw Rachmaninoff into other worlds was made by the Moscow Art Theater, by inviting him to write the music for their production of Alexander Blok's poetic play, *The Rose and the Cross.* After one conference with the author, the producer, and the designer, Rachmaninoff begged out of a task that would involve him with so many new acquaintances.

In his southern tour this summer, Rachmaninoff played at Rostov. Knowing that Shaginyan was living in Nakhichevan, a town near Rostov, he wrote to ask if he might go there on the day after his concert. She recalls the dark mood of his visit:

He was obsessed with a fear of death. I remember that he asked my mother to tell his fortune with cards—was he to live much longer? A story by Artzibashev, about death, had made a terrible impression on him—"It's impossible to live while one knows one must die after all. How can you bear the thought of dying?" While saying this, he had unconsciously begun to eat from a plate of roasted salted pistachio nuts that we always had ready for him. He shifted a little nearer the plate, then looked at it, realized the incongruity, and broke into laughter—"The pistachio nuts have made my fear go away. Do you know where?" My mother gave him a whole sack of them to take along to Moscow to cure his fear of death.

Soon after Rachmaninoff joined his family at Ivanovka a pain in his right temple made them anxious, and the doctor sent him to the Caucasus to drink mineral waters and take mineral baths for a few weeks. In his absence his father came to Ivanovka to wait for his son's return and to remain there for the summer. Since 1892 the father had seen little of his son, and the lonely city dweller had long looked forward to these months with his son's family in the country.

In the Caucasus, at the resort of Essentuki, Rachmaninoff renewed acquaintance with Nina Koshetz, a young soprano whom he had admired, and met, and accompanied the previous winter. The first of his extant letters to Nina Koshetz—this correspondence has a worldly, gay tone in contrast to the gently paternal voice of his letters to Marietta Shaginyan—is a brief note of apology and appointment:

Dear Nina Pavlovna, I've had my bath and am now resting. Last evening Stanislavsky dropped in unexpectedly and stayed the whole evening. I am very sorry I couldn't come to you. Today I hoped to see you, but "the rain came, and stopped, and came again."* Perhaps we'll see each other at 5:30, in our pleasant pavilion near Spring No. 3? Or could you come here at 4:30, or for supper? All these plans are good. Which do you prefer? Till we meet. I send with this your umbrella—for the rain and to deceive the eyes. I kiss your hands.   S. R.

Before leaving Essentuki, Rachmaninoff and Koshetz agreed to perform a group of his songs at one of Siloti's chamber concerts in the fall. When Rachmaninoff returned to Ivanovka in mid-August, he found a mourning household: his father had just died of a heart attack.

---

* From *The Miserly Knight.*

On September 1 Rachmaninoff wrote to Nina Koshetz:

Highly esteemed Nina Pavlovna, or dear Ninochka, or Ninushka, or *perfidious* Naina! So you've abandoned the Caucasus, and it can enjoy a peace and quiet undisturbed by your mischief and deviltry. The patients there can now recuperate. I rejoice for them. And Moscow is much better for you. There, at least, some watch can be kept over you. . . .

As for your appearance at the Siloti concert, I wrote Siloti the day I received your telegram, asking him to change the order of the concerts. But my request came too late; the schedule had been set by then, as he wired you. So there's nothing to be done about that. As for the program, we have plenty of time. Let him print whatever he wants now, and we can change it as *we* wish. You must sing new songs that I'll give you when I come to Moscow. How much I'll have written and how satisfactory by then—I don't know. But I should think that the first and third parts of the program should be old songs, and that the second part should contain new ones. I'll arrive about September 10.

Op. 38, Rachmaninoff's only completed composition of 1916, is a group of six songs, dedicated to Nina Koshetz. One song, the famous "Daisies," is undated, but four of the six are dated September 12 and 14.* All six use texts by modern Russian poets, and this may have reminded him of the young poet who had always urged these new poems on him. He wrote to Marietta Shaginyan on September 20:

In cleaning my desk today I reread some of your letters to me, dear *Re!* . . . I felt so much tenderness, gratitude, and something more that is bright and good, that I was stabbed by a need to see you this very minute, to hear your voice, to sit by you, and to have a good, hearty talk with you, to talk about you, about me, about anything you wish. Perhaps to be silent, but mainly—to see you and sit next to you. . . . Where are you, dear *Re?* And how soon shall I see you?

Before his Moscow concert season began, Rachmaninoff composed some piano pieces that were to be included in the later *Etudes-Tableaux* of Op. 39. The new songs of Op. 38 were sung in a Mos-

---

* There are two more songs of this year, left in sketch and unpublished: "Prayer," to a poem by K[onstantin] R[omanov], and "All Wish to Sing," to a poem by Fyodor Sologub. These manuscripts are owned by Mme. Koshetz, to whom they were given by the composer.

cow recital by Nina Koshetz on October 24, with the composer as accompanist. Engel wrote:

On such occasions the singer is usually the center of attention, and no one cares about the accompanist. For once it was the other way round. The accompanist was the center of the evening, not only *de jure* as the creator of all that was performed, but *de facto* as well, as an incomparable artist who gave his compositions the flesh and blood of sound, and kindled them with a vital breath that penetrated the interpretation by both performers. . . .

The unpublished new songs that occupied the final section of the program are written to texts by modernist poets who had not previously attracted Rachmaninoff's attention (Belyi, Blok, Severyanin, Sologub, and others). His approach to the problem of giving musical embodiment to new literary forms seems to have been a correct one: he did not emulate those composers who may be closer to the new poetry, but sought in himself those chords that responded independently to this poetry.

This season fresh critical attitudes toward Rachmaninoff can be detected in the reception of his works and his recitals. Rachmaninoff as pianist was gaining stature, and a new element was noticed in his recent compositions. His Petrograd recitals surprised the critic of *Russkaya Muzykalnaya Gazeta*:

In the *Etudes*, opus 39, Rachmaninoff appears in a new light. The soft lyricist begins to employ a more severe, concentrated, and deepened mode of expression. We noticed a dramatic mood, in the E-flat minor *étude*, and even a demoniac one in the F-sharp minor, the best of the group! Some significant change has taken place in this interesting creative talent, and we shall doubtless witness new vistas that are thus opening to the composer of *Francesca* and *The Miserly Knight*.

In Moscow, where he played eight of these new *Etudes-Tableaux*, Engel wrote:

"Who among Russian pianists is strongest, and most radiant?" For me the choice is clear: Rachmaninoff. . . .

It is not amazing that with such pianism the music itself, though his own, should seem merely accessory to his pianism, even a by-product of it—and that it should seem less important than his performance of it. When I recently expressed such an idea, after hearing him accompany some new songs, I received an anonymous letter from a group in Petrograd, reproaching me bitterly. But what should I have said?! I wrote what I believed, and this was dictated by no lack of respect for him as a composer, but on the contrary, by love and faith in him. . . .

Yet I could not repeat this comment after hearing him play the new series of *Etudes-Tableaux*. . . . These are lovely pieces, independent of their performer even when he is Rachmaninoff himself (though always more captivating in his performance, I'm sure). Seven of the eight are in a minor key. . . . A new feeling hangs suspended over the entire opus. In one the shadows are faint (2, A minor), in another, tempests gather force (6, A minor),* in another a break can be seen through heavy, heavy clouds (5, E-flat minor), but nowhere do we find happiness, calm, ease. . . . Yet throughout them all, life pulses, saying in sound what has to be said, and saying it beautifully. . . . The most attractive of the group is probably that in B minor—a wonderful piece, somewhat "humoresque," sharply rhythmic.

Leonid Sabaneyev wrote in *Muzykalni Sovremennik,* the organ of young Russian music:

This great talent is now in a period of search. Evidently the individuality originally formed by the composer (the culminating point of which I consider to be the extraordinary Second Concerto) has for some reason ceased to satisfy the composer. . . .

The searches of a great talent are always interesting. Although personally I cannot consider Rachmaninoff a musical phenomenon of the highest order (for me his personality as musician, as conductor, and especially as pianist must be placed above his career as composer, in which I acknowledge him as an outstanding talent—no more), nevertheless one senses in him a tremendous inner power, a potentiality that some barrier prevents from emerging fully . . . his artistic personality contains the promise of something greater than he has yet given us.

The Rachmaninoff-Koshetz program was successfully repeated in Petrograd and in Kharkov. While plans were being made to take it to Kiev and other southern cities, Rachmaninoff heard that Nina Koshetz had signed a contract, and wrote to her at once:

Is this really true? Why didn't you tell me about it? And is it possible that

* For comparison of these critical "programs" with the composer's own programs for these two *études,* as he described them to Respighi, see pages 262–63.

before signing you showed it to no "grownup"? In such matters you are worse than a child. I am afraid that merely because you've chatted with some acquaintances about an attractive proposal, you are ready to sign anything. This is, unfortunately, very like you. Did you limit the length of the tour? Has the itinerary been shown to you? ...

Greetings on the approaching holiday. I wish for you all that you could wish for yourself, though I fear this may mean general catastrophe to all pilots, a complete havoc in every shop that sells precious objects, and a universal fainting at every concert where you appear.

I stay in the country for about three more days, and then I go to Moscow, to visit the Koussevitzkys if my family has gone out there.

The second concert of the Bolshoi Theater Orchestra on January 7, 1917 was a triumphant climax of Moscow's adulation of Rachmaninoff. He conducted his three programmatic works, *The Crag, The Isle of the Dead,* and *The Bells,* and the audience's enthusiasm for their musical hero turned the occasion into an ovation.

Following this concert and a recital of his works on January 9, Rachmaninoff left on a three-week tour of southern cities—Kiev, Kharkov, Rostov, Taganrog. Marietta Shaginyan and her mother had moved into Rostov, and when Rachmaninoff arrived there for his recital at the Music School on January 26, he sent her a message:

Dear *Re,* I've just arrived after enormous delays. I leave tomorrow morning, and I'll not be coming back here.

I want very much to see you, but I can't come to you. Perhaps you can come to me before the concert, at the Music School!? I promise we'll be alone. If you come at 6:30, we can sit together for about an hour and a half. I'll play for you, and you'll tell me things—all right? Here are my songs.

This was his last meeting with *Re,* but it could not have been a completely sad hour and a half, for there was, in the new group of songs, some tangible result of their relationship. From its beginning Shaginyan had campaigned to have Rachmaninoff use better poems, more genuine, living poets, for his songs, and the songs of Op. 38 were a vindication of her efforts.

Sergei Prokofiev gives us a glimpse of Sergei Rachmaninoff on his return to Moscow. At an Evening of Modern Music (February 5) the program was devoted to Prokofiev's chamber music, including the first performance of his songs on Akhmatova's poems.

Among those invited were Rachmaninoff and Medtner. Throughout the concert Medtner fumed and fussed, "If that's music, I'm no musician." Rachmaninoff, though, sat like a stone idol, and the Moscow audience, that usually received me well, was confused as it watched its hero's reaction to my music.

February was a month of demonstrations—for bread, against the war, against the government and its policies; the demonstrations developed into a general strike, in Petrograd on February 26 the strike had gained the power to push, and the Tzar and his government toppled. In Moscow on that afternoon Rachmaninoff gave a recital, a charity concert with fifty per cent of the proceeds to go to the All-Russia Cities Union to help the sick and wounded of the army. By the next morning Russia was a different country; when Rachmaninoff received his fee for the concert he sent his thousand rubles to be spent for the benefit of released political prisoners and to buy gifts for the army of "my now liberated country."

That was Rachmaninoff's last piano recital in his "now liberated country" of Russia. When he appeared as a soloist in the March orchestral concerts conducted by Koussevitzky and Emil Cooper, these were his last appearances—forever—before Moscow audiences. The concerts conducted by Koussevitzky on March 13 and 20 were a Tchaikovsky program, in which Rachmaninoff played the B-flat minor concerto, and a Liszt-Scriabin program, with Rachmaninoff playing the Liszt E-flat major concerto. To these two concertos he added his own Second Concerto in a charity concert on March 25 "for the needs of the army," with Cooper conducting. Few members of that audience at the Bolshoi Theater were ever to see Rachmaninoff again.

Immediately afterward he left for Ivanovka to look after the spring sowing. As the children were in school and his wife remained with them in Moscow, Rachmaninoff joined them at the end of the school term, and they spent a troubled summer together in the Crimea. The joy that Rachmaninoff had felt in the February Revolution was displaced by anxiety at the look of events. The inactivity and impotence of the Provisional Government distressed him. The charm of the Crimean summer shore did little to dispel his presentiments. Previously, on June 1 he had written desperately to Siloti from Essentuki:

I have a favor that I beg you to act on as quickly as possible. I'll be brief. First a few sentences of explanation: I've spent almost my entire earnings on the Ivanovka estate. It now represents an investment of about 120 thousand rubles. Yet I am ready to write this off, for I see another crash in store for me. Besides, living conditions here seem so much better than there that I've decided not to return there. I have about 30 thousand left— which is "something," especially if I can work and continue to earn.

But I fear another crash: everything around me affects me so that I can't work and I'm afraid of going completely sour. Everyone advises me to leave Russia temporarily. But where and how? Is it possible?

Can you possibly catch M. I. T[ereshchenko, Foreign Minister] at a free moment to consult him about this? Could I count on receiving a passport for all our family to go at least to Norway, Denmark, Sweden? It makes no difference where! Anywhere!

Could I obtain such a permit by July? Can any money be taken? How much?

Please talk with him! Perhaps he can suggest something else! He who is at the summit has the widest view! Please talk with him, and answer me, quickly.

Your S. R.

Siloti seems to have been able to do little in the matter at this hectic time. The summer's news from Petrograd grew worse. Antigovernment demonstrations were countered with wholesale arrests. The Russian Army was defeated in Galicia, and in August General Kornilov attempted to seize Petrograd and power. On September 5, in Yalta, Rachmaninoff made his last public appearance in Russia, playing the Liszt concerto.

The family returned to their Moscow apartment on Strastnoi Boulevard, and to take his mind off surrounding pressures Rachmaninoff began a long-delayed task: the revision of his First Concerto. He became so engrossed in this work as not to notice that the shots and machine gun rattlings on the night of October 25 meant another change of Government. He had no taste for the first duty imposed upon him by the new government: to attend house com-

mittee meetings with the other tenants and to take his turn at guarding the house at night.

Public musical activity was suspended until the return of
"normal" conditions, and an atmosphere conducive to composition
never seemed more remote from Rachmaninoff than now. After completing his revision of Op. 1, on November 10, there was a gap that
he could fill only with piano practice and with thinking. The thinking did not make him happy. In the two weeks since the Bolshevik
revolution he had felt an increasing antagonism to the new regime.
All three sides of his career appeared blocked, no one could guess for
how long. He had to break through the impasse, somehow. A
solution to his immediate problem was offered to him, but his ac-
ceptance created far more serious problems that remained with him
till his dying day as an émigré.

Some three weeks after the Revolution he received a telegram—an
invitation from a Swedish concert manager to appear in Stockholm.
This was his first offer from abroad since the beginning of the war,
and its arrival at this moment was attributed by Rachmaninoff "to
the grace of God." He replied at once that he would accept the engagement. Money had to be borrowed from friends, and Swedish
visas had to be obtained for the family. No one questioned this
strangely large-scale departure for concerts in Sweden. When he
showed some concern lest a collapsed exchange rate wipe out his
borrowed funds (500 rubles were permitted each traveler), a friend
pointed to Rachmaninoff's hands: "You needn't worry—there's your
exchange rate!" The last pieces of music he composed in Russia are
dated November 14 and 15, 1917. One is a 63-bar sketch, a speeding,
irresistible rhythm that sounds a desperate wish to break through to
some other life—a piece of music that was later to be nicknamed the
"Orient Express." Another is an equally short piece that he was to
publish under a subtly tragic title—"Fragments." And there is an unpublished piano work in D minor, dated November 14—a dark and
harsh piece.

In order to obtain permits to leave Russia, Rachmaninoff went on
to Petrograd alone, a few days ahead of his wife and daughters. At
six o'clock one evening at the end of November he and his sister-in-
law Sophia boarded a streetcar that jerked them through the unlit

streets of Moscow to the Nikolayevski Station. Through the drizzle and dusk they could hear scattered shots. The ride was a grim and bleak ordeal. Rachmaninoff carried one small suitcase; the only music in it was his first act of *Monna Vanna,* sketchbooks containing the new piano pieces, and the score of Rimsky-Korsakov's *Golden Cockerel.* He had turned over the revised First Concerto to Koussevitzky's firm. At the station they met an employee of the Diederichs piano company who had bought the ticket and promised to find him a seat on the jammed overnight train to Petrograd. Only Sophia Satina and a stranger were there to say farewell to Rachmaninoff as he left Moscow forever.

The Rachmaninoffs left Russia on December 23, accompanied by the composer's best friend, Nikolai Struve. No one saw them off at the Petrograd station—though Chaliapin sent them a note attached to a package of caviar and homemade white bread for the journey, an attention that deeply touched Rachmaninoff. None of the expected complications or misunderstandings occurred, either on the train or in crossing the Finnish frontier. The customs inspector who searched their luggage showed interest only in the books that he found, until he saw that these were the children's schoolbooks. He bade the family a polite farewell, wishing Rachmaninoff success in his concerts. The road from the Finnish to the Swedish border was traveled in an open sledge, and it was long after midnight when they reached their last stage, the train to Stockholm.

From the manuscript of *Monna Vanna*; Act I is dated April 15, 1907, Dresden.

First page of an unpublished piano piece, dated November 14, 1917.

Virtuoso

WHEN the weary Rachmaninoffs arrived in Stockholm on the afternoon of December 24, the gaiety of the holiday shoppers only increased the loneliness and anguish of the exiles. On Christmas Eve Rachmaninoff, surrounded by his family, sat in their hotel room, feeling more desolate than he had ever felt—even when he had tried not to hear the fiasco of his First Symphony.

The Stockholm invitation was put aside until his mind and fingers were more willing to work, and as their one friend, Struve, had joined his family in Denmark, the Rachmaninoffs moved there as soon as a landlord could be found who permitted a piano. The ground floor of a house was finally rented in the suburbs of Copenhagen, and Rachmaninoff plunged into practice for his Scandinavian concerts.

This first winter and spring of exile were dreary indeed. The whole burden of the household was on Mme. Rachmaninoff alone, for her husband had to take the utmost care of his hands. His single chore was to light the stubborn stoves each morning, but on a marketing trip to town his wife slipped and broke her arm, and for a while he assumed all household duties. The summer at Charlottenlund, in a villa shared with the Struves, was not very restful: the servant girl they engaged for the summer had not mentioned that she was epileptic.

Rachmaninoff's first appearance as an émigré artist was on February 15, 1918 with the Copenhagen Symphony Orchestra, conducted by Hoberg. He played his Second Concerto. A week later he gave a recital of his own compositions in Copenhagen before playing his delayed concerts in Stockholm. There, on March 12, he played his Second Concerto and Liszt's First Concerto, and on March 14 Tchaikovsky's First Concerto, both concerts being conducted by Georg Schneevoigt. His first piano recital in Stockholm, on March 18, was of his own works, a program repeated in Malmö on March

22. After this month alone and away from his family, he took an offer to play his Second Concerto and the Tchaikovsky concerto in Copenhagen on April 16; then to Oslo for his Second Concerto and the Liszt concerto on April 20, followed by two piano recitals here on April 24 and 26. On May 2 he shared a program with the singer Skalontz in her Stockholm performance of his songs. His concert season ended on July 10 in Copenhagen, where he played his Second Concerto for the third time.

With the fees for these twelve concerts Rachmaninoff was able to get back on his feet, pay his debts, and rest long enough to look around before making his next move. One thing was clear: he would have to give up composition for a long time. In order to give his daughters an education and to provide some security for the family, he would need a regular income. Beneath these practical, reasonable motives, there ran a deeper, less "reasonable," and increasingly habitual motive: a refusal to compose, so firm a refusal that he had to interpret it to himself as an *inability* to compose. Uprooted, isolated from all that was native and familiar, Rachmaninoff had a difficult decision to make; yet he was not aware of all that compelled him to make it.

The adoption of a pianist's career, and the preparation for it, would require a maximum effort. He realized that the engagements of a composer pianist would always be limited; he must transform himself into a virtuoso pianist. For this his daily life would have to be changed, his long-neglected technique would have to be overhauled —and a large new repertory would have to be built. All the demands he made on himself in playing his own compositions were multiplied in playing the works of other composers. In this respect (as in most others) his scrupulousness was severe and taxing. At the age of forty-five this great artist went to work on his new career with the energy and persistence of a young and ambitious musician.

Rachmaninoff had rarely played recitals in which his own music occupied a minor place. His first two recitals of the next season, at Lund and Malmö on September 18 and 19, were therefore trials for the new career. These two programs displayed most of his summer work: Mozart, Schubert, Beethoven (Op. 10, No. 3), Chopin, Tchaikovsky. Between September 18 and October 18 Rachmaninoff gave 14 concerts. At one more concert in Stockholm, conducted by Schneevoigt, he played both his Second Concerto and his Third—the last performances before his next big step.

With the end of Karl Muck's contract with the Boston Symphony Orchestra, its manager Charles Ellis sought a successor for Muck. One approach was made to Ossip Gabrilowitsch in New York, and his response to Ellis, on April 23, gallantly suggested another:

I hear that Rachmaninoff, the great Russian composer, is in great distress, his entire money having been confiscated and his country estate devastated during recent disturbances in Russia. He is at present a refugee in Denmark. Although I have not heard from him direct, I am sure that he would be glad to come to America, and I can think of no man better fitted for the position of Boston Symphony conductor than he. I do not have to tell you that Rachmaninoff is one of the greatest musicians of today, you know that as well as I do. Moreover, having heard him direct his compositions in Boston some years ago, you know what a splendid orchestra conductor he is.

I sincerely hope, Mr. Ellis, that you will not misunderstand the spirit which prompts me to make this suggestion to you, nor think that I do not appreciate highly enough the possibility of the Boston conductorship being offered to me. No one admires the Boston Symphony Orchestra more than I do, and indeed I fully realize that an offer to become its conductor—if such an offer were made to me—would be a very great honor, but I am willing to see that honor bestowed on one who is worthier of it.

To get Rachmaninoff would, in my opinion, be a splendid thing for Boston and a splendid thing for Rachmaninoff in his present situation, particularly.

The newly organized Board of Trustees for the Boston Symphony Orchestra adopted the recommendation by Gabrilowitsch and cabled Rachmaninoff an offer to conduct 110 concerts in thirty weeks. This was the third cabled proposal from the United States that he had received: the Wolfsohn Bureau offered him the post of conductor (for two years) of the Cincinnati Symphony; the Metropolitan Concert Bureau sent him Altschuler's proposal of 25 piano recitals. Though the Boston offer seemed the most attractive of the three, the number of concerts disturbed Rachmaninoff; he had no programs ready, and time would be too short to prepare so extended a schedule. After a brief hesitation he declined all three offers, but they had helped him make up his mind.

The idea of moving to America, far from the scene of war and outside the tiny circuit of neutral countries open to him in Europe, had for some time seemed advantageous. The three offers showed him that he would surely find work and audiences somewhere in America. With October ending he realized that it was too late to organize tours or to hire halls for the current American season: yet he decided to take his family there on pure speculation, with no contract, relying solely on his powers and his hopes. He had money for the journey, but little more. When the émigré Russian banker Kamenka heard of the risk that Rachmaninoff was taking—to live in the United States for a while before being able to work there—he advanced him enough to cover a considerable delay in employment, an assistance that the composer always recalled with deep gratitude.

The last hours in Europe were crowded. Another cable came from Boston, and was declined. An American visa was needed, and the American Consul in Copenhagen issued one promptly when he saw the three invitations. At the last minute, when the family were already aboard the small Norwegian steamer in Oslo harbor, a box was thrust into Rachmaninoff's hands: more money for his security.

The *Bergensfjord* steamed from Oslo on November 1, 1918 out into the center of the war: on the North Sea and the Atlantic all lights were blacked out at night, and on one gray day the British fleet sighted and signaled the little steamer, but did not halt her; their quarry was the German fleet. By November 10 the *Bergensfjord* was anchored in New York harbor.

The Rachmaninoff family were finally deposited at the Sherry-Netherland Hotel, but their first night in America was not to be a quiet one. They were roused from their beds by a nightmare uproar from the streets below—shouts, whistles, automobile horns. The startled family tried to explain it to each other. Perhaps a revolution had started here, too, or some new gas had sent everyone at street level crazy, or this was what the war had done to the Americans. A satisfactory explanation came with the morning paper: news of an armistice had reached New York early that morning!

For musicians the arrival of Rachmaninoff was news more immediately joyful than the armistice. Visitors squeezed through rejoicing crowds on the streets to bring greetings, welcomes—and advice. In New York at that time were Hofmann, Kreisler, Zimbalist, Elman, Ysaye, and Prokofiev, who had also just arrived from Russia by coming the other way around the world. Everyone had something to offer the newcomer. Some offered him money, some recommended their favorite concert bureaus, others tutored him in what to say and how to behave in doing business with Americans. Prokofiev paid his tribute by including works by Rachmaninoff in his first New York recital. Rachmaninoff told reporters, "I have come to America to rest and work."

Among the letters of welcome was one from Dagmar Rybner, a Danish-American musician who had corresponded with Rachmaninoff before the war. She offered any assistance that she could give from her experience of the New York musical world, but she was surprised to be telephoned the next morning by Mme. Rachmaninoff, asking her "to come at once" to their hotel, as Rachmaninoff needed her help.

Needless to say, I dropped all my plans for that day (and many to follow) and rushed to the hotel, grabbing a bunch of roses on the way. I was greeted by Mme. Rachmaninoff, though there was no sign of him, but after a little while the curtains of the adjoining room moved slightly, and out of the corner of my eye—I saw him peering at me. Soon, very timidly, he came in, with his equally shy younger daughter Tatiana. I understood his aversion to meeting strangers, yet after a few moments of halting conversation, I sensed his decision that I seemed to be a safe person and was to be trusted. He pointed to his piano covered with letters, telegrams, and messages and asked me to help him with "all that." From then on I took charge, unraveling the tangle of mail and telephone calls, and later attending to the mass of problems that he was unable to cope with, partly from not knowing the English language, as well as being unaccustomed to American ways. I saw that he had to be relieved of all details in order to prepare himself for his coming concerts, so I did all I could to bring order out of that chaos—and remained to keep his life running smoothly.

Another American music lover offered him her studio and her piano, at which he could practice all day without disturbing any neighbors; he accepted the offer, grateful to be relieved of the embarrassment of playing for an involuntary hotel audience. Offers and recommendations of managers continued to come. Before Rachmaninoff's arrival, Hofmann had told two or three managers he knew that, for their own good, they should not allow this Russian to escape them; and every important concert bureau in America seemed to have been given the same advice by someone. Recording companies and player piano companies also besieged Rachmaninoff. Hofmann later enjoyed reminding him how attentively and gratefully he listened to Hofmann's advice—and then acted on his own. He signed a contract with the concert bureau of Charles Ellis, whose manner and efficiency in the Boston Symphony's negotiation with Rachmaninoff had inspired his confidence. Of the several pianos offered him, he chose the Steinway, and received with it the lifelong friendship of Frederick Steinway and his wife. The first recording contract was signed with the Edison Company.

This whirlwind of arrangements came to an abrupt halt when he and both his daughters were attacked by the "Spanish influenza," then epidemic in American seaports. Only Natalia Alexandrovna was spared the frustrating idleness of weeks in bed. The doctor who treated Rachmaninoff insisted on a long rest after his recovery, but concert contracts had been signed, and the patient would allow nothing to spoil this good fortune; as soon as he left his sickbed he went to work strenuously on his new American career.

Though far from fully recovered, he made his first appearance four weeks after arrival on December 8, in Providence—his American Malmö before the Stockholm of Boston. By a small margin of chance Rachmaninoff came to Symphony Hall not as conductor of the Boston Symphony, but as a pianist. On the afternoon of December 15, before what Philip Hale described as "a very large, enthusiastic and bronchial audience," a program prepared in a Copenhagen summer (but opened with Rachmaninoff's transcription of "The Star-Spangled Banner") began one of the most enduring musical successes ever known in America. In the next day's *Transcript* H. T. Parker gave his benediction to Rachmaninoff's American future:

No more impressive figure has crossed the stage of Symphony Hall these many years than Mr. Rakhmaninov when he came first to the piano yesterday afternoon. Nine years of absence had dimmed memories of his aspect; perhaps materially altered it. . . . His height nearly topped the doorway through which he entered; the breadth of his spare body nearly fitted it; the black that clothed him heightened this austerity of presence. As of old, the head, the face were unmistakably Russian from the close-cropped dark hair to the long jaw, the firm chin. The well-remembered brown color had not turned to pallor; the forehead sloped upward broad and high; the eyes kept the old gravity of contemplation—deepened. Plainly the past had worn him, yet had not left him in the present wearied. Obviously Mr. Rakhmaninov lives much within himself, wears no surface-moods and emotions, cultivates no manner for audiences, shuts himself from the world except so far as his music and his playing may reveal him. Therein speaks the man who, having found his means of self-expression, first makes himself unobtrusive master of them; who by this mastery discloses more amply, more exactly the treasures of a penetrating, reflective, many-sided mind, of a grave yet ardent imagination, of a quick, yet measuring spirit—a man in whom all things run deep and strong, devotions and ideals, passions and affections, sensations and achievement. He has given himself to music—to the writing of it, to the playing of it as conductor and pianist; yet, as with Mr. Paderewski, it is possible to feel that upon any other career he would have stamped his individual mark. . . .

Once embarked upon performance . . . he neither regards nor disregards his hearers; he merely bids them hear. With hands, with body he has not a trick of physical or technical display. There he sits, wholly absorbed in his task, entirely concentrated upon it, summoning, marshalling into it all that his faculties may give. . . . The piece ends; with grave courtesy Mr. Rakhmaninov acknowledges the applause with which the audience yesterday heaped him: seeks neither to emphasize nor to prolong it; returns as quietly, as briefly, to the next item in the programme of the day. . . . Similarly with the inevitable extra pieces. The pianist waits not to play them until time and again clapping has recalled him. He sets to them at once, plays them generously; quite understands that sooner or later, before an English or an American audience, he must play his Prelude in C-sharp minor. With grave good will he fulfills every obligation to his hearers—and vanishes.

The first New York recital of December 21 was greeted by the habitual acid tone of James Gibbons Huneker in the *Times*. In a program that he waved aside as "old-fashioned," he singled out the opening Beethoven Sonata for comment:

The oldsters were reminded of von Bülow. The same cold white light of analysis, the incisive touch, the strongly marked rhythms, the intellectual grasp of the musical ideas, and the sense of the relative importance in phrase-groupings proclaimed that Rachmaninoff is a cerebral, not an emotional artist. Not Woodrow Wilson himself could have held the academic balance so dispassionately. Even the staccato Princeton touch was not absent.

The "inevitable" encore was not played, and Huneker was amused:

. . . the Rachmaninoff "fans"—and there were thousands of them in the audience—clamored for the favorite piece of Flatbush "flappers." They surged toward Serge in serried masses. They clustered about the stage. . . . But the chief thing is the fact that Rachmaninoff did not play It. All Flapperdom sorrowed last night, for there are amiable fanatics who follow this pianist from place to place hoping to hear him in this particular Prelude; like the Englishman who attended every performance of the lady lion tamer hoping to see her swallowed by one of her pets.

Rachmaninoff's second Boston program, on January 10, 1919, was criticized by H. T. Parker for including too many novelties and showpieces, though it opened with Haydn's Variations in F minor and Beethoven's 32 Variations in C minor. His first appearance with orchestra this season was on January 12 with the New York Symphony Society, conducted by Walter Damrosch, in Rachmaninoff's Second Concerto. A fellow composer, Reginald de Koven, writing in the *New York Herald,* saluted this performance:

In all my critical experience I have seldom seen a New York concert audience more moved, excited and wrought up to and above, so to speak, concert pitch; and the enthusiastic and prolonged applause which greeted Mr. Rachmaninoff at the close of the concerto was an unusual, spontaneous and heartfelt tribute to the composer as pianist and to his work.

I feel I am not overstating the case by saying that this noble concerto, broad and vigorous in constructive treatment, truly romantic and poetic in conception, wholly grateful and effective for the solo instrument, with an orchestral color and development scintillating and never extravagant, which adds notably to the strongly emotional grip of the composition as a whole, is one of the best and most truly inspirational works of its class written in our time.

Two weeks later Rachmaninoff attempted to make an equally secure place in the repertory for his revised First Concerto, playing it with Modeste Altschuler and the Russian Symphony Society Orchestra. Dismissing the concerto as "singularly effective," Huneker confined his comment to the composer himself, concluding, "It would seem that this is a Rachmaninoff season."

For his third Boston recital of the season, Rachmaninoff played on February 22 an all-Russian program of music new to the city, beginning with his Variations on a Theme by Chopin, ending with the six *Etudes-Tableaux* of Op. 33, and including a large Scriabin group and three of Medtner's *Fairy-Tales*. When a reporter questioned him afterward on the programs of his *études*, he gave an answer that he was to repeat many times: "Ah, that is for me and not for the public. I do not believe in the artist disclosing too much his images. Let them paint for themselves what it most suggests."

Before the close of his first season, rules for the reception of Rachmaninoff's music among American intellectuals were laid down by Paul Rosenfeld, in *The New Republic*:

But there is an essential that his music wants. It wants the imprint of a decided and important individuality. . . . Nor is the music of M. Rachmaninoff ever quite completely new-minted. Has it a melodic line quite properly its own? One doubts it. . . . Nor can one discover in this music a distinctly original sense of either rhythm or harmony or tone-color. . . . In all the music of M. Rachmaninoff there is something strangely twice-told. From it there flows the sadness distilled by all things that are a little useless.

The rest of Rachmaninoff's career in America, no matter what he played nor what he composed, was haunted by this superior voice: intellectual American criticism rarely deviated from the Rosenfeld fiat. The English parallel of this line was laid down a few years later when Edward Sackville West heard the Second Symphony at a Promenade Concert:

Few artists have proved to be ultimately negligible on so large a scale as Rachmaninoff. . . . Metaphorically speaking, Rachmaninoff shut himself up in a dark room, frightened himself to death, and then translated his soul-storm into the language of music. . . . I look forward to the time when people will be ashamed to listen to Scriabin, Tchaikovsky, Rachmaninoff, *Tod und Verklärung,* and the symphonies of Gustav Mahler.

The first season of Rachmaninoff's American career ended with three charity concerts. On April 8, in a concert with Geraldine Farrar at the Metropolitan Opera conducted by Stokowski, he played his Second Concerto; on April 14, with Pablo Casals, he played his sonata for piano and cello; on April 27, for the Victory Liberty Loan, two numbers were programed, "The Star-Spangled Banner" and Liszt's Second Hungarian Rhapsody (with a new cadenza) but the audience got its prélude, too. Then the family escaped for the summer to the West Coast, where they rented a house near San Francisco, Menlo Park, in Palo Alto. He wrote to his secretary on June 15:

My dear Miss Rybner,

We've arrived in fine shape and it's almost a week now that we've been living in our villa.

Здесь хо-ро-шо и воздух как в раю!

Here it is nice—and the air is heavenly!

We've set up our own housekeeping: we have a gardener who is also the chauffeur—an American; the cook is Japanese and the maid is Swedish. Nearly all nationalities—in the style of the Paris Conference.

I've been practicing for three days.

A young admirer, Henry Cowell, made a pilgrimage to Rachmaninoff, to ask advice:

I was very young—'teen age, I guess. He kindly received me and, picking out one ["Fleeting"] of a great pile of works I brought, looked at it intently with no comment for two hours, upon which he marked tiny red circles around 42 notes, saying "You have 42 wrong notes." Seeing my confusion, he quickly and kindly added, "I too have sinned with wrong notes in my youth, and therefore you may be forgiven." After that time he followed my career with great interest, and I always visited him whenever I was at a place where he was playing.

Practice made this a full summer: the Third Concerto was pro- gramed for next season (including a tenth anniversary performance with its first conductor, Damrosch); Monteux had asked him also to play the Liszt Concerto with the Boston Symphony on its tour; and one of his new programs was to be the first of his "idea-programs," of *études* from Chopin and Schumann to Scriabin and himself, through Rubinstein and Liszt.

The Etude, dedicating its October issue to Rachmaninoff wel- comed him as "America's new artist." There were appreciations and tributes from the great of music, and to give the magazine a "first," the composer provided one of the pencil sketches he had written in his last month in Russia; "Fragments" occupied a single page.

H. T. Parker was impressed by his first hearing of the Third Con- certo, which Rachmaninoff played with Monteux and the Boston Symphony on October 31, in a program that included Stravinsky's *Fire Bird Suite.* But the young critic of the *Boston Post,* Olin Downes, was not impressed with the concerto, and carried his doubts into an interview with Rachmaninoff that the interviewer never forgot:

... the young man launched a question which he believed he phrased in a manner both crafty and subtle. He asked Rachmaninoff, "Do you be- lieve that a composer can have real genius, sincerity, profundity of feeling, and at the same time be popular?"

Rachmaninoff: "Yes, I believe it is possible to be very serious, to have something to say, and at the same time to be popular. I believe that. Others do not. They think—what *you* think," with a long indicating finger and a look of such evident comprehension that Mr. Rachmaninoff's questioner was suddenly left high and dry, with not a word to say!

Another Russian composer pianist looked on Rachmaninoff's suc- cess and was discouraged; Sergei Prokofiev wrote to a Moscow magazine:

The public here isn't used to listening to a whole evening of compositions by one composer. They demand a varicolored program from which popular pieces can peep out. Rachmaninoff accepted this compromise. I could not even dream of his tremendous concert success. In my disappointment I've begun a new five-act opera [*The Flaming Angel*].

Stokowski conducted the Philadelphia Orchestra in an all-Rachmaninoff program on February 6, 1920, with the composer playing the Third Concerto; this included the first American performance of *The Bells* (announced as "Rachmaninoff's Third Symphony"), with Florence Hinkle, Arthur Hackett, and Frederick Patton as soloists. When the program was repeated in New York, Pitts Sanborn, in the *Telegram,* was unmoved by *The Bells:*

. . . this music is conspicuously lacking in invention, rhythmic or melodic. The means employed are gigantic; the results are banal. It is a great deal of noise about very little indeed, and one suspects that a second hearing of it would be an indescribable bore . . . one regrets the more keenly the time and labor lost in composing this symphony, which is so far beneath its author's abilities.

A Rachmaninoff program of broader scope was announced by Walter Damrosch for his New York music festival in the 71st Regiment Armory in April. Rachmaninoff was promised in a threefold capacity—as composer, conductor, and pianist—in a program built around *The Bells* and the Second Concerto, but at the last minute the program was changed, with *The Bells* replaced by the less ambitious choral work, *Spring;* this was conducted by Mr. Damrosch, the program explaining that Rachmaninoff was suffering from "an attack of neurosis [neuritis?] in the upper arm" that prevented him from conducting and playing on the same evening. In addition to *Spring* and the Second Concerto, Mr. Damrosch conducted *The Isle of the Dead,* the orchestrated *Vocalise,* an *a cappella* work, "Laud Ye the Name of the Lord" (from the *Night Vigil*), and three songs sung by Sophie Breslau.

The summer of 1920 was spent in Goshen, New York, a quiet village that seemed farther than it actually was from the noise of New York City. Rachmaninoff's favorite amusement was to take long automobile trips as he had done through the black earth country of

Russia. A mechanic went along, for mishaps, but Rachmaninoff always drove. In an interview of a few years later he gave a reason for his enjoyment of driving: "When I conduct, I experience much the same feeling as when I drive my car—an inner calm that gives me complete mastery of myself and of the forces, musical or mechanical, at my disposal." Summer practice for the new season's programs was enlivened by the first composing spark since 1917: he arranged a Russian song, "The Splinter," for the voice of John McCormack.

Rachmaninoff's season was to begin late, on November 11, at Ann Arbor, Michigan, and there was to be a heavy schedule: 41 recitals and 13 appearances as soloist with orchestra, playing his Second and Third Concertos and Tchaikovsky's First Concerto, the tour to end on April 2. Early in the autumn Avierino, reduced to playing in an Athens hotel orchestra, wrote to him, and Rachmaninoff answered with money and somewhat embittered advice:

I am sending you 1500 drachmas today. Forgive me for sending so little! I can't manage more. It seems to me that no matter how poorly you may be living now, it can't be compared with life in Russia at present. This should make us happy! For example, I have a mother and sister [Sophia Satina] there—and there's nothing I can do for them.*

You ask about America? God keep you from trying to come here. There are ten candidates for every musical position. Besides, you'd never be given a visa with the recent ruling of this government, caused by an unprecedented flood of immigrants. Go to Paris, or London, or wherever you wish in Europe, but forget the "Dollar Princess."

Just before leaving for his first concert in Michigan, Rachmaninoff received shocking news of his best friend: Nikolai Struve had been killed in Paris in an elevator accident.

While on tour Rachmaninoff received from Rome another kind of news: along with Paul Dukas and Henri Rabaud, he had been elected an honorary member of the Royal Academy of Santa Cecilia.

For many years Rachmaninoff had suffered with an acute pain in the right temple, increasing every year in frequency and severity. While in Russia he had associated these pains with writing, bending

* Later, with the help of the American Relief Administration, Rachmaninoff sent regular checks to his mother.

over manuscript, or any tense work, and he declared that if doctors could not help him, he would have to give up composition. Here in America, with composition put altogether aside, the pain nonetheless progressed steadily. One doctor diagnosed it as neuralgia of a facial nerve; another as an infection, possibly in the jaw or teeth. Temporary relief came only when he faced an audience from the concert stage: there was then, no necessity for reducing his concert schedule. After this season, in the spring of 1921, he submitted to surgery (starting a rumor in Moscow of his death), but the operation brought him no appreciable help.

For the following summer's rest the family found a residence fifty miles from New York City, on the shore of a bay, at Locust Point, New Jersey. Here Rachmaninoff began his summer habit of re-creating a microcosm of Russia, surrounding himself with Russian customs and foods. In this he was abetted by his neighbor, Yevgeni Somov, who had first met the composer in Moscow through the Satins. Summer driving was discouraged this year by an embarassing failure in the oral examination for his New Jersey license; however, a motor boat, swimming, and long rests on the beach in the sun refreshed the exhausted artist. Before leaving New York Rachmaninoff had made the gesture of a permanent resident by buying a house on Riverside Drive, and by autumn it was ready for occupancy.

This year Nikolai Medtner also left Moscow and Soviet Russia. He wrote to Rachmaninoff from Reval, on his way to Germany; Rachmaninoff's answer was dictated in German to Miss Rybner:

> 33 Riverside Drive, New York City
> October 29, 1921

Mein lieber Herr Medtner:

First, forgive me for not writing this myself, but I have to play so much this winter and my hands are so tired that I fear to tire them more with writing.

Your welcome letter of October 4 from Reval gave me great pleasure, and I am really happy that you are safely there. Now, certainly, The Art of the Fugue will proceed much more easily.

He discusses Medtner's contracts with Steinway, Duo-Art, and his concert prospects:

Of course I'll do my utmost to get the best terms for you, but don't forget that conditions here, too, have changed for artists, and that when you come—you will be heard here *for the first time.*

As you'll be in Germany for that long, I strongly advise you to give concerts there. It would be wise for you to write Koussevitzky about your compositions because it is only in Europe that they can now be published, as long as conditions for composers here are so terrible.

Rachmaninoff's new program, with a group of three Ballades—by Chopin, Liszt, and Grieg—was first played on November 10 in St. Paul. It made new Boston admirers for him when he played it there on December 7. H. T. Parker concluded a detailed study of his art: "Again the puritan of pianists was by puritans applauded," and Philip Hale wrote in the *Boston Herald:* "Mr. Rachmaninoff's playing is distinguished by its clarity. His dissection of a composition is not, however, pedagogic. He is far from being a dry analyst, but he delights in exposing the structure of a work in an eloquent manner. In this he has no rival."

When he played the Second Concerto on December 15 with the New York Philharmonic under Stransky, Richard Strauss, whose *Til Eulenspiegel* was also programed, was in the audience. In Rachmaninoff's short Christmas vacation at home he continued his advice to Medtner, now in Berlin:

What would you say to an alternative plan?—to send back the 25,000 marks to Koussevitzky with thanks for his help, explaining that you would prefer to have this money deposited with the Russischer Musikverlag for printing your compositions. I like this plan very much—more than the others—and if you agree to it, I'll send you 50,000 marks, begging you sincerely not to refuse it. This will enable you to live quite comfortably in Germany without financial worries for a few months, while you compose. . . .

He adds a postcript, in Russian:

I am so happy that you are in Europe, where I can "get at" you, and where you'll be able to live peacefully and work. As for the estrangement you sense, I must confess I feel it here, too. I see very few real, sincere musicians. Apparently you are the only one left.

His first formal American honor was presented when he came to play in Lincoln, Nebraska, on January 24, 1922; *The Lincoln State Journal* reported:

"I am very sorry that my poor English prevents me from telling how proud and glad I am. I thank you very much for this honor." In this brief speech, Sergius Wasiliewitsch Rachmaninoff expressed appreciation of the degree of doctor of music conferred upon him Tuesday morning by Chancelor Avery in the name of the University of Nebraska.

The Boston recital of February 18 showed H. T. Parker for the first time that Rachmaninoff as a pianist was too delicately balanced an instrument to give a superlative performance in every concert:

Possibly, on Saturday afternoon in Symphony Hall, he was depressed, out of the mood, beyond the power of usual audience or an expectant occasion to quicken him. It is hard to believe him wilfully indifferent to his work or to the public; yet as hard to recall him so inert and mechanical as he was from his beginnings in an Air and Variations of Handel through his own inevitable "Study-Picture" and Prelude. Not that he was careless after the manner of sundry pianists when they are out of the vein. Rather he was dry exactitude to the last curl of the last letter. Not once, until, at the end of the concert, he played Liszt's Second Rhapsody, did he let his hearers forget the piano as an instrument . . . only the native wildness of Liszt's Rhapsody, laced and interlaced with his own ornament as well as the composer's, warmed Mr. Rakhmaninov out of his dry and dull mechanics.

Obviously, a change was in order. He ended his American tour with two benefit concerts, on April 2 playing his Second and Third concertos with Damrosch,* and on April 21 playing for the relief of Russian students in the United States. Four days later he sailed on the *Mauretania* to give his first postwar recitals abroad: May 6 and 20 in London. He sailed alone, for Natalia Alexandrovna had to remain while her daughters took examinations in their schools. The family was to meet again in Dresden.

* "On Saturday night Mr. Rachmaninoff celebrated the forty-ninth anniversary of his birth, and last night he made the day memorable by giving a concert in Carnegie Hall, the proceeds of which are to be devoted to the relief of artists, musicians and men of letters in his native Russia . . . the receipts amounting to about $7,500, will be distributed by the American Relief Administration."—*New York Tribune,* April 3, 1922.

According to the London *Observer*, it was not an exclusively musical affair on May 6:

Rachmaninoff filled the Queen's Hall yesterday, and sent people away disappointed. Hofmann half fills the Queen's Hall, and Busoni plays in the Wigmore Hall. . . . But they never composed "The Prelude."
 . . . Would he actually play It, Itself? Rachmaninoff bowed to the inevitable, sat down wearily, and played the piece which (as an interviewer in the *Morning Post* of that very day had revealed) of all pieces he most hates. . . .

The Musical Times proposed the impossible: "It would be a great treat to hear this fine and singularly unassuming pianist in a small hall from which all Prelude-maniacs had been barred." Rachmaninoff sent his own report to Miss Rybner:

The concert went off successfully. I played well and the hall was "sold out." Someone scolded me in the papers but that's of course. They will praise me, as others are praised, only after I die, when everyone does it. I'm very bored here and I think of America very often. I extol America to all the English and they get so angry.

After leaving Russia the Satin family had settled in Dresden, and the Rachmaninoffs were to spend part of their summer there with them. A villa was rented for Rachmaninoff where he could be visited by his cousins and be joined later in June by his wife and daughters. Riesemann tells of the natural but awkward question asked Rachmaninoff by his old Dresden acquaintances:

"Is it possible that in all these years you have not written a single note?"

"Oh yes," with a wry smile, "I have written a cadenza to Liszt's Second Rhapsody."

Despite the reunion with the Satins Rachmaninoff could not recover his good spirits in Dresden. When he wrote to Miss Rybner, soon to be married, it was a sad letter:

Do not forget to show much love and attention to your parents. If you have to part, it will be very hard for them, as I can well understand, being myself a father. All pessimists, faced by two possibilities—one joyous and the other sorrowful—always prefer the latter.

Rachmaninoff tried to see Medtner before leaving Europe:

August 4, 1922

Dear Nikolai Karlovich,

I cannot come to you: my family here "frowns at me" too much for that. Besides, I have to visit a doctor daily for electrical treatments—my head and hands still ache. So, if you can't get here, my last tiny hope is to sneak over to you [in Stettin] from Hamburg, where we'll arrive on the evening of August 19 . . . before leaving for America on the 22nd.

On the eve of his departure from Dresden Rachmaninoff heard from another old friend still living in Moscow, Vladimir Wilshaw, whom he answered as soon as the family was safe again at Locust Point:

As for myself and family I shall say only a few words. I dislike my occupation intensely! For this whole time I have not composed one line. I only play the piano and give a great many concerts. For four years now I practice—practice. I make some progress, but actually the more I play the more clearly do I see my inadequacies. If I ever learn this business thoroughly, it may be on the eve of my death. Materially I am quite secure. Bourgeois! But my health fails—yet it would be strange to expect the opposite when you remember that my dissatisfaction with myself throughout my life has scarcely ever allowed me to feel repose. In the past, when I composed, I suffered because I was composing poorly, and now—because I play poorly. Inside I feel some firm assurance that I can better both the one and the other. This keeps me alive!

My wife has changed little. She remains the same, though perhaps with a few more gray hairs. The children are well. The older one graduates from the University [Barnard College] in two years. She loves life and is very fond of America. The younger one graduates from high school in three years—she is gloomy and cannot bear America. And this is not the only difference between them: they might have been born of different parents! . . .

Good-by, Vladimir Robertovich. I shan't be writing you for a long time. Don't be cross—it's just that during the season I have no time at all. Following the winter season I have accepted more concerts in Australia. If you write me again, I'll be very, very grateful.

Greetings to you with all my heart. Salute for me all whom I love.

S. Rachmaninoff

Chapter 14

Ties with Russia

ACHMANINOFF'S ties with Russia at this period were closer than they had been since he emigrated. Seeing the Satins at Dresden awoke many memories. In addition to more regular messages from his mother, brother, and other relatives in Russia, the restored correspondence with Wilshaw put him again in touch with Russian musical life and his old friends. When Wilshaw wrote him that Nikita Morozov was recovering from a serious illness, Rachmaninoff sent good wishes at once to Morozov ("I'd still certainly like to talk with you and, of course, to argue as we used to"), even though his approaching season had brought down the bars on all correspondence. His parcels to needy persons in Russia grew more numerous, facilitated by the American Relief Administration. One of the most moving sections of the Rachmaninoff Archive contains the large group of responses to his gifts from musicians and writers, from artists, actors, teachers, from universities, conservatories, theaters. The chorus of the Marinsky Opera in Petrograd signed seventy signatures to their note of thanks. From the Kiev Conservatory, in the center of the famine area, came a reply that almost sobs its thanks. Stanislavsky wrote from the Moscow Art Theater: "You cannot know how your attention and memories touch our hearts. It is a very fine thing that you are doing, for the artists are really starving," and he signed this "Your eternal debtors." For years the parcels went and the letters came, not only from Russia, but from Russians all over the world— Paris, Prague, Harbin, San Francisco. The greetings that came to Rachmaninoff on his sixtieth birthday were chiefly from individuals and groups whom he had helped and fed. When morale was needed, that too he would try to supply. *Musical America* carried an appeal from him for help to the State Institute of Musical Science:

The organizers of this institution have sent me a letter containing two requests and a report covering ten months of their work. According to that report several manuscripts of articles on the science of music were prepared by the members of the institution,* but could not be published owing to lack of funds.

The requests contained in the letter of the organizers are:

1. They appeal through me to your country "which has such esteem for Science, Culture and Art" and they hope that perhaps "there could be found persons interested in the Science of Music, who would and could bring material help to a cultural work of international importance." This material help is needed exclusively for the publication of scientific articles and researches.

2. Their second request is to bring to the attention of the American people through the press the fact of the existence of their institution.

When Felix Blumenfeld sent Rachmaninoff a list of needs among his colleagues in Kiev, he also sent a cheering account of musical activity:

From August 1918 up to last spring I had as a graduate student an extremely talented youth of 17, Vladimir Horowitz—a passionate admirer of your music and of Medtner's. He graduated, by the way, with your Third Concerto; at the Conservatory concert and later at his own concert he also played your B-flat minor Sonata quite well. As you see, here you are warmly loved. *Aleko* is often performed at the City Theater and at the studios. I write you about this with the thought that it is pleasant to know what goes on in the homeland.

The house on Riverside Drive became a center for Russian artists living in or passing through New York City. This phase of its existence was climaxed by the arrival of the touring Moscow Art Theater. One of the authors of this book first met Rachmaninoff at that time:

Sergei Vasilyevich had always been a devoted worshiper of the Art Theater; his attitude towards Stanislavsky was based on extraordinary admiration—I may even say tenderness. It is easily understood how happy Rachmaninoff must have been when his beloved Muscovites arrived in New York City. After several years of separation from Russia, it was like a meeting with Moscow herself. He and his family came to see each play of our repertory several times, visiting us backstage, which is where we first met. Soon I was invited with other members of our com-

---

* Among the papers are "The Law of the Golden Section in Poetry and Music," by Rozanov; "Phenomena of Color Hearing," by Sabaneyev; and "Review of Modern Russian Musical Literature," by Kuznetzov.

pany to visit the Rachmaninoffs at their hospitable home on Riverside Drive. We came on nights after the performance, and what memorable nights these were! There were lively theatrical and musical recollections, discussions of the day's events, stories told by our host, his cousin Alexander Siloti, the choreographer Michael Fokine, Stanislavsky, Knipper-Chekhova, Kachalov, and Moskvin. It was a delight to watch Rachmaninoff listening to the sharp and lively stories by Moskvin about the backstage life of our theatrical family, told in the "juicy" flavor of typical Moscow speech. Catching every word and watching every movement of Moskvin's expressive features, Rachmaninoff's face, usually so pensive and concentrated, would be transformed: it became almost childlike, even his deeply graven wrinkles would vanish, and he surrendered himself to the happiest and most carefree laughter, throwing back his head, and brushing away tears of joy with the back of his hand.

With the area of his tour widening (this year he went to Canada and to Cuba) and his schedule packed tight with 71 appearances between November 10 and March 31, 1923, he was tempted to hire a special railway observation car, equipped for his full establishment, where he could live free of hotels and practice without thought of other tenants. But this luxury, that had seemed at first so efficient, was soon given up: life in it grew too monotonous, and the very sight of the car became repulsive to him. In general the season of 1922–23 was undertaken with less enthusiasm than usual. One of the few satisfactions of this season was his new Russian secretary and correspondent, Yevgeni Somov, to whom he could write frankly:

As for me, I am so-so [he wrote from Dallas, Texas]. I groan and moan a bit and take pleasure in deducting the passing days from my life account. Both the material and moral satisfaction afforded by my concerts are middling. But no one's material affairs are very good now, so I seem to be no exception. As for the moral side, better not to speak of it. I was born a failure and therefore I bear all the burdens that are inseparably part of this status. Five years ago, starting to play, I thought I should get some satisfaction from this piano business; now I have convinced myself that that is not to be attained.

Even Chaliapin's attempt to make Rachmaninoff's Chicago stay warmer with a "homemade" dinner did not help much. The tour ended the day before his fiftieth birthday, April 2. A clue to his dis-

satisfaction with this life is to be found in his letter to Morozov of
April 15:

I received all your letters as numbered. I didn't answer you, for till
April I was on tour, and only passed through New York. I played and
played. Now that I've returned, I'll stay here all summer and must bring
myself back to order. I am very tired and my hands ache. In the past
4 months I gave about 75 concerts. Every superfluous motion of the
hands tires me, so I am dictating this to you. Because of this fatigue I
canceled my tour to Australia, where I was supposed to go on April 20. . . .

Your main question, that I find in all your letters, as to my creative
work, I must answer thus: either from overfatigue or from loss of the
composing habit (it's been five years since I worked on composition),
I am not drawn to this matter, or rarely drawn. This does take place when
I think about my two major compositions that I started not long before
leaving Russia.* When I think of these, I long to finish them. This,
apparently, would be the only possibility of moving me from this dead
halt. To begin something new seems to me unattainably difficult. If I
should get a little stronger and rested, I'll try to get to this this summer.
Thus your advice and new subjects must go, for the time, into my portfolio, and lie there until my "awakening" or rebirth.

In an interview given to *The Etude* there is a hint of Rachmaninoff's
next step in composition:

I believe in what might be called indigenous music for the piano;
that is, music which the Germans would describe as *klaviermässig*. So
much has been written for the instrument that is really alien. Brahms is
a notable example. Rimsky-Korsakov is possibly the greatest of Russian
composers; yet no one ever plays his concerto in these days, because it
is not *klaviermässig*. On the other hand the concertos of Tchaikovsky are
frequently heard because they lie well under the fingers! Even with
my own concertos I much prefer the third, because my second is uncomfortable to play, and therefore not susceptible of so successful effects.
Grieg, although he could not be classed as a great master pianist, had the
gift of writing beautifully for the piano and in pure *klaviermässig* style.

* Igumnov has said that Rachmaninoff spoke with him in Russia about a Fourth
Concerto, and, indeed, the Russian press mentioned the preparation of this Concerto
in April 1914; the second of these "two major compositions" may have been
Monna Vanna, though this was abandoned ten years before his departure from
Russia.

A birthday present sent from Moscow in December finally arrived: a tiny cantata with text by Wilshaw:

> From your far-off native country
> We send you joy and our greeting,
> And from our hearts and souls we say
> Long live Rachmaninoff Sergei!

The music was by Gliere, and the gift bore the signatures of twenty musicians. It too was difficult to answer:

May 1, 1923

My dear Vladimir Robertovich,

I have received the letter with your many signatures, and the "cantata" of greeting.

I was very much touched, by the words as well as by the sounds. Many thanks to all of you.

I can write no more. I have finished the season and my hands seem nearly paralyzed.

Health to all of you, and accept my greeting.

In the same week Rachmaninoff answered a letter from the son of Rimsky-Korsakov; after apologizing for the delay caused by his tour and exhaustion:

I must tell you how highly the works of Nikolai Andreyevich are valued here. Such compositions as *The Golden Cockerel, Scheherazade,* the *Easter Overture,* and *Capriccio Espagnole* are played each season by every symphony society, and they invariably rouse the same rapture. The first three of these compositions always affect me painfully. Because of sentimentality (perhaps characteristic of me) or because of my advanced age, or because of the loss of my native land, with which the music of Nikolai Andreyevich is so closely bound (only Russia could create such an artist), to hear a performance of these works always brings tears.

Accept my sincere greetings and my low bow—to you, the children and grandchildren of the unforgettable Nikolai Andreyevich. If there ever should be anything you need, please let me know.

S. Rachmaninoff

Before the return to Europe of the Art Theater, the group visited Rachmaninoff at the Locust Point house. After dinner everyone performed in his honor, with Chaliapin, who had come along, as star: he gave imitations of a breathless accordion, the drunken accordion player hauled to the police station, a lady adjusting her veil before a mirror, an old woman praying in church. At two in the morning, when the guests seemed about to go, Chaliapin barred their exit: "Where are you going? I only stopped for breath—Sergei Vasilyevich and I will really show you something!" With Rachmaninoff at the piano Chaliapin sang on and on—peasant songs, bits of opera, gypsy songs, and finally, at Rachmaninoff's request, "Dark Eyes." One of the guests, Ivan Ostromislensky, recalled the occasion:

On that hot July night at Rachmaninoff's house the small drawing room was divided in two, for the stage and the audience, the first row on the floor in Turkish style. With Sergei Vasilyevich at the piano Chaliapin pranked and charmed us all night. . . . Our party broke up only at 5 A.M.

Next day at lunch I saw Rachmaninoff again. The creases in the parchmentlike skin of his face and the pouches under his eyes had been made more conspicuous by the night's party. But his mood was cheerful. "Tell me, Ivan Ivanovich, what made the greatest impression on you last night?" Without waiting for my answer, he went on, "I'm sure it was 'Dark Eyes'—I don't doubt it. How he sighed, that villain, how he sobbed 'you have ruined me!'—I couldn't sleep, for thinking, 'How God endowed you beyond other men!' . . . Oh, that sigh!"

Rachmaninoff treasured a Chaliapin record of this song, and he always drew attention to the singer's sob at this dramatic moment.

With the exhaustion of the previous season fresh in Rachmaninoff's memory, Mme. Rachmaninoff and Charles Foley (who had assumed Rachmaninoff's management after the retirement of Charles Ellis), the number of engagements was reduced for the season of 1923–24. As this began, Rachmaninoff dictated a letter to Morozov:

I've just begun my season—in other words, my harvest time has begun. True, this year my season has been shortened to the minimum; that is, from today till December 15 I have 15 concerts, then from December 15 to January 15 I rest (studying my next program), from January 15 till February 20 I have 15 concerts, after which I go on strike.

All your advice and my projects are postponed indefinitely. If I had felt a little better this summer, I would certainly have started work. But this didn't happen. At our age it is usual to be sick and grow weak.

He opened this season's program with the same English Suite by Bach that he had played at the age of twelve for Anton Rubinstein. The *Boston Herald* reviewer found the opening moment of the recital worth comment:

Yesterday he began the Prélude to the Bach Suite and paused. He gazed placidly, but keenly, into the open mechanism of the piano, as if he suspected an atom was out of the place given it by the makers of the instrument or an ion was a bit wild in seeking its proper electrons. He tried again, seemed satisfied that each element was functioning normally and went on as if nothing had happened.

The New York recital of December 2 closed with a surprise: not the tossed bouquet of violets that had so embarrassed him at a New York appearance of 1920, but a laurel wreath presented by representatives of the Moscow Art Theater, inscribed, "With love and admiration."

During Rachmaninoff's monthlong interval a letter came from Morozov that he answered at once:

Today is Christmas, and in your letter you and Vera Alexandrovna congratulate me on the holidays. I also want to congratulate you both and to wish you all the best. These wishes are sent, you know, from the heart itself. How much I enjoyed your conversation with Vera Alexandrovna, repeated in your letter, about the money I sent you. She "didn't even care to hear" all your restless talking, saying only: "Thank him, and have done with the talk." Golden words, especially the last ones. I'd shorten them even more, cutting the beginning. But what is bad is that after you read several books and proposed to write me about them, you didn't, after all. How many times I've told you that I love your letters and that they bring me joy. My life here goes along much as you imagine it, with concerts day after day, and piano practice in the intervals. During these holidays I have no concerts, but then I must make gramophone and player piano recordings. . . .

This year the season is short: I finish the concerts on February 1 and plan to go to Europe at the end of March. For rest and treatment. If you ask me for what, I'd find it difficult to answer; mostly for old age, I suppose. . . . I am sorry that the rumor about my composing a whole series of fox trots is untrue.* I'd gladly have written them, for I like their original and inimitable rhythm.

There is confirmation of Rachmaninoff's interest in jazz: his name appears among the patrons of Whiteman's epoch-making Aeolian Hall concert of February 12, 1924.

On April 5 the Rachmaninoffs arrived in Naples on the *Duilio*, and one of the first words home from the travelers came on a post card to Dagmar Rybner, chiefly to tell of Rachmaninoff's joy that he had arrived "in time to see everything in blossom." From Florence, just before leaving for Dresden, Rachmaninoff wrote to the Somovs on May 12:

We've been here in Florence for 3½ weeks. I'm somewhat improved and seem to have gained weight. Altogether my life here has been very pleasant. I've also been entertained by Medtner and his wife, who were here when we came and who are going with us now to Zurich. I have listened many times to his playing and I can't tell you what sincere pleasure and satisfaction I gained from both his compositions and his playing. I've also seen some of the Russians in the colony here. They discovered us when we attended the Russian church for the bringing out of Christ's effigy on Good Friday, and for the midnight service. And these Russians, mostly titled, turn out to be nice, affable, and amiable. . . . Now I feel I've had enough tourism, and it wouldn't be bad to sit down, solidly, somewhere! So I contemplate Dresden and the life there with anticipation.

In their Florentine conversations Medtner asked a question that had to be asked, and later told John Culshaw of Rachmaninoff's reply: "I asked him why he no longer composed. He smiled, and in return asked, 'How can I compose without melody?'" Back in Dresden, the setting of almost as much work as Ivanovka, the long-immobile composing mind of Rachmaninoff began to turn once again. On June 20 he wrote Medtner: "I've already started to work. Am moving slowly," but he also spent time on assisting Medtner to arrange an American engagement. Whenever letters came from Rach-

* During the twenties a large number of jazz "arrangements" (some anonymous) were made of the Prélude in C-sharp minor, including *That Russian Rag*, a saxophone sextette by the Six Brown Brothers, and an arrangement by Duke Ellington. The earliest of these popular American arrangements of the Prélude was William Lorraine's *Salome*, in 1898, just after Siloti introduced the work to America.

maninoff, his family and friends knew that he was not composing; they had long since come to realize that letters were rather a symptom of dissatisfaction with himself.

One of the joys of this summer was a visit from the loving and be-loved Masha Ivanova (now, by marriage, Shatalina), who had been the maid in the Satin household and later with the Rachmaninoffs until their departure seven years before. No matter how they im-plored her to sell the belongings they had left behind, to buy food and clothing for herself, she refused, guarding them, untouched, pre-ferring to crowd her Moscow room with the "sacred" trunks of Rachmaninoff.*

Another surprise this summer was a serious change in the family. Prince Peter Wolkonsky asked for the hand of Irina, and the family decided to stay in Dresden till the wedding.

Though composition sketches were shelved for calmer times, prac-tice had to continue for the coming concert season. On August 21, as Rachmaninoff worked at the piano, he dictated letters to Tatiana, including a brief report to Wilshaw:

I want to write you only a few lines about myself and about all of us. We still sit in Germany. This happened unexpectedly. My older daugh-ter Irina decided on marriage (to P. Wolkonsky). We changed all our plans and we'll live here until the wedding, which will take place here on September 24; on the 25th I leave for England, where after October 2 I have three weeks of concerts. My wife and the one who writes these lines will come for me in London, and from there all of us—but there are only three of us left now (Irina and her husband will spend the winter in Munich)—will leave on October 22 for America.

Hearing that Chaliapin was in Berlin, he urged him to visit them in Dresden, but there was a disappointing but hearty reply addressed to "My dear Seryozhenka!":

I can't take advantage of your nice invitation, for today I am singing and tomorrow morning I am *obliged* to go to Paris. My beloved Seryozha! If I had known that you are in Dresden I would have darted there without any invitation—but they told me that you're living in Italy.—I also heard

---

* Two years after Masha's return to Moscow the family heard she had died of a painful cancer.

today that you have given in marriage, or are just about to, your daughter. Congratulations on your *grandfatherhood,* and I wish your daughter all happiness.—I kiss my dear little Dulcinea [Tatiana]!

Do please convey my warmest greetings to all, *"throw a loving look to all,"* and you I embrace till your bones crack.

Your Fyodor.

After the religious ceremony a saddened family of three left Dresden. Eight concerts in England, and then the Rachmaninoffs left for the American winter. In Boston, before his opening recital on the afternoon of November 23, he listened to *The Isle of the Dead* at a concert of the Boston Symphony. When the audience discovered him, they gave him as much of an ovation as is decorous in Symphony Hall.

Following his Providence recital on December 7, he stayed on to hear Paul Whiteman and his orchestra, and later gave an enthusiastic comment on the experience:

Mr. Rachmaninoff said: "My compliments to Mr. Whiteman! He has the finest orchestra of its size I have ever heard. I have long been an admirer of his work, and each month I send to my daughter in Europe the records made by this remarkable organization.

"The charm and interest of this orchestra for the musician is that it is undoubtedly new. That is to say, it expands and develops its material in a characteristic and novel fashion which to me is absolutely fascinating. This may certainly be called authentic American music, for it can be heard nowhere else that I know of.

"My friend Medtner calls Mr. Whiteman the best storyteller he knows in music; storytelling is exactly what Mr. Whiteman's short pieces are. Excellent pointed anecdotes, crisply told, with all the human breeziness and snap that are so characteristic of the American people.

"And the arrangements of these pieces are a marvel to me. 'By the Waters of the Minnetonka,' for instance, is a beautiful theme developed in an ingenious manner that could not be excelled."

In Washington he began his last letter to Morozov:

First I'll answer your questions. To your first question, for how long will I send you a "pension"?—I'll reply: I'll send it as long as I can! To your second question, why do I do it? I'll tell you in your own words: so that you'll "feel a little warmer and brighter" whenever it arrives! You don't absolutely have to write whenever it comes. Write when you feel like it! But I am always glad to receive your letters.

That's all for "business." Now I sit in Washington. My concert here was yesterday, and if I sit still one more day it's only because I am to play for the President at the White House.* And then begins the *Perpetuum mobile* till April 1st. . . . On the 2nd and 3rd I play in New York with orchestra. . . . Now I go to California, traveling from city to city across the American land, and from there I'll return in the same way across the Canadian territory. . . .

I didn't have time to finish this letter. Began it on January 15. Today is the 19th. Have just come from a concert here in Norfolk. I want to finish this before going to sleep. I am tired, so very tired, dear friend! My health is so-so. Only neuralgia torments me (right side of the face). And the more tired I get the more painful it gets and the more often the pains come. This means that by the end of a season the pains are almost incessant. Next season I'll change my way of work radically.

From New Orleans he sent Somov instructions and an excuse:

First, about the sale of the house. See, though I play the *Business-Man*, actually (this is confidential) I don't understand a thing about business and I hate it. That's why I spend half my American life with lawyers.

In a review of Rachmaninoff's concert in Stockton, California, we get a glimpse of the conditions often faced by a touring musician:

The stage of the high school auditorium, where the concert was held, was barren and unattractive. The background suggested cheap melodrama and rats running about. By reason of a temporary heating system, which bellows out the curtain in an annoying way, it has been difficult to give a proper setting for a concert, yet, if the "Red Mill" set, used in last year's high school opera, had been put up, it would have been far better than the set used.

May 16, 1925, New York

Dear friend of mine Vladimir Robertovich, yesterday, at last, I finished my work. No concerts this past month, but there were records to be made

---

* The program for President Coolidge on January 16, except for a Chopin group and the *Faust Fantasia* by Gounod-Liszt, reads like a list of his encores. Rachmaninoff had given his first White House concert on March 10, 1924.

for the phonograph, player piano, etc., and a mass of all sorts of matters before leaving. All of us, that is: I, Natasha, Tania, and the two Wolkonskys, leave in a week for Europe. Natasha and the Wolkonskys will land in France. . . . Tania and I continue by ship to Holland, and from there to Dresden, where I plan to stay in a sanitarium for five weeks, while Tanyushka lives with the Satins. As soon as I recuperate a little, we'll join the family in Paris. . . .

Next year I am drastically altering my mode of living. My concert season here will last altogether 5 weeks, from November 2 to December 5. In that time I'll give no more than 22–25 concerts. Then two weeks recording for the phonograph and player piano, and then *Schluss*. Where I'll live the rest of the time I haven't decided. Probably here part of the time, with my wife (Tania will stay on in Paris with the Wolkonskys), and part of the time in Europe with the children. I've liquidated my affairs here, including the house, which we all loved very much and which I've now sold. I have also arranged all my affairs in reference to my wife and children, so that I have a full right to die "when I choose" or when it comes.

Well, I'm joking, of course. But to be serious and sincere: I love you very much, I value your friendship greatly, and I await news from you.

The sanitarium played so regular a role in Rachmaninoff's European summers that some explanation may be necessary. The American acceptation of "sanitarium" is a place for the treatment of invalids and convalescents. It is quite possible that Rachmaninoff regarded himself as convalescent after giving concerts from November to May. The European notion of a sanitarium, however, as a more loosely supervised rest home with medical attention at hand if required, is the image to keep in mind during these repeated references to his "sanitarium existence." He wrote Wilshaw again from the Dresden sanitarium on July 2:

. . . we arrived June 3 and, eluding relatives and friends, went straight from the station to the sanitarium, from where I now write you. I—to be treated! Tanyechka to chaperon me! Tomorrow we'll have been here a whole month. (I seem to be writing badly: my hands are trembling—old age is no sweetheart!) I am somewhat better, but only somewhat. The postwar sanitarium has changed along with the rest of the world. Tomorrow I move to a hotel, for a few days of freedom, and then we go to

Paris, where, 40 kilometers away, Natasha has rented a villa where we'll stay till October 15.

My vacation ends with my departure from here. In France I shall again sit down at the piano and at the exercises for the 4th and 5th fingers. About five years ago Hofmann told me that our second finger is "the lazy one"! I fixed my attention on this finger and began to "check" it! Soon I noticed that the third finger has the same fault. And now, the longer I live the more I am convinced that both the fourth and fifth work in bad faith. Only the thumb remains honest, and that only temporarily! So I have begun to look at him, too, with suspicion! I have three months to get ready.

The family experienced tragedy in August. Prince Wolkonsky died shortly before the birth of his child, leaving Rachmaninoff's daughter a widow and a mother. Rachmaninoff wrote to an American friend of his new grandchild:

I only want to tell you that I have a granddaughter—Sophie, who is an exact likeness of her father. Tomorrow is her birthday: she will be a week old. I like her so much and go to see her every day. Irene is well so far, and I hope to bring them both here the 15th of September, when I will wheel Sophie around in her carriage.

This crisis affected him so deeply that, but for his contracts, he would have stayed with his widowed daughter and not returned to America that year. It was at this time that Rachmaninoff established the publishing house called "Tair," from the names of his daughters Tatiana and Irina. It was first intended as a means to give them occupation by the printing of worthy Russian works that could not find publication. Tair became the European publisher of Rachmaninoff's later works and transcriptions for the piano.

On his program this season were two new piano transcriptions, actually closer in form to variations or the fantasia. The *Boston Evening Transcript* gave these new works some detailed attention; of Schubert's "Brooklet":

In this new piece—for thoroughly new piece it is—the composer raises a question. The style of the new accompaniment is quite frankly, though mildly, chromatic; while nothing could be more naïvely diatonic than the song-melody. One can hardly deny that the combination of such melody with such ornamental figuration presents an anachronism. To many, this will be a complete answer, and a damning one. Yet, if one looks more deeply, one finds that this gently modern background does no violence to the melody, that the two fit as hand in glove, that Mr. Rachmaninov has written brook-music such as has probably never been penned, such as completely justifies itself. And through it all, ever-present, like the song of a simple peasant by the side of the turbulent brook runs the simple, heartfelt melody.

Of the Kreisler *Liebesfreud*:

The things that the transcriber has not done to the work of the composer would be hard to discover. The first feeling one has in listening to this new piece is one of wonder at the originality and resourcefulness of the treatment. But there is in this feeling no element indicating that such resourcefulness has in any way brought to the piece anything essentially foreign to the spirit in which the original was conceived. Through the surprising transitions, the outré harmonies, the startling cadenzas, the sudden modulations whisking the hearer aside from the expected course, the final glissando, the Kreisler themes, and extensions of the Kreisler moods as well, were always in evidence. . . . Yet, through all the cleverness, all the artfully contrived consistencies with the original Kreisler, one could not down the questions, "Did the transcriber have his tongue in his cheek in writing this; was the notion of burlesque entirely foreign to him?"

In December 1925 the Musical Studio of the Moscow Art Theater opened its American tour with a performance of *Lysistrata*. After the performance the entire company was invited to Chaliapin's for a party. The Studio's repertory included a program of short operas based on Pushkin subjects; one of these was Rachmaninoff's *Aleko*, so that the company was especially thrilled to meet its composer at Chaliapin's supper. A singer in the company, Julia Fatova, met him there:

Observing those two Russian geniuses, I was amazed at how "unlike" they were. Chaliapin—dynamics, fire, unrest. Rachmaninoff—concentrated, calm, self-contained. Chaliapin talked continuously, gesticulated, "acted." Rachmaninoff listened, smiled his kind smile. As I left I timidly went up to Sergei Vasilyevich and asked him whether he would be present when we played his *Aleko*. His answer was firm: "Not only will I not come, but I am ashamed to have written such nonsense." I was completely taken aback by such a cruel remark about my favorite opera. . . .

When, at the beginning of January 1926, Rachmaninoff received new complaints from Medtner on his negotiations to print some of his music, Rachmaninoff sent off a cable advising his friend to accept the conditions offered, and followed it on January 14 with some of his bitterest conclusions:

Now I can explain myself in greater detail. There are three categories of composers: 1) those who compose popular music, that is, "for the market"; 2) fashionable music, that is, *moderne;* and finally 3) "serious, very serious music," as the ladies say, to which category you and I have the honor to belong. Publishers are very willing to print works in the first two categories, for this is easily marketable merchandise! And very unwilling to touch the last category—this merchandise moves very sluggishly. The two first are for the pocket. The last is more "for the soul"! Once in a while, however, a publisher holds a tiny spark of hope in the future, that by the time the composer of serious music is about to reach his hundredth birthday, or, better yet, after he's quite dead, his compositions may land in the first category, and become popular. But this is never a serious hope.

The world has many publishers exclusively for the music of each of the first two categories; there are publishers exclusively for popular music, or exclusively for modern music. But there isn't one publisher in the world who prints exclusively "serious music." Belayev seems to have been the sole exception to this rule, but it cost him his entire fortune. . . . Or there are publishers exclusively for classical music, but these are the ones who wait for composers to die and achieve fame, as I've mentioned. So, if contemporary "serious" music ever sees the light of day, that is only because of the publishers' habit of a *mélange:* alongside the 75 per cent of popular or fashionable music, they risk 25 per cent from the third category—"ours." The late Gutheil, who was able to stand a large quantity of my music, died a natural death only because, in addition to my compositions, he printed thousands of popular songs. Otherwise he would have gone bankrupt or hanged himself! . . . I also consider as acceptable the proposal made to you for outright payment rather than royalties. "Royalties" is a word that sounds very pleasant, but that's all. More for the

soul, rarely for the pocket! Again I'm thinking of us, of "serious" composers. Both your contracts and mine mention royalties, but when did
we ever receive any? If we did, it was so little it's better forgotten!
Nothing but shame! Z. offers you 1200 marks for the songs. Translated
into francs, this means a whole year of your apartment. The violin
sonata—that's six months of rent. No, it's not much! But that's what keeps
us "serious."

I've just remembered that even Belayev couldn't keep up with Rimsky-
Korsakov, and that two of his operas, *Voyevoda* and the *Cockerel*, went
to Bessel. And here's something more. Publication might be arranged
here somewhere for one of your violin sonatas. I'm not sure, but I think
so. The terms here: nothing in advance, and a certain percentage from
each copy sold. An accounting once or twice a year. But here there are
even fewer lovers of serious music than in Europe.

Chapter 15

The Composer Resumes

AFTER seven long, full concert seasons Rachmaninoff considered
that he deserved a sabbatical year. Bookings for the season of
1925–26 were cut short—no recital dates were accepted after December 11, 1925—and after too long an interval Rachmaninoff, secretly
as of old, began another major work, his fourth concerto.

Without leaving the New York apartment for the winter he went
into deeper seclusion than usual. A good start was made on the concerto, but its composer had underestimated the intrusive powers of his
friends armed with unavoidable obligations of all sorts. He had to
participate in the composition of an "address" sent to Glazunov at the
Leningrad Conservatory on Glazunov's sixtieth birthday. He had to
hear the progress of Nemirovich-Danchenko's project (with Morris
Gest as go-between) of persuading Otto Kahn to have Rachmaninoff
conduct *The Queen of Spades* at the Metropolitan (Gatti-Cassaza
would not hear of it). Through March and April Josef Hofmann
tried to trap him into listening "to a piano concerto of an American
lady who plays the piano quite well; the orchestral accompaniment
would be done by her husband, on the 'Duo-Art,' *completely private,*
and without any obligations on your part—do you care to take a
chance?" This was not the atmosphere for composition. Rachmaninoff
wrote to Wilshaw on April 19:

My dear Vladimir Robertovich, it gives me great joy to receive your
letters and truly, if it weren't for this accursed life here that robs one of
work as well as one's whole day, and the continuous rush to do what has
to be done and what doesn't have to be done, such as various pointless
visits, notes, pesterings, proposals, and so on—if not for all this I would
write you oftener. I've grown used to this country and I love it, but
there's one thing it doesn't have—quiet. However, it has become difficult
to obtain this in Europe, too. Either I don't know how to organize it, or
perhaps it doesn't exist anywhere. So I'm always rushing about, eternally
conscious that I shan't be in time! Now, before our departure for Europe,
this seems even worse. . . . We're going to our children in Paris, whom

I have missed terribly! As in the old days—they are "the light in the window"! They are really nice, and their treatment of me, grown old, is quite touching. I think to myself that evidently somewhere in my life I did one good deed, for which God sends me this joy. I also had a son-in-law who was as good and whose treatment of me was like that of my children! But he did not survive. . . .

We plan to stay in Paris till June 1, not later than the 15th. Then to Germany, where we've taken a villa in Weisser Hirsch. We'll all be together there. Only Irina will go to the Wolkonskys for a month. We hope to stay in Germany for about three months. . . .

Separately I send you some of my piano arrangements. I hope they reach you.

The composition of the concerto, begun in a New York apartment, was completed in Weisser Hirsch by the end of August. Even a crippling boil on his hand does not check the relieved tone of his letter to the Somovs, on August 28:

Only in the last few days have our plans grown clear, not the plans for the far future, but for the most immediate. Thus the mad rush! . . . Natasha, alone, leaves on Tuesday for Nice via Paris. On that day Irina and I also go there, but by automobile, and by a shorter route. . . . On account of the Italian and Austrian visas that I didn't get in New York, we'll have to take an altered route through countries "within the pale" for us poor Russians; in other words, again through Germany and France.

 . . . My hand is still bandaged, but the wound is healing, and I can play a little. Only the little finger functions badly because its movement somewhat pains the wound. With great strain I managed to finish my work day before yesterday. And that lifts some burden from my soul. Now I contemplate with horror my pianist activities. I've not played for eight months. Shall I have time to do all that must be done?

On September 7 the family landed in Cannes. A piano followed them from Paris—Rachmaninoff felt even less ready for the coming season—and there were new antagonists to describe to the Somovs:

We arrived yesterday, and only then did Natasha find us this villa and we moved in. It belongs to Rothschild. Price to match! We have our own passage (*under* the railroad) to the sea. The garden is full of great palms. The heat is stunning, and the mosquitoes are beasts. All last night, till six in the morning, the three of us spent catching them, each in his room.

The ladies didn't count their kill! But I did. Nineteen corpses lay on my bed. . . . Towards morning all of us lost our strength, and besides that, my hands and forehead look pock-marked. The ladies show no external marks. I explain that this is due to my skin's being more tender than theirs, and they grow angry. . . . My hand is still bandaged and heals slowly. No piano yet, and how I, slave of God, am to give concerts I dread to think.

On the following day he gave Medtner an even more stirring account of the Battle of the Mosquitoes, and also told him of a more important anxiety:

Just before leaving Dresden I received the copied piano score of my new concerto. I glanced at its size—110 pages—and I was terrified! Out of sheer cowardice I haven't yet checked its time. It will have to be performed like the *Ring:* on several evenings in succession. And I recalled my idle talk with you on the matter of length and the need to abridge, compress, and not to be loquacious. I was ashamed! Apparently the whole trouble lies in the third movement. What I must have piled up there! I have already started (in my mind) to look for cuts. Found one, but only eight bars, and besides, it's in the first movement, which isn't so frightening in length. And I "see" that the orchestra is almost never silent, which I regard as a great sin. This means that it's not a concerto for piano, but a concerto for piano *and* orchestra.

I also notice that the theme of the second movement is the theme of the first movement in Schumann's concerto. How is it that you didn't point this out to me?

On September 13 Medtner wrote to his friend of his troubles with his own new concerto, and of Rachmaninoff's fear of length:

True, we have no mosquitoes, but I have been literally beaten down by bassoons and clarinets that, like invisible spirits, pester me day and night ever since I completed the new concerto. . . .

I cannot agree with you, either in the particular fear that your new concerto is too long, or in general on your attitude to length. Actually, your concerto amazed me by the fewness of its pages, considering its importance. . . . Is it possible that music in general is so unpleasant that the less of it the better? Naturally there are limitations to the lengths of musical works, just as there are dimensions for canvases. But within these human limitations, it is *not the length* of musical compositions that creates an impression of boredom, but it is rather the *boredom* that creates the impression of length. . . . A song of two pages lacking inspiration seems longer to me than Bizet's *Carmen,* and Schubert's *Doppelgänger* seems to me more grandiose than a Bruckner symphony. I can hear you exclaim, "Why does he say all this!"—Of course you know all this better than I, and *this* is really what you are speaking about, except that you speak in that strange language of *figures,* pages, minutes.

Rachmaninoff sent some comfort on September 22—"There are always small corrections to be made, and it's easier to get to them after hearing the whole composition . . ."—and some news on October 9: "I'm still working on the corrections of my concerto, and I see no end to this."

When Rachmaninoff returned to New York, on November 10, the new concerto (dedicated to Medtner) was ready for performance. He brought another newly completed work, a choral and orchestral arrangement of three Russian folk songs. This may have been the result of several years' work at odd intervals; the first ("Over the little river") he had long admired in a collection of Russian songs, the second ("Oh, Vanka, you bold fellow") Chaliapin had sung for him, and the last ("Quickly, quickly, from my cheeks") he first heard as sung by Nadezhda Plevitskaya, a concert singer of folk songs. The choruses were dedicated to the conductor of his favorite orchestra, Leopold Stokowski, and arrangements were made for the Philadelphia Orchestra to give the first performance of both works.

Before these premières, Rachmaninoff's recital season began. At his first New York program, on February 19, 1927, Olga Samaroff estimated the pianist more highly than his program:

Rachmaninoff has a curiously complex personality. Reserved and inscrutable as a man, he is singularly frank and simple as a pianist, presenting music with a magnificent pianism and imposing general mastery, but with a sometimes almost matter-of-fact directness, as in the E-flat minor Intermezzo of Brahms.

This destroys, in my opinion, the mystery and "half-lights" which under the fingers of a Gabrilowitsch seem to form the undeniably characteristic note of the piece. Brahms clearly indicated the establishment of this general mood in the opening section of the said work by marking the first four measures "piano," "sotto voce" and the repetition of the phrase beginning at the fifth measure pianissimo in the treble with a triple pianissimo in the bass. Mr. Rachmaninoff played all these measures forte or mezzo forte, thus throwing a clear, decisive light on the outlines of the music.

Again, as a pianist, Rachmaninoff seldom displays in my opinion the emotional warmth and sensuous color so characteristic of his own creative muse. So we have in one person a triple personality, highly interesting, intriguing and often furnishing the unexpected. My most thrilling impressions of Rachmaninoff, the pianist, have been those given by his playing of his own piano concertos with orchestra, notably the third. There, in his double role of creator and interpreter, he is stupendous.

Hofmann, to whom he had shown the new concerto, came to this concert, but could not stay to talk about the work. He wrote to Rachmaninoff the following day from Philadelphia:

. . . I like your new concerto extremely well. Although it seemed to me that it would be rather difficult to play with an orchestra; particularly because of its frequent metric changes.

I sincerely hope that this won't be an obstacle to other performances of the concerto. It certainly deserves them from a musical as well as a pianistic point of view!

After two Philadelphia performances of this Fourth Concerto and the choruses on March 18 and 19 the new works were displayed on March 22 before the enthusiastic audience and skeptical critics of New York. Lawrence Gilman, who had written the program notes, was more subjective in his review of the concerto for the *Herald Tribune*:

For all its somewhat naïve camouflage of whole-tone scales and occasionally dissonant harmony, Mr. Rachmaninoff's new concerto (his Fourth, in the key of G minor) remains as essentially nineteenth century as if Tchaikovsky had signed it. Somber it is, at times, but it never exhibits the fathomless melancholy of such authentic masters of tragical speech as Moussorgsky. There is a Mendelssohnian strain in Rachmaninoff which relates him more intimately to the salon than to the steppes; and this strain comes out in his new concerto, as it does in all his music, sooner or later.

The new work is neither so expressive nor so effective as its famous companion in C minor. Nor is it so resourceful in development. There is thinness and monotony in the treatment of the thematic material of the slow movement, and the finale begins to weary before its end. The imposing, the seductive Rachmaninoff is still the unashamed and dramatizing sentimentalist of the Second Concerto.

Samuel Chotzinoff, in the *World,* was frankly disappointed:

When Mr. Rachmaninoff last night launched into his "Fourth" concerto . . . the first theme, after a few introductory measures, seemed like an assurance that the eminent Russian was only taking up the thread where he had left off, all seemed so right and true for the moment. Here were the same characteristics, the vaulted architecture of phrase, the undercurrent of romantic sadness, the harmonic solidity. But as the movement progressed the artistic tension began slowly to relax. Succeeding parts did not attain a natural fusion, new material appeared without the sanction of a musical necessity, piano and orchestra went skirmishing afield. One's attention began to wander.

The first movement came to a close with unexplained abruptness. One's hopes were centered on the largo. Rachmaninoff is always at home in slow movements in which his long, supple melodies move luxuriantly, albeit with aristocratic dignity. But the melody of the largo of the new concerto was not even characteristically Rachmaninoff. It was reminiscent, but only of Schumann's piano concerto, the opening theme of which appeared in the Rachmaninoff like a pale emanation of itself. The last movement had even fewer moments of inspiration than the preceding two, and left one with the impression that a lot was said, but not of any particular importance.

Pitts Sanborn's review in the *Telegram* was devastating. He found the concerto "long-winded, tiresome, unimportant, in places tawdry":

The concerto in question is an interminable, loosely knit hodgepodge of this and that, all the way from Liszt to Puccini, from Chopin to Tchaikovsky. Even Mendelssohn enjoys a passing compliment. The orchestral scoring has the richness of nougat and the piano part glitters with innumerable stock tricks and figurations. As music it is now weepily sentimental, now of an elfin prettiness, now swelling toward bombast in a fluent orotundity.

It is neither futuristic music nor music of the future. Its past was a present in Continental capitals half a century ago. Taken by and large—

and it is even longer than it is large—this work could fittingly be described as super-salon music. Mme. Cécile Chaminade might safely have perpetrated it on her third glass of vodka.

For Richard Stokes, of *The Evening World,* the Three Russian Songs saved the day:

> Like Napoleon at Marengo, Sergei Rachmaninoff yesterday evening at Carnegie Hall turned the most disastrous rout of his career into decisive victory. The opening attack was made with a new concerto. . . . It came reeling back from the charge in disorder and defeat. . . .
>
> After the intermission a chorus of twenty contraltos and basses took its place with the orchestra and proceeded to redeem the catastrophe with Mr. Rachmaninoff's three latest compositions. These are settings for voices and orchestra of Russian folk songs. . . .
>
> The chorus, singing mostly in unison, had the effect of a twenty-fold soloist. The composer used the folk melodies as well as text, so that his creative office was restricted to the orchestra. But its comment on the narrative of the verses was that of a music drama.

The reception of the new concerto was distinctly a defeat. After completing its scheduled performances with the Philadelphia Orchestra, Rachmaninoff withdrew it from further American hearings. The blow was so heavy that it was many years before the composer could face the problem of revision of the Fourth Concerto.

After closing his season with a performance of the doomed concerto, Rachmaninoff left for Europe. He stayed first in a villa near Dresden. One task was to keep Medtner's spirits high; he wrote to him on June 25:

> I consider that a splendid idea of yours to submit a new chamber music composition to the Philadelphia contest. Perhaps you'll have time to do it before the beginning of November? I could then take care of the delivery of the manuscript, demanding a hearing of it as reward. . . .
>
> The dedication to me of either the concerto or the variations will make me happy, but I refuse to make the choice. *You* must do it.
>
> Don't grumble about the sanitarium regimen—bear it to the end. And the time you lose from work can be made up when you're well.

On September 27 he wrote again to Medtner:

> I am so sorry that the place you chose for the summer turned out so

badly, with the "outrageous screams" of roosters and dogs irritating you. I just happened to remember the thrush that disturbed your repose near Dresden—and no matter how wicked of me this is, I can't help smiling. Worst of all for me, and this is serious, was your news that the composition for the contest isn't ready. I was so happy when you decided to send something to America. Is this really final? Couldn't you really finish the work by the deadline? You still have two months.

A summer excursion was reported to the Somovs:

Exactly a week ago we left Dresden for Switzerland. By reason of my infinite kindness, little acknowledged and insufficiently appreciated by my wife, I have decided to extend the two-week term of our stay here— to 17 days. Let her drink my blood! Our place, Glion, is 700 meters above Montreux, and the Lake of Geneva is just under our feet, always admired by us from our balcony. No, I have no intention of describing the beauties of Switzerland for you. Baedeker has done that. I'll say only a few words about myself and our pastimes. As promised, my whole day is devoted to health: that is, I remain outdoors except at night and for the afternoon nap. And at night we sleep with both doors on to the balcony open. For these six days I've tramped at least several hundred kilometers. And in six days we've eaten enough for 18 days. I'll return to Dresden looking like Pyotr Petrovich Petukh.* . . . Each day we go up some neighboring mountain top by *funiculaire* and come back on our own feet. And no matter how we sweat or how much certain little bones in the loins ache— we endure and go on. Tomorrow, for the first time, we are to have an automobile trip. We're renting, just like the bourgeoisie, a car and going to St. Bernard—just the two of us, not in a crowd as the English proletarians do it. There and back is about 150 kilometers, and to get there we have to cross several mountains. I can imagine what a lot of food we'll gulp down!

We've had two letters from our girls. They also lose no time and everything there goes on—whirlingly. Enchanted admirers from all corners of Europe! After our departure the attraction seems to have increased. We probably left just in time, too! I seem to find it easier to climb hills than to endure this cascade of the enchanted. It is wisely arranged that death removes the older generation, leaving the way free for the young. Just think what could happen without this! What a roar of grumbling and rumbling, what a thunder of discontent. Forever and everywhere!

* A well-fed character in Gogol's *Dead Souls*.

In every family, in every house, city—the whole world! The old ones should always live apart. They can agree with one another and talk on endlessly, mostly about the mistakes of the younger generation. . . .

Yours,

P. P. Petukh.

For this year—and the next year, and the next too—Rachmaninoff's family were not to live on his earnings as a composer. They were to be supported not by the new Fourth Concerto or by the Three Russian Songs, but by Rachmaninoff as a pianist. His income season resumed in January 1928, with a program built around three fantasia-sonatas—by Beethoven, Liszt, and Chopin. Before going to work Rachmaninoff attended this month two musical events of contrasting significance: a concert demonstration of the electronic instrument invented by Leon Thérémin, and the American debut of Blumenfeld's young pupil, Vladimir Horowitz.

Among Rachmaninoff's most memorable recordings are those made with Fritz Kreisler—a diplomatic miracle arranged by Charles Foley, who was manager for both artists. The first of these was for Grieg's Sonata for Violin and Piano; two years later Rachmaninoff spoke jocularly of the circumstances of this recording:

Do the critics who have praised those Grieg records so highly realise the immense amount of hard work and patience necessary to achieve such results? The six sides of the Grieg set we recorded no fewer than five times each. From these thirty discs we finally selected the best, destroying the remainder. Perhaps so much labour did not altogether please Fritz Kreisler. He is a great artist, but does not care to work too hard. Being an optimist, he will declare with enthusiasm that the first set of proofs we make are wonderful, marvelous. But my own pessimism invariably causes me to feel, and argue, that they could be better. So when we work together, Fritz and I, we are always fighting.

The American season ended on Sunday afternoon, April 22, 1928, with a benefit " for the relief of Russian sufferers from the late war." By Tuesday the receipts were counted and Rachmaninoff addressed a letter to The New York Times, thanking "all those who attended," and attaching an itemized account of receipts, expenses, and disposition of the funds.

The single London recital of the year gave pleasure to its hearers, including Ernest Newman:

> He is one of the very few musicians who can fill Queen's Hall in these days; but whether he manages this because he is one of the finest of pianists or because he wrote the C sharp minor Prelude I should not like to say . . . he has amusingly confessed that it still pursues him everywhere. That little effort of his Byronic youth has been the making of him; for the general public, Rachmaninov is that Prelude, just as Charlie Chaplin is a pair of baggy trousers and hypertrophied boots, and George Robey is a pair of arched eyebrows. Lucky Rachmaninov, and no less lucky us, for were it not for the world-popularity brought him by the Prelude we might not have been listening to him last Saturday.
>
> . . . While his Bach and his Chopin playing was a pure delight, we listened with special interest to his performance of Liszt's Fantasia quasi Sonata, "Après une lecture de Dante." For it is out of the Lisztian rhetoric that a good deal of Rachmaninov's own music has come. He makes a more worthy thing of the Fantasia, I fancy, than Liszt himself was in the habit of doing.

Rachmaninoff was less satisfied with his performance. He wrote to the Somovs the next day, May 24: "The hall was about three quarters filled. I had a very great artistic success, but played only so-so. The Steinway is quite satisfactory and in its melodiousness and *piano* it is even better than the American make. The only thing it lacks is the American power."

The family took a pleasant country house in Normandy for the summer, "Les Pelouses," near Villers-sur-Mer, surrounded by flowers and orchards and meadows. The Somovs received an enthusiastic report and a list of errands, dated June 17:

> We've lived here five days and we are all extremely pleased with the location and the air and the view all around. . . . For exercise here there is tennis and, a kilometer away, there is the sea for swimming. It seems to me, however, that this sea will serve more for backdrop—it's so cold. . . . I'm satisfied with the climate! In old age heat seems harder to bear! I lead an exemplary life: doing gymnastics, walking a lot, going to bed on time, drinking milk and smoking "on schedule," meaning little, or considerably less than I smoked before. . . . Results already appear. I sleep better, headaches are less frequent, and I eat more.

Just a kilometer away live Nikolai Karlovich [Medtner] and his wife. They kindly waited till we found something so that they could take a place near us. We see them every day, which pleases and entertains me greatly. . . .

1. Send me, care of Paichadze, a thousand cigarettes.

2. Find the Liszt "Eroica" (in my cabinet) and send it too. It's a little thing of six pages that I can't get here.

3. With the "Eroica" send the volume of Chopin Préludes and Rondos. . . .

4. Alert Fischer by telephone that two copies of the "Russian songs" have been sent him for Washington, to register the copyright.

5. Salute everyone, embrace and express *my love*.

By August 12 enough friends had discovered the pleasures of "Les Pelouses" for Rachmaninoff to tell Somov, "We have a full house here. From morning to night—walks, racing, swimming, poker, gymnastics." Among the visitors were Somov's uncle, the famous painter Konstantin Somov (who had painted Rachmaninoff's portrait in the unhappy summer of 1925), and the Swans, who give a picture of the household:

In accordance with the Russian fashion, every night the family and their friends gathered in the big dining room of "Les Pelouses," and tea was served. Mrs. Rachmaninoff, a very gracious hostess, presided over the table. The two daughters—the lively Irina, who is the widow of the young Prince Peter Wolkonsky, and the younger Tatiana . . . added much animation. . . .

On one occasion—August 29, 1928—a different mood prevailed and there was music. Rachmaninoff showed his friends [his new two-piano arrangement of the Fourth Concerto dedicated to Medtner, who was present with his wife]. Rachmaninoff played his new work with Leo Eduardovich Conus, his lifelong friend and classmate at the Moscow Conservatory.

The summer ended in Dresden, where he had a chance to get some work done, as well as to practice for an "experimental" European tour, starting on October 2. The first concert, in Copenhagen, left pleasant memories; in speaking with Swan two years later, Rachmaninoff said, "Most of all, I love to go to Denmark. It is not very profitable to go there, but I do it out of sentiment. The Danes are about one hundred years behind in music, as also in their technical development; that is why they still have a heart. It is so wonderful to see a whole nation that still has a heart. Very soon this organ will generally become atrophied because of its uselessness; it will soon be a curiosity." Then Oslo, Bergen, Stockholm, Upsala, The Hague, Amsterdam, Rotterdam—

By Berlin the experimental campaign was a triumphal progress. About his recital on November 9 the Berlin critics were unanimous; the 8 *Uhr Abendblatt* wrote:

. . . the evening's climax was Chopin. One has almost forgotten how Chopin must be played, for there is no piano classic so much sinned against. Rachmaninoff approaches him with the incomparable craft and unpretentious virtuosity, the charm and fantasy that this witty and sensuous music requires. Only a great personality, a poet, can take a Nocturne in this slow tempo and still produce breathless tension that never lags. And how Rachmaninoff plays a rondo, a scherzo—how rhythm, tempo, color, and form are forged together into a unity, and with what direct comprehension!

Commenting on the long absence of Rachmaninoff from Berlin, and the growth of his world fame, one critic was wryly ironic: "So it is possible to grow famous away from Berlin, too!" On November 11 and 12 Rachmaninoff played the Third Concerto with the Philharmonic conducted by Furtwängler, and there was no longer any doubt as to the success of the "experiment." After recitals in Dresden, Prague, Vienna, and Budapest, the tour ended in Paris on December 2, and an annual European tour was established as a part of Rachmaninoff's year.

While in Paris Rachmaninoff gave an interview that produced international repercussions:

"Radio is not perfect enough really to do justice to good music," he said. "That is why I have steadily refused to play for it. But my chief objection is on other grounds.

"It makes listening to music too comfortable. You often hear people say, 'Why should I pay for an uncomfortable seat at a concert when I can stay at home and smoke my pipe and put my feet up and be perfectly comfortable?'

"I believe one shouldn't be too comfortable when listening to really great music. To appreciate good music, one must be mentally alert and emotionally receptive. You can't be that when you are sitting at home with your feet on a chair.

"No, listening to music is more strenuous than that. Music is like poetry; it is a passion and a problem. You can't enjoy and understand it merely by sitting still and letting it soak into your ears."

British and American papers reacted to this frank opinion in editorials, cartoons, letters from readers. *The New York Times* of December 23 carried a reply sent by Walter Damrosch from his office at the National Broadcasting Company:

Mr. Rachmaninoff is so fine an artist that I think I could convince him of the error of his ways if he would sit in with us for one of our radio symphony hours and then during the following week read the letters that pour in from that great audience which he believes to be too lazy and comfortable to enjoy music. . . . If Rachmaninoff is correctly reported in this cable, he must be woefully ignorant of the enormous factor the radio has become in the development of good music.

Rachmaninoff's only hint of a response to this invitation shows in a second interview he gave early in January 1929:

Sergei Rachmaninoff told his Paris interviewers that New York had become the musical capital of the world. . . .

"Year by year, the thing that impresses me more and more about America is the wonderful improvement in public taste and appreciation that has taken place within an astonishingly short period of time. When I first went to America in 1909 audiences were not one tenth so large or so discriminating as they are now.

"New York has replaced Berlin as the bright particular heart of music," Rachmaninoff added, "and Philadelphia possesses one of the greatest orchestras the world has ever heard."

On his return to the "music capital of the world" Rachmaninoff faced a schedule of thirty-one recitals, to end on April 7. From Pittsburgh, on February 7, he wrote to Somov:

I send you the Detroit reviews. At last I too have joined the Pyrotechnicians. First time in my career. Incidentally, neither Natasha nor I could understand the places I've underlined: do they scold or praise us?* We await your instructions. There was also a Russian review, but so ridiculously laudatory that it's not decent to send it.

Before Rachmaninoff left for Europe, Alexander Greiner of the Steinway Company asked him if he would conduct three concerts of the New York Philharmonic during the next season. The programs would include his works, but the composer was not enthusiastic, according to Greiner's memorandum:

Rachmaninoff replied that the public did not care for any of his compositions except the C-sharp minor Prelude and that apparently the public believes that he can compose nothing else. He said that he wouldn't think of approaching any conductor to perform his works; that if the public did not care to hear his compositions, they might leave them alone. He furthermore said that he had no desire to go into orchestra conducting. He also said that he would not receive sufficient remuneration to make it worth his while. . . . However, he said that there was no use speaking about it—that if he wants to conduct and make money, he can hire an orchestra and perform whatever he pleases.

He then spoke of his forthcoming tour in Europe; he said that he had more dates than he could take care of, that the doctor had strongly advised him to pause for a year and that he insists that he rest at least a month between his American and European engagements. . . . He said that he would gladly stop playing but that he could not yet afford to do so.

By May the Rachmaninoffs were in Paris, and they wrote the Somovs on May 30, the day after they occupied their new summer home: "Yesterday, with Natasha, and the former cook and a new chauffeur (a new broom, if it's Russian, sweeps clean), we moved out to the villa. We're not quite satisfied with it, but it was the best to be had—according to Natasha." The villa of "Le Pavillon" turned out to be satisfactory enough for several Rachmaninoff summers. It was in the village of Clairefontaine, an hour's drive from Paris; Swan,

* The review was by Ralph Holmes, in the *Detroit Evening News:* "Something seems to have come over Rachmaninoff these past few seasons. Not only did he take to smiling a couple of years ago, but now he has definitely joined the ranks of the pianistic pyrotechnicians, and in Orchestra Hall Tuesday evening gave a performance that was positively dazzling."

who visited them the following summer, described the place and the life there:

The chateaulike house [was] protected from the street by a solid wrought-iron fence. . . . The wide steps of the open veranda led into the park. The view was lovely: an unpretentious green in front of the house, a tennis court tucked away among shrubs, sandy avenues flanked with tall old trees, leading into the depth of the park, where there was a large pond. This whole arrangement was very much like that of an old Russian estate. The park of "Le Pavillon" adjoined the summer residence [Ram- bouillet] of the President of France. A small gate opened into the vast hunting grounds: pinewoods with innumerable rabbits. Rachmaninoff loved to sit under the pine trees and watch the games and pranks of the rabbits.

In the morning the big table in the dining room was set for breakfast. As in the country in Russia, tea was served and with it cream, ham, cheese, hard-boiled eggs. Everybody strolled in leisurely. There were no rigid rules or schedules to disturb the morning sleep.

Except for visits to a doctor in Paris, the rest continued. The Satins visited Clairefontaine, and Boris Chaliapin came to paint a portrait of Rachmaninoff.

Somehow I've grown lazy lately [he wrote the Somovs on July 14]. . . . I've nothing to do: I drink a glass of cream at 11 A.M. That is all I do. And I also lie on a cot in the garden or in the woods. This amazing life ends soon. In three months concerts begin, and I must begin "the prepara- tory exercises," as Medtner says. Well, we'll start in a few days!

As for my health, the treatments have had results, of course. I've gained a few pounds and I don't feel my heart, which must have calmed down from doing nothing. Headaches have also lessened. In June there were even three weeks when they almost completely ceased. . . . In any case I look much better. Everybody notices it. Even Natashechka, who, as you know, is hardly ever satisfied with the way I look!

Before the summer's end the tone of Rachmaninoff's letters was changed by the news from Novgorod of the death of his mother on September 19. This, and the approaching concert season, changed the letters from relaxed talk of cream and cots to business arrange- ments, recordings, and the ever thorny matter of broadcasting. To Somov, on September 29:

I enclose a letter from Stokowski. Give it to Foley for his consideration. In my reply to Stokowski I emphasized that the decision [to broadcast] rests with Foley.

And there are two other matters on which I want his advice. According to the manager, my Berlin recital [on December 5] will be a sellout. A radio company asks to broadcast it. Should I consent, and what fee should I ask? My net profit last year was about 9 thousand marks. Similarly, if such a proposition is made in London, should I agree and how much should I ask? . . .

Has the recording of my Second Concerto come out? I play it on October 19 at The Hague with Mengelberg, and it would be good to have the records there at the same time.

After three recitals and two concerts with orchestra in Holland, he gave his first London recital of the season in Albert Hall on November 3. Within ten minutes of his return to the hotel he wrote the Somovs:

A cable came yesterday which in free translation read: "Why are you devils so silent!" I was quite embarrassed and cabled you at once my promise to write you after the London concert. . . . Beyond my expectations this barn's acoustics turned out to be very good. The instant I touched the piano I was assured of this. I calmed down and played quite successfully—in other words, I am pleased with myself. Thank God! The audience was large, but I have no idea how many more thousands might have been seated. The hall holds nine thousand.

Ibbs has sent Foley my list of concerts for November. I have 15 concerts in England. . . . I'll add only that on November 18 I play the 4th Concerto with Coates and the contract provides for two rehearsals. I hope all will go satisfactorily.

On November 21, *The Bells* will ring in Manchester. Sir H. Harty conducts. A fine musician! But I'll not be able to hear them, for that day I play in another town, from where I go to Manchester on the 22nd—one day too late. What a shame! Natasha has decided to abandon me and go there for the concert.

I gave five concerts in Holland. They spoiled me so there that if now the entire audience *in corpore* does not rise at my entrance and after the completion of a big work, I am displeased. I demand respect! . . .

In Paris lately I was treated lengthily and stubbornly by Kastritzky [a dentist] and by a French hypnotist. Both were charming! I was helped

and my neuralgia was considerably lessened. If you should ask me which
doctor saved me, I would unhesitatingly reply: the former. . . .

How glad I am that Sasha's [Siloti's] concert went brilliantly.

In the *Sunday Times* Newman echoed Rachmaninoff's satisfaction
with the London recital:

In a world that teems with fine pianists I know none finer than Rachmaninoff. Even the Albert Hall cannot obscure his superfine quality.
Last Sunday he employed an extraordinary variety of nuance and colour
in Mozart, Chopin and other composers. In every work his reading was
entirely his own; yet in not a single phrase could I find myself venturing
to disagree with him, sharply as his interpretation often cut across my
own notion of the work.

The *Manchester Guardian*, in reviewing the recital of November 23,
summed up the meaning of Rachmaninoff for an English audience:

Consider the programme, the main works in it: Beethoven's F-sharp, Op.
78; the Schumann Novelette in F-sharp minor; the Nocturne in D-flat and
the Valse in E-flat of Chopin; the Chopin Scherzo in C-sharp minor;
Tchaikovsky's Variations from his Op. 19—who would cross the street to
hear music so hackneyed? This music, one would have sworn until
Rachmaninoff had played it for us, could contain no new delights, no
pleasures that long and mechanical acquaintance had not staled years
ago. It was Rachmaninoff's achievement to make these standard works
seem fresh from the forge, every note vital and full of meaning. Incidentally he caused us to think we had never before heard them played, save
in a mild, commonplace fashion. He expresses his power by keeping,
like an artist, within the range of his instrument. His sonority is unforced,
a matter of intensity, not of noise. His songfulness, of which he is sparing,
is never too yielding in line; he seems always proud of the piano's essential
keenness of tone. He uses the pedal dexterously in his production of light
and shade. But he does not abuse this device; indeed he is often austere in
the niceness with which, by a perfection of timing, he releases the sus-
taining pedal to avoid dissonance. His attack is so intense that he commands our ears—and our minds—at once. He has the composer's instinct
for what is important in a structure: he seems to see the end in the beginning and to lay out his proportions accordingly. Yet we never get the
effect of a merely studied interpretation; the sense of form is quick and
instinctive with Rachmaninoff.

The Albert Hall recital of November 24 was an agony, for Rachmaninoff was forced to play almost two hours torn by neuralgic pain. Yet the standard of the performance was not impaired; the audience was unaware that anything was wrong until the newspapers of the next day announced that Rachmaninoff had canceled his two remaining English recitals in order to see his doctor in Paris.

Resuming his schedule with the Paris recital of December 1, he made eleven more appearances in Europe before returning to America, including two Berlin performances with Bruno Walter of the Second Concerto. The cool reception of the Fourth Concerto by London critics after its performance with Albert Coates appears to have confirmed the American opinions of it, and after four more performances in Europe next season, he played it no more until he could find the time and mind for revision of it.

As he left England on the *Berengaria,* on which Prokofiev and Elman were also sailing, an incident took place that Rachmaninoff could never speak of later without being overcome with laughter. On boarding the ship he noticed a great group of photographers bearing down on him. With the sinking heart he always experienced when confronted by a news photographer, he steeled himself, bowed to the inevitable, and awaited the onslaught. The phalanx of photographers advanced—and rushed past him! With a twinge of disappointment he turned to see that their target was the prizefighter, Primo Carnera.

Chapter 16

Work and Rest

O N RETURNING to New York Rachmaninoff found a happy suggestion awaiting him. Paichadze, managing director of Koussevitzky's music publishing house, passed on to Rachmaninoff a proposal from Koussevitzky: Would the composer select a group of his *Etudes-Tableaux* to be turned over for orchestration to Ottorino Respighi? The commissioned orchestrations would be published by Koussevitzky's firm, and Koussevitzky would conduct their first performances by the Boston Symphony. Previously, others had attempted to translate the color of Rachmaninoff's piano pieces into orchestral color, but no one had yet orchestrated his own favorite piano works, and Respighi seemed an ideal choice, in temperament and in skill. The proposal was enthusiastically endorsed by Rachmaninoff, and by January 2, 1930 he personally entered the negotiations with Respighi, writing to him directly. He had chosen five *Etudes-Tableaux*, from Op. 33 and 39, works whose programmatic contents he had been careful to conceal since their composition; but now these programs might be useful to Respighi. Rachmaninoff's letter to the Italian composer was sent to Paichadze, with this covering note: "If your financial negotiations with Respighi are concluded happily, kindly forward to him the enclosed letter."

Mon cher Maître!

La Société Anonyme des Grandes Editions Musicales [Koussevitzky's firm] informs me that you have agreed to orchestrate certain of my "Etudes Tableaux."

This good news gives me great joy, for I am sure that in your masterly hands these Etudes will be made to sound marvelous.

Will you permit me, Maître, to give you the secret explanations of their composer? These will certainly make the character of these pieces more comprehensible and help you to find the necessary colors for their orchestration. Here are the programs of these Etudes:

The first Etude in A minor [Op. 39, No. 2] represents the Sea and Seagulls. [This program was suggested by Mme. Rachmaninoff.]

The second Etude in A minor [Op. 39, No. 6] was inspired by the tale of Little Red Riding Hood and the Wolf.

The third Etude in E-flat major [Op. 33, No. 4] is a scene at a Fair.

The fourth Etude in D major [Op. 39, No. 9] has a similar character, resembling an oriental march.

The fifth Etude in C minor [Op. 39, No. 7] is a funeral march. Let me dwell on this a moment longer. I am sure you will not mock a composer's caprices. The initial theme is a march. The other theme represents the singing of a choir. Commencing with the movement in 16ths in C minor and a little further on in E-flat minor a fine rain is suggested, incessant and hopeless. This movement develops, culminating in C minor—the chimes of a church. The Finale returns to the first theme, a march.

That is all. If these details are not too boring to you, and you see some advantage in having them—I can develop them further.

When Respighi answered him on March 20 from the Palazzo Borghese, terms had evidently been agreed on:

Thank you very much for your kind letter and for the explanations of the études, which will be priceless for my work on their orchestration. I am really very pleased to be orchestrating these admirable compositions, and I hope you will be pleased with me. . . .

Ottorino Respighi

Unfortunately, Respighi did not ask for more details; and more were not again offered.

Before beginning his American tour in Hanover, New Hampshire, on January 21, Rachmaninoff had an opportunity to hear his favorite pianist Josef Hofmann, in a New York recital. He wrote to Hofmann afterwards:

What a delight you gave me with your Suite and how marvelously you played it! The first part only seemed to me a trifle monotonous.

Am I allowed to make one more remark? Why was the second half of the Valse not played in the same character as the first one? The first one was beautiful!

I hope you are not angry with me?

To which Hofmann replied:

I was very happy to learn that you liked my Suite and the way I played it. The reason I try to play it well is that the composition happens to be so poor.

As regards the Chopin Valse, I dare say that I do not plan how to treat a composition and occasionally it happens to sound well. This also explains why, on returning to the first part, it did not sound so well.

Angry with you? Certainly not! I am never angry with people I love and admire.

When Rachmaninoff returned to New York after the recitals in New England and Canada, he found that there were several days before his Carnegie Hall recital. He told Swan: "They were to be wasted days. So I asked Foley, 'Get me a couple of concerts in the vicinity of New York.' He got busy and arranged two concerts in comparatively small places, Englewood, New Jersey, and Mount Vernon, New York. All the tickets were sold, and everything went very well. This can happen only in America. I had tea at home, drove there and back in the car, played, earned some money, and at night I again had tea at home."

The New York recital of February 15 was particularly noted by the critics for Rachmaninoff's new interpretation of the Chopin sonata. W. J. Henderson, in the *Sun,* wrote:

He is not only a composer, but a pianist, a real pianist—not a composer-pianist. The third number on his list was Chopin's B-flat minor sonata, and the distinguished master played it entirely in his own way. He threw overboard all the old fashions and he even made adaptations of the composer's marks of expression. What he gave us was Sergei Rachmaninoff's translation of the text, and a tremendous version it was. . . .

For one listener this interpretation of the B-flat minor sonata—in which even the funeral march was played differently—closed itself with a magisterial *quod erat demonstrandum* which left no ground for argument. The logic of the thing was impervious; the plan was invulnerable; the proclamation was imperial. There was nothing left for us but to thank our stars that we had lived when Rachmaninoff did and heard him, out of the divine might of his genius, re-create a masterpiece. It was a day of genius understanding genius. One does not often get the opportunity to be present when such forces are at work. But one thing must not be forgotten: there was no iconoclast engaged; Chopin was still Chopin.

Posterity can also participate in this experience, for three days after

this recital Rachmaninoff recorded his performance of the Chopin
sonata at the Camden studios of the Victor Company. By six that day
he had finished and was visiting the Swans in Philadelphia, where
he talked about the recording session, among many other things:

"I get very nervous when I am making records, and all whom I
have asked say they get nervous too. When the test records are made,
I know that I can hear them played back to me, and then everything
is all right. But when the stage is set for the final recording and I
realize that this will remain for good, I get nervous and my hands get
tense. I am very pleased with the Schumann *Carnaval*. It has come
out very well. Today I recorded the B-flat minor Sonata by Chopin,
and I do not know yet how it has come out. I shall hear the test
records tomorrow. If it is not good, I can always have the records
destroyed and play it over again. . . . [The records were approved.]
You know how severely I judge myself and my compositions. But
I want to tell you that I have found some old records of mine. They
are very well played, without a hitch. There is some Johann Strauss,
Gluck, I think. They are very good."

Farther along on the tour of his Chopin-Liszt program he wrote
to Somov from Chicago:

Dear Yevgeni Ivanovich, how I regretted that Yelena Konstantinovna
wasn't at yesterday's concert. I experienced several bitter moments. . . .
I played well and was pleased with myself. After the concert I awaited
some "expression of delight." The first to come was Natasha, who—said
nothing. Let us assume that she speaks rarely. Then came two antiquated
Russians, one of whom is the local priest. These two thanked me for
playing my "wonderful Moscow bells," meaning my Prélude. This was
the first reaction I heard to my concert of the works of Chopin and Liszt.
And the last reaction came from a Russian woman I encountered; she said
wouldn't I "please play my piano sonata at my next concert." Today I
awaited the reviews. . . . I thought they might be laudatory. But they are
more than dubious. I enclose them. So I thought: if only Yelena Konstantinovna had been present there would have been none of these bitter
moments—I would have been praised. Positively, there is something in
my playing that is either not understood or not perceived, or—worst of
all—something so bad that I myself can't realize it. The outer success was
very great, but none of the musicians came to me. And Natasha has even
just now expressed the suspicion that X, who had promised to see us and

take us to dinner, hasn't done so because he didn't like the way I played. So that's what I'm "experiencing"! Yes, and I was left without dinner!

After his Philadelphia recital, also, he experienced some "bitter moments." Swan was present:

There was much commotion and mysterious whispering in the artists' room after the Philadelphia recital on March 29, 1930, when Rachmaninoff played a Chopin-Liszt program. Mrs. Rachmaninoff with some friends had come from New York. Rachmaninoff invited us to dine with them. Where? This was the cause of the whispering. It turned out to be a small, dark restaurant in the slummy part of the town, but—wine was served there. Those were prohibition days, when sedate, sober people would get excited at the prospect of a drink. But Rachmaninoff hardly drank at all—he just sipped the wine slowly without any particular satisfaction. He had come to this place not to spoil the fun of others, and mainly not to hurt the person who had arranged this rather gloomy affair. We sat down to table in a private dining room. In the adjoining room a man was playing the banjo and tearing violently at the strings. Rachmaninoff winced under a neuralgic pain in his left [right] temple, which he rubbed now and then, trying to do it as inconspicuously as possible. I asked Rachmaninoff's permission to stop the unexpected accompaniment to our meal.

"No, no," he said, as if a bit frightened, "please don't, they might think that I am displeased with something."

Mrs. Rachmaninoff and the friends left in a taxi after dinner to catch a New York train. We walked back to the hotel with Rachmaninoff. He was leaving alone at midnight for Boston, where he was to play the following day. The slummy streets were dirty and crowded. Rachmaninoff walked quietly and rather slowly. He looked at the squalid world with that peculiar gaze of his—somewhat aloof, quiet, wise, and at the same time sharp, noticing everything about him.

"Look, look here!" he said suddenly, stopping in front of a smelly fish stand. "Look, this dealer is cheating this old man. He is not giving him the full weight. The scoundrel! Look!"

At the next corner we saw the weird shape of an old Negress. Wrapped in dirty rags, she sat on a box, stretching out her trembling hand and looking somewhere into empty space with her blind eyes. Her eye lids were red and swollen.

"Oh, what is this? Look," said Rachmaninoff, with a shudder, and pulled out his wallet.

A postscript to the Philadelphia recital was provided by Hofmann, who wrote on April 4:

There were many high spots in this recital, but the Chopin Mazurka was probably, musically, the highest. Rubinstein told me, in one of my lessons with him, that if I get to the point where I know how to play a Chopin Mazurka, there would be no reason to worry about anything else. So, why should you worry?

Another thing that struck me as very unusual was that when you do not play as well as you are able to, your execution still bears the stamp of mastery.

In April Rachmaninoff left for Europe and reported to Somov from Paris:

We made the voyage well. Absolutely no tossing. Ship was good—food was bad.—I don't know why, but this time I felt unusual anguish. This is never gay, but this time especially. And my wife also felt anguish. . . .

Haven't been to the doctors yet. Am quite well. We're mostly loafing. Or we go visiting, or are visited. Natasha, from morning till seven o'clock, is on the rue de la Paix. We are getting our villa back. Hope to move there May 10.

Among interesting events in prospect: Toscanini's concerts, [Alexei] Remizov's evening, in which he'll recite from the works of Turgenev and Gogol as well as his own, and then a Russian assembly, where Russians will try to "unite." I've never been at such gatherings. That's for tomorrow.

Back in Clairefontaine for the summer with all its sounds and smells that reminded Rachmaninoff of Ivanovka—the ponds of croaking frogs, the nightingales, the aromas of fields and woods, the blossoming lindens—he would walk about the estate, delightedly sniffing the air with its smoke of bonfires, one of his favorite odors.

Alfred Swan and his wife received an invitation from "Le Pavillon":

Dear Alfred Alfredovich, Our hearty greetings to the Swans. Yesterday we moved here, into the country. The tennis court is being lengthened and widened. The surface is being rolled and improved. I have bought new rackets. New balls. I am bankrupt. When will you come?

Even before the Swans' arrival there was a stream of visitors through

"Le Pavillon," mostly friends of the girls. More than tennis, the great game this summer was film making, organized by young Fedya Chaliapin and played by all with great intensity; Rachmaninoff assumed the thankless role of the Father, either in the background or in the ensemble of the "happy ending." Officially he was referred to as "the one who suffers the financial losses."

We are all well [he wrote Somov on June 13]. I am working quite a lot. Work on the film has started. This means that our house is Babel and that half Paris spends its week ends at our place.

In August Rachmaninoff was compelled to take a two-week vacation from his vacation, driving with Tatiana to Vichy and Cannes; but the Swans' memories of this summer show us an almost carefree Rachmaninoff:

. . . everybody was possessed by the Russian passion for gathering mushrooms. Rivalries ran high, mushrooms were counted and compared, their beauty was discussed. Rachmaninoff was an early riser and often went alone for a walk in the woods. He used to return contented and start teasing (he was a great teaser). One day he badgered us with: "Oh, you don't know how to find the mushrooms? Look. A whole meadow, right here, round the corner, next to the house, and you missed them all. And I counted twenty."

A gay crowd rushed out to the meadow, and actually it was covered with mushrooms. But on touching them we discovered that they were not growing, but had merely been tucked into the moss and grass. Rachmaninoff had picked them in the woods while everybody was still asleep, had stuck them in, and now teased everybody with a contented smile. . . .

After tea, no matter how many guests there were, the big house would plunge into silence. Quietly and very inconspicuously, Rachmaninoff closed the doors of the drawing room and sat down at the piano. He did not practice in the strict sense of the word; he played something through, went with his fingers over the keyboard meditatively, and then suddenly the loud and victorious sounds of Beethoven's "Les Adieux" would be heard. Then he would again appear in the garden or in the dining room. . . .

On one of the last days of June 1930, the mood at Clairefontaine was particularly light and jolly. A great many people had gathered. After dinner, spirits rose high. A loud game of poker was organized, in which

Medtner was the principal loser. Then Rachmaninoff went to the piano.

"Father, play 'Bublichki!" the girls called.

This was a vaudeville song that had just been imported from Russia . . .
To Rachmaninoff's accompaniment, everybody sang "Bublichki." [Then
he announced:]

"And now Natashechka and I will play you the Italian Polka. This is
the only thing Natashechka knows. . . ."

The next morning Medtner found Rachmaninoff standing at the piano.
Medtner always longed to talk to him about music, especially composition, but Rachmaninoff invariably evaded the issue. . . .

"I know Rachmaninoff from my early years," Medtner once said; "all
my life has passed parallel to his, but with no one have I talked so little
about music as with him. Once I even told him how I wanted to discuss
with him the subject of harmony. Immediately his face became very distant and he said, 'Yes, yes, we must, sometime.' But he never broached
the subject again."

Rachmaninoff's avoidance of theoretical discussion was of course
most noticed in the field of music. With musicians he was always
ready, even eager, to discuss immediate or practical problems in music, but when theory and principles were mentioned, he would grow
so restive that the subject was soon dropped. Outside music, too, his
refusal to talk in abstract terms was so evident that a legend grew
that Rachmaninoff was "anti-intellectual," and even that "he never
read a book." His reading was actually wide and varied, but in his
choice of books, too, he emphasized *experience;* in these latter years
of much travel he read few novels, but absorbed enormous quantities of memoirs and social histories. But some factor of modesty or
shyness prevented conversation outside the family circle on these
unsuspected interests.

As for his own memoirs, the risk was exposure of the privacies behind the carefully austere façade maintained for the public. He
believed that a musician should communicate with his audience in
music alone. Nevertheless, at this summer's end some decision was
reached on the several biographical suggestions offered him. That
he was concerned with this subject was indicated by an interview
published in *The Musical Times,* in June. The article began:

Human beings keep on learning as long as they live. They gather experiences and impressions, from which they should draw lessons and conclusions to be utilized when they are getting old and have time to reflect on their memories. This, however, applies to those who have leisure wherein to assimilate impressions, and not to artists who rush about all the time giving concerts.

The Russian writer Mark Aldanov read this article as translated in *Candide,* on September 4, and immediately encouraged a Paris literary agent to approach Rachmaninoff with a request for his memoirs; but Rachmaninoff refused to use his time for this purpose. Two acquaintances of many years suggested that Rachmaninoff help them write his biography: Richard Holt, in London, and Oskar von Riesemann, then living in Switzerland. Rachmaninoff consented to help on the conditions that little of his time should be required, and that his poor memory for dates should be checked by his sister-in-law, Sophia Satina, who would also supply the factual basis for both books. Materials were sent to both biographers: Holt changed his mind, and Riesemann asked permission to talk over with Rachmaninoff some unclear periods of his career. Riesemann was invited to Clairefontaine for several days, and during this time he accompanied Rachmaninoff in his walks in the woods, talking of many matters, but without taking any notes. Rachmaninoff later remarked that he never saw a pencil in Riesemann's hand at this time.

On tour the Rachmaninoffs were persuaded to visit Riesemann again in his Swiss home. An indirect result of this visit was their decision to acquire a permanent European home. For years Rachmaninoff dreamed of buying a small estate; he wished to put aside all these rented villas and feverish movings and to settle down *at home.* Germany was considered, but Natalia Alexandrovna, who disliked Germany, urged him to look farther. Czechoslovakia was pleasant, but too far away from the rest of their world. The family preferred France, but Rachmaninoff put little trust in the mode of life there. Near Riesemann's home the Rachmaninoffs passed the shores of Lake Lucerne, where they had visited on their honeymoon twenty-eight years before. Here they found a lot on the lake front, purchased it to build later, and named it for

SErgei and NAtalia Rachmaninoff—SENAR.

Chapter 17

Exile Reinforced

RACHMANINOFF's autumn tour of the Continent and England lasted from October 25 in Oslo to December 10 in Zurich. After it he returned to the United States, where his American tour was to begin in New Haven on January 23, 1931. One request awaiting him was from Ossip Gabrilowitsch, inviting him to attend one of the New York or Philadelphia concerts of the Philadelphia Orchestra, which Gabrilowitsch was to conduct in Rachmaninoff's Second Symphony. After outlining a possibly conflicting schedule of dates, Rachmaninoff replied:

I agree with pleasure to attend the concert in which you will perform my Symphony, but on two conditions: first, that together we shall go over the tempo of the Symphony in advance, and secondly that "the presence of the composer in the audience" shall not be officially known to the conductor.

I consider it my duty to thank you sincerely for the wish to perform my work.

The symphony was performed without benefit of the composer's advice or attendance.

A request that had louder reverberations came from "The Circle of Russian Culture": to sign a protest against remarks made by Rabindranath Tagore praising Soviet achievements in the field of public education. Heretofore Rachmaninoff had always been unusually circumspect in avoiding political reference in his public statements—possibly because of unwillingness to embarrass his several relatives then living in Russia, including his mother and his brother Arkady. Now Rachmaninoff added his signature to those of Ivan Ostromislensky and Count Ilya Tolstoy, and over these three names *The New York Times* of January 15 printed a long, furious letter, sprinkled with heavy sarcasm, built on this motif:

By eulogizing the dubious pedagogical achievements of the Soviets, and by carefully omitting every reference to the indescribable torture to which the Soviets have been subjecting the Russian people for a period of over thirteen years, [Tagore] has created a false impression that no outrages actually exist under the blessings of the Soviet regime.

Within two months this gesture was to have a serious effect on Rachmaninoff's relations with his native land.

In the meantime more compliments passed between the two greatest pianists. Josef Hofmann addressed a letter to "Premier Sergei Rachmaninoff":

By "Premier" I mean the "Premier of Pianists," in spite of my artistic attempt of Sunday last!

After thinking over your offer to exchange hands with me, which you were so good as to suggest at the Zimbalist party, I accept. So I am to trade you my 20 fingers, according to your count, for your 10, which I still swear—despite the smaller number—are far superior. The only difficulty is how to close our deal—and in a painless fashion. Any suggestions?

January 19, 1931

My dear Mr. Hofmann:

There is a story that goes as follows: "Once upon a time in Paris there were a great many tailors. When one of them succeeded in renting a shop in a street devoid of tailors, he wrote on his sign: THE BEST TAILOR IN PARIS. The next tailor who opened a shop in the same street was forced to write on his sign: THE BEST TAILOR IN THE WHOLE WORLD. What was there left for the third tailor, who rented a shop between these two?—He wrote with becoming modesty: THE BEST TAILOR IN THIS STREET. . . ."

Your touching modesty, as expressed in your letter of January 15, as well as your incomparable professional knowledge, gives you full right to that last title:

You are the best in this street.

After Rachmaninoff's Chicago recital he sent Somov clippings and complaints:

Here are the reviews. I played well and I'm pleased with myself. But the critics are sour. What does it mean? What did I do to them? Ten years ago, when I played about ten times worse, the tone of the newspapers was ten times better. There's something here beyond my understanding. But the main thing is that I can't change, nor do I wish to.

On his way to Canada Rachmaninoff paused again in Chicago from where he wrote to Somov on February 20:

It's good that we stopped over in Chicago. It's been a sort of breathing spell, a rest. Took a walk, had a good sleep, and practiced. This last always cheers me up. I've just had dinner at the Congress, then I'll write letters and go to the train. Just before leaving I'll play the Bach once more. . . .

And in Chicago too I was awaited by two photographers and a lady reporter. I behaved courteously to the photographers, but I barked a bit at the reporter! Don't push in where you're not invited!

The tour swung west and down to Los Angeles, and as they crossed the continent to complete the season on the east coast, they heard most unwelcome news from Moscow. On the occasion of a concert performance at the Moscow Conservatory of *The Bells,* conducted by Coates, Moscow newspapers ran attacks on the work and its composer, calling for a halt to Soviet performances of his music as an answer to his anti-Soviet actions. The quality of these denunciations varied according to the character of the paper: *Pravda* was fierce but factual, mentioning the correspondence on Tagore; the chatty evening paper, *Vechernaya Moskva,* printed a malicious feuilleton on the concert:

The Bells Toll . . .

You enter the hall, sit down, and listen to the music. Church choirs, now heathenishly wild, now mystically awful. At the beginning they try to put you "to blissful sleep," with "silvery little bells," with languid violins, with a general monotonously lullaby movement; they end in a frightful desperate howling against a background of church liturgy. They try to induce hysteria. . . .

You look around, astonished. Yes, this is certainly a very peculiar audience. Some old men in tail coats and old women in ancient silks reeking of naphthalene. Bare skulls—quivering necks—swollen eyes—long gloves—lorgnettes—

Who is the author of this text, and who wrote this mystical music?

The music is by an emigrant, a violent enemy of Soviet Russia, Rachmaninoff. The words (after Poe) are also by an emigrant—the mystic, Balmont; on the conductor's podium was the former conductor of the

Marinsky Opera, Albert Coates, who left Russia in 1917 and now returns here with a foreign passport. . . .

Incomprehensible!—For whom was this concert intended?

The only musicians who took part in the discussion were those who supported the resolutions in the Moscow and Leningrad Conservatories to stop the teaching and performance of Rachmaninoff's works there.

Rachmaninoff refused to comment on this boycott when he arrived in New York, and he took the news more calmly than did his friends, for he felt sure that this was only a temporary penalty for his signature on the *Times* letter. But he had ended *The Musical Times* interview, "Only one place is closed to me, and that is my own country—Russia," and now Russia was closed to his music, too. His East Coast concerts were played without the spirit that always made the most familiar music so fresh an experience in his hands; he said it was his right temple, not the boycott, that caused this. Of his last concert, Edward Cushing wrote in the *Brooklyn Eagle:*

. . . despite his classic impersonality that is one of its most striking characteristics, his art reflects the fluctuations of his moods to a degree not observable in the performances of pianists equally gifted, equally accomplished. When he is not at his best, as was the case last evening, he can be very dull. His emotional detachment then is translated into terms of indifference, and one feels that Mr. Rachmaninoff has neither head nor heart for his task; nothing is expressed in his playing but weariness and lassitude of spirit. He is sufficiently the master of his instrument, sufficiently the musician always to play brilliantly, in a sense effectively; neither his technique nor his sense of values, of proportion, of style deserts him; but his pianism becomes spiritually, emotionally barren, conveys to us little or nothing of the meaning of the music, seems to us a mere repetition of interpretative formulae, devoid of conviction on Mr. Rachmaninoff's part.

Even Paris was less welcome to Rachmaninoff this year. ("Here they tear me to pieces, so the less I live here the better for my health.") After inspecting the Senar site he moved to a *Kurhaus* in nearby Lucerne for a two-week rest; he looked forward to summer work in a postscript to Somov: "Do send me from the music closet, Scriabin's

2nd sonata (Sonata Fantasia) and Liszt's Tarantella, 'Venezia e Napoli.'" The family settled again in "Le Pavillon," and Rachmaninoff wrote Somov on July 16:

A few words about us: Ever the same. Guests, guests, and guests! Now they stay in the middle of the week, too. If I should buy "Pavillon," I suppose the caretaker's little house would be adapted for guests, and it would never be empty. Just as well that purchase didn't work out. . . .

Work saves me from the guests. I am working a lot. Letters and requests besiege me as usual and my lack of promptness in answering them torments me somewhat. The latest political events have swooped down on us like a thunderstorm! It's no longer good to be living on this earth!

And it seems to me that the worst times are still ahead.

Guests may have conflicted with his work, but he enjoyed them. One visitor of this summer, Michael Chekhov, actor and nephew of Anton Chekhov, tells that his host would emerge from regular morning scales with a face as serious and severe as at concerts. Then Rachmaninoff would stroll over to the tennis court and light a cigarette as he watched the players, and his face would gradually relax. Chekhov also witnessed Chaliapin's visit to Clairefontaine:

S. V. beamed—he loved Fyodor Ivanovich dearly. They walked through the garden, both tall and graceful (each in his own way), and talked: F. I. the louder, S. V. the softer. S. V. would lift his right eyebrow slyly, look askance at his friend, and then laugh heartily. . . .

When they returned to the big study, "Fedya, please—" F. I. guesses the appeal and refuses—no, he can't, he's not in good voice, and in general— "No, I won't," and then, suddenly, consents.

At the piano S. V. touched a few chords; and then, as Fedya sang, S. V. looked so joyful, so young, now and then glancing at us as if successfully performing a trick. The singing ended. S. V. laughed and patted Fedya's powerful shoulder, and I noticed tears in his eyes.

In early August Rachmaninoff and his wife drove to Senar to occupy the first structure there, an apartment over the garage, while watching progress on the building of the house proper; he wrote to his sister-in-law:

Of our four days here two have been very hot, and two have had uninterrupted rain. Today, for instance, it's been pouring since morning, and it's now seven in the evening. Nevertheless, I feel wonderful! I walked a little—if not in the yard, then on the covered balcony; and—I work a lot. Stillness disturbed by no one. Yesterday, however, we had guests: Riesemann came with the violinist Milstein, and they stayed all evening. As I had worked to my heart's content up to their arrival, I spent the evening pleasantly, chattering....

As for our property—I am very well satisfied with it. We have a fine cottage.... As yet I can only dream of the big house, for which a large area has been leveled, just by the cliff over the lake. I stand here, feast on the view, and imagine what beauty there will be in my room through the big window. In my thoughts I have also found a place where they can bury me, if necessary.

He did not mind when his wife made fun of his efforts to transform Senar into another Ivanovka. The debris, the noise and explosions that began when the workmen arrived at 6 A.M., the incessant rains that washed earth and rocks down onto the laboriously leveled space —all this drove Natalia Alexandrovna to despair, but Rachmaninoff was stimulated by the idea of a new home, and a great deal of composition was accomplished this summer. Old works were brought out for revision, and a large new piano work was undertaken. The rift with his native land may have had the positive effect of forcing him to depend again on himself alone. On leaving Senar he wrote to Somov:

We've been in Switzerland for three weeks. Tomorrow at 7 A.M. we leave for Paris. Natasha leaves here with pleasure, I with reluctance. Both living and working have been more quiet and pleasant for me here.

Before beginning his American season Rachmaninoff returned to Clairefontaine, where one evening he talked with Swan about work:

Medtner had just composed his three "Hymns to Toil," and when Rachmaninoff saw them he responded with a one-word telegram to the composer: "*Superbe.*" Yet he criticized the great length of some of Medtner's works—for example, the length of his sonata developments—and sometimes urged him to cut them. Rachmaninoff was himself at that time cutting and rewriting some of his early compositions. This is what he said:

"I look at my early works and see how much there is that is superfluous. Even in this sonata [referring to his second Sonata in B-flat minor] so

many voices are moving simultaneously, and it is too long. Chopin's
Sonata lasts nineteen minutes, and all has been said. I have rewritten my
First Concerto; it is really good now. All the youthful freshness is there,
and yet it plays itself so much more easily. And nobody pays any attention. When I tell them in America that I will play the First Concerto,
they do not protest, but I can see by their faces that they would prefer
the Second or Third. . . . It is incredible how many stupid things I did
at the age of nineteen. All composers do it. Only Medtner has, from the
beginning, published works that it would be hard for him to equal in
later life. He stands alone in this."

I asked him about his last works.

"I have just written a set of Variations on a theme of Corelli," he said.
"You know, with all my travels and the absence of a permanent abode,
I really have no time to compose, and when I now sit down to write it does
not come to me very easily. Not as in former years."

I then asked him to show me the Variations. . . .

Sitting down at the piano, half reading from the manuscript and half
playing from memory, with a miraculous facility, he went from one variation to another. . . . In twelve variations Rachmaninoff leads us through
an ever-winding labyrinth of rhythmic and melodic figures. Then the
onslaught on the tonality is made with a torrent of cadenzas. While playing it he said: "All this mad running about is necessary in order to efface
the theme." And out of the turmoil emerged a lovely, luxurious D-flat
major, first in blocks of chords (Variation 14) and then in the form of
an enchanting Rachmaninoff nocturne. But its life was brief. The D
minor hurried in once more and finally engulfed all. Here Rachmaninoff
hit upon an entirely novel device. The final variation (*coda*) was neither
a climax nor a return to the beginning. It opened up new perspectives,
drew the conquered D-flat major into its orbit, and ended on a quiet,
meditative note.

After Rachmaninoff had played the Variations he looked at his hands:

"The blood-vessels on my fingertips have begun to burst; bruises are
forming. I don't say much about it at home. But it can happen at any
concert. Then I can't play with that spot for about two minutes; I have
to strum some chords. It is probably old age. And yet take away from me
these concerts and it will be the end of me."

The first public performance of the new Variations—dedicated to
Kreisler—was at Rachmaninoff's first concert of the season, in Mont-

real on October 12, 1931. The reception generally was faintly condescending; one Boston critic found in them "a great deal that will intrigue pianists willing to tackle new problems." In New York one of the attendant critics was Joseph Yasser, who wrote enthusiastically of the new work in *Novoye Russkoye Slovo,* but pointed out Rachmaninoff's error in crediting Corelli with a theme that had been previously used by other seventeenth-century composers.

On the day after this article appeared [Yasser recollects], I received an invitation to see S. V. . . . On the desk lay the opened newspaper with my article. With this he began the conversation:
"First, I want to thank you for your review and for pointing out my error. . . ."
In the detailed discussion that ensued Rachmaninoff was evidently seeking a substantial pretext for leaving the first title of his piano work unchanged, as it had already appeared in this form in concert programs, in the press, and in advance notices of his approaching tour. (Later, in publication, Rachmaninoff settled this dilemma with a compromise: he omitted Corelli's name on the cover, but retained his original title inside.)
But the "Corelli problem" was, for Rachmaninoff, only of secondary importance in our conversation. . . .
He began to tell me that he was then very much interested in the familiar mediaeval chant, *Dies Irae,* usually known to musicians (including himself) only by its first lines, used so often in various musical works as a "Death theme." However, he wished to obtain the whole music of this funeral chant, if it existed (though he wasn't sure of this); he would be extremely grateful for my help in this matter, for he had not time for the necessary research.
He also asked about the significance of the original Latin text of this chant, and asked some questions as to its history—particularly as to fixing an approximate period for its origin—without offering a word of explanation for his keen interest in this. . . .
When I dropped in on Siloti to tell him about the conversation with Rachmaninoff, he indicated a "tactical error" on my part in not seizing upon S. V.'s general question about my new tonal system, to which I had referred in passing in an earlier encounter. I said that I was reluctant to talk about this "in general," but that I would prefer a full discussion, which might take as much as two hours. Knowing how busy S. V. was, Siloti doubted that such a long session could be arranged, but said that he would speak to him about it at a timely moment.

Another Rachmaninoff interview, on interpretation, was given to Florence Leonard for *The Etude*:

As the talented student grows older he must seek within himself his interpretation. Does he wish to know how to play the *cantilena* of Beethoven or of Chopin? He must feel it himself! Talent is feeling, the feeling that every player experiences in his innermost consciousness. . . . It takes years of work to understand and think out problems in music. Every player must ponder them and decide them for himself after his conservatory training is finished. . . .

Chopin! From the time when I was nineteen years old I felt his greatness; and I marvel at it still. He is today more modern than many moderns . . . he remains for me one of the greatest of the giants.

In Philadelphia Rachmaninoff met the Swans again after his concert of December 5:

Mrs. Rachmaninoff begged him to change his clothes. But he would not listen. He was invariably in good humor after the enthusiastic reception of the public. I remember he once said in New York: "The musicians and critics were always waiting to devour me. One would say: 'Rachmaninoff is not a composer, but a pianist!' and another: 'He is primarily a conductor.' But the public—I love it. Everywhere and at all times it has treated me wonderfully."

So Rachmaninoff did not want to change.

"Please wait, Natasha—I am not tired. How did you like my Oriental Sketch? Ah, you did not listen to it very attentively! Then I will play it to you again!"

"Seryozha, you are tired!" said Mrs. Rachmaninoff.

"Oh, no," answered Rachmaninoff, and he went to the piano and played the Oriental Sketch with much zest.

"Do you like it now? I can see, you have not taken it in properly. I will play it again."

He played it again and again. Every time he took a faster tempo, and every time, at the end, he got up and with a mischievous gleam in his eyes, hummed:

"Fritz [Kreisler] calls it the Orient Express."

A table was brought in, and we sat down for supper.

"A lady from here, from Philadelphia, has been pestering me a long time," said Rachmaninoff. . . . "She writes on music. At last Foley arranged for an interview at my house in New York. She is a very nice lady, but she does not understand much about music. No sooner had she come than she began to put to me questions, like this: 'How should one play Chopin? How does one develop proper pedaling?' For heaven's sake! What could I tell her? She does not understand that a teacher has to work for years on the feet of his pupils. She comes and wants me to take a recipe out of my pocket. So I told her: 'This is how we learn to play in Russia! Rubinstein would give his historical concerts in St. Petersburg and Moscow. I had the great good luck to attend them. He would come out on the platform and merely say: "Every note of Chopin's is pure gold. Listen." And then he played and we listened.'"

Rachmaninoff was in a gay mood, although he was not very well. Befor coming to Philadelphia he had to see a doctor, who told him that his heart was tired. That same night he suddenly had a pouch under his eye. But he still had the reserve from which to draw for twelve more years.

When Rachmaninoff came again to New York for his second recital there and his annual midseason vacation, Fritz Kreisler introduced him to a young friend in the world of Broadway music, Robert Russell Bennett:

I was at that time working on the arrangements for *Of Thee I Sing* with music by George Gershwin. I had to excuse myself rather early during the afternoon because I had to begin work on the overture for the play. Mr. Rachmaninoff asked me when I had to finish it, and I told him that the orchestra was rehearsing it the following afternoon at 4 p.m. He looked at me very gravely and said, "That is too little time," and he was perfectly right, but he understood already that that was show business in the U.S.A.

Rachmaninoff was also hurrying in a matter of orchestration: final corrections were made in the Respighi orchestrations of the five *Etudes,* and Rachmaninoff and Koussevitzky, by mail, agreed on all tempi before their performance this month.

He sent Medtner the new Variations:

I've played them here about fifteen times, but of these fifteen performances, only one was good. The others were sloppy. I can't play my own compositions! And it's so boring! Not once have I played these all in continuity. I was guided by the coughing of the audience. Whenever the coughing increased, I would skip the next variation. Whenever there was no coughing, I would play them in proper order. In one concert, I don't remember where—some small town—the coughing was so violent that I played only 10 variations (out of 20). My best record was set in New York, where I played 18 variations.* However, I hope that *you* will play all of them, and won't "cough." . . . We shall meet the New Year in Cleveland, where I play on January 1 and 2. I'm left with very few concerts. In this respect it's bad here. And bad in general. "The Christians have now turned stingy! They love their money, they hide their money" [Varlaam in Pushkin's *Boris Godunov*]. Well, so far there is a loss.

Siloti kept his word to Joseph Yasser and arranged an appointment for him with Rachmaninoff on an afternoon in January 1932:

At that time my work (*A Theory of Evolving Tonality*) had just been accepted for publication, but as it had not yet gone to press, I looked forward to Rachmaninoff's criticisms—certainly harsh, I thought, coming from this alleged "conservative," but helpful for this very reason.

However, nothing of this sort happened. Throughout my entire visit of two hours, I heard from him neither praise nor reproof, though this seemed far from being any indication of indifference on his part to this matter. His chief intention seemed to be not so much to criticize me as to absorb information himself on facts, attitudes, and theoretical structures new to him.

While I gave him an account of each page of my manuscript (which took about an hour and a half), Sergei Vasilyevich sat near me and listened intently to my words and to the illustrations I played on the piano. Occasionally he interrupted me with questions or remarks on some point not quite clear to him. At the end of my expositions he busied himself for a few minutes with my musical tabulations and acoustical diagrams that were scattered over the piano. He finally sat down in a more comfortable armchair, lit a cigarette, and began to talk in his typically "leisurely" way, expressing ideas that were essentially more a reflection of his own musical views than an attitude to my work.

* In Washington, Ruth Howell of the *Daily News* wrote: "There were, perhaps, too many variations. The piece grew long, boring, and the theme thickened so that even Corelli couldn't have found it. If the finale had been put in five minutes before, it would have been perfect. When it was finished, even Rachmaninoff looked a little disgusted."

Rachmaninoff began by saying that though one cannot *theoretically* deny the logic of my structures, only with difficulty could he *musically* imagine any system that goes beyond the limits of twelve tones within an octave, to say nothing of his inability to understand many things in contemporary music, even within the limits of this generally adopted scale norm.

"Perhaps," he said, "my opinion would change if I could actually hear your new 19-tone scale, but you did happen to say that no instruments tuned to it yet exist, and even that your entire theory requires further, longer experimental verification. As for the musical evolution that you declare invariably occurs throughout history, this of course cannot be denied altogether; yet it seems to me personally—and not to me alone— that tonal systems tend to change themselves much more slowly and imperceptibly than many people imagine. You probably know how Sergei Ivanovich Taneyev liked to demonstrate the various stages of musical evolution?"

I said I did not.

"No?" There was a hint of surprise in his voice. "Then it's worth showing!"

He sat at the piano and played several bars of some banal Viennese waltz and, smiling broadly, said:

"This, according to Taneyev, represents the first stage of the evolution, and this—as Sergei Ivanovich said—is the second stage" (Rachmaninoff repeated the bars)—"and finally, Taneyev would always end by saying, Here is the third stage!" (Rachmaninoff again played the same bars.)

As a living illustration of the characteristic Taneyev "method of discussion," this musical joke was certainly curious. However, I must confess that I was much more impressed by the way in which Rachmaninoff had played this passage three times in succession. Though the fragments seemed exact repetitions, each was distinguished by a different "breath" that can be recorded neither in words nor in written notes. As far as I could then understand, the sense of Taneyev's illustration lay in his subtle conveyance of these scarcely perceptible interpretative differences. . . .

Some minutes later, when I attempted to draw an analogy from contemporary music, interpreting it as an intermediate "hybrid" stage between the tonal system of the passing present and that of an as yet unguessed future, he slightly squinted his raised eyes, as if minutely examining something within, and after a slight pause he said with a little grin, "Hm! *Se non è vero . . .*"

I answered, "So be it! But if one accepts the basic theses of some theory, one can't evade the inevitable conclusions."

"Perhaps you are right theoretically," he observed, again making his distinction between the "theoretical" and the "practical," "but when I think that from this very 'hybridity,' as you call it, came all this present-day filth, an involuntary doubt creeps in as to whether the road chosen by contemporary music is correct, as well as doubt as to the sincerity of its representatives."

With these words Sergei Vasilyevich rose from his seat and began slowly and hesitatingly to move about the room. In reply to his last remark, I said that, in the end, all general trends of music, including the "modernistic," are the result not so much of someone's conscious choice as of the irresistible march of history. As for those individual representatives of contemporary music—living and dead—surely all of them, in this respect, could not deserve equal blame. "Doesn't it seem to you," I concluded, "that in our time it is a little too late to doubt, let us say, the sincerity of Debussy or Scriabin?"

Rachmaninoff took a few more steps, leaned his shoulder against the window frame, looking outside, and said, as if deeply absorbed in recollections: "Well, Scriabin—that was a quite special case."

The January tour of the Midwest was triumphal: in Minneapolis Ormandy made a program of the Second Symphony and the Second Concerto; in Chicago, Stock conducted another all-Rachmaninoff program—*Vocalise, The Isle of the Dead,* the Respighi transcriptions of the five *Etudes-Tableaux,* and the Third Concerto. In the *Herald and Examiner* Gunn wrote:

With one impulse the audience rose and shouted its approval. . . . Once on their feet the listeners remained to cheer long after the orchestra had trumpeted and thundered its fanfare and long after the composer-pianist had brought Dr. Stock to the footlights to share his honors.

Never have I witnessed such a tribute, not in symphony, opera or recital. And never, it is my sincere conviction, has such response been so richly deserved. For the imperishable beauty of this music is added to the spiritual wealth of the world, a solace, a joy to treasure always in grateful memory.

Chapter 18

Senar and *Rapsodie*

TWO DAYS before leaving on the *Europa* for concerts in London and Paris, and a summer at Senar, the new Swiss home, Rachmaninoff spoke with unusual bluntness to a reporter for *The New York Times:*

Sergei Rachmaninoff took issue yesterday with the current opinion that modern music represents a period of evolution. To him, he said, it represents only retrogression. He did not believe that anything worth while could grow out of it, because it lacked the one great essential—heart.

Mr. Rachmaninoff said that he will devote at least part of the Summer to composition. He refused to divulge the nature of the new works which he plans to write. . . .

Speaking of his reactions to modern music, he added: "The poet Heine once said, 'What life takes away, music restores.' He would not be moved to say this if he could hear the music of today. For the most part it gives nothing. Music should bring relief. It should rehabilitate minds and souls, and modern music does not do this. If we are to have great music we must return to the fundamentals which made the music of the past great. Music cannot be just color and rhythm; it must reveal the emotions of the heart."

. . . He named Josef Hofmann as the greatest living pianist, not only technically but in every way. . . . For his own part, he said he enjoyed playing the piano professionally and had no intention of giving up concert appearances to devote himself exclusively to composition. He said he never tried to compose during the periods that he is giving recitals. His best works, he thinks are *Evening Mass* [*Night Vigil*], and his symphony *The Bells,* neither of which is well known in this country.

Senar and composition had to wait for Rachmaninoff the pianist to finish his season's work. The London concert with Sir Henry Wood was greeted by Ernest Newman with the attitude of quizzical admiration that had become habitual with him in writing of Rachmaninoff's appearances:

The great thing of the evening was the playing of the incomparable Rachmaninoff in his own third piano concerto. This work will never be as popular as the second, but pianists of the first rank will probably come more and more to prefer it for public purposes. Its virtue resides less in its basic ideas than in the beauty and ingeniosity of the writing for the solo instrument; the inlay on the casket is so dexterous that one can be made to forget that the underlying metal is not always precious. As usual, Rachmaninoff gave us the impression of being, all in all, the first among living pianists. A Feinschmecker could have sat there all night merely observing how many shades, how many inflections—and shades and inflections of what incredible delicacy!—he could manage to give to the opening subject alone. At the conclusion of the performance Rachmaninoff was presented by the Duchess of Athol with the Society's gold medal. I hope this intrusion of his into the sacred circle will not be resented by some of the other initiates. . . .

Rachmaninoff was astonished to hear an English audience shouting. His annual benefit concert in Paris was not so happy an experience; after it, on March 20, he wrote to the Somovs:

. . . my life in Paris, where I've been for a week, is very tiring, as usual. I sit a great deal "among people," chatter a lot, don't get enough sleep, and I played too much before the concert—which made me extremely tired and weak. . . .

In general the concert went successfully. . . . The only thing missing [in the newspaper accounts] is the main thing: that I played *badly* and suffered a great deal for two days after the concert. That pain has now passed.

The sooner they reached the haven of Senar, the better. There is an almost audible sigh of relief in a report on Senar's domestic details sent to Rachmaninoff's sister-in-law:

Natasha and I arrived here on March 26. Most of the mountains are still covered with deep snow. . . . Today was sunny, but the barometer and the old inhabitants predict rain for tomorrow. This is how they make their forecast: when Pilatus, the mountain facing our windows, seems near and is plainly visible—this means that rain is coming. When Pilatus seems far away—the weather will be fine. Or, more simply: south wind— rain; north wind—sun. And I've learned many things here in these four days. The most useful knowledge is that here, as everywhere, it's the "rainy people" who prevail—the sunny ones are rare. And if you don't want to be cheated—do everything yourself. That, Sonichka, means I've taken over the management of the estate. I dismissed the gardener and hired a helper by the day. My neighbor, for whom I had the forethought to bring some cigars, gives me very helpful advice. Today we plowed— with a real two-bottom plow and a team of horses. As my fields are "boundless," the plowing won't be finished before tomorrow evening, if rain holds off. . . .

All day I walk round and round my estate, looking at the work, at the way the men are working, and examining each tree, hoping to see buds. The only buds so far, and big ones too, are on the lilacs. . . .

So you can see I am up to my ears in work—not my real work, of course! No time!

The letter is signed "Wilhelm Tell." A letter to Somov a few days later is even cheerier:

Pardon, Sir, this crumpled paper! We live in the provinces! Working hours! Up to my chin in business! No time to buy paper, not even to go to the W.C., as Chaliapin used to say. . . .

Tomorrow, first thing in the morning, we'll have the last and biggest planting. There will be five day laborers besides the chief gardener from the nursery where I bought the trees. A big truck will bring: four large cypresses, two larches, three silver firs, two birches, two maples, one *Tulpenbaum* (God only knows what sort of tree this is), ten plum trees, 20 rose bushes, etc. Today we finished planting five birches, two pines, weeping willows, and shrubs along the edge of the lake. Do you sense, Sir, the grandeur of the plans? You'd better!

Sowing grass is a less easy matter. The tilling and harrowing are done, but the soil is no good, too stony—there should be a thicker layer of topsoil, but this isn't to be had now for any money. All of this should have been done last winter . . . but the owner (according to an old Russian custom) was busy not with his estate, but with the Devil knows what!

"Wilhelm Tell of Senar" also wrote to Mrs. Barclay, on April 19:

Over here we earn our daily bread with hard labor—from morning till night we dig, plow, plant flowers, bushes, and trees—we blow up rocks and build roads—we go to bed with the hens and rise with the roosters. How hard the life of a Swiss *Bürger!*

On May 8 Tatiana was married to Boris Conus, son of the violinist Jules Conus, of a musical family that had been friends of the Rachmaninoffs and Satins since Conservatory days. After a honeymoon in Italy, Boris and Tatiana Conus made their home in Paris, where Boris was employed.

Summer advanced with no sign of composition, though not without music. Horowitz and Milstein (both living a few miles away) came over to Senar to read Beethoven sonatas together. Arrangements were finally made to have Alfred and Katherine Swan visit in July, urged by Rachmaninoff's note to the "Dear Swans":

Your post card received. Its contents sound fishy. You are trying to fool us. The sea, the empty hotel, and the grapes we will grant you. But as for the sun, you are bragging! Don't you think we read the papers that say, "Rain everywhere, rain at the seashore, rain at the Swans'"? When are you coming? No fooling here: we have a lake, fish, and walks and rain in abundance. There is also a splendid little hotel, not far from us, where the rates are the same as where you are—where you will also be living alone, as it is empty. Do you suffer from rheumatism? There are wonderful baths in that hotel—four days ago I began a cure there. Don't turn up your noses—come.

Yet when the Swans came, they heard words that were not so lighthearted as their invitation. Senar was obviously costing too much in time and distraction. The conversation on the veranda turning to Tolstoy, Rachmaninoff said:

"I think that Sophia Andreyevna was a charming woman and that Tolstoy tormented her, and now all the world is 'down' on her. Ah, this is one of the most difficult questions: What sort of a wife should a great man have?"

Rachmaninoff was quite roused by this thought. He took a deep breath, and his nostrils quivered:

"A creator is a very limited person. Always he revolves round his own axis. There is nothing for him but his own creative work. I agree that the wife has to forget herself, her own personality. She must take upon herself all the physical care and material worries. The only thing she should tell her husband is that he is a genius. Rubinstein was right when he said that a creator needed only three things—'praise, praise, and praise.' The most frequent mistake of the wives is that they take the creator for an ordinary man. There is not enough understanding. Take Tolstoy: if he had a stomach pain, he talked about it all day long. But the trouble was not in the stomach at all; it was in the fact that he could not work that day. This is what made him suffer. There is not enough understanding of what a creative artist needs. This is why Tolstoy was so miserable. Yes, this is tragic." And in a low voice he added: "We are all like this."

[He went on:]

"Mrs. Medtner is a remarkable wife. With great effort and very limited material resources she has produced ideal conditions for her husband's creative work. The fact that he can devote every day of his life to his compositions without any hindrance, that he can work uninterruptedly, this in itself is worth a lot. . . ."

By evening the inspiration of the day had worn off, and Rachmaninoff said: "I've been very tired by these household cares. I should never have started it all. And the worst is that they are swindlers here, as everywhere else. Disgusting!"

He became quite perturbed when asked if he had any new compositions.

"How can I work? Even for my concerts I am working very little, and the season will start quite soon. Besides, my studio is not ready. I have no proper room to work in."

To see the summer slipping away with no progress on the new works he had promised so publicly was deeply frustrating to the composer. His conscience expressed itself in irritation with everyone and everything; he wrote the Somovs on August 15:

At Senar domestic matters never decrease—they increase. Now laborers wake us every morning at 6:30. It all costs a lot of money and affords little pleasure. Less than before. And I am pretty well bored with all this, though I force myself to pretend interest. On about September 15 Natasha and I move to Paris, where we'll probably live at the Majestic, and on October 4 we sail for America on the *Europa*.

He refused to discuss new compositions with the ship reporters in New York on October 9. (He did not say that that was because there were no compositions.) But he talked freely of Ferde Grofé, a young American composer who had won Rachmaninoff's admiration in an unexpected way. His party had entered a London restaurant just as the jazz orchestra was playing Grofé's arrangement of It—the hated

Prélude. His British manager later described the awkward moment: ". . . the soloist started the famous chords—and then proceeded to do a jazz arrangement of it, and all who knew expected the worst. But Rachmaninoff listened and his eyes lighted up. 'Stay,' he said gently. And they stayed to the end, when the composer, with glistening eyes, exclaimed, 'What a fine piece of music! I enjoyed every note of that.'" When the orchestra further dared to play Grofé's arrangement of the Queen of Shemakha's aria from Rimsky-Korsakov's *Golden Cockerel,* Rachmaninoff went so far as to say that its composer would have applauded the new version! He told the ship reporters that he would certainly hear the Paul Whiteman concert on November 4, when Grofé's *Grand Canyon Suite* would be played for the first time.

David Schor, the pianist who had attended the St. Petersburg Conservatory during the short time Rachmaninoff, in his boyhood, was there, wrote to Rachmaninoff from Tel Aviv, praising his new homeland. Before beginning his concert season Rachmaninoff replied, somewhat skeptically:

Dear David Solomonovich,

You write of Palestine, of the gifts scattered there by Nature, and about the "harmony" established there by virtue of those gifts.

That word sounds rather strange to me. According to the news we get from there, there is little "harmony" in Palestine. The whole world is now a troubled sea. If you feel it, an inner harmony and peace can be achieved, or gained by hard work.—Can it be achieved?—or is it received from God as a talent, and a rare talent at that? Happy is its possessor! With such harmony and peace of soul one could live peacefully even in New York—I speak of you. On the other hand: without this it would be difficult to live even in Palestine—I speak of myself. I thank you sincerely for your wish to include me in this "harmony," and to take me from the "heights of glory" upon which you yourself placed me. I am also grateful for your remembrance of me.

With a wish of further peace for you . . .

Forty years after the Moscow autumn when he made his debut as a piano virtuoso, Rachmaninoff, worried by the financial depression in America and by the increased expenses of his Swiss estate, began an unusually heavy schedule of fifty concerts. The only celebration of the anniversary, by the Russian colony in Paris, doubled the years, making it his eightieth jubilee! He tried to joke about the mistake, but it had made the advancing years sound heavier.

His new recital program was the expansion of an earlier "idea program." He played six fantasias: Scriabin's *Sonata Fantasia* (Op. 19), Haydn's Fantasia in C major, three of Schumann's Fantasy-pieces, Chopin's Fantasia, and, in the second half, Beethoven's *Sonata quasi una fantasia* and Liszt's *Fantasia quasi sonata* (*après une lecture de Dante*). One of the Chicago critics suspected, "Is he, perhaps, about to offer the world a piano fantasy?"

Rachmaninoff wrote to Somov from Shreveport, Louisiana, on November 15:

Business is lamentable! We play in an empty but huge hall, which is very painful. (Correction: "huge, but empty"!) Today the local paper writes about the absence of the public! Furthermore, a few people dropped in to apologize because "there were so few of us." The day before yesterday there was a football game here, with 15 thousand spectators. Well, wasn't I right to say over and over that our day is interested only in muscles? Within five or ten years concerts will no longer be given. Only Paderewski will perhaps be able to attract an audience—as a former "premier"—and an army of hungry artists will march on Washington, where they'll be dispersed with clubs. Serves them right! Shouldn't play the piano or busy themselves with nonsense!

As if to rub salt into Rachmaninoff's wounded pride, one of the Shreveport papers reviewed his concert in the imagery of a football victory, headlined: "Rachmaninoff Wins by Large Margin in Monday Night Game!"

It was, of course, because Rachmaninoff's art required an audience that he could show such deep resentment when they stayed away. In New York a month later he confirmed this need in speaking about radio broadcasting, in a *Times* interview:

"I cannot conceive of playing without an audience. If I were shut up in a little 'cigar-box' of a room and were told that my audience was listening somewhere outside I could not play well. The most precious thing for me when I play is the feeling of contact established with my audience.

Anticipation of this contact, on days when I play, gives me the utmost pleasure.

"An artist's performance depends so much on his audience that I cannot imagine even playing without one. If I should broadcast, it would have to be under the same conditions that exist when I appear in Carnegie Hall. In order to play well inside a radio studio I should find it necessary to think only of my visible audience, rather than of the millions listening outside."

Newspapers, however, were given a guarded announcement that Rachmaninoff was planning to go on the air "sometime, depending upon circumstances."

A group of Rachmaninoff's friends, headed by Somov and Ostromislensky, were determined to celebrate his anniversary before the year ended. They secretly prepared a ceremony as a surprise item in his concert with the New York Philharmonic on December 22; Oscar Thompson reported the occasion for the *Evening Post*:

His debut as a pianist in 1892 was remembered last night, when a delegation of his transplanted compatriots took the stage at Carnegie Hall and presented him with an emblazoned scroll and a wreath. The presentation was made in the name of the Russian Academic Society of the United States.

Among the mail accumulated in his New York home Rachmaninoff found a request from Walter E. Koons that he define music. He replied:

What is music!? How can one define it? Music is a calm moonlit night, a rustling of summer foliage. Music is the distant peal of bells at eventide! Music is born only in the heart and it appeals only to the heart; it is Love! The sister of Music is Poesy, and its mother is Sorrow!

There was also a letter from Glazunov, thanking Rachmaninoff (whom he usually addressed as "Sir Gay") for his financial help and adding his good wishes on the anniversary, but it was a sad synopsis of a musician's life.

Yesterday morning, following your advice and taking advantage of a warm, sunny day, I took a rather long walk in the Bois de Boulogne. Because of the beautiful weather my "excursion" brought me no punishment, but what will happen on a bad day? Besides a *si,* wouldn't some cracked *fa♯* drive like a nail into my final C major chord to cause fresh pangs?

During the tour through the South and West, Rachmaninoff's aging body gave him a sharp warning. In San Antonio he had so painful an attack of lumbago that he could not reach the piano stool unassisted. It was only after being placed in position that he permitted the curtain to be raised. While playing the pain did not disturb him, but when at the intermission he found that he could not rise, he signaled for the curtain to be lowered while he remained sitting. The important thing was to let the audience be conscious of nothing but music.

From Oklahoma City on January 29, 1933, he sent Sophia Satina a detailed account of his troubles, but the letter ends on another note:

I'm just finishing the second volume of Chekhov's letters. What a delight! It's impossible to tear oneself away from them! What a wise and charming man! *Charmeur!* And what a pity that it was only after his death that I came to know him for what he really was. But, this is what usually happens: we appreciate and understand the good ones only after we lose them! Another reason for this is that good people conceal themselves! Only fools and scoundrels are open to all.

When Rachmaninoff arrived at the Philadelphia Academy of Music to give his March 18 recital, he found a messenger and letter waiting for him:

Dear Mr. Rachmaninoff,

I did not realize you were playing here this afternoon but just by chance we are playing your *Isle of the Dead* to-night at 8:20. Would you care to hear it and if so may I arrange for the tickets for you and how many would you like?

After studying *The Isle of the Dead* again for these performances I have been so deeply impressed by its unity of style and form. Its psychic power is to me greater than ever but I had never before realized the perfection of its organism. It grows from the roots out to the branches and leaves and flowers and fruit—just as does a tree and just as does the music of Bach.

I hope you will not mind—I have not followed the cuts you made but am playing it in its entirety without cuts. I had someone else conduct it in rehearsal so that I could listen to it and it seemed to me that it was perfect without cuts.

Lately I have not had the pleasure of seeing you but I am always the same in spite of this and my admiration for you and friendship is—if anything—increasing, no matter whether I meet you personally or not.

Sincerely your friend
Leopold Stokowski.

Rachmaninoff could not attend this concert: he had made other arrangements to occupy his time between the recital and his departure for Boston to give a concert there the following afternoon. The Rachmaninoffs and the Swans dined together at an Italian restaurant on Broad Street, partly in celebration of Tatiana's recently born son, Alexander. Rachmaninoff boasted to the Swans of his other grandchild, Sophie, nicknamed Pupik:

"Pupik has a very good memory and her mother teaches her all sorts of things. Ah! only Irina can do this. She makes Pupik learn long and difficult poems, such as the later poems of Balmont. So Pupik, in one of her last letters, says that she now often writes in blank verse. Here's an example:

> All the joy went out
> Of the heart of the old man.
> He lay down and died.

"I have written music to these verses—poetry by granddaughter, music by grandfather. I tried to make it as easy as possible, within the compass of an octave. She is musical, so she can play and sing it. . . ."

The conversation shifted to the question of money. He said:

"Yes, again I have lost between one half and two thirds of all I had. Not in any of the banks that have failed, but through the depreciation of stocks and bonds.

"I am glad you liked the Schubert Impromptu. I love it. How wonderful, the middle part. Yes, it is a gem."

They talked of the past, of memories of Tolstoy and Chekhov, before it was time to catch the Boston train:

It was time to go. Mrs. Rachmaninoff was worrying about the spicy sauce which we had eaten and which was not good for Rachmaninoff.

Again she mentioned that he had had to see a doctor, who had advised him to play less, since he was tired.

"Oh no," Rachmaninoff said with sudden ardor, "this is my only joy—the concerts. If you deprive me of them, I should wither away. If I have a pain, it stops when I am playing. Sometimes this neuralgia in the left [right] side of my face and head torments me for twenty-four hours,* but before a concert it disappears as if by magic. . . . No, I cannot play less. If I am not working, I wither away. No—it is best to die on the concert platform."

On April 2 Rachmaninoff was sixty years old, and when he arrived in Paris he became uncomfortably aware of plans to celebrate his birthday publicly, despite his wish to have it ignored. In an interview with Andrei Sedikh he tried to discourage all such plans:

As I am about to ring the bell my hand freezes. Rachmaninoff is playing. I stand in the corridor and listen.** . . .

"Monsieur, qu'est-ce que vous faites ici?" An attendant in striped waistcoat looks suspiciously at an unfamiliar person standing motionless at a door that is clearly not his. . . . I am forced to ring the bell.

The music breaks off instantly. When I enter, the piano is already closed. Sergei Vasilyevich, hand extended, rises to meet me. He has a strange, oblong face that seems not to know how to smile. And four deep furrows in his forehead only add to the external impression of sternness.

On April 2 Rachmaninoff was sixty years old, but the venerable composer doesn't care to hear about a jubilee.

"Then you will ask me about my debuts, about my teachers, about Tchaikovsky and Rimsky-Korsakov. This is all too complicated; a whole book could be written about it. . . .

"For the past fifteen seasons I have played about 750 concerts. Before I became a person of jubilees I played 70 or 80 concerts a year. But as I approach the age of jubilees, I've had to scale down a little. Concerts require very serious preparation. I work with pleasure on the compositions of other composers. When I work on my own—it is more difficult. Only a month, a month and a half, is left for rest."

* Dr. Kastritzky's treatments, during Rachmaninoff's visits to Paris, eventually eliminated this pain altogether.

** Recollections of Rachmaninoff are sprinkled with listeners in hotel corridors. In *My Melodious Memories,* Herman Finck tells a similar story of hearing him in a Glasgow hotel.

"Doesn't Rachmaninoff the pianist hurt Rachmaninoff the composer?"

"Yes, very much. I never could do two things at the same time. I either played only, or conducted only, or composed only. Now there's no opportunity to think of composition. And somehow, since leaving Russia, I don't feel like composing. Change of air, perhaps. Forever traveling, working. Instead of hunting three hares at once, I'm sticking to one. No, I do not regret it. I love to play. I have a powerful craving for the concert platform. When there are no concerts to give I rest poorly. So I grumble on—too much work—and then when there are no concerts, I begin to feel bored. . . ."

For a moment the conversation turns to events in Germany: Bruno Walter can no longer conduct in Germany.

"Such an act cannot be justified from any point of view. The single consolation for me is that his banishment has turned into a genuine triumph for him. Never has he been received so warmly in London. All, for him, has turned out for the best."

Before his London recital of April 28 he spoke with H. E. Wortham, of *The Daily Telegraph,* of this same choice between composing and concerts:

"Some pianists say they are the slaves of their instrument. If I am its slave, all I can say is—I have a very kind master," he said with a smile. "I practice two hours a day, and though I find it rather tiring to give many recitals—as I have to do on my American tours—still I know I should be more tired if I gave none at all."

Did it not interfere with his composing? At this question, Mr. Rachmaninoff smiled again, now gravely. . . .

"For seventeen years," he said, "since I lost my country, I have felt unable to compose. When I was on my farm in Russia during the summers I had joy in my work. Certainly I still write music—but it does not mean the same thing to me now."

As usual, London papers said more about one encore than about the whole program of his recital. The *News Chronicle* headline:

THE PRELUDE: RACHMANINOFF MUFFS IT.

In the midst of the applause he struck the famous opening chords of IT. He did not even wait for the applause to die down, but flung it at the audience like a bone to a dog.

And here is news which will be a consolation to thousands of amateur pianists: he played it, and he muffed it. Yes, in the rapid middle section, which is such a trial to the amateur, Rachmaninoff himself played two wrong notes.

And a reporter from the *Star* cornered Ibbs, Rachmaninoff's European manager, for the "inside" story of IT:

"It is quite a mistake to assume that Rachmaninoff hates it," he explained. "He thinks it is a very good bit of work. What troubles him is the fact that he is expected to play it every time he is seen near a piano.

"It worries him also to think that the vast majority of people know him only by it, whereas he has written other things as good and better.

"But he faced the inevitable many years ago. At Saturday's concert he said to me, 'Don't worry, I know my duty. I shall play it.'"

When Benno Moiseiwitsch made his American debut in 1919, he had included Rachmaninoff's unfamiliar Prélude in B minor on his program, and the composer, in congratulating him, asked why he had played that particular prélude. Moiseiwitsch said that it was his favorite among the préludes, and Rachmaninoff happily agreed that it was his favorite, too. Now in London, in this spring of 1933, they met again:

I was with him after luncheon one day when he smilingly showed me a post card from a lady admirer asking him if the C-sharp minor Prélude meant to describe the agonies of a man having been nailed down in a coffin while still alive. When I asked what reply he was going to give, he said, "If the Prélude conjures up a certain picture in her mind, then I would not disillusion her."

This gave me courage to ask him something that had been on my mind for very many years. It concerned his Prélude in B minor, for which I had so visualized a certain picture that I could almost translate every bar into words.

They were both amazed to learn that Moiseiwitsch's mental picture and Rachmaninoff's actual source were the same painting—"The Return," by Böcklin.

At the beginning of May Rachmaninoff went to Brussels to play in the Palais des Beaux-Arts for the benefit of Russian students in Belgian universities. One interviewer asked:

May I have your opinion of the American public?

Oh, it is no different, at least not in the larger cities, from that which I find in Europe. There are musical societies in which the best traditions are cultivated. In Boston, Philadelphia, Chicago, and a hundred other communities an artist may be sure to find a circle of intelligent amateurs whose sympathies are ready for him. There as well as here are those who love Beethoven, Tchaikovsky, Mendelssohn, Schubert. . . .

I have heard that you knew Tchaikovsky well: did you study with him at the Moscow Conservatory?

No, he was not teaching then. But he was a member of the jury for my final examination. And he frequently visited the professor at whose house I was living. . . . He was such a remarkable man. And what a talent!

Speaking of composers, may I ask which of your own compositions you value most?

That would be my cantata, *The Bells,* which unfortunately is rarely performed.

And your operas?

They have less interest for me, and there is none among them that I value particularly.

What about your conducting?

My arms have lost their flexibility, and handling the baton requires an energy that I must conserve for my recitals. . . .

A last question, Monsieur: was there any event that determined your vocation or that confirmed it?

No. I owe to God the gifts given me, to God alone. Without him, I am nothing.

Another interviewer (for *La Nation Belge*) opened a more difficult matter:

In the program you play here, there is no music of today. . . .

Rachmaninoff looks at us with an ironical smile:

The reason is simple, and there is no need to conceal it; I understand nothing in the music of today.

So you have never played modern music?

A single work has found favor alongside my undiminishing passion for the classics: this is Poulenc's *Toccata.* This is distinguished by spontaneous inspiration, and it is written for a musician of temperament.

You have given up composing?

Not entirely. During my summer rests from the fatigue of my tours as a pianist, I return to composition. My last works were transcriptions for piano of a work by Bach and the *Scherzo* from Mendelssohn's music for *A Midsummer Night's Dream.*

The Paris concert at the Salle Pleyel on May 5 was made the occasion for a public demonstration of Rachmaninoff's jubilee—a demonstration made to serve for both his sixtieth birthday and (belatedly) the fortieth anniversary of his debut. There were innumerable addresses; Cortot spoke for the Conservatoire; and Rachmaninoff would gladly have been anywhere else that evening. A few days later he wrote to Somov:

All the testimonials I received at the jubilee—there are about 1500 of them—go with me to Senar. It would be worth your while to travel there just to read them.

Now a few words about the concerts. In London—full. Played very well. In Brussels, half empty—played middling. In Paris, almost full—played well with a minus. In this city I do not live—I burn. Every day I receive 10 letters with requests for money.

Of the many tributes written and published in honor of Rachmaninoff's jubilee, none was more sensitive than Medtner's, in one of the Russian papers of Paris:

It is precisely because of his fame that it is difficult to speak of Rachmaninoff. This fame is more than his: it is the glory of our art. This rare identification of his personal fame with our whole art is evidence of the authenticity of his inspiration. This unbroken contact of his entire being with art itself can be sensed each time his touch produces sound. This sound, in score or keyboard, is never neutral, impersonal, empty. It is as distinct from other sounds as a bell is different from street noises; it is the result of incomparable intensity, flame, and the saturation of beauty. . . .

His value and power as pianist and conductor reside in his imagination, in his inner perception of the original musical image. His performance is always creative, always as if the composer were playing it—and always as if it were "for the first time." He seems to be improvising, making a song not heard before. . . .

His own music's chief themes are the themes of his life—not the facts of life, but the unique themes of an unique life.

It seemed a pity to live on the shore of one of the world's most beautiful lakes without exploring it, and the novelty that this summer brought forth at Senar was a large motorboat that Rachmaninoff bought at auction. Every letter reported some new detail of its excellence. He sent snapshots to Somov on June 25:

Enclosed herewith (1) my new grandson, who smiles at you; (2) my new house, photographed from the lake. . . . The motorboat isn't photographed yet—the bronze letters aren't ready, and without its name it's not worth a photograph.

For the information of Yevgeni Ivanovich, it has a four-cylinder motor. In spite of old age (I refer to the motor, not to myself) it works splendidly. I've not had a single misunderstanding with it . . . but I should like greater speed. Yet the wooden body of the boat—of redwood—is beautiful and will serve another hundred years. So if I also last that long, I shan't have to change the boat.

By replacing the motor Rachmaninoff achieved his wish for greater speed, and racing the steamers on Lake Lucerne became a favorite game.

The summer looked promising for composition, but an unexpected crisis wrecked this prospect. Oskar von Riesemann had completed his biography of Rachmaninoff, and proofs arrived at Senar for approval. The first shock was to see the title: *Rachmaninoff's Recollections*. Rachmaninoff's indignation at this unwarranted liberty mounted to anger when he found that the proofs contained long passages supposedly said by him about himself. Especially infuriating was a chapter in which Rachmaninoff praised himself and his work. Though he found himself accurately quoted on many episodes of his youth and musical career, he could not tolerate the several embroidered and invented quotations in which he was made to judge and explain his compositions. A representative of Rachmaninoff told Riesemann that he could write whatever he chose, but that the title would have to be altered, and some of the direct quotations would have to be omitted; if the title and text should remain as they were in proof, Rachmaninoff would have to protest against so unceremonious a use of his name. Riesemann's reply was piteous: he said that the publisher would never consent to change the title, because it had been the publisher's own idea, and if any serious trouble were made about title or text, the whole project would collapse and Riesemann's investment of time and money would all be lost. And then Riesemann suffered a severe heart attack.

To prevent the further infliction of personal financial loss on Riesemann, Rachmaninoff paid for the major cuts that he insisted on, including most of the offending chapter of self-praise. He even agreed to furnish an ambiguously phrased letter that Riesemann could print in the book as an "endorsement." Efforts to have the title changed were unsuccessful, and throughout the rest of his life any reference to his _"Recollections"_ irritated the composer. The book was published in 1934 in England and in the United States.

A happier episode took place in Paris, where he saw his eight months-old grandson, Alexander Conus. Rachmaninoff wrote to his Aunt Trubnikova:

I have a charming grandson. Calm, quiet, happy. Whenever I don't feel quite myself, I go to him and sit beside his bed for a while. We sit, we are silent. I look at him, he looks at me—and he smiles! And I at once feel more peaceful. But such pastimes are only for the summer.

At the end of October the Rachmaninoffs returned to America. In November the United States had finally granted _de jure_ recognition to the Soviet Government, and during his Christmas vacation Rachmaninoff was questioned by the _Evening Post_ on his feelings about Russia:

Mr. Rachmaninoff still prefers to pretend that he is a subject of the Tzar of All the Russias. This tall, stooped man of sixty, who smiles seldom on his audiences, yet confesses that concert playing is his very life, can have spiritual integrity only by identifying himself with Russia's past, and so he does, both as man and musician.

"You cannot know," he said, " the feeling of a man who has no home. Perhaps no others can understand the hopeless homesickness of us older Russians. . . . Even the air in your country is different. No, I cannot say just how."

Though he no longer hoped to return to Russia, he had taken no steps to acquire United States citizenship:

"My attachment to the old Russia is too strong," he said. "If good Americans cannot understand how I feel, then I am sorry, but still it seems right to me to remain as I am."

It has cheered Mr. Rachmaninoff greatly to learn that his own music, long under the Soviet ban, is being played again in Russia. . . . A letter from a musician [Albert Coates] who formerly was a conductor of the Imperial opera informs Mr. Rachmaninoff that programs of his compositions recently were presented repeatedly at Moscow.

His American season completed, Rachmaninoff sailed for England on February 28. When ship reporters questioned him about the child prodigy, Ruth Slenczynski, he shook his head sadly. "All these public appearances are bad for her. It is too bad, too bad. . . . And I told her father so. I warned him that she should not play so much. She should practice, practice, practice, all the time through these years. All the pieces she plays are too big. She is playing things she can't afford to play at her age."

Between London and Paris he reported to the Somovs:

The London concert went very well: plenty of people—nearly filled! and I played successfully. As for the welcome, it would seem that nowhere am I received with such pomp as here. Before the concert I didn't feel so well and came out on the platform rather "sourly." But the welcome touched me so that I at once decided to play well.

In a London interview with Norman Cameron (for the *Monthly Musical Record*) Rachmaninoff gave a fuller rationale of his adjustment to concert conditions:

I am well aware that my playing varies from day to day. A pianist is the slave of acoustics. Only when I have played my first item, tested the acoustics of the hall, and felt the general atmosphere do I know in what mood I shall find myself at a recital. In a way this is unsatisfactory for me, but, artistically, it is perhaps a better thing never to be certain what one will do than to attain an unvarying level of performance that may easily develop into mere mechanical routine.

On April 6, just before driving to the freedom of Senar, Rachmaninoff wrote from Paris to Wilshaw, in Moscow:

Now the concerts are over (until October 3 in America) and I feel, appropriately, like a squeezed lemon: tired, irritable, and generally unpleasant for those around me. With each year this fatigue progresses perceptibly, even though I cut down the number of concerts each year. I won't try to explain this phenomenon. You can understand it—

In three days I go to Switzerland. There on Lake Lucerne I have a small place where I'll live all summer. I love to be there. My occupations there: landscaping and gardening. . . . This year I must undergo a minor operation as soon as I arrive. Fear not! They say it's not serious. Perhaps by May first I'll be allowed out of the hospital, only I'll be late for the flower-planting.

This was the first year that the "small place" was to be formally occupied. The master and mistress of Senar arrived in a properly ceremonial mood and in the best humor. Rachmaninoff told the Somovs about it on April 11:

We drove through the gate of Senar just after seven that evening. It was already dark. But anyway, I went alone to inspect places around the big house, though I didn't go inside. Even in the darkness the impression was quite imposing. Then I went through the garden to examine all the trees. Everything is still rather bare, but there are tiny buds on some trees. This means we've come at my very favorite time—every day I'll be able to watch the trees and flowers opening. We retired early [in the lodge]. Natasha begged me not to wake her until half past eight. I promised! But inwardly I decided that at eight o'clock I would have to begin a fit of coughing. I woke at half past six and waited patiently. At ten to eight I rejoiced to hear Natasha's sleepy voice, "You can get up." I didn't have to be told twice. I raised our heavy Venetian blinds and saw a cloudless blue sky and a glittering sun. Then I got Natasha up, too. As I dressed I looked through every window in every direction at the garden and at the house. After coffee Natasha and I went downstairs with Rossi [the builder] to look at his work: the new stone wall by the water and the work he has done on the rock where the big house stands. . . . And only then did Natasha and I go to the house. Well, Sir! stupendous! Our chauffeur, whom Natasha today took through the house, was right to say, "You can charge just for looking!"
I walk through the house and feel like a millionaire—though not every millionaire has such a house.

To cap his pride in Senar the Steinway people sent Rachmaninoff a gift; he wrote about it to Greiner, his friend at the Steinway Company:

. . . today my new piano was delivered to me. It stands in the new studio. Wrapped and wound up in a paper. As the house is not yet ready and the furniture is not yet all delivered, I don't want to open the piano. Only I did lift its lid softly and softly played "God save the Tzar!" The piano looks splendid to me. I wanted so much to cable at once to the Steinway firm in New York to express my delight and gratitude for the gift—a gift that could not have pleased me more. And only my vile ignorance of English hindered me. I am forced to send a Russian text to my children in Paris so they can send on a translation to New York.

This was the third summer that Rachmaninoff had promised himself to bring a new work from Senar, and this year the promises were to be kept. As if to put himself in tune for composition he asked Somov to include some scores in the boxes of books being sent from New York: in addition to his own *Night Vigil* he asked for two operas, *The Golden Cockerel* and *The Legend of the Invisible City of Kitezh.* Rachmaninoff's opinion of Rimsky-Korsakov's music had soared so high that he could now say, "Just to read a score by Rimsky-Korsakov puts me in a better mood, whenever I feel restless or sad." His growing happiness was increased by a rapturous letter from Wilshaw, bringing confirmation of the news from Coates:

Now I'll tell you of several great, great joys you have given me. First, thanks to the kindness of Goldenweiser, my wife and I heard your new Variations on a Theme of Corelli, played in a concert by one of his pupils. . . . She played well, and for an encore played your transcription of the minuet from *L'Arlésienne.* This was all a tremendous pleasure and I listened with the greediest of attention. The Variations, or as much as I could grasp of them, seem not at all like your previous Variations of Op. 22 (which I love very much—with the possible exception of the finale-coda that you suggest omitting?), but the new ones surpass those in complexity and profundity. . . . I suddenly thought what a long way you have come from the past; I don't mean from Op. 22, but from all that group of ideals that saturated, say, your 3rd Concerto. . . . Since the *Etudes-Tableaux* of Op. 39 (do you remember breaking a string when you played these at the Polytechnic Museum?) you have definitely departed from your saintly hierarchy (forgive me!) and arrived at your Op. 40 and 41. A few words about the latter—your Three Choruses on Russian Songs: I was sitting in the first row at the Bolshoi Theater when the program included Scriabin's *Prometheus* and *Poem of Ecstasy,* Musorgsky's Choruses on Jewish Themes (which, by the way, I didn't like at all), and then your three choruses. This I awaited with great emotion, and finally it came. The curtain parted. There was the orchestra, and behind it two rows of the seated chorus—the second row stands up. Silence, not a cough, not a whisper—my heart thumps. Golovanov moves his baton almost imperceptibly, and suddenly, very loud, the voices of "Over the little river"—it ends far too quickly! When the women's voices of the second began, "Oh, Vanka!," all as if with exclamation marks, my heart began to pound so that my attention was distracted. But in the third, "Quickly, quickly," with the increasing speed of the pizzicato, I simply grew numb; my soul could take no more, and tears began to flow! I can't tell you how deeply I was impressed. A kiss would be too little for these songs. Only a man who loves his fatherland could compose this way. Only a man who in his inmost soul is a Russian. Only Rachmaninoff could have composed this. I was the first to yell *Bis!* Its success was enormous, and the chorus repeated it.

The expected minor operation was performed on May 23, and the stay in the hospital was almost a pleasure. For one thing, his grand-daughter Sophie was in an adjoining ward, after an appendectomy; for another, he could work out in his mind the design of his new composition. In less than two weeks Rachmaninoff was brought back to Senar, thinned and weakened; a vacation was recommended and most of June was spent by Lake Como and at Monte Carlo. When he returned to Senar on July 1, all social duties and correspondence were sacrificed to his first Senar opus. By August 19 he had news for his sister-in-law Sophia:

. . . it's been long since I wrote you—but ever since the very day of my return from Como and Monte Carlo on July 1, I've kept myself at work, working literally from morn to night, as they say. This work is rather a large one, and only yesterday, late at night, I finished it. Since morning my chief aim has been to write you. This piece is written for piano and orchestra, about 20–25 minutes in length. But it is no "concerto"! It is called Symphonic Variations on a theme by Paganini. I'll tell Foley to arrange for me to play it this coming season, in Philadelphia or Chicago. If he does arrange it, and there is little doubt of this, then you too will hear it. I am happy that I managed to write this piece during my first year in the new Senar. It's some compensation for the many stupidities I al-lowed myself in building Senar. Truth! I believe it!

Now, for the three or four weeks remaining before we leave, I'll try to rest, devoting about three hours daily to practice at the piano; I'll re-sume my regular motorboat trips, etc. . . .

You may speak of the "Variations" *only* to Somov, but to no one else.

Yet when he wrote to the Somovs at the end of August, not a word about the new work: "Ibbs is now staying here; he treats me to the news that I have exactly 40 concerts to give in Europe. If you add to these something like 25 concerts in America, the total should wind up with a funeral procession and a memorial dinner." Similar complaints went to his old friend Wilshaw on September 8, but with a description of the new composition (still seeking its final title):

My vacation now ends, so I'll not be writing you before next May, if I live. I leave here September 15 for Paris and on September 27 I go on to America. I begin playing on October 12. This time my season in America ends at Christmas. I return to Europe in January, and on January 22 I begin to drag myself through Europe—till May 10. For the past three years I haven't allowed more than 40–45 concerts to be arranged for me. Well, this season they talked me into giving 29 in America and 40 in Europe. Shall I hold out? I begin to evaporate. It's often more than I can bear just to play. In short—I've grown old.

Two weeks ago I finished a new piece: it's called a Fantasia for piano and orchestra in the form of variations on a theme by Paganini (the same theme on which Liszt and Brahms wrote variations). The piece is rather long, 20–25 minutes, about the length of a piano concerto. I'll give it to the printer next spring—after I try to play it in New York and London, which will give me time to make necessary corrections. The thing's rather difficult; I must begin learning it, but I get lazier every year with work on my fingers. I try to get by with some old piece that already sits in the fingers.

Chapter 19

The "Russian" Symphony

ITH THE first performance of the new Rhapsody only four
days away, Rachmaninoff was at his best for his New York
recital of November 3.

When Mr. Rachmaninoff plays the piano as magnificently as he did
at his recital on Saturday afternoon at Carnegie Hall [Chotzinoff wrote],
the listener cannot help wondering when the composer of the piano concertos, the etudes, the preludes, etc., had found the time to become one
of the world's greatest pianists. Or vice versa. In the heroic days of music
and music-making no one, I dare say, ever gave such a phenomenon a
thought. But in these days of specialization we cannot easily envisage it,
and we almost hope to find a flaw in at least one of Mr. Rachmaninoff's
occupations. I, for one, have been unable to find it.

In the *Sun* W. J. Henderson wrote:

What other pianist could have played the [A minor] mazurka more ex-
quisitely? Yet Rachmaninoff is not registered among the Chopin special-
ists. Then came one of the grand achievements of the afternoon, a reading
of the C-sharp minor scherzo delivered as only a giant of the keyboard
could deliver it. This indeed was mighty piano playing, a mighty re-
vitalizing of the tremendous outburst of Chopin's genius. . . .
    The last group consisted of Liszt's *Funerailles,* and Eleventh Rhapsody.
One does not hear Liszt played this way often, not as a mere maker of
piano pieces, but with a fastidious regard for every musical quality in
each work. And the artist showed no slightest sign of weariness as he
neared the end of his recital. His fingers were as supple, his tone as full
of color and variety, his revelation of form as clear and his enthusiasm as
warm as at the beginning. Rachmaninoff may have had a year of depression, but he has got bravely over it.

One critic, Leonard Liebling, was moved to send a personal tribute:

My dear Mr. Rachmaninoff,
    I have just come home from your recital of this afternoon and I feel

impelled to do something which has never occurred before in my career as a critic; that is, to write a private letter of admiration to an artist. . . .

You gave performances of such loftiness, fancy, and fire, that you altogether captured my mind, heart, and imagination.

I pride myself on knowing the piano and its eminent players intimately almost from the days of my babyhood, but I have rarely been stirred so completely as by your art of this afternoon. It was superb, soulful, and supreme. I wish to thank you as warmly as I feel at this moment.

My gratitude, too, for giving generous place to the too much neglected Liszt.

As author of the Philadelphia program notes, Lawrence Gilman had a chance to see and hear the new score in advance of its public performance, and he wrote of it in his Sunday column:

Mr. Rachmaninoff's new work, his first major product since the Fourth Concerto for Piano heard here in 1927, is a "Rapsodie" (so-called) for Piano and Orchestra. It is, in form, a series of [24] variations on a theme of Paganini's, and the manuscript score originally bore the title, "Rapsodie (en forme de Variations) sur un Thème de Paganini." Mr. Rachmaninoff afterward struck out the parenthetical phrase—but, happily, preserved the variations! For they are among the most engaging and brilliant of this composer's achievements as a master of musical structure and design.

The new work was begun on July 3 of the present year, at Mr. Rachmaninoff's summer home on the Lake of Lucerne. Mr. Rachmaninoff arrived in New York October 4 with the score of the new composition in his portfolio. Within the brief period of eight days the parts were extracted, photostated, and bound, and (with the helpful co-operation of Mr. Stokowski) the work had its first reading in the foyer of the Academy of Music, Philadelphia.

The Paganini theme chosen by Rachmaninoff for beneficent exploitation is that of the last of the "Ventiquattro Capricci per Violin Solo," Op. 1, for which Paganini himself composed eleven variations and a finale. The theme is known to all musicians and most music-lovers as that employed by Brahms in his famous Variations for piano, Op. 35.

Mr. Rachmaninoff appears to have made something of a mystery about the structure of the piece, "the exact nature of which," it is said, "he desires to conceal until the performance." But perhaps there is no harm in noting at least one point, without giving the whole show away. Rachmananinoff's "Rapsodie" begins with an introduction of nine measures

(*Allegro vivace,* 2/4) in which the theme is foreshadowed. Then comes a sort of musical analogue of the singular court procedure in *Alice in Wonderland,* as announced by the Queen: "Sentence first, verdict afterwards!" For we hear, first, Variation I ("precedente"), in which the orchestra toys with fragments of the theme, and then the formal statement of the Theme itself, by the first violins, rhythmically punctuated by the piano, *poco marcato.* This is followed by Variation II.

The first performance of the Rhapsody, in Baltimore on November 7, made little impression on the correspondent for the *Musical Courier,* who summed it up as "Not an important opus, in all probability, but one eminently worth hearing." But in general the reception was so enthusiastic that the composer, recalling the reaction to his last two major works, was disturbed: "It somehow looks suspicious that the Rhapsody has had such an immediate success with everybody."

On tour Rachmaninoff took along proofs of the Rhapsody; he wrote Somov on November 14 from Boston:

Make one more—no! *two* more—copies of my corrections on the Rhapsody. Send one for me to check, and give the other to Shvedov, so that when he sees a change he won't think it a mistake. Whenever he feels doubt, let him look at the list of corrections. . . .

[P.S.] Forgot the main thing: write a letter to Nikolai Afonsky [conductor of a Russian chorus in Paris]—"Rachmaninoff is on tour—your letter has been forwarded to him. Presume your request will be granted. As for your suggestion to perform something from Rachmaninoff's *Liturgy,* I don't think it will please Rachmaninoff very much. I know definitely that he is not 'in sympathy' with this composition."

While on tour, he kept in touch with Medtner:

[December 8, 1934, Chicago]

I received the first part of your book in California, where I've just been. I'm staying here only three hours before I go on, to Washington. I read it at a single sitting and want to congratulate you on your achievement in a new field. What a lot of interesting, pointed, witty, and profound things are in it! And so timely, too. If this present sickness should some day pass away, though I must confess I don't see this as imminent, your description of it will last forever. And what a well-turned title [*The Muse and Current Fashion*] you have given your book! I am fully satisfied and will gladly publish your book as soon as I get to Europe. I await the second part impatiently. I've had another difficult season. I am playing a great deal and doing much proofreading (the new Rhapsody). I am quite exhausted. I can look forward to a rest only in May, and then but a brief one.

[December 17, 1934, New York]

Just home from a long journey (forty days and forty nights!). All day yesterday, on the train, I read the second part of your book. What a wonderfully wise man you are!

I'll be here until the 29th, then to Mexico. [This trip was canceled.] On January 17 we'll be home, and on the 19th we'll be on board ship. Hope to see you between January 26 and 29 in Paris.

The New York Philharmonic Symphony played the Rhapsody with Bruno Walter conducting. Reviews showed a program-seeking tendency; *Musical America* wrote, "Almost as prominent as the Paganini quotation is the Dies Irae. The two subjects seem pitted against each other, in a bitter, ironical struggle; as if some concealed programmatic idea governed their use." But in *The New Yorker* Robert A. Simon cheered:

After the business of composing variations on a theme had been pretty well upset by an untimely revival of Reger's variations on a theme by Hiller, Mr. Rachmaninoff restored the industry with a Rhapsody on a Theme by Paganini.

The Rachmaninoff variations, written with all of the composer's skill, turned out to be the most successful novelty that the Philharmonic Symphony has had since Mr. Toscanini overwhelmed the subscribers with Ravel's Bolero. Of course, the Rhapsody had the advantage of Mr. Rachmaninoff's pianism and Mr. Walter's adroit direction of ensemble music, but the succession of brilliances for the piano, dramatic references to the Dies Irae, wide-open Schmalz for divided strings, and old-fashioned bravura was enough to insure success. The Rhapsody isn't philosophical, significant, or even artistic. It's something for audiences, and what our orchestras need at the moment is more music for audiences. More music for audiences means more audiences for music, and with this sage apothegm, I conclude another salute to Mr. Rachmaninoff.

Abram Chasins sent his salute directly:

The work is magnificent. It is truly a Rhapsody and you have managed to make a completely individual and self-revealing comment on the same theme which Liszt and Brahms both used before. It seemed to me that there was not very much left to do with this theme, that the possibilities had been exhausted, but you have conclusively proven the contrary by this latest opus.

The marvelous orchestral color, the ingenuity of your invention and complete mastery of form are all overwhelmingly beautiful. Although these comments are as unnecessary as the statement that you played the piano as only Rachmaninoff can, I nevertheless felt that I would like to tell you of my enthusiastic reaction.

Rachmaninoff's written acknowledgment was conventional—"I sincerely thank you for your very kind letter of yesterday, and it makes me happy that you liked my new composition"—but a telephoned addendum to it contained the highest tribute that one musician can pay another: "You probably noticed that one variation [the 22nd], with the fifths in the bass, is very much influenced by Chasins' Parade."

The European tour did not begin auspiciously. The Somovs heard from Stockholm:

The day after my first concert, in Copenhagen, I caught a slight cold and stayed in bed for two days. On the advice of a doctor friend—I have one in Copenhagen—I telegraphed to Oslo to cancel the first concert there. Next day I felt better and had time to cancel this instruction, appearing in Oslo on schedule. The box office was not full, but the success was. Yet to give myself some rest—my cheeks are quite sunken—I canceled the second Oslo concert despite all the managers' entreaties and the promise of a sold-out house. This cancellation has allowed me to live here in Stockholm for five days without moving anywhere.

The first English performance of the Rhapsody, conducted by Nikolai Malko in Manchester, restored his spirits; he wrote from Edinburgh in early March:

Dear Somovs,
    I send you a review of the first performance of the Rhapsody in Manchester. . . . At the end there was a real storm. However, if one can

ignore the receipts, which, except for London and Manchester, were middling, such storms accompany me everywhere. I even suggest to Natashechka that she address me only as Maestro, but she responds poorly to the suggestion.

An hour ago I finished my recital here and we leave on the night train for London, where I'll have two days without concerts. Pleasant!

Just received the letters from you and Yelena Konstantinovna in which you write about M. A. Chekhov.* I knew you'd like him, and if you can pry out of him in conversation, say, something of his memories of Stanislavsky, about his rehearsals of *Revizor* with him, you will be rewarded. Try. Meanwhile give them my greetings and watch out that he's not swindled with some new proposition....

Good-by! Hand is tired!

There were more concerts in England before the Rachmaninoffs reached the Continent again, and there, after appearances in Zurich and Paris, Natalia Alexandrovna achieved a long-harbored wish. For years she had coaxed Rachmaninoff to take engagements in Spain, and four recitals were arranged in Spanish cities during April. They were bitterly disappointed, not only by the amazing hotel accommodations, but also by the audiences that chatted throughout the concerts—and concerts were never begun before 11 P.M. Their only pleasant experience in Spain was a meeting with the conductor Arbos; when they left Spain, they resolved never to try it again.

When they returned to Senar, Rachmaninoff answered an inquiry from Yasser:

You are correct in saying that Russian folk song and orthodox church chants have influenced the creative work of Russian composers. . . . I would only add—"some of them!" As to whether this influence be "unconscious" (which would appear "most essential" for your conclusions) or "conscious"—it would be difficult to say. Especially about the *un*conscious! This *is* obscure! But the latter case, which could more simply be called

* Tatiana Conus had written to Somov on January 30 from Paris: "Papa asks you earnestly to meet Mikhail Alexandrovich Chekhov, who is sailing on the *Lafayette* February 6. He scarcely speaks English and is very afraid of New York, the customs, the inspection of passports, and generally any kind of formalities. Both he and his wife, Xenia Karlovna, are very nice and I'm sure you'll like them. They were here yesterday and Papa promised to ask you to meet him, which touched M. A. deeply."

"counterfeit style," is obvious. And the composers themselves, if they should care to, can show you instances of this. I too can point to one. In accordance with the rules of the Orthodox Church, certain chants of the *Night Vigil* must be written on themes from the ritual. For example: "Bless, my soul, the Lord"; "Allow thy servant, Lord, to depart in peace"; "Glorification," etc. Others, however, can be original. In my *Vigil* all that applied to this second instance was a conscious counterfeit of the ritual. For example: "Blessed is He," "Mother of God," etc.

Now for your questions:

1. The first theme of my 3rd Concerto is borrowed *neither* from folk song forms nor from church sources. It simply "wrote itself"! You will probably refer this to the "unconscious"! If I had any plan in composing this theme, I was thinking only of sound. I wanted to "sing" the melody on the piano, as a singer would sing it—and to find a suitable orchestral accompaniment, or rather one that would not muffle this singing. That is all!

2. Thus, I aspired to impart neither a folk song nor a liturgical character to this theme. Had that been so, I would doubtless have "consciously" maintained the mode, not admitting the C-sharp, but keeping the C natural throughout. At the same time I realize that this theme has, involuntarily, taken on a folkish or ritual character. I have mentioned such a possible influence above. . . . And, finally:

3. Somehow I cannot recall any variations that would display hesitation on my part in choosing the melodic turns of this theme. As I have said: the theme "wrote itself" easily and simply! This eliminates the possibility of any "creative history" for the theme! Did you speak yourself of the "unconscious"?

Reading your letter, I thought: How, then, is it with creators of *non-*Russian nationality? Let us say, the French? How are they born? How do they compose? Do they take something from their songs or from Catholic church chants? (Wonderful in quality, by the way!)

Forgive me if I have expressed myself with insufficient clarity, or at insufficient length. . . .

I've now been "in paradise" for six days, here in my Swiss place. The weather is cursed! But, you see, paradise is possible at a low temperature, too. . . .

He wrote to his former American secretary:

The past season was a very tiring one. . . . In the future I must cut down the number of concerts or find some remedy against old age. . . .

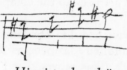

Hier ist sehr schön

I might even say *wunderschön,* but this wouldn't fit the music. . . . Recently I went to a famous doctor in Zurich. . . . All in order—including the 50 francs.

As usual, Natalie and I begin the summer alone here. The children won't be here until the middle of May, at the earliest.

Have you heard the great news—that my dear Foley (who has been quite ill) has freed me from the South American tour? That was a real joy!

Rachmaninoff wrote no one, however, a greater piece of news: that on June 18 he had begun a new symphony. There were few visitors this summer, but fatigue persistently interrupted his work; on July 3 he wrote Somov that his health forced them to go to Baden-Baden for three weeks. On their return from there he wrote Somov again:

Beginning today [August 22] I have another interruption in my work—of twelve days. My doctor compels me to travel 20 kilometers from here to take pine-electrical baths; I'll have to take ten baths that will consume each time, with rest and massage, about four and a half hours—which obliges me to stop work altogether for this time.

But, according to his letter to Somov of September 1, he did squeeze in a little work during the mornings of his treatments, and on the day after his last bath he began "to work strenuously." He had completed the first movement on August 22; the second movement was begun on August 26 and completed on September 18. Without the last movement a fully satisfactory report could not be sent to Wilshaw on September 26:

My work is not yet finished. Only two thirds nearly ready. I must give it up and sit down at the piano, which I have not been very diligent about lately. In four days I leave for Paris, and 12 days later I sail for America. Concerts there start on October 25, and as they will go on till April 2, you can see that I shan't get back to the completion of my work before next summer.

My health has been wretched. I'm breaking up rapidly! When I had health—I possessed extraordinary laziness; as that begins to disappear—all I can think of is work. This proves that I don't belong among the genuine talents, for I consider that real talent, even ability, is due to efficient work from the first day that you realize you have talent.* And in my youth I did all I could—to smother this. Rebirth can't be expected in old age! Thus, to increase the total of my activity is now difficult. This means that in my lifetime I have not done all I could have done, and this realization will not make my remaining days happy.

I stop here. Forgive the minor key.

Wilshaw answered at once:

Your letter was so pessimistic that I could never have suspected such a mood in you, but—the chief thing is that you are so unjust to yourself! I understand that there are no roses without thorns, and I understand that you have had to endure all sorts of bad luck and dissatisfaction. But all this passes, and swiftly, too—and in looking back over your creative road one sees how wrong it is to draw such conclusions as you do! . . . Who is there among your contemporaries who can boast such gifts as you have, as pianist, composer, conductor? Even in the near past only one man can be mentioned without hesitation—Liszt. No one need feel sorry for you—no, one must only wish that your love for your work may not dry up.

At the New York recital of November 2:

The bell rings and a very tall, spare, grave gentleman, in afternoon garb of irreproachable correctness and sobriety, steps without smiling upon the stage. He seats himself at the piano and plays. He does not smile once through the whole occasion. In no way does he gesticulate or parade. All that he communicates he says with two wrists and ten fingers, without the raising of an eyebrow. The performance is one of mind sovereign over matter, spirit that transfigures digital gymnastics. So it has always been with Rachmaninoff, and so it will be for the years to come. It is his fine tribute to art.

* He repeated this thought in 1937 in response to an inquiry—about heredity! "I am inclined to believe that HEREDITY and TRAINING are inseparable and indispensable in any ART achievement. I consider that a capacity for hard work is also a Talent, and only those few artists who have inherited both musical and working talents attain the highest peak of their profession."

This concert was also attended by two Soviet citizens, the visiting humorists, Ilf and Petrov:

The night we went to hear him he appeared tall, bent, and thin, with a long sad face, his hair closely clipped; he sat down at the piano, separated the folds of his old-fashioned black swallowtail, adjusted one of his cuffs with his large hand, and turned to the audience. His expression seemed to say: "Yes, I am an unfortunate exile and am obliged to play before you for your contemptible dollars, and for this humiliation I ask very little— silence!"

This description appeared the following year in their American travel book, *One-Storied America* (later translated here as *Little Golden America*), but in the earlier magazine publication, the authors gave the performance itself more attention: "His playing was rhythmically sculptured and clear, worked out in the most minute details. There was nothing of an old man in his performance, but it had become too settled and crystallized."

The Chicago performance of the Rhapsody, under Stock, was greeted so enthusiastically that its composer was compelled to repeat its latter half after an already long program that had begun with his Second Symphony and Lyadov's Eight Russian Folk Songs. In Minneapolis Ormandy built another all-Russian program around Rachmaninoff and the Rhapsody, with the Lyadov Folk Songs, Stravinsky's *Fire Bird* Suite, and Ravel's orchestration of Musorgsky's *Pictures at an Exhibition*. In the *Minneapolis Star,* John K. Sherman wrote:

If Nino Martini can draw a packed house, there is comfort in the fact that Sergei Rachmaninoff can draw a packed house, too. Last night's phenomenon might give rise to the philosophical reflection that genuine greatness often receives as much recognition as specious greatness.

For Rachmaninoff, greeted by an audience that overflowed into the pit at Northrop Auditorium, has the aura and aspect of greatness, and it is sensed the moment he steps on to the platform. He is the same crafty sorcerer, the gaunt, wise ogre in evening dress who shambles to the piano to draw from it the blazing fires of eloquence and the slow flame of poetry.

And as usual, the experience of hearing Rachmaninoff goes down as one of the deep and authentic experiences of the season. What may have surprised many last night was that from the man who looks like an oracle of remote and superior wisdom should have come the brilliance, the Lisztian pyrotechnics, the sheer mischief of the composition he chose to play with the orchestra—the Rhapsody on a Theme of Paganini, composed only last year.

When the Rhapsody was again played with Stokowski, Rachmaninoff was so pleased that he told the conductor, "We must play it together in New York." And it was with this New York performance of the Rhapsody that Rachmaninoff ended his American season on January 13, 1936.

Cortot conducted the Paris performance of the Rhapsody, and Rachmaninoff's recital tour took him through Switzerland (with only a day to spare at Senar) to Poland for both a concert with orchestra and a recital. This was his first visit to Warsaw since he had left Russia. True, this was not Russia, but the nearness of its border and the recollections of Warsaw concerts of long ago made the visit an emotional experience for him.

When he got to Vienna, for a recital on February 26, the Swans were in his audience:

The hall was packed. The atmosphere was quiet and serious. There was an expectation of a real musical event, and the element of sensation was absent. The Viennese had gathered to hear Rachmaninoff, and the mood was probably the same as in bygone days at the concerts of Brahms and Clara Schumann. Rachmaninoff fully justified their expectations. . . .

We had supper at the Hotel Bristol, where the Rachmaninoffs stayed. At the end of the day Rachmaninoff quite instinctively longed for privacy. In the dining room he chose a table at the door, from which it was hidden by a high screen. As usual, he seemed a little aloof, as if, after all, there was a barrier—imperceptible perhaps, but still a barrier—between him and the rest of the world. His movements were quiet and rather slow. But the moment he felt secure behind the screen that shielded him, he smiled and was joking and teasing in his charming, harmless way. . . .

When asked why he did not relax and enjoy himself a little oftener, Rachmaninoff gave a sly look and said:

"I will tell you something. You see, I am like an old grisette. She is skinny and worn, but the urge to walk the streets is so strong that in spite of her years she goes out every night. And so it is with me. I am old and wrinkled, and still I have to play. Oh no, I could not play any less. I want to play all I can."

In London, after a performance of his Third Concerto, on March 30, with Malcolm Sargent and the Philharmonic, the *Times* shook a kind finger at Rachmaninoff the next morning:

We have a grudge against Mr. Rachmaninoff's concertos. He plays them so wonderfully and his music and his performance belong so completely to one another that we very rarely get a chance of hearing him play anything else with orchestra. As no doubt he would be the first to declare, there are greater concertos for piano and orchestra than his own, and we want to hear them played by him, since he is a great musician as well as a great pianist. We would willingly have foregone Borodin's Symphony in B minor to hear Mr. Rachmaninoff again in one of the classics.

Enclosing this clipping, Rachmaninoff wrote to Wilshaw on April 15, as soon as he arrived at his Swiss home:

By the end of every season I move only "under the whip." . . . How strangely life is arranged. When one is young, strong—one just waits for engagements. But they do not come. And when one becomes weak, one doesn't know how to protect oneself from them! I cannot satisfy half of them—that is, by accepting them. For the last ten years Natasha travels everywhere with me. She helps me get things ready, for one often arrives at a city only a few hours before a concert and leaves immediately afterwards. My programs are made up mostly of the compositions of others. I don't like to play my own things.* I put in the program two or three little things "for appearance sake." What do I play? I've played so many programs! My favorite is a concert in two parts: in the first Chopin, in the latter Liszt. One needn't add oneself to such a program. . . . Kreisler is considered the best violinist. After him, or rather alongside him, comes Jascha Heifetz. The best pianist, I daresay, is still Hofmann, but on the condition that he's in the mood, or "in form." . . . The best orchestras in America: in Philadelphia (with which I make records) and in New York. He who hasn't heard these can't know what an orchestra is.—I have not

* Mme. Rachmaninoff's explanation of this remark was that her husband often expressed such a severe attitude towards his own compositions, but that this usually happened when a composition was not going well and he was overcome by doubts. These moods were of short duration. In general his letters to friends show an exaggerated attitude of self-criticism.

published my recollections. You must have heard of Riesemann's book, which is called "Rachmaninoff's Recollections told to Riesemann." It is published in America and England—in English, of course. If you wish— I'll send it to you. The book is superdull. Incidentally it contains a great deal of untruth to prove that I did not dictate this book, but that Riesemann largely composed it. While I was in England in March they sent me another book [by Watson Lyle] about me, with a request to permit its publication. I gave the permission, but I could read only its first three chapters. Patience didn't last beyond this! For God's sake, don't think I am posing. Even in such writing one should sense the talent of the writer! And here it wasn't noticeable, either in Riesemann (he died last year, which is why I scold him so little) or in the Englishman. . . . You also ask after Natasha and my children. Of them one may say only that it would be difficult to find a better wife and children. It's about them that a book should be written!

Letters came to Senar from conductor friends and pianist friends, with gifts of grapes from South Africa (where Moiseiwitsch was playing the Rhapsody) as well as bids for the new symphony and renewed efforts to break down Rachmaninoff's resistance to the radio. On his way to Europe in May, Eugene Ormandy wrote asking for the score of *The Bells*, suggesting that its composer conduct the performance, and:

Now another question. Have you finished your new Symphony yet? I would feel honored if I could give its world première. As a matter of fact I am planning to make your appearance with the Philadelphia Orchestra an All Rachmaninoff Festival. I should greatly value your suggestions for a program.

In his reply on May 11, Rachmaninoff tells Ormandy that the score of *The Bells* is being sent him from Paris, but that some new work has been done on it:

The work is being performed in England by Sir Henry Wood on October 18 at the Sheffield Festival. I have rewritten the vocal parts for the entire third movement and Sir Henry will give the first performance of the revised version. . . .

I hope to finish my new work for orchestra in time for performance this coming October. I shall be only too happy to have its world première given by the Philadelphia Orchestra. I believe Mr. Foley has already mentioned this to Mr. Stokowski, and I am not sure whether he made any promise to Mr. Stokowski in regard to the first performance. This, however, can be adjusted between Mr. Stokowski and yourself.

When Stokowski wrote on May 20, the symphony's première had been settled, so that his persuasive powers could be concentrated on a more difficult problem:

Dear Friend,

I have often been thinking of our performance of your new Variations, and I am so glad we were able to play them again in New York. I feel more and more convinced that we ought to broadcast this work some time so as to give millions of people who live in remote places the opportunity of hearing this remarkable music. Of course this could only be well done if we have exceptionally good transmission equipment and a specially planned pick-up. Although these will be difficult to obtain, I feel confident we can have them.

In that case we would be able to offer all music lovers four unique things, combined in one—your extraordinary composition, your unique way of playing it, the unusual qualities of the Philadelphia Orchestra, and a specially prepared high quality transmission and pick-up.

I am not going to try in any way to persuade you to do this because I know your intense dislike of the distortion which in radio so often ruins music. I fully agree with you about this and hate these distortions just as intensely as you do. But there are ways of broadcasting music so that the music is not spoiled but can give pleasure to literally millions of people. This cannot be done by the wholesale method in which radio is now being carried on, but for a special occasion like the one I am dreaming of such a high quality of broadcasting is possible.*

Swan, visiting Senar at the end of May, witnessed an unpleasant incident with the boat:

Rachmaninoff was a great lover of motorboating and used to go out every day. He always steered himself. Often he went out alone. This

---

* Rachmaninoff's antipathy to radio was possibly reinforced by a children's program of 1935 that purported to be a biography. The text of it, which was sent to him, concluded: "And that, boys and girls, is the story of Sergei Rachmaninoff, and how he overcame those wretched fellows who try to stop all of us—old Mr. Laziness and all his family—you know them—Fun, who wants us to play during study hours— Dreamy, who would rather have us wander with him than do our lessons—and all those other fellows."

hobby of his nearly proved fatal during that stay of ours. About an hour before dinner he said:

"I think I shall go for a spin on the lake."

He got up quietly. He did everything quietly and firmly; hesitation was alien to his nature. It was a lovely afternoon, one of those rare and bright afternoons in the Swiss mountains in May. We joined him. At the last minute Mr. Ibbs, Rachmaninoff's agent in England, asked permission to come along also. He was a corpulent man with a round, ruddy face.

The lake was as still as a fishpond. Rachmaninoff took the wheel, and we glided smoothly out of the boathouse on to the lake. We were well out of sight of the house when Mr. Ibbs asked if he could try his hand at the steering wheel. Rachmaninoff handed it over to him and joined us on the back bench. No sooner had he sat down than something very strange happened. Evidently Mr. Ibbs had decided to make a sharp turn. But, instead of turning, the boat began to spin and bend over to one side. We slid on the back seat and watched Mr. Ibbs in dead silence. But when his face had turned as red as a beetroot, Rachmaninoff got up quietly, as if he had merely given Mr. Ibbs time to correct his mistake, reached the wheel with a few big strides, and pushed Mr. Ibbs aside. The screw was already thumping loudly in the air, and the left rim of the boat was touching the water. Just as the heavy boat was about to capsize and bury us under it, Rachmaninoff set it right and we glided back to the embankment of the Villa Senar. Nobody said a word. Silently we got out of the boat. On the way up to the house Rachmaninoff touched his left side several times and frowned. When we were quite near the veranda, he said:

"Don't say anything to Natasha. She won't let me go boating any more."

The Symphony and its third and last movement were resumed on June 6, and on June 30 Rachmaninoff sent news to his sister-in-law:

Yesterday morning I finished my work and you are the first to be notified of it. It is a Symphony. The first performance is promised to Stokowski. Apparently in November. With each of my thoughts I thank God that I was able to do it.* No need to be secretive about the symphony. You may tell whom you wish.

Next day he and his wife motored 344 kilometers to Aix-les-Bains. He had been bothered by symptoms of arthritis: the little finger on

* At the end of the new symphony's score he wrote, "Finished. I thank God! 6–30 June 1936, Senar."

his right hand was slightly swollen and pained him in playing. Fear that this might spread to the other fingers forced Rachmaninoff to consent to take a cure at Aix. His letters from the Regina Hotel show no willing invalid. In his first week he wrote the Somovs:

We are being given the treatment! Natasha vigorously and I lightly. Both prescribed by the doctor. I am slightly contemptuous of doctors, and doctors are slightly scared of me, and that's why my prescription is a light one. In the three weeks of our treatment there are many empty days for me, described by the doctor as "rest." But there's nothing to rest from! Perhaps he thinks, "Better not get mixed up with him, for he may be 'playing himself into the coffin'—and then I'd have to answer for it!" So I'm drinking two little glasses of water daily and warming my hands in vapors. Very pleasant sensation! As for the water, as God is my judge, this spring seems to me to give the most ordinary water. At least it tastes that way. Something like the water you find in washbasins! Just to throw dust in the eyes, a beautiful building and baths have been built for this water. . . . I have rescued myself by bringing some work with me. More than half [the Symphony] has been copied, and I am proofreading. When this is finished I don't know what I'll do. . . . The phlox and lilies are flowering there [at Senar] now.

His "cure" progressed. On July 18 he wrote to Wilshaw:

The sanitarium regimen can be defined in two words: boring and perspiring! Both inseparable parts of sanitarium treatments. I don't care to play roulette; already too late for me to court ladies; I don't make acquaintances; I'm not allowed to work; even reading is not recommended. Well, and so? Green anguish! I count the days remaining before our departure, which, if all goes well, will be on July 25 early in the morning. . . . It will be pleasant to skip out of here! . . .

Just before coming here from Senar I finished writing a symphony. Its first performance I've given, as usual, to my very favorite orchestra, in Philadelphia. How I should like you to hear this orchestra at least once.

Chapter 20

The Composer Rebuffed

BEFORE leaving Senar, Rachmaninoff wrote to Somov: "Has the copying of the Symphony started? If the orchestra parts are ready by September 25, then perhaps the score could be copied, too; *four* copyists could do it in a week, easily."

While the copying was pushed ahead in America, Rachmaninoff, impatient to attend the Philadelphia rehearsals, filled two English dates: a performance of the Rhapsody with the London Symphony Orchestra, and an appearance at the Sheffield Festival, where he was to play the Second Concerto and to hear the long-delayed Sheffield performance of *The Bells*. A program note by the conductor, Sir Henry Wood, explained the delay and described the revisions made for this performance of *The Bells*:

The Sheffield Festival Committee had entered into correspondence with Serge Rachmaninoff in 1913, with a view to giving this work the first performance in this country, at their forthcoming Festival, but the Great War intervened, and naturally caused the abandonment of the Festival, and the work was not produced until I gave the first performance in this country on the 15th March, 1921, at a Liverpool Philharmonic Society's Concert. . . .

The voice parts of this [third] movement were entirely rewritten for the Sheffield Festival last October, 1936, and published separately, as the composer told me he found the choral writing too complicated, that it did not make the effect he intended. Certainly at Liverpool in 1921, I had the utmost difficulty in getting the chorus to keep up the speed and maintain any clarity, amongst the great mass of chromatic passages, and certainly vocal power was out of the question, and I feel the composer did very wisely in re-writing this section of the work. As it now stands, the chorus writing is splendidly distinctive, full of colour, and easily "gets over" the brilliant orchestral texture. . . .

An amusing incident occurred when the composer first played through his work to me, remarking that the piano arrangement in the published vocal score by A. Goldenweiser, was much too difficult for him to tackle, but he would do his best with it. Certainly it is the most difficult vocal score that I have ever seen.

The work made a negative impression on the chorus in their rehearsals without orchestra, but with their first orchestral rehearsal they revised their opinion. The *Times* reported the performance:

The Bells is largely pictorial, in contrast to the C minor Piano Concerto, played to-night by the composer, which is primarily psychological. Its first number, depicting sleigh bells, is entrancing as sheer sound, and is wholly satisfying as a *scherzo* in which a huge orchestra produces an effect of fairy-like transparency. The second number deals with wedding bells, and here we have no peals such as an Englishman associates with espousals, but an evocation of love against a background of the Russian Orthodox Church. Fire bells and funeral bells complete the suite. Though they are faithfully done, they sound a less distinctive note, and at one point come to the verge of bathos by a sudden flight of fancy into the *macabre* of Poe's words.

Rachmaninoff arrived in America just in time for the final rehearsals of his symphony's première in Philadelphia; a *Times* reporter watched the composer during the performance:

During the playing of the symphony, Mr. Rachmaninoff sat in a box near the back of the auditorium, following the music intently and several times smiling at companions when the orchestra seemingly reproduced passages just as he had intended them to be interpreted.

At other times he clenched a fist and half rose in his seat, while still again he sat immobile with chin resting on his cupped hand.

Edwin Schloss reported the première for the *Philadelphia Record*:

Novelty added to the glamour of the occasion. Of the four numbers on the program, Dr. Stokowski offered three never before heard in Philadelphia. Leading these in importance (at least on paper) was the world premiere of Sergei Rachmaninoff's Third Symphony. . . .

The new Rachmaninoff symphony was a disappointment at least to one member of yesterday's audience. Written in three movements, there are echoes in the music of the composer's earlier lyric spaciousness of style. But sterility seems largely written in the pages of the new score.

Samuel L. Laciar, of the *Public Ledger,* was more pleased:

The symphony . . . is a most excellent work in musical conception, composition and orchestration. Emotionally, it is full of that defiant melancholy which is one of the outstanding characteristics of the composer. Mr. Rachmaninoff, as always, has been conservative in his harmonizations, and he has given us another example in this work that it is not necessary to write dissonant music in order to get the originality which is the greatest—and usually the single—demand of the ultra-moderns. This symphony is thoroughly understandable musically at a single hearing, although several will be required before all the complexities of the technical side of the composition will be entirely clear, especially the contrapuntal writing of the final movement. Its single drawback seemed to be insufficient contrast in tonality and mood.

The Philadelphia Orchestra when it brought the Third Symphony to New York, encountered a wide range of opinion, all the way from B. H. Haggin's (in the *Brooklyn Eagle*), "a chewing over again of something that never had importance to start with," to the politeness of W. J. Henderson, in the *Sun:*

It is the creation of a genial mind laboring in a field well known and loved by it, but not seeking now to raise the fruits of heroic proportions. . . .
    The first movement is orthodox in its initial statement of two contrasting chief subjects. They are contrasted in the customary way, in temper and tonality. But the working out section pays only polite respect to tradition. . . . The development of themes immediately follows their statement and this is Rachmaninoff's method. The cantabile theme of the first movement is especially attractive in its lyric and plaintive character and the leading subject has virility and possibilities which are not neglected later. In fact, we suspect, after this insufficient first hearing, that there is more organic unity in this symphony through consanguinity of themes than is instantly discernible.

Even Olin Downes wavered in his faith:

What does it say? Mr. Rachmaninoff would never explain. His work is done with the last note of the scoring and some find his personal reticence reflected in his art, which is prevailingly somber in tone and passionately introspective.
    The outward characteristics of Rachmaninoff's style are evident in the

work heard on this occasion. There are the broad, curving Slavic melodies, which can say so much with a simple instrumentation confined principally to the choir of strings. There are the throbbing rhythms; the relapses, at one moment, to a point when the whole orchestra seems to lie supine and without strength, only to rise with fresh accumulation of force and to shake with fury. There is the impression of frustrated strength, which gathers, to crash helplessly against some obstacle. . . .

It cannot be said, however, that in these pages Mr. Rachmaninoff says things which are new, even though his idiom is more his own than ever before, and free of the indebtedness it once had to Tchaikovsky. Nor is it easy to avoid the impression, at a first hearing of this work, of a certain diffuseness. There is a tendency to over-elaboration of detail, and to unnecessary extensions, so that the last movement, in particular, appears too long.

Would not a pair of shears benefit the proportions of this work?

When Alexander Aslanov sent Rachmaninoff his personal reactions to the symphony, the composer replied: "I send you a thousand thanks for your complimentary, and for me most touching, letter. I shall preserve and remember it when the inescapable waves of doubt and pain come upon me."

Rachmaninoff often had occasion to deny that his music was "nationalist" or "Russian." In the ears of the émigré Russians who heard the first American performances of his last symphony, this new work contradicted his protestations, however, for the music was saturated with "Russianness," more than in any work he had composed since 1917. He was consistent in one claim, that he composed only "the music I hear within me," for here he heard his nation. This was a richly detailed dramatization of his feelings about Russia, his memories, love and friendships there, his loss—an articulation in music of thoughts otherwise unspoken. As usual, he provided no key; but even his family remarked the symphony's unusually Russian sound. American audiences and critics alike may have been deaf to this quality, but when the symphony was later introduced to Russian audiences, no one there missed the point: it was recognized as Rachmaninoff's "Russian" symphony.

In St. Louis and Pittsburgh, respectively, Vladimir Golschmann and Antonio Modarelli conducted the new symphony; on each program the composer played one of his concertos. The symphony was played in Chicago without the composer present; he was at that moment playing a Washington recital that appears to have been affected by his symphony's failure:

Once upon a time Sergei Rachmaninoff was a great pianist. But his piano playing last evening was that of a successful composer.

Composers, of course, seldom play well. Absorbed by their own creative work they seldom have the time or inclination for painstaking, conscientious re-creation of other men's works.

Following the example of Siloti, pupil of Liszt, in calling attention to the fiftieth anniversary of the master's death, Rachmaninoff's program this season concluded with a group of Liszt compositions. For the critic of the *Boston Herald*, this illuminated an essential quality in his playing:

. . . there is a romantic element in Rachmaninoff's personality, which is accentuated by the apparent coldness of his demeanor. . . . Unquestionably the beauty of his playing of romantic composers, such as Chopin and —for the matter of that—himself, is enhanced by this inversely dramatic approach.

Ormandy's planned Rachmaninoff festival program came off, though without the new symphony. With the Second Concerto and *The Bells*, the Philadelphia Orchestra and Rachmaninoff toured New York, Philadelphia, Washington, and Baltimore for the first half of January, and then Rachmaninoff departed for the Middle and Far West. The score of the Third Symphony, in proof, accompanied the Rachmaninoffs on their tour. From Denver, where he played on January 19, Rachmaninoff wrote to Somov the next morning:

I am sending you the cello parts! In the score make a correction five bars before ☐74☐, Celli and Bassi

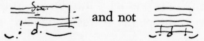 and not

that is, one note has to be taken out in these. . . .

I feel B number two! Yesterday I played like a cobbler. Occasionally there's no one who can play worse than I do!

On the following day he answered an inquiry from Nicolas Slonimsky on his work since leaving Russia. Itemizing five works, from Op. 40 to Op. 44, he wrote: "I list all that I have composed 'as a refugee.' It's not difficult; little has been accomplished!" Slonimsky had also asked for the dates of the compositions, but these Rachmaninoff was not able to remember, except for the new symphony, whose dated manuscript was on the desk before him in the Denver hotel.

Then to Portland, Oregon:

A press delegation met the artist in the hotel lobby. The composer, famous as an interview dodger, looked down on the delegation, frowned, and then, in slow, measured words, announced: "I have not so many words for you, I have no words for you at all; there are too many."

"I was told this is your farewell tour; that we'll never see you any more," the writer stated.

"I have no such thoughts; who told you this is my last trip?" replied the visitor, real snappily for him, "I have not thought this is my last trip; I may see you many times." . . .

"Where do you make your home now?" was inquired.

"On the train, in the Pullman car," came the answer, proving the stern pianist really has a sense of humor. "I must travel so much in your country. I will sail from New York February 28 and be in England March 3 to start my tour there March 9. My little grandson is waiting for me in Paris to see what I bring him."

He gave another morning press interview in San Francisco; the *Chronicle* reported:

Of all the dissatisfactions of his long career one among three stands out.

"The big annoyance of my concert life," asserted the sallow, lank Russian master, "is my C sharp minor Prelude.

"I'm not sorry I wrote it. It has helped me. But people ALWAYS make me play it. By now I play it without feeling—like a machine.

"For annoyance No. 2," he said, "take the press interview before breakfast." And since he had had his breakfast, his sleepy Oriental eyes became magically friendly in a smile.

But instantly a slow anguish seized his expression. Some one had asked him whether modern composers are writing great works for piano.

"About modern music," was his grave reply, "I feel as about interviews without breakfast. I am very pessimistic about modern music."

The *Call-Bulletin* reporter asked him whether he considered himself primarily a pianist, conductor, or composer. He did not know:

"And the critics don't help me. . . .

"No, the critics are not helpful. When my first symphony was first played they said that it was so-so. Then when my second was played they said the first was good, but that the second was so-so. Now that my third has been played—just this fall—they say my first and second are good but that my—oh, well, you see how it is."

The Philadelphia performances of *The Bells* were mentioned. " 'I have an affinity for bells. Whenever I hear deep-throated bells I think of Russia,' he sighed."

Corrections of the symphony continued to be made during the tour; they reached Somov from Kansas and from Canada. Even while waiting in railway stations Rachmaninoff would take out the green proof sheets and bend over their correction.

In Detroit a rehearsal of the Second Concerto was described in the *Detroit Free Press*:

Down the stairs leading from the soloist's private room sounded a military tread, in regular beats. . . .

He looked straight ahead. He spoke to no one. He wore a dark suit, and loosely fitting brown gloves.

At the door he hesitated a minute. Victor Kolar nodded, turned to the orchestra and said:

"Gentlemen, Mr. Rachmaninoff."

Applause broke forth from the musicians. . . .

A moment's pause while the pianist settled himself, took off his gloves, glanced at the keyboard and then up at the leader. Kolar tapped for attention, moved for the downbeat, and the music started.

The rehearsal was more formal than most concerts.

Even when Kolar stopped the music, or when Rachmaninoff himself stopped to give his suggestions on how his own composition should be played, he maintained that solemn air of a man who has attained the heights of his own field. It was obvious that he would brook no deviation from the straight line of business. . . .

Between his last recital in Columbus, Ohio, on February 26 and his first English recital in Birmingham on March 10 there was no opportunity for rest at either end. He wrote Somov from London on March 24:

Dear Yevgeni Ivanovich, yesterday I played my last concert here and in half an hour we leave for Paris. . . .

   The concerts here went well. Very big success. But the criticisms here in London are only so-so. Ibbs doesn't even want to show me the *Times*. Says he could kill that man; that he daren't write so dishonestly. In the provinces, of course, the picture is different. There the newspapers are in seventh heaven. I feel well.

Tomorrow we shall have been here a week [he wrote the Somovs on April 24, from Senar]. The weather alters slightly—meaning that the rain is somewhat less, but squalls still rattle the blinds and shake the house. I also shake in fear that one of my trees will be broken—and the cold is un-poetically referred to as "a dog's cold"! After an icy morning the wind changed direction and it grew warm. Someone even claims to have seen the sun! Be that as it may, I crept out of my sweater, holding on to my rubbers, scarf, and a fall coat. The cherry trees have flowered a little today. All trees remain bare. To exploit the late spring I am planting a few more trees. . . . Of course I'm not working yet—aside from the hour of practice that I have to do for the sake of the sore finger. I am reading and walking a lot and sleep much better—and that's all so far. By Natasha's definition I am not yet "in good shape," but this will soon pass. . . . I'll rest for about two more weeks. Positively! . . . Incidentally, bad weather pursued us from our first day in Europe. Even in Milan it poured. The last sunny day was in New York, on the day we left. . . .

   Here, at Senar, the Medtners spent a day with us. We were glad to see them.

More visitors were reported on May 4: "Day after tomorrow the Horowitzes arrive here, intending to stay about a month. Haven't seen him yet, for I missed him in Basel." Some four-hand playing with Horowitz, recuperating from a long illness, was anticipated in the second item of a list of needs sent to Somov:

At the first opportunity, send me:
1. My 4th concerto, the score, only the score.
2. The Godowsky pieces for 4 hands. I believe I have 24 of them.

A visitor to Senar, Mrs. A. M. Henderson, leaves a pleasant picture of life there:

An evening spent at the Villa Senar is a memory to treasure. Dining, the family sit long at table, in the leisurely Russian fashion; for, with them, a meal is not just a means of satisfying hunger, but is regarded as an opportunity for an exchange of ideas in friendly conversation . . . With many interests and friends in common, conversation is a delight, and if it ultimately drifts into the realms of music, it is not to be wondered at; for, with the great artist, music is not simply a profession, it is his life.

Rachmaninoff sent Wilshaw, on June 7, a complete report on his plans and his feelings:

Now that I'm old and tired and sick and I try to overcome it all—there's no end to the concerts. I have a manager (in Russian, *impresario*) with whom I have worked in America for 19 years. We've already become friends! So now my work with him consists in deciding which engagements to accept and which to decline. I've turned over to him, too, the general representation of me in Europe. This is how we've arranged next season: from October 17 to December 20, 32 concerts in America. January—rest. February—12 concerts in Scandinavia, Holland (that's 4), and Vienna, Budapest, Paris, and other places (one in each). March—12 concerts in England, and finally, on April 10, a last concert in Vienna, where, after a long interval of 20 years, I have consented to conduct. Program: my 3rd Symphony and *The Bells*.

Besides these tours I have two extra trips, both at a time usually set aside for my rest. On September 5 I have to record my 3rd Symphony in London. For this they give me the Philharmonic Orchestra and three rehearsals—[September] 2, 3, 4. And because the record sale of such long works goes poorly and the orchestra costs much and the Company loses on it, they accepted as a bribe from me that I would make a recording of my First Piano Concerto. As my hands have completely lost the habit of conducting, I cannot make both recordings at the same time, so I've decided to come back home and return again to London on September 21 and 22. And I sail for America on October 1.

A few more words on the new symphony. It was played in New York, Philadelphia, Chicago, etc. I was present at the first two performances. It was played wonderfully. (The Philadelphia Orchestra, about which I've written you—Stokowski conducting.) Both audience and critics responded sourly. Personally, I'm firmly convinced that this is a good work. But—

sometimes the author is wrong, too! However, I maintain my opinion.
The symphony (only score and parts) was published two weeks ago.

Today I begin to study my 1st Concerto. Thanks be that it's not very
difficult! As the records will appear this winter, I've promised to play it
at my second concert in London on April 2, which is with orchestra.
Program: my first, Beethoven's first (there's divine music!)* and my
Rhapsody. Enough about myself. It turned out a little too much! Excuse
me. . . .

[P.S.] I am now reading Ilf and Petrov's *Little Golden America*. Read
it, absolutely, if you wish to get acquainted with America and know it.
There's much of interest in it! There are a few funny lines about myself.
This was the only place where I found untruth!

Wilshaw's response was spirited: "I have read your letter about your
new symphony, and of course I was vexed that the reviews said so
much less than it deserves. So?! Just recall how the press received
most of Tchaikovsky's works—usually they were charged with bayo-
nets! Though this grieved him, he wasn't disturbed but went on composing, composing."

An Italian excursion was announced to Somov on June 17:

In two weeks we plan to leave for Italy. Irina, with the children and
dogs, goes there the day after tomorrow. Don't imagine that this trip was
prescribed by the doctor! No! some friends only slightly acquainted with
medicine advised us to treat our arthritic sores with hot sea sand. They
argued with great eloquence! Impossible to contradict. So we decided
to go! Irina and I, in advance, without a chauffeur, drove to a place
[Riccione] where Charley found a villa for us that turned out to be quite
suitable, and the trip was set.

After the family's return to Senar they were visited by Vera and
Michael Fokine, who came to talk with Rachmaninoff about col-
laborating on a ballet. Rachmaninoff suggested the Paganini
Rhapsody as suitable, but Fokine was dubious, and so wrote:

[August 23, 1937]

We want to thank you and Natalia Alexandrovna for the wonderful

---

* After years of capitulation to local managers who refused to let him play any
concertos besides his own, Rachmaninoff this year insisted on playing this Beethoven
Concerto (numerically the First, but actually composed two years after the "Second"
Concerto, Op. 19).

evening we spent in your "Little Paradise." We're very grateful to have
been introduced to the Rhapsody. Long ago I heard you play it in New
York, and I was completely fascinated by it. But I must hear it more often
before I can feel that I know it. If after studying your Rhapsody I feel able
to create a suitable and worthy setting of it for the stage, I hope you will
allow me to do so and give me your blessing for it. I confess that I vaguely
hoped that our meeting would result in the new ballet that I've dreamt
about for so long. As yet this hasn't happened. You've become busy with
something else and I haven't yet found a theme that seems *absolutely*
suitable for you. I've read a mass of books in my search for a subject, and
I can't really understand why the results have been so fruitless! After hearing a Bach Suite recently I worked out in a single day a complete ballet
idea that didn't seem so bad. I need some sort of push. Sometimes this is
music or, less often, a book. It is probably my uncertainty as to what would
interest you that blocks me. I've just been re-reading the myths of Ovid—
in which there is rich material for both composer and choreographer. But
I remember your rather sour look at the thought of Perseus—"What does
this Perseus feel? How should I know?" you said. "The Shepherdess and
the Sweep" or "The Flying Carpet" by Andersen, Pushkin's "Hussar"—
these would make lovely little ballets. But I don't want to propose trifles
of this sort to you. And then I think of the tempting elements in Peter's
epoch: Peter himself, the assemblies, Tzarevich Alexei in Italy. A mix-
ture of cruelty and the will of a genius—debauchery—drunkenness—sacri-
lege. The tragedy of father and son. . . . And then I think of the reign of
the Empress Anna—the Ice Palace—the contrasting costumes of Prince
Golitzin, who, after his marriage in Italy to an Italian woman, was forced
to divorce her, become a jester, and marry a Kalmuck female jester—but
all this shows monarchs in such a light that you wouldn't care to under-
take a theme of this sort. I haven't found anything in Pushkin, Lermontov,
Byron, Shelley, Zhukovsky, Oscar Wilde, Poe, in Russian fairy tales, in
the 1001 Nights, in the Decameron—anything that would be a suitable
subject for you and me, anything that hasn't already been used. Now I'm
going to look through Carlo Gozzi and Hoffmann, and all of Andersen's
tales. . . . Vera Petrovna has just told me that you have often said you require a ballet that represents something mighty, a struggle of the elements, for example something in the manner of my last ballet to Bach's
music. Why shouldn't we create a "creation of the world"? There's a
theme for music! It is wonderfully described by Ovid at the very beginning of his Metamorphoses. Though this letter is growing too long, I want
to tell you how interesting I found your thoughts on the importance of

the theme in music. I learn the art of dance from music and verify my thoughts about dance by listening to substantial discussion about music. In ballets at present the quality of themes is replaced by quantity, as with most new composers. So the theme is too weak to bear repetition, and one must take up another, though it's just as empty as the first. We found nothing suitable on Lake Lucerne and finally landed here in Montreux. It was lovely when we arrived, but it's raining now—perhaps for the best. I work every day on the *Cockerel*.

After receiving this letter a more persistent image for Fokine's use of the Rhapsody occurred to Rachmaninoff. He tried to telephone Fokine in Montreux, and then sent a letter to London.

Last night I was thinking about a subject and here is what came to mind. I'll give you only the main outlines, for the details are still foggy. Consider the Paganini legend—about the sale of his soul to the evil spirit in exchange for perfection in art, and for a woman. All variations on the Dies Irae would be for the evil spirit. The whole middle from the 11th variation to the 18th—these are the love episodes. Paganini himself makes his first appearance at the "Theme" and, defeated, appears for the last time at the 23rd variation—the first 12 bars—after which, to the end, is the triumph of his conquerors. The first appearance of the evil spirit is in the 7th variation, where, at #19, there can be a dialogue with Paganini during his theme as it merges with the Dies Irae. Variations 8, 9, 10—progress of the evil spirit. Variation 11 is the transition to the realm of love. Variation 12—the minuet—is the first appearance of the woman—through the 18th variation. Variation 13 is the first understanding between the woman and Paganini. Variation 19 is the triumph of Paganini's art, his diabolic pizzicato. It would be good to show Paganini with a violin—not, of course, a real one, but some devised, fantastic violin. And it also seems to me that at the conclusion of the play the several personages [representing] the evil spirit should be caricatures, absolute caricatures, of Paganini himself. And they should here have violins that are even more fantastically monstrous. You're not laughing at me? How I wish I could see you, to tell you more fully about all this—if my ideas and subject seem interesting and of value to you.

With Fokine's reply, a new ballet was close to being born:

[September 9, 1937, London]

I was very happy to receive your letter and to learn your thoughts about the Rhapsody. All that you say is extremely interesting. If any further details grow clear to you, do send them to me. Each word can be valuable and may push a whole scene into being. Where can I find details on the Paganini legend? I know very little about it. And too: what is this Dies Irae? Is this the same Dies Irae that is in the Catholic service? Do the words of this hymn have any relation to Paganini? I'm now very occupied with the *Cockerel* and have no opportunity to search for material on Paganini. This explains why I can't answer your letter at once in the way I should like to answer it. As soon as I finish work on *The Golden Cockerel* (by September 21) I'll concentrate on the Rhapsody. But if you send me any further explanation this will be very helpful.

Chapter 21

Retreat from Europe

O<small>N</small> R<small>ACHMANINOFF</small>'<small>S</small> return to New York he was interviewed by a reporter from the *Sun,* who asked about a rumored new work given to a British conductor:

"No," he said, drawing out the monosyllable, "nothing new." He sighed deeply, and added: "I have been a little bit lazy. I have nothing in mind now, either. Only in the summer do I have the time to compose—and last summer, I was lazy. One grows older. Now, I can play only about sixty concerts a year—thirty or so in America, the rest in Europe. That is my limit." He passed his strong blunt-fingered right hand over his closely cropped hair.

"You remember they gave my Third Symphony here last season. It was not a great success."

"But, Maestro," I protested, "It takes time for the general public to know and understand such things—"

"Ah, yes!" he said. "Only the critics can understand everything after a single hearing. Sometimes, such quick understanding is a dangerous thing. I should not be brave enough to say whether a work is good or bad after a first hearing."

Rachmaninoff is one of the few major artists who have steadfastly refused to have anything to do with the radio or the motion pictures. Last summer, he bought a radio—"but I bought it for the gramophone attachment," he explained. "Some one of my family tuned in Moscow. Always, they were trying to hear things from Russia. Sometimes I was near, and I listened. I was astonished at how conservative the programs were. I heard songs by Glinka, Tchaikovsky—some of my own. . . ."

Rachmaninoff has no interests outside of music, his family and friends. "I am myself only in music," he said. "Music is enough for a whole life-time—but a lifetime is not enough for music."

One critic, notwithstanding his praise of Rachmaninoff's St. Louis recital, remarked that the "program could have been performed before gas foot lamps, with horses hitched to carriages outside," that the year might well have been 1900—for the works did not touch this century. To add to the Old World atmosphere of the occasion, Kreisler was also in St. Louis and in the audience—so Rachmaninoff added to the encores his transcription of the *Liebesleid*.

In Philadelphia he prefaced another encore with the remark, "A new composition by myself," in a theatrically heavy voice, as he struck the too familiar chords of the C-sharp minor Prélude. Another encore, after the New York recital, brought praise from *The New Yorker*: "It takes a great artist like Mr. Rachmaninoff to remind us that the *Liebestraum* is good piano music and not a meditation in molasses."

In Bonavia's London letter to *The New York Times* Rachmaninoff read discouraging news of his new symphony, conducted by Beecham at a concert of the Royal Philharmonic Society:

The symphony has had a bad press. Not one critic appears to have enjoyed it; all of them lament the total absence of those warmhearted melodies which attracted in Rachmaninoff's earlier compositions. . . .

Has the symphonic plan plus motto hampered his creative faculty, or can it be that Rachmaninoff has lost the stimulus of having to do battle for his convictions, that he has come to believe that nothing is worth struggling against? This great danger is ever present in the case of the successful international artist, who has no opportunity to strengthen and nourish his genius in seclusion.

Fortunately, he received a more enthusiastic report from Sir Henry:

November 26, 1937

My dear Mr. Rachmaninoff,

Just a few lines to tell you we dashed from Southport to London last Thursday and arrived in Queen's Hall at 9:30 P.M. just in time to hear your splendid 3rd Symphony—it scored a real success—what a lovely work it is—I thought the Orchestra gave a fine performance of it.

I am playing it twice after Christmas, at a Liverpool Philharmonic Concert on March 22nd and at a Studio Concert on April 3rd. If there is any advice you can offer me as regards your feelings or readings, of the Symphony, please do so and I shall be most grateful, on the other hand if you think it is all right, please don't trouble to answer this.

My wife and I have booked seats for your recital at Queen's Hall and perhaps we may get a word with you afterwards in the artists' room.

Michael, our dear dog, sends you his compliments and greetings.
With our united kindest regards and best wishes

Always sincerely yours

Henry J. Wood.

P.S. My Jubilee Concert is going splendidly and the Charing Cross Hospital *believe* they can raise a large sum of money for a Ward, dedicated to Orchestral musicians, all this comes about by your superb offer to come over and be my *one* solo artist. Orchestra of 300 (but they will not *all* play in your Piano Concerto) so don't be frightened.

For this Rachmaninoff thanked him on December 15:

My dear Sir Henry:

About ten days ago I read in the New York Times a letter from London in which it was said that the first performance of my Third Symphony had received a very poor press.

This news afflicted me, of course, but when I read your kind letter of November 26 and found that you liked my new composition I was very glad and forgot all my griefs. Thank you!

I expect to meet you in London at the beginning of March and to have a talk with you about the Symphony.

The only young American composer to acknowledge Rachmaninoff as a master also cheered him:

December 2, 1937

Beloved Master:

On Saturday last, my wife and I heard you in your New York recital, and we are still under the spell of your magical art. We planned to come backstage, for she is so very anxious to meet you, and I was anxious for you to know how deeply touched I was, but there was a big crowd, and we could not get up enough courage to add our presence to so many others.

Everything that pertains to you, every new work, every performance in short, all that belongs to your musical world is continually of the greatest personal concern to me, and I merely write to tell you, quite simply, that admiring thoughts and deepest devotion are always in my mind and heart. When critics, meaning to scold me for not indulging in "ultra-modernisms," have said that I followed in your footsteps, they never realized how complimentary I considered it, and how proud it always makes me.

It was a pleasure to see Mrs. Rachmaninoff at the Steinway dinner for Hofmann. On that occasion, I told your good wife that for several months I have been at work revising my 2nd Piano Concerto, and that only one opinion of it would matter to me—and that is yours. When time permits, and you would be so gracious, I would consider it a great privilege could I show the completed score to you, for advice, not approbation. Also this summer, I did a "Carmen" Fantasy for two pianos, and that, too, I would like to burden you with.

Devotedly yours,
Abram Chasins.

A few days later Rachmaninoff met Chasins at Steinway's and asked him with whom he was practicing the revised concerto in preparation for the performance with the Philharmonic. Mr. Chasins later wrote of this:

I said, "With nobody, for there is no piano reduction of the orchestral score." He then offered to practice it with me if I sent him the score! I sent it, and sure enough, two weeks later, Mr. Rachmaninoff came to my studio and practiced it with me for hours. His spirit of generosity was only matched by the magnificence of the piano reduction he played on the 2nd piano. Think of his doing that! I was absolutely overwhelmed, and have told this many times to those unfortunate people who thought that Mr. Rachmaninoff was a cold and distant man. Also, at that time, I showed him a picture I had cut out of *Life* magazine [December 7, 1936] by Steichen. He looked at it. . . . "Hm !. . . very dramatic!" He autographed it "To Abram Chasins . . . Bravo." I treasure it not only because of the signature, but because it brings back that unforgettable day in the life of a *composer-pianist* who was shown extraordinary courtesy and kindness on the part of the man he will always regard as *the composer-pianist*.

January 10, 1938

Dear Mr. Chasins:
    I want to tell you how very much pleasure it gave me to play with you your Second Piano Concerto. It is greatly to Mr. Stokowski's credit that he conducted it so soon after you completed it. I think that your revisions are a still further improvement on a remarkably beautiful work. You should have a great success with it with Barbirolli in April.
    It is impossible for me to understand why you have had to wait five

years for another series of performances for this composition. It reflects very badly upon the honesty and knowledge of the conductors in your country. Are they impressed only by music that they and no one else can understand? Are they only interested in "First Performances"? It seems that ASCAP or other organizations should educate the American people to realize how much they owe native musicians like yourself and native music that speaks simply, originally, and directly to the public. Perhaps you should go to Europe again. I am sure that complete recognition as a great pianist and composer would come to you without the need for expensive publicity or belonging to the clique.

The Viennese plans for *The Bells* collided with history. Under the windows of his hotel Rachmaninoff heard crowds shouting for Hitler and *Anschluss*. He was not surprised when, three days before the scheduled performance, all concerts in Vienna were canceled because of the political unrest. Catastrophe was in the air of Europe.

March was a crowded month, with Rachmaninoff covering more of the British Isles than on earlier tours. On Friday, March 10, in Manchester, he played the ever-surprising happy "First" Concerto by Beethoven. On Sunday he gave his only London recital of the season at Queen's Hall, and unconsciously gave the critics a little test. Clinton Gray-Fiske (in the *Hampstead News and Advertiser*) explained the embarrassing incident:

The programme told us that Rachmaninoff was going to play Liszt's well-known variations, "Weinen, Klagen," on a theme of Bach. The writer of the excellent analytical notes (Richard Holt) naturally assumed that Rachmaninoff intended to play what had been announced and accordingly described it in detail. There exist, however, three versions of the work—one for organ and two for piano—and Rachmaninoff had chosen the shorter and virtually unknown version without, apparently, making the fact clear. He duly played it, but the audience, having read the programme notes, expected the longer version, and instead of applauding, sat for a few minutes in mute bewilderment which was eventually relieved by semi-apologetic clapping. One cannot blame the audience, for they cannot be expected to know obscure works, but our great (?) critics (?) subsequently treated us to a fine exhibition of ignorance and inanity. The next day we read in the Press. "Bach-Liszt variations abandoned" [the *Times*], "Rachmaninoff began in unusual style by stopping halfway

through Liszt variations," etc. Even if they did not realize that Rachmaninoff was playing an entirely different piece, their commonsense
should have told them that an artist of such eminence would never stop
playing as a result of mere caprice, irritation, or memory lapse. So much,
or so little, for critical infallibility!

Before leaving London Rachmaninoff gave a press interview that
was reported (entitled "Ritual") in *Cavalcade*:

Alone in his suite in London's Piccadilly Hotel last week wandered a
tall, mournful-looking man with a high, stiff collar, a sombre blue double-
breasted suit. He was S. V. Rachmaninoff, a composer and one of the
greatest current pianists, and he was waiting to give the Press interview
that would embark him on his English-Irish tour. . . .

Several minutes after the appointed hour one reporter and two photographers arrived. With the attitude that to him one reporter was ample
Rachmaninoff detachedly sat down to give his interview, was interrupted
by the arrival of a crowd of newspapermen, more photographers, his
impresario.

Rachmaninoff shook hands with his impresario, resignedly changed
his plans. He thought he would surrender to the photographers first, as he
wanted to "get the worst part over." He sat at the piano, but refused one
photographer's request that he put his thick, medium-length fingers on
the keys. He forced a smile, would wearily close his green eyes when the
flashing bulbs became too bright. Afterwards he shook hands with the
photographers, took special pains to shake that of the photographer whose
request he had refused.

In slow English the Russian pianist admitted heavily that critics
thought his compositions were old-fashioned, but that he did not care what
they thought. . . .

The close-cropped composer recalled his last year's tour through the
U. S. without excitement, considered that his compositions had not been
much of a success, said without bitterness that his critics never used to
bother to converse with him. . . .

Many people, Rachmaninoff said, had asked him if he did not want to
retire. The tall pianist would reply that he did not. He shyly revealed
that being in the public eye gave him as much pleasure as it would a
schoolgirl.

In the suite overhead pianist Dr. Edwin Fischer was playing. While
Rachmaninoff frowned towards the ceiling as the notes came down he
replied to an interviewer who had sympathised about his famous C-sharp

minor being turned into a dance tune. Said Rachmaninoff: "I think that I prefer it that way."

Before his Dublin concert, his first in that city, a reporter asked him:

"Where do you find the best audiences?" He replied, with the faintest ghost of a smile—the first and last I saw on his face: "No audience is bad. There are only bad artists."

On March 27, after this concert, he wrote to the Somovs:

Well-ll! my season draws to an end. I played here yesterday afternoon. (Last evening I went to the movies with Natasha and Ibbs: *The Life of Emile Zola*—wonderful picture!) . . . I've cancelled Vienna, of course. What we'll do next I really don't know. I've written Sonichka that here in Europe we live as on a volcano. Nobody knows what will happen tomorrow. But everyone thinks it probable that war may break out to-morrow. And you know what a very irresolute man I am, and I'm at a loss where to begin. I realize only one thing: if we go to Senar and things begin to boil, we'll find ourselves in something of a mousetrap. On the other hand, to go from Europe to America, leaving Tanyushka here—my heart doesn't allow me to do this—and so on.

As for my artistic affairs, they've never been so successful and brilliant as this year. From both the artistic and the financial points of view! Even my 3rd Symphony, just now performed in Liverpool by Wood, had a great success. Isn't that good luck? He repeats it for the radio on April 3rd. I'll be present at one rehearsal and try to direct Wood a little further along the right path.* . . .

Where are the Fokines? Are they coming to Europe? . . . I've thought of a few more plot details [for *Paganini*]. Don't know whether it's worth writing to them? Would be rather difficult to explain on paper.

In addition to his promised help at the B.B.C. rehearsal, Rachmaninoff gave one more London concert, with the Philharmonic and Sir Thomas Beecham, on April 2.

Disturbed by news of Chaliapin's serious illness, Rachmaninoff

* According to Sir Henry Wood's *About Conducting,* he also had an exhaustive piano rehearsal of the symphony with the composer: "I remember when I wanted to give an authentic performance of Rachmaninoff's Third Symphony in 1938, he came to my home and gave me two hours going through the work on the piano; two hours chock full of interesting and intensive study, marking my score with a precision I could not better, which remains for all time."

left London for Paris to see his old friend immediately after this concert. Chaliapin's death on April 11 was so great a loss that Rachmaninoff could neither speak nor write about it for some days afterwards. From Senar he finally wrote to his sister-in-law Sophia:

My dear Sonichka, it is now eight days since Fedya died. . . . In Paris I went in to see him twice a day. The last time I saw him was on April 10. As I always used to do, I succeeded in amusing him a little. Just before I left, he began to tell me that after getting well he wanted to write another book, for artists, the theme of which would be the art of the stage. Of course he spoke very, very slowly. He was suffocating! The heart was scarcely functioning. I let him finish and as I stood I said that I also have a plan: that when I retire I too shall write a book, the theme of which will be Chaliapin. He gave me a smile and stroked my hand. On that we parted. Forever! On the next day, April 11, I stopped in only in the evening. They had given him a morphine injection; he was in a coma, and I didn't see him. . . . He died at 5:15. . . . Ended is the Chaliapin epoch! Never has his like been seen and never again shall we see it!

Well, our life here flows on peacefully and quietly. . . . I am not working. I read, walk, and lie on the balcony. Natasha busies herself all day with the flowers and her concern for this, as always, is extraordinary. This trait of hers touches me very much. . . .

Asked by Milyukov to write a long article on Chaliapin for the Paris newspaper, *Posledniye Novosti*, Rachmaninoff made his only public statement, a brief one, on his friend's death:

"Dead only is he who is forgotten." I once read such an inscription in a cemetery. If this is true, then Chaliapin will never die. He cannot die. For this miracle of art, with the genuine genius of legend, is unforgettable. In the past forty-one years, from almost the very beginning of his career, of which I was a witness, he quickly ascended to a pedestal from which he never descended, never slipped, till the end of his days. All concurred in the worship of his talent—ordinary people as well as the great. . . . And news of him swept through the whole world, and not through Russia alone.

Chaliapin's death appeared to have an immediate physical effect on Rachmaninoff, as if some strong prop of friendship and of the past had been suddenly removed. After some reminders sent to Somov on April 29, he attempted some grisly jesting:

. . . about everything else I've forgotten. Sclerosis! At some time it showed only in my forgetting things. . . . Lately, the action of the sclerosis has made considerable progress and I'm already finding it difficult to choose and recall the Russian words necessary for the household. It's amazing how Natasha understands me sometimes: for instead of words I utter only sounds. So let's put off speaking of business matters until later, when I'll remember them! I still have lucid intervals now and then—but more and more rarely. And my visual judgment is also deteriorating! (Not my vision, which long since worsened.) Both today and yesterday I scraped my car against the entrance sidewalk, and this never happened to me before. And of course I grow deaf as well. . . .

So far Natasha and I live alone at Senar. We've had drought all this while. Only today did it begin to rain for the first time. We had planned a prayer service. Everything was dried up. We live quietly and peacefully! Yesterday we listened to a speech about Maître Rachmaninoff, and then six of my records were played. And all this was happening in Paris! Miracles! And they used such big words! They don't realize I have sclerosis. Now would be the time to start living.

The Senar summer was chiefly filled with practice for next season's recitals and corrections of the Third Symphony. From his summer place in New Hampshire, Ormandy again tempted Rachmaninoff: ". . . how would you react to my suggestion that you conduct your own symphony? I know that you are a Great Conductor and I believe that the public would enjoy seeing you lead your own work." Rachmaninoff replied: "It is very kind of you to offer to let me lead your orchestra, but I could not do it this season." He sent the Somovs a more cheerful report than usual, on July 19:

. . . I don't have much to do: I play three hours a day. And that's nearly all I do! True, even these few hours tire me. Also busying myself with the corrections of my last symphony. There are not many, and they're all trifling—but considering them took two weeks. Now I've given everything to the copyist for insertion into the orchestral parts: in August it will be performed again in London, by Henry Wood. I think I wrote you, in the spring, that he is fascinated by this symphony. Since I began a record of those who love this work, I have turned down *three* fingers. Its second lover is the violinist Busch, and the third—excuse me—is I! When I run out of fingers on both hands, I'll give up counting! Only—when will this be?

To write something new—I have no plans as yet. I have always noticed that a desire for composition comes with physical cheerfulness, which I don't notice in myself just now. Hence my "gloom," about which, in Natasha's words, you ask. This summer I should also like to correct my 4th Concerto, and this would not be difficult for the first two movements. But the catch is in the last movement, where a whole episode has to be recomposed anew, and I don't feel up to that.

On the same day he wrote to a friend whose daughter had asked for foreign stamps: "In my young days I met many musicians, but never saw collectors of stamps. Now it is just the opposite. There seem to be only philatelists left."

By July 31 he could send Somov the corrected score of the symphony and one corrected part for each instrument; his final instruction: "The parts I send you have been attentively checked by me, which means that *they must be followed blindly*."

The summer ended grandly with a dinner at Senar following Toscanini's open-air concert at Triebschen. Among the twenty-two guests were the Toscaninis, their daughter with her husband, Vladimir Horowitz, and the Milsteins.

The American season began pleasurably, with Rachmaninoff playing his First Concerto and listening to his corrected Third Symphony in an all-Rachmaninoff program under Ormandy, in the Philadelphia Orchestra's tour of the East Coast.

One reporter, after the Philadelphia opening, asked about swing. Rachmaninoff replied that he disliked swing but greatly admired the jazz of fifteen years ago—"Ah, if I could hear that fine pianist, Eddy Duchin, playing Irving Berlin's 'Blue Skies,' I'd be very happy." Free as Rachmaninoff was from affectation, this can be believed; whenever New York permitted a relaxed evening, he enjoyed dropping in to the Persian Room of the Plaza, where Duchin played. He admired his arrangements and his handling of piano "color." And Duchin, whenever he noticed Rachmaninoff there, would swing his band into that favorite arrangement of "Blue Skies."

Rachmaninoff's program this season began with the Rameau variations and Bach's Toccata and Fugue in E minor (cleansed of Busoni's ornament), followed by Beethoven's "Les Adieux" and two Schubert pieces, to complete the first half. A Pittsburgh critic called this program (completed with twelve of the 24 Preludes of Chopin and two works by Liszt) "more pianistic than scholarly"—"a conservative, sixth grade assortment of piano works." But in San Francisco Alfred Frankenstein saluted Rachmaninoff in the *Chronicle:*

Today Sergei Rachmaninoff stands at the pinnacle of his gigantic career. His recital last night at the Opera House demonstrated that at this moment we are privileged to witness a kind of pianistic kingship that in future years will be enshrined in the mythology of music as one of the colossal and incredible achievements of the great old times, much as the performances of Liszt are now regarded.

For Rachmaninoff, despite his pessimism regarding the present state of music and his almost total reliance on the literature of the past, is one of the four or five very great lords of the interpretative realm, so far as the piano is concerned. He has held that enviable position for long, but, if the recollection of past recitals can be relied on, his art has ripened even further and more gloriously in recent years.

In Seattle he received the expected news from Somov that he would no longer be working as his secretary; Rachmaninoff replied:

Dear Zhenichka, an hour ago I received your letter, to which I must give the name of the first movement of the Beethoven sonata now on my program. This movement is called "Les Adieux." I won't conceal from you how very sorrowful I felt. I have grown old and it's hard for me to part from people whom I love, from those to whom I've become—accustomed. Nevertheless, just as two years ago, I say: go, go! Financially it will be better for you, and more interesting from a business viewpoint. As for your attitude and your touching wish to act as it would be better for *me*— I thank you heartily.

But Somov's departure as secretary did not mean his departure as friend; when Somov questioned him on rumors of illness during the tour, Rachmaninoff wrote: "There's nothing alarming with me! I'm tired—that's true! But I have no intention of dying just yet. And little ailments are natural at my age. . . . (Though you all forbid me to mention my age, it is just this mentioning that explains everything.)"

During the fortnight of "rest" in New York at Christmas time, he enjoyed hearing his thirteen-year-old granddaughter continue her musical career by singing the role of Gretel in a production of the

Humperdinck opera at the Brearley School. Before returning to the tour he wrote to Medtner:

I've received your letter and new sonata. Thank you! I played the sonata at once. I liked the second part right away, but haven't made out the first part yet. I wanted to play it once more before writing you—but I didn't get around to it. You will say immediately: That means I didn't like it! And you will be wrong! No! I've been pushed onto a merry-go-round here —guests—going to parties—business up to my neck in addition to the daily practice. So I decided at least to write a few lines of gratitude. And to postpone the sonata until London, when I hope you will play it for me yourself.

One of the first letters Rachmaninoff received on arriving in London was from Auckland, where Fokine was on tour:

I write you from New Zealand, where I'm preparing "Paganini." The ballet will be given in London by the end of June, or in July. I have already set most of it—we've reached the 22d variation. I'm working with great enthusiasm. All goes well. Vera Petrovna approves. I vouch for the "critics." I think the rest will be interesting, too. In work it became clear that the 2nd scene—the Florentine beauty with the girls and youths— would gain by a repeat of the 12th variation. I'm very pleased with the splendid contrast between the diabolic dances of the first scene and this dainty dance of the girls on the meadow. It is pleasing, soothing . . . but too short. So I ask your consent to a repeat. Conductor Dorati is very much opposed to this repeat in full without some change. But this is exactly what my heart desires. . . .
    P.S. May I program it in this way?
Paganini
(Rapsodie sur un thème de Paganini)
A ballet by S. Rachmaninoff and M. Fokine
Music by S. Rachmaninoff
Choreography by M. Fokine.

The program played in London evoked a new complaint:

What the programme lacked [wrote the *Glasgow Herald's* correspondent] was some recognition of the mass of neglected and deserving music, written to-day or yesterday, that needs a helping hand from some crowd-compelling player such as Rachmaninoff.

Yet one is little inclined to reproach Rachmaninoff on this score. To see him approach the piano, a weary Titan, is to exempt him from all artistic duties, but those he has made up his mind about long ago, such as the right way to play Beethoven.

He *was* weary, and after his Sheffield recital the weariness developed into illness, but by the following week he resumed his engagements, appearing in Middlesbrough:

When this great pianist stepped on the stage at the Town Hall he was wondering whether his physical condition would enable him to justify his reputation.

Late last night he told the *Northern Echo* that he had been ill for the last five days and that until noon on Monday he was not sure whether he would be fit enough to travel to Middlesbrough. But like all "troupers" he decided to appear, although his doctor would have preferred him to remain in bed for a few more days. When he took his final bow, after the treble encore, he announced to his friends that he was back again to normal health.

The Evening News reported his last social engagement in London:

Mr. Rachmaninoff is staid and serious and at 65 looks as if he had worked himself hard. He is sharp featured and thin and pale—but has a most charming smile.

After his concert at Queen's Hall on Saturday afternoon he was taken [by Moiseiwitsch] to the Savage Club, where, to his surprise, they made him an honorary member. A musician friend of mine who was a guest tells me it was amusing to see the great pianist's reaction to the carefree abandon of the gathering.

If the Savages expected their new member to play "a few pieces" in return for their hospitality, they were disappointed.

On April 2, 1939 Rachmaninoff wrote to the Somovs from his Paris hotel:

Day before yesterday I finished my concerts. They all turned out successfully and there was a lot of noise. Gradually I begin to be recognized. I fear I won't have time to live up to full recognition! Now Ysaye, here in Paris, pesters about a concert. As Natasha works for the same aim, it is possible I shall have to play here. . . . If this concert takes place (decision tomorrow), it will be at the end of April,* so I'll still be able to

---

* The concert did take place, on April 25, for the benefit of L'Action Artistique.

get to Senar for about ten days before coming back here. However, I repeat, I'm not sure if Hitler will approve my plans.

For three or four days I am allowing myself a rest from the piano. Tanichka and I are going to drive through the suburbs of Paris to find her some villa or farm where she could live and shelter if Hitler flies here. Very hard to find anything. All Paris seems busy with the same thing.

Next day Rachmaninoff wrote Fokine about the changes suggested by Fokine and Dorati:

At the end of the published score you make an addition of twelve bars from the variation preceding the minuet and the 18th variation, which is now transposed into A major. . . . the 18th variation won't sound good in this key. Here is what must be done: play all twelve bars without alteration, as I wrote them—and then begin the 18th variation not in A major, but in D major, i.e. a halftone higher than originally. It will sound with even more tension! . . .

The titling of the ballet is left entirely to your discretion. I agree to everything. Received the sketches for the décor. I like them very much. But—why has Paganini changed his profession and become a guitar player?

From gray Senar Rachmaninoff answered Somov's anxious queries on the European situation:

I've stated my doubts and anxieties many times in my letters to Irina and Sonia. And these anxieties are not yet lifted from me! I can't understand how those who don't share my anxieties can risk assuming such responsibility! In any case, thus far I think of staying. This decision was mostly influenced by a letter from Sonichka, whose advice has always brought me luck! This is not a logical explanation, but—I am a weak man! I love my Senar very much. Whenever the sun peeps out, I walk in the garden and think, "God, how good—if only war would not come."—But we have little sun now. Very little! The weather is Hitlerian! . . .

As you can see, so far the mood isn't very courageous! What's to be done!

When Fokine brought the Russian Ballet to London, he invited Rachmaninoff to come for the première of *Paganini;* he received bad news from Senar:

Do you recall the miraculous escape—long ago—of Their Majesties at Borki Station on October 17? Something similar has happened to me. I slipped on the parquet and banged to the floor. The miracle is that I broke nothing. But the bruise was so bad that for three weeks I limp and walk with a cane. I couldn't appear this way. The doctor recommends patience and believes I shall be lame for about two more weeks. Perhaps I can come on later.

This was a lameness that lasted for two more *years,* and perhaps left a more serious permanent injury. His wife wrote to her sister about the circumstances of the accident:

On May 27, Irina's birthday, Seryozha slipped on the dining room floor and fell heavily. The shock was so severe that he almost lost consciousness. When I ran over to him, I was horrified: he was deathly pale. It was a miracle how we got him into the elevator and upstairs to his bed. I was sure that he had broken a hip or a wrist. . . . A doctor was called. He tormented him a long while but finally found that no bones were broken. . . . For this whole month Seryozha has hardly been able to move, and only with a cane, and painfully. Now the doctor has ordered him to walk as much as possible.

Fokine sent a report from London:

I do regret that you won't be present at the first performance. But we can console ourselves that you won't have to endure the unpleasant moments of a "ballet composer." There are many such moments as the opening night approaches, when finished costumes are delivered with mistakes, the dancers' hats fall off, there's not enough space for the dancers, some of them get confused when they don't recognize their music, now coming from an orchestra rather than from a piano . . . and the ballet master gets horribly angry and yells, trying to put everything in order. All the time you think that the performance can't possibly go through without mishap—that the wrong curtain will be raised, that the wrong dancers will be spotlighted, that the dancers won't have time to change, and so on. In *Paganini* most of the dancers have two or three changes, doing it by the second, which I've measured with stop watch, metronome, and music in hand. In a word, the birth pangs of a ballet are not small ones. Usually everything goes off smoothly, except that the ballet master goes home with a sore throat. I'm sure that this time, too, everything will go as usual— disorderly, noisy, nervous . . . and a good ballet will be born. . . . I've written you about everything that might go wrong so that if you should come you wouldn't be shocked and distressed by all the mistakes at the rehearsals. Now almost everything has been carefully gone over with the newcomers, and we still have a week to spare. . . . The leading dancers have not been changed, and they'll be splendid—Rostoff as Paganini, Riabushinskaya as the Florentine girl, Baronova as Paganini's genius. Grigorieva as the Lie, Lazovsky and Alonzo as the gossips, 9 good dancers as Paganini's doubles. In short—the best of casts. The production is a very complicated one in sets, costumes, lights, and dances. There are many difficult and virtuoso dances. I've not heard the pianist yet. The one Dorati rehearsed with couldn't get a working permit for London. He's found another [Eric Harrison]—a young man, 20 years old, who plays the Rhapsody by heart and, Dorati says, very well. So I look forward to a good performance. And then? Stupid, perhaps even malicious reviews. One "balletomane" critic told me, jokingly: "I hear you are portraying critics? Critics are untouchable! The critic is a holy personage." I replied, also jokingly: "I am aware of the holiness of critics—and therefore I show them with the music of the Dies Irae. So we have both holiness and—the Last Judgment; everything they could wish."

Paganini was first presented on June 30, at Covent Garden. The *Times* wrote:

Fokine's latest composition is a fantastic ballet of the romantic period on the subject of Paganini, set to Rachmaninoff's Rhapsody for piano and orchestra, which makes an unexpectedly good score for dancing as it stands without modification, except for a new quiet ending provided by the composer.

Immediately after the performance, Fokine wrote to Rachmaninoff:

Congratulations on the newborn. Our first ballet has turned out very successfully and was received enthusiastically. The curtain kept going up endlessly. . . .

The three ballerinas danced beautifully, Paganini-Rostoff was very good, handsome and demoniac. . . . The music sounded very good and the young pianist did not spoil matters. I don't suppose Irina Sergeyevna and Tatiana Sergeyevna derived much pleasure from the piano. They hear your performance in their ears. . . .

Amusing: the "music" critics approved the ballet's ending, which you composed "especially," without noticing that it is an exact repeat of music they had heard 7 minutes before!

And so, Sergei Vasilyevich, I thank you heartily, sincerely, for this first but, I trust, not last collaboration of ours.

Rachmaninoff replied:

> Thank you for your detailed letter, the reviews, programs, etc.
>
> Only in looking them over did I learn of your birthday. So, first of all, allow me to congratulate you and Vera Petrovna on your birthday and to wish you, for many years to come, good theater, good artists, pianists, good orchestra and good composers. And may the latter, with scores for ballets under their arms, queue up before the door of your waiting room, awaiting only your shout: "Next!"

On the following day he sent the Somovs some of the *Paganini* reviews, along with some gloomy thoughts:

> We live as before—that is, not very calmly. Evidently calm has departed from those who live in Europe, even though war does not come.
>
> As you know, I've tied myself to a festival in Lucerne. My concert is on August 11. To be the first to run away seems improper in every way. But after the 11th I shall consider myself justified in displaying weakness. Perhaps we can then leave, or rather, take to our heels. . . .
>
> I just broke off this letter to glance at the local afternoon paper. News is again worse! So it goes from day to day. That there could be such possibilities in the world! Unthinkable!

The Musical Courier prepared a symposium on modern music, and Leonard Liebling asked for Rachmaninoff's comments. Unexpectedly, his reply was full, frank, and very personal:

> I feel like a ghost wandering in a world grown alien. I cannot cast out the old way of writing, and I cannot acquire the new. I have made intense effort to feel the musical manner of today, but it will not come to me. Unlike Madame Butterfly with her quick religious conversion, I cannot cast out my musical gods in a moment and bend the knee to new ones. Even with the disaster of living through what has befallen the Russia where I spent my happiest years, yet I always feel that my own music and my reactions to all music, remained spiritually the same, unendingly obedient in trying to create beauty. . . .
>
> The new kind of music seems to come, not from the heart, but from the head. Its composers think rather than feel. They have not the capacity to make their works "exult," as Hans von Bülow called it. They meditate, protest, analyze, reason, calculate, and brood—but they do not exult. It may be that they compose in the spirit of the times; but it may be, too,

that the spirit of the times does not call for expression in music. If that is the case, rather than compile music that is thought but not felt, composers should remain silent and leave contemporary expression to those authors and playwrights who are masters of the factual and literal, and do not concern themselves with soul states.

I hope that with these thoughts I have answered your question regarding my opinion of what is called modern music. Why modern in this case? It grows old almost as soon as born, for it comes into being contaminated with dry rot.

Is it necessary to add that I do not mind telling you all this confidentially as a friend, but that I should not in any circumstances like you to publish it—at least, not while I am alive, for I should not enjoy having some of the "modernists" rap me over the fingers, as I need them for my piano playing. It is not politic for me even to have written to you as I have. I mostly keep my opinions to myself, and in consequence I am generally regarded as a silent man. So be it. In silence lies safety.

Wilshaw wrote from Moscow:

The lilacs are in bloom, and though we don't see them blooming, they have them in the market. This time of year and these lilacs always remind me of you, especially. . . . Everyone here plays your works: the 2nd, 3rd, 4th Concertos, the Rhapsody, the Corelli Variations, the Préludes of Op. 32 and 23. . . . They play well but not like you! It's seldom that a concert takes place at which your works are not sung or played. See how appreciated you are. At someone's concert lately, either Igumnov's or Goldenweiser's, I met some young pianists, and they asked me, what is heard from Rachmaninoff? Do you write him? And does he write you? Ah, if he were only here, they said, we would carry him on our shoulders. . . .

Just now a boy, a student at the Conservatory, came and asked me to lend him your 4th Concerto. He didn't know it, for he was ill when Igumnov played it. How could I refuse him!

In reply, Rachmaninoff wrote Wilshaw for the last time on July 26:

First, to express my joy that you are all alive. I hesitate to ask about health. Young people usually answer, "Thank you, I am well!" But we have to alter this wording slightly, and answer, "Thank you, I am alive!"

This year my wife and I leave for America earlier than usual. I'll settle my concert duties in Lucerne, on August 11. . . . In America this season, besides the usual concerts, a *Festival* is arranged, but only of three concerts and only of my compositions. In the first two I'll play my four concertos, and the orchestra the 2nd Symphony and *Spring*. The third concert: the 3rd Symphony and *The Bells*. I am to conduct this one myself. By the way, I'll be conducting for the first time in twenty years, so they'll give me a three weeks' rest after this concert. The orchestra is the Philadelphia, i.e. the best of the best. This *Festival* seems to be, for some reason, a "totaling of the sum."

Comes the time when one doesn't walk by oneself, but is led by the arms. In one way this is a sort of honor, but in another way, it's as if you're being held up so you won't fall to pieces. Still, last season, I gave 59 concerts. There will probably be, in the approaching season, just as many. Well, how many more such seasons I can take—I don't know. I know only one thing, that while working I somehow feel inwardly stronger than without work. Therefore may God grant me to work up to the last days.

Europe heard Rachmaninoff play for the last time at Lucerne's International Music Festival, transferred from Salzburg: neutral Switzerland was garnering the artist refugees—Toscanini, Bruno Walter, Casals. On August 11, with Ansermet conducting, Rachmaninoff played Beethoven's first piano concerto and his own Paganini Rhapsody.

Only then did he consider himself justified in limping back to safer America. The family's tickets were for the *Queen Mary's* last crossing on August 16, and then, clinging to Europe for one more week, they changed their reservations to the *Aquitania* on the 23rd, and Rachmaninoff wrote to Somov, "There will be no further changes. At least, not on *our* part."

Before his farewell to Senar Rachmaninoff had a social duty. After the concert of August 11, he was visited in his dressing room by the Maharajah of Mysore, who attended the concert with his retinue of forty, and who expressed a desire to visit Senar. Neither Senar nor its host was in a hospitable mood at this hectic moment of history, but it was inconvenient to withhold an invitation so powerfully suggested. Two days later, then, the Maharajah's family arrived at Senar —without the Maharajah. He arrived with fresh guests as the first contingent was leaving—not without a conflict between Russian and Hindu customs that kept the host immobile on his porch and the departing guests likewise immobile in their cars. The Maharajah's special mission was to ask Rachmaninoff to listen to his pianist daughter, a great admirer of the composer. Rachmaninoff's departure for Paris on the following morning was of minor importance to the admirer's father; the Maharajah implored him to stop at his Lucerne hotel for breakfast the next morning before leaving for Paris. Refusal was out of the question. After breakfast the following morning Rachmaninoff listened to the daughter play a few pieces (which she played well, to his surprise) and was shown a film of the wedding of the heir to the throne of Mysore. Only then were the Rachmaninoffs allowed to hurry off to Paris.

In the few days before the *Aquitania's* sailing, Tatiana's parents said good-by to her against a background of French mobilization. Irina and Sophie were to follow them to America as soon as possible. The war also boarded the *Aquitania:* antisubmarine precautions were taken, and portholes were blacked out. The Rachmaninoffs again escaped from warring Europe as they had in 1918.

Chapter 22

Symphonic Dances

O̲N THE American tour Rachmaninoff arrived in Minneapolis after a sleepless night on the train. He was to play both the First Concerto of Beethoven and Liszt's *Todtentanz;* conducted by Mitropoulos, the program was also to include Rachmaninoff's Third Symphony, and it was to be an exhausting concert. A reporter asked him if and when he expected to retire, and the weary musician said, "Certainly I will retire," thinking fondly of bed; "this trip was especially tiring." These words were the source of a widely circulated newspaper report that on this thirtieth anniversary of his first American concerts Rachmaninoff was making his farewell tour. But American audiences were to hear him for three more seasons.

The celebration of this thirtieth anniversary was to be more glorious than retirement. The Philadelphia Orchestra announced for its New York concerts:

THE RACHMANINOFF CYCLE

November 26th   Eugene Ormandy, *Conducting*

Symphony No. 2 in E minor, Opus 27
Concerto No. 1 in F sharp minor, for Piano and Orchestra, Opus 1
         Sergei Rachmaninoff, *Soloist*

———

"Rhapsodie" on a Theme of Paganini, Opus 43
         Sergei Rachmaninoff, *Soloist*

December 3rd   Eugene Ormandy, *Conducting*

Concerto No. 2 in C minor, for Piano and Orchestra, Opus 18
         Sergei Rachmaninoff, *Soloist*

———

The Isle of the Dead, Opus 29
Concerto No. 3 in D minor, for Piano and Orchestra, Opus 30
         Sergei Rachmaninoff, *Soloist*

December 10th   Sergei Rachmaninoff, *Conducting*

Symphony No. 3 in A minor, Opus 44

———————

The Bells (for Soprano, Tenor and Baritone Solos, Chorus of
     Mixed Voices, and Orchestra) Opus 35
Susanne Fisher, soprano; Jan Peerce, tenor; Mack Harrell, baritone;
The Westminster Choir, with John F. Williamson assisting

The last week end of November was a full one, even for New York's
musical life: Koussevitzky conducted the Boston Symphony in an all-
American program, Toscanini and the NBC Orchestra broadcast the
fifth concert in their Beethoven cycle, and Ormandy opened the
Rachmaninoff cycle:

When Mr. Rachmaninoff appeared for the first time on the stage to play
his concerto most of the audience rose in his honor, from those on the
floor to those near the roof. Their admiration for him and their enjoyment
of his music were more evident there than words can make them here.
The occasion was a memorable tribute to a great artist.

Each work in the second program was linked to his first American
visit. His first performance with orchestra in this country was of the
Second Concerto, with the Boston Symphony in Philadelphia, on
November 8, 1909. He had himself conducted the first American
performance of *The Isle of the Dead* with the Theodore Thomas
Orchestra in Chicago that December. It was in anticipation of his
American visit that he had composed his Third Concerto. One pro-
gram summed up the peaks of his first American experiences.

The third program brought a new experience to all but the few in
the New York audience who had heard Rachmaninoff conduct his
own music in 1910. A touching and youthful tribute to him as a
conductor was forwarded by Dr. Williamson, director of the Westminster Choir:

Dear Mr. Rachmaninoff,

One of the greatest privileges that ever came to our young people was
the privilege they had in singing under your baton with the Philadelphia
Orchestra.

As you know, they fell in love with you as a man. This sounds rather
funny, I know, but they all say you are the sweetest person they have ever
met. Perhaps you have never had young people use that adjective before

with you, but they so fell in love with your absolute sincerity, with your simplicity and your great honesty, and they used that word "sweet" in its right meaning, not any sentimental meaning. . . .

Rachmaninoff sent Arthur Hirst his own reaction to the "totaling of the sum":

The cycle was rather successful. . . . we are well, although I am very tired.

My elder daughter and my granddaughter had great difficulty in reaching New York. If it weren't for the efforts of Foley it is doubtful whether they would have succeeded at all. They came and brought four dogs with them, which is a little too much for wartime.

I am sad and worried about Tatiana. Before leaving Europe, I bought her a little estate within forty miles of Paris, where she is living all alone, if you don't count her little boy. Her husband, happily, is not at the front but is serving, at present, as an instructor somewhere in France. It is only possible to bear up under such conditions with as strong a character as Tatiana's. In the last two months she managed to obtain a French passport and a driver's license. This last fact worries me no less than the war. I never felt that she had any talent for driving.

The Festival represented, physically, only eight concerts in a season of forty-one appearances. The tour now wove back and forth across the continent; with the West Coast seeming more attractive this year than on previous tours. Chaliapin's son Fyodor was now a resident of Hollywood, and the Rachmaninoffs, who had known him since his childhood, spent much of their leisure time with him. He introduced them to the Ratoffs and the Tamiroffs, and Rachmaninoff, though he saw films irregularly, eagerly employed this opportunity to inquire into the whole process of film making and how actors and directors worked in these unusual conditions. He clearly enjoyed the atmosphere of the colony of Russian artists that he found in Hollywood. The enthusiastic reception by the whole glittering film community of his performance of the Second Concerto in a Stokowski concert made a distinct impression on Mme. Rachmaninoff; she wrote to the Somovs: "The mimosa is in blossom, there are occasional showers, and the air is wonderful. Two days ago at the beach it was so warm that many were swimming. Seryozha doesn't want to leave. Last night we spent with Bertensson, talking a great deal and recalling the Art Theater."

When reporters along the tour were forbidden interviews they resorted to their powers of observation.

His punctuality is a legend. If a reporter asks for two minutes of his time, two minutes and no more are given. Consequently he arrives at a concert hall on the dot of 8 and goes on the stage precisely at 8:30. If the concert is unavoidably delayed he becomes extremely impatient.*

As he waits in the wings before a performance, he puts his hands in an electric muff to keep them warm and flexible. They are very tender, those hands, insured with Lloyds' and carefully shielded from athletic handshakes.

While he plays, his wife listens in the wings so that she may tell him the concert went well. Afterward, he sips a cherry malted milk float (his favorite drink) unless he has to catch a train. His conversation ranges in four languages over everything except death and politics, two topics he refuses to discuss.

For his life on the trains, friends and secretaries sent new books, usually Russian ones, to reach him along his itinerary, so that he would have to resort as little as possible to the mystery novels ever plentiful in the compartment. The reading problem was not always so luckily solved as it was on one tour when he had Kluchevsky's *History of Russia* to absorb all his reading time. And there were always Tolstoy and Chekhov to reread, and Dickens—*in Russian*. For emergencies there were the jigsaw puzzles especially manufactured for this puzzle enthusiast by those two "masters," Somov and granddaughter Sophie.

When France fell in June, Rachmaninoff's anxiety for his daughter Tatiana merged with his anguish at the national catastrophe; and the calm necessary for composition seemed more remote than ever.

A minor operation in May had so weakened him that the family insisted on a really restful summer for him. "Orchard Point," the Honeyman estate near Huntington, Long Island, represented seventeen acres of seclusion, with groves, orchards, a mile-long beach, and pier for a new cabin cruiser, the *Senar*. Rachmaninoff's studio was isolated from all other living quarters, and he could practice and compose unembarrassed by the possibility of disturbing anyone. Com-

---

* Observers often remarked on the big gold watch (the gift of Zverev) that went in and out of his pocket, *accelerando,* as concert time neared.

position was possible only when he could feel sure that no one could hear or listen to him. On the other hand he could not face being *actually* alone, especially in the evenings; he preferred to know that people were nearby; just out of ear range. The arrangements of the Honeyman house were ideally convenient in this respect. Within motoring radius he had the Somovs, the Greiners, the Fokines, and the Horowitz couple for neighbors, Boris Chaliapin* and others as guests, and the *Senar* was used even more than the automobile. It had a cabin and kitchen, and Rachmaninoff was usually at the wheel himself. In it, the family often crossed the Sound to visit Chekhov's studio in Connecticut.

In midsummer, in the midst of his preparations for the coming season, he began the composition of his last symphonic work. With concert practice and the new composition proceeding simultaneously against his usual policy, his schedule was increased almost incredibly: a working day lasted from nine in the morning till eleven at night, with only an hour's interruption for an afternoon's rest. On August 21 he was able to offer a new work to the Philadelphia Orchestra:

My dear Mr. Ormandy:

Last week I finished a new symphonic piece, which I naturally want to give first to you and your orchestra. It is called "Fantastic Dances." I shall now begin the orchestration. Unfortunately my concert tour begins on October 14. I have a great deal of practice to do and I don't know whether I shall be able to finish the orchestration before November.

I should be very glad if, upon your return, you would drop over to our place. I should like to play the piece for you. We are staying at the Honeyman Estate, Huntington, Long Island, and only forty miles from New York, so that you can easily reach us.

By August 28, when he acknowledged Ormandy's enthusiastic response to his proposal that the conductor hear him go through the work in mid-September, the work was referred to by its permanent title: *Symphonic Dances*. He may have noticed that Shostakovich had a work called *Fantastic Dances* and may for that reason have

* Chaliapin painted two more portraits at Huntington: of Rachmaninoff in shirtsleeves (so as not to interfere with his practice), and of his granddaughter Sophie.

preferred a title used by Grieg, and once considered but not used by Scriabin—"Symphonic Dances." His original plan was to give the movements separate titles—Noon, Twilight, Midnight—but he finally ruled out even this programmatic hint.

One of his earliest hopes for *Symphonic Dances* was to interest Fokine in a ballet to follow their successful *Paganini*. Even before playing it for its first conductor, Rachmaninoff gave its choreographer-to-be a hearing. Fokine's reactions were sent to the composer on September 23:

Thank you for introducing me to your wonderful composition that I have so wanted to know. I trust that it will be brought to as successful a conclusion, and that I shall become acquainted with it "generally and wholly" very soon. . . . Though I'm a poor musician and I don't grasp everything immediately, the music has caught me up and I feel that I have mastered all that you played and that I can guess the whole. Perhaps fragments, with a few words, sneak into the head better than a harmonious and unbroken performance. Before the hearing I was a little scared of the Russian element that you had mentioned, but yesterday I fell in love with it, and it seemed to me appropriate and beautiful. Here is what I wasn't able to tell you, and is my chief purpose in writing you: about this one-ta-ta, one-ta-ta. This valse rhythm seems to disturb you, to handicap you. I gathered this, not from the music, but from your words (of five weeks ago). If this valse element seems intrusive to you, and you hold on to it because it gives a dancing quality, or facilitates dancing to the music, or facilitates the composition or creation of a dance, or justifies the title then I consider it necessary to discard the ta-ta as soon as you lose your musical appetite for it. The thought of dancing is a side issue. If the joy of creating dances to your music is again given me, I should not at all feel the need for this rhythmic support. I'm not able to speak of music, and even less to write of it, but I am now writing because it seems to me that you are binding yourself to dance requirements.

With his tour to begin in Detroit on October 14, the orchestration of the new work was crowded into every working minute. Ormandy had scheduled its first performance for January and the copied score had to be in his hands by this December. From this hectic autumn there is a characteristic note, addressed to Harry Glantz, first trumpet player of the New York Philharmonic:

My dear Mr. Glantz:

Will you be so kind as to answer my question? Is such a passage possible?

to which Mr. Glantz replied that it was easily possible.

Rachmaninoff also applied to his friend, Robert Russell Bennett, for advice on an instrument unfamiliar to him:

When he was doing his *Symphonic Dances,* he wanted to use a saxophone tone in the first movement and got in touch with me to advise him as to which of the saxophone family to use and just how to include it in his score—his experience with saxophones being extremely limited. . . . At that time he played over his score for me on the piano and I was delighted to see his approach to the piano was quite the same as that of all of us when we try to imitate the sound of an orchestra at the keyboard. He sang, whistled, stomped, rolled his chords, and otherwise conducted himself not as one would except of so great and impeccable a piano virtuoso.

Some days later we had luncheon together at his place in Huntington. When he met my wife and me at the railroad station he was driving the car and after driving about one hundred yards, he stopped the car, turned to me, and said "I start on A sharp?" I said, "That's right," and he said "Right" and drove on out to his place.

Before leaving New York to begin his season in Detroit, the *Symphonic Dances* and its coming première by the Philadelphia Symphony were announced, and he gave the *New York World-Telegram* an interview on his new composition:

"It should have been called just *Dances,*" he said, grinning, "but I was afraid people would think I had written dance music for jazz orchestras. . . ."

Mr. Rachmaninoff declined to tell anything of the new work.

"A composer always has his own ideas of his works, but I do not believe he ever should reveal them. Each listener should find his own meaning in music," he said. . . .

"I do not know which gives me more pleasure—to compose music or to play it," he said. "When I have worked and worked and have finished a phrase that I know is good it fills me with the greatest of satisfaction. Only when I am playing in concert and I have a good day—some days are not so good, you know—then I think this must be the greatest happiness."

It was "a good day" in Detroit on October 14:

The long, lean and stooped figure of Sergei Rachmaninoff came out on the stage of the Masonic Auditorium Monday evening, with the great hall crammed full and extra customers in the pit, and sat down at the piano and delivered a program which, for power and spirit and musicianship and the tokens of intellect, has not been surpassed hereabouts by anybody, not even by Rachmaninoff. That a pianist at the age of 67 should continue to get better and better is surely a marvel. But it actually appears that Rachmaninoff is pursuing an upward curve; that his facility is easily as great as 20 years ago and that the mind and heart of him employ that unimpaired facility to speak more movingly every season.

The legend states that Liszt was the greatest pianist the world has ever known. But Liszt, as many forget, ended his career as a virtuoso when he was 36 years old. The legend refers to his achievements while his muscles were still a-throb with youth and his mind without that mellowness which is the long result of years. Our age is providing a greater legend for the aftertime, a legend of a tremendous man who, while neighboring his threescore-and-ten, can summon all the power of youth to his fingers and control them with a sounder musical brain, in its full development than ever was possessed by the youthful Liszt.

Proofs of orchestral parts for *Symphonic Dances* followed him from town to town. This season the tour took in Havana, where he had not played since 1923. On a December afternoon, before his recital for the Pro-Arte, he spoke with an interviewer about public taste:

"Taken individually the people in an audience may be poor critics of music, but as a complete body, the audience never errs."

But asked if he considered the taste of his audience in drawing up his program, he said, "No, I think only of my own taste."

It amuses him to point out how newspaper critics occasionally chide him because he does not play the C Sharp Minor Prelude the way he wrote it.

"I have revised it since it was published," he explains.

. . . he was asked if he was disturbed by the way other musicians played his works.

"To be quite honest, no," he answered. "It is interesting to see how some other pianist will give a piece you have written yourself an entirely different musical color. . . .

"I will miss playing Europe this year, but no one there has time for the arts now." He glanced out over the patio to the city beyond as he added, "Music can only succeed where there is peace and quiet—as here."

The schedule never relaxed, no matter how many promises were made his wife and family. Their only victory was to obtain greater intervals within a season. Two free weeks were gained after Havana. Christmas in the West End Avenue apartment was as gay as it could be with no word from Tatiana in Paris. On December 25 three generations celebrated an American Christmas around a big fir tree with Rachmaninoff himself in the role of Santa Claus.

The two-week vacation from recitals included the pleasant task of attending rehearsals of *Symphonic Dances*. At the final rehearsal he turned to the men of the Philadelphia Orchestra, and said, "Years ago I composed for the great Chaliapin. Now he is dead and so I compose for a new kind of artist, the Philadelphia Orchestra."

After a Philadelphia performance on January 3 (attended by the composer), the orchestra brought the work to New York, where it did not receive a warm critical reception. A frankly harsh notice was given it by the *World-Telegram*:

The composer took a bow from the stage. The prolonged applause was doubtless a tribute to himself rather than to his music, for the novelty nowhere rises to his best standards.

The work is long and derivative. It might serve for a ballet with a macabre theme. The Dies Irae rings out in the finale in the midst of a rattling poor imitation of Saint-Saëns' *Danse Macabre*.

The piece teems with weird sounds, some of them just plain echoes. Mr. Rachmaninoff's orchestra is definitely haunted, especially the wind section, which is a real rendezvous of ghosts.

The middle waltz section is best, with its ironic retards. A lugubrious ennui shuffles through it, and Ravel, Richard Strauss, and Sibelius join the dance in deep purple. The memories crowd in thick and fast.

Of course, Mr. Rachmaninoff does what he wants with the orchestra. His arsenal of effects is large, and he can send shivers quivering tautly down the length and breadth of the string section. But the work sounds like a rehash of old tricks, and the performance did nothing to rescue it from itself.

The only critic to show interest in the new work was Olin Downes, in the *Times:*

The dances are simple in outline, symphonic in texture and proportion. The first one, vigorously rhythmed and somewhat in a pastoral vein, is festive in the first part and more lyrical and tranquil in the middle section. The second Dance begins with a muted summons, or evocation, of the brass, a motto repeated in certain places, and for the rest there are sensuous melodies, sometimes bitter-sweet, sometimes to a Viennese lilt—and Vienna is gone.

In the last Dance, the shortest, the most energetic and fantastical of the three, an idea obtrudes which has obsessed the musical thinking of Rachmaninoff these many years—the apparition, in the rhythmical maze, of the terrible old plain chant, the *Dies Irae.*

If one asked Mr. Rachmaninoff what he meant by these Dances he would undoubtedly give the sincere, correct and eminently logical reply that he meant to write some music. It is also true that music springs from a source in the individual which is deeper than any a surgeon has yet probed, and of which the artist himself may be unconscious, and it is from this source only that there emanates significant, living art. A melancholy, a fatalism not frantic or exhibitionist, inhabits many of Rachmaninoff's pages. The Dances have no ostensible connection with each other. They could easily reflect a series of moods, presented in a certain loose sequence —of Nature, and memories, and reveries with some Dead Sea fruit in them—all unpretentious, melodic, sensuously colored and admirably composed music.

A pleasant postscript to the Philadelphia Orchestra performances came from Ormandy on January 10:

On Wednesday morning I talked to the orchestra men, thanked them for their wonderful cooperation as well as for the beautiful concerts they played from Friday until Tuesday. I told them of the superlative remarks you, the Kreislers and many other friends and colleagues who were present Tuesday evening made about them. . . .

They were very happy and proud, and asked me to thank you for everything.

May I for my own self, express to you my very deep thanks for letting us have the first performance of your latest creation, and hope that our performances of it didn't disappoint you and justified your confidence in us. I am deeply grateful to you for this. I am also grateful to you for the personal friendship we have, in which I admire you as much as I admire Toscanini.

Recital duties were resumed, outwardly unaffected by the discouraging reception of the new work.

On the tour reporters assigned to interview the unwilling, protected master were often hard put to it for something to write. A typical example of such column-filling sleuthing was displayed by the frustrated interviewer of the *Corpus Christi Caller-Times*, acting on the principle that ordinary activities by an extraordinary person may also be "news":

Rachmaninoff, accompanied by his wife and manager, R. C. Heck, arrived in Corpus Christi from Harlingen Friday afternoon at 12:45 o'clock. They traveled in a hired automobile. After registering at the Nueces Hotel, he lunched with Mrs. Rachmaninoff in the public dining room. Both ate avocado stuffed with lobster salad, sea-food chowder and a health salad. The pianist signed the $1.10 check with an almost illegible scrawl and left a 25-cent tip for the waitress. Mr. Rachmaninoff is said to have smiled occasionally at his wife as he read the menu to her [etc., etc.]. . . . Saturday morning's heavy fog provided a natural screen to hide his departure on an early train.

From Texas the Rachmaninoff entourage went to the West Coast where Mme. Rachmaninoff achieved a restful interval at Hollywood's Garden of Allah and he saw his Russian friends in the film industry. In Chicago he paid homage to Frederick Stock and the Chicago Symphony on its Golden Jubilee, by conducting a program of his Third Symphony and *The Bells,* assisted by the Apollo Musical Club. In the *Daily Times* Robert Pollak summed up the impression on Chicagoans:

Rachmaninoff as a composer may be too conservative for our tastes a quarter of a century hence, but as a composer, pianist or conductor he is unfailingly impressive. His technical genius in a variety of fields, his absolute musical integrity, the spell of his own person, all these lead you to spontaneous tribute, "What a wonderful old man!"

But the Chicago concert was an unpleasant revelation to the "old man" himself that conducting put more strain on his arms than a pianist could afford to suffer. He was willing to conduct once more before retiring for good from that profession. He was to conduct the Philadelphia Orchestra in a recording of *Symphonic Dances,* but the schedules of the orchestra and the Victor Company conflicted, and the recording was postponed. Later Victor's Charles O'Connell presented their side of the matter:

My only disagreement with Mr. Rachmaninoff came about because of the *Symphonic Dances.* I have never felt that this music added a great degree of lustre to the composer's name, but what was more important, it was not notably a success with the public. The work was dedicated to the Philadelphia Orchestra, which Rachmaninoff admired more than any other. He wished to record the Dances with the Philadelphia Orchestra and to conduct the work himself. For various reasons irrelevant here, this was not practicable, and I discreetly postponed the matter until it was not only impracticable but impossible. A little later we engaged the Chicago Symphony to make Red Seal records and one of the first things on their program that season was Rachmaninoff's *Symphonic Dances,* whereupon, conditions being quite different from those existing in Philadelphia, I proposed that the Chicago Orchestra record the *Symphonic Dances.* Rachmaninoff was not at all enthusiastic, and when it developed that Dr. Stock and not Rachmaninoff would conduct, the composer became actively resentful and things were rather uncomfortable between us for a time. When I was in a position to tell him the whole story, however, I was restored to his good graces.

The tour ended, the Rachmaninoffs moved back to New York and then into the Honeyman house. The absence of news from Tatiana, his helplessness in not being able to assist her in any way, and the continuing reports of Hitler's triumphs all had a darkening effect on Rachmaninoff's mood and when, on June 22, news came of the German attack on Russia, his worry and depression deepened.

Work that he had determined to do this summer was hampered but not canceled by events in the world outside Huntington. For a second time he tackled the long-wished-for revisions of the Fourth Concerto. Without altering the thematic material, he largely revised its orchestration and the final movement was rewritten. A small work of this summer was a piano transcription of Tchaikovsky's *Lullaby*. And there were new additions to the concert repertoire to be practiced, including Schumann's Concerto.

Sophie Wolkonsky gave her grandfather some needful pleasure with her musical gifts, working hard at both piano and composition, and the celebration of her sixteenth birthday made a happy end to the summer at Huntington. Rachmaninoff acted as master of ceremonies, led the family in a march around the table, and made a solemn speech of congratulation in Russian.

After opening the recital season in Syracuse and Utica, Rachmaninoff played the new version of the Fourth Concerto for the first time on October 17, with Ormandy and the Philadelphia Orchestra. Edwin Schloss wrote, in the *Philadelphia Record*:

The Fourth Concerto as heard yesterday is a revision of a work first heard here 14 years ago from Rachmaninoff's hands. The revision, which is extensive, was made last summer and yesterday's performance was the concerto's first anywhere in its present form. It turned out to be nobly-meant and darkly romantic music, somewhat fragmentary in shape and typically Rachmaninovian in spirit. And, with all due respect to the great artist who wrote it, and for all its fine pianism, a trifle dull. Its playing, however, added up to news in any season—news that becomes increasingly miraculous as the years go by, namely, that for all his 68 years, Rachmaninoff is still one of the most virile and brilliant young pianists before the public today.

Ormandy and Rachmaninoff played the "new" Fourth Concerto (with the Second Symphony) in Washington, Baltimore, and, later, New York.

Since the attack on Russia in June, the downward course of the war had darkened Rachmaninoff's days. However, he refused to echo the defeatism he heard all around him, from other Russian émigrés: the Germans marched on and on, but the Russians did not surrender, and Rachmaninoff's desperation turned to hope, and this hope sought some way to help his native land. Among Americans he found such a total lack of understanding of both Russian geography and spirit that he was compelled to interpret current news reports wherever he went, even though he never heard them directly from the radio; he was unable to listen to "commentators" and to the admixture of advertisement, and three times a day some member of the family would bring him an undiluted report of the radio's news.

Through the summer and fall a wish ripened to do something, anything, for his country, though resident in the United States, but he realized that such an act might offend many groups. By midautumn he decided to come into the open and by his example encourage all to forget differences in the succor of Russia's agony. He wished all advertisements for his recital of November 1 to announce that the entire receipts were to be turned over "to the war sufferers of his native Russia," but Americans close to him dissuaded him, and he had to be content to print this unequivocally in the program. Rachmaninoff sent two tickets for this concert to his cousin and former teacher, Alexander Siloti, now a seventy-eight-year-old resident of New York. When Siloti heard that the proceeds were going to Russia, he sent a check to pay for the tickets. He too wanted to help Russia.*

Before leaving New York Rachmaninoff gave an interview to David Ewen for *The Etude*:

Composing is as essential a part of my being as breathing or eating; it is one of the necessary functions of living. My constant desire to compose music is actually the urge within me to give tonal expression to my thoughts. . . . That, I believe, is the function that music should serve in the life of every composer; any other function it may fill is purely incidental.

I have no sympathy with the composer who produces works according to preconceived formulas or preconceived theories. Or with the composer who writes in a certain style because it is the fashion to do so. Great music has never been produced in that way—and I dare say it never will. Music should, in the final analysis, be the expression of a composer's complex personality. It should not be arrived at mentally, tailor-made to fit certain specifications—a tendency, I regret to say, all too prevalent during the past twenty years or so. A composer's music should express the country of his birth, his love affairs, his religion, the books which have

* "A special shipment of medical and surgical supplies, valued at $3,973.29 and bearing the inscription 'Gift of Sergei Rachmaninoff,' will soon be on its way to Russia. The sum which made this purchase possible represents the entire net proceeds of the composer-pianist's recent Carnegie Hall recital. Soviet Russia's consul in New York, representing the country from which Rachmaninoff has long been an exile, is cooperating in assembling and shipping these supplies for Russian war sufferers." *New York Herald Tribune,* December 7, 1941.

influenced him, the pictures he loves. It should be the product of the sum total of a composer's experiences. Study the masterpieces of every great composer, and you will find every aspect of the composer's personality and background in his music. Time may change the technic of music, but it can never alter its mission. . . .

In my own compositions, no conscious effort has been made to be original, or Romantic, or Nationalistic, or anything else. I write down on paper the music I hear within me, as naturally as possible. I am a Russian composer, and the land of my birth has influenced my temperament and outlook. My music is the product of my temperament, and so it is Russian music; I never consciously attempted to write Russian music, or any other kind of music. I have been strongly influenced by Tchaikovsky and Rimsky-Korsakov; but I have never, to the best of my knowledge, imitated anyone. What I try to do, when writing down my music, is to make it say simply and directly that which is in my heart when I am composing. If there is love there, or bitterness, or sadness, or religion, these moods become a part of my music, and it becomes either beautiful or bitter or sad or religious.

To those who may have wondered why his only short piano works since leaving Russia had been transcriptions, he said:

Young composers are often apt to look condescendingly upon the smaller forms of music. . . . A small piece can become as lasting a masterpiece as a large work. As a matter of fact, I have often found that a short piece for the piano has always given me much more pain, and has presented to me many more problems, than a symphony or a concerto. Somehow, in writing for the orchestra, the variety of colors provided by the instruments brings me many different ideas and effects. But when I write a small piece for the piano, I am at the mercy of my thematic idea, which must be presented concisely and without digression. . . . After all, to say what you have to say, and to say it briefly, lucidly, and without any circumlocution, is still the most difficult problem facing the creative artist.

The Chicago Symphony concerts of November 6 and 7 conducted by Stock were devoted to Rachmaninoff—*Vocalise, Isle of the Dead,* the Fourth Concerto, the Third Symphony. Chicago critics did not agree with Chicago audience:

In spite of the rain outside, the hall was jammed and the ovations frequent and loud, yet the cumulative effect of the concert was depressing.

Somebody described a noted Chicagoan as "a man with one of the finest minds of the 14th century." Rachmaninoff owns one of the intriguing composing talents of the 19th century. But, to listen to an all-Rachmaninoff program is like sitting down to a seven-course dinner with Beluga caviar for each course. He no more deserves a concentrated evening than Reger, Franck or Saint-Saëns and, in 20 years, he won't get one.

The Third Symphony, beautifully read by Dr. Stock and the orchestra on this occasion, is magnificently plush, full of those overstuffed melodies, the drugged lyricism, the brief military passages marcato and those familiar rising chords of the ninth.

But an hour more of the same is too much. Then following, "Isle of the Dead" seems rhetorical and self-conscious. As for the Fourth, and most recent piano concerto, it is an unbelievably empty piece of music with a slow movement that sounds like an Alec Templeton improvisation on "Three Blind Mice" and a finale devoid of anything but decoration.

Rachmaninoff played his Rhapsody and the Schumann Concerto in A minor (for his first time in America) with the Pittsburgh Symphony, conducted by Vladimir Bakaleinikoff, on November 28 and 30. When he arrived in St. Louis for his recital of December 9 his audience was at war:

For once radio divided interest with the artist at a concert here, for many were anxious to hear President Roosevelt's statement on the Japanese war situation. So the Refectory was filled with listeners in the intermission, and on the foyer of the orchestra floor several pocket radios were in evidence, around which audiences were thronged as deep as listening was possible.

Though Rachmaninoff had said, "Music can only succeed where there is peace and quiet," the war did not stop his music making.

Chapter 23

California

THE RACHMANINOFFS decided to try southern California for the summer, perhaps with a plan of longer range in mind, and, because I (Bertensson) knew Rachmaninoff's tastes, I was asked to aid a real estate agent in renting a house. Together we found a Beverly Hills estate with a large house, a swimming pool, the all-important garden, and a big music room that could hold two grand pianos. Its high elevation afforded several broad views, including one of the Pacific. It was a sunny, delightful place, and its nearest neighbors were at the right distance, at the bottom of the hill. The owner, Eleanor Boardman, arranged for the Rachmaninoffs to move in by the middle of May.

In the interval before occupying the Boardman house Rachmaninoff made his last recordings, in the Hollywood studio of the Victor Company. Only one of these was left unreleased: his transcription of Tchaikovsky's *Lullaby*. A more ambitious and valuable project suggested by Rachmaninoff—to record a series of his recital programs—was rejected by the company.

Vladimir Horowitz, with his wife and daughter, lived not far from the new Tower Road house. Sergei Vasilyevich was fond of the entire Horowitz family, and I heard him repeatedly express his admiration for the talent of the famous pianist. Horowitz frequently visited Rachmaninoff, and they played duets for their own pleasure, without an "audience"—a pleasant practice that had begun in Switzerland. I was once invited to attend one of these exclusive concerts, and except for the members of both families I was the sole auditor. The program included a Mozart sonata, Mozart's D major piano concerto, and Rachmaninoff's second suite for two pianos. It is impossible to word my impression of this event. "Power" and "joy" are the two words that come first to mind—expressive power, and joy experienced by the two players, each fully aware of the other's greatness. After the last note no one spoke—time seemed to have stopped. I, for one, forgot that I was living in Hollywood, where the word "art" has a habit of slipping from one's memory. When I came home that night I wrote down the date of this extraordinary evening so that it could not slip away: June 15, 1942.

I was so fortunate as to hear another of these exquisite concerts: the two Mozart works were repeated, but Rachmaninoff's second suite was replaced by his transcription for two pianos of his *Symphonic Dances.* The brilliance of this performance was such that for the first time I guessed what an experience it must have been to hear Liszt and Chopin playing together, or Anton and Nikolai Rubinstein.

Another occasion enjoyed together by the two Russian artists was a visit to the Disney studio:

Part of the program was the running of Disney's early film *Mickey's Opry House,* in which the tiny hero was seen as a concert pianist playing Rachmaninoff's most famed Prelude. Its composer told Walt, "I have heard my inescapable piece done marvellously by some of the best pianists, and murdered cruelly by amateurs, but never was I more stirred than by the performance of the great maestro Mouse."

California presented her most attractive aspects to the Rachmaninoffs and gained two more admirers; settlers, too, for a house on Elm Drive was purchased as a permanent home. Rachmaninoff told Mandrovsky, on June 29:

It's true, I've bought a house. Not a "country-seat," as Aldanov says, but a small, neat house on a good residential street in Beverly Hills. It has a tiny garden with lots of flowers and several trees: an orange tree, a lemon, and a nectarine. In general I'm not lucky with houses. In my lifetime I've bought six houses. Of these only the one in New York was a success, and I sold it satisfactorily. The others I've either lost, as in Russia, or practically lost, as in Germany and Switzerland. This last one here will probably be taken from me by the Japanese, though, frankly, I scarcely believe they will get here. If they do come, it will be only for the sake of my house. Such is fortune!

The war with Japan provided a curious but pleasant incident that has been recorded by Julia Fatova. She was one of a small group of Rachmaninoff's friends invited to the home of Leonid Raab for a shashlik dinner. In the midst of the quiet evening the air raid sirens sounded. All lights were extinguished, but the guests' alarm was somewhat soothed by the host, who explained that he was the neighborhood air warden, and that this was only a test of Los Angeles' precautionary measures. Everyone in the darkened, airy room spoke in whispers, without moving from their seats. Someone sounded a few chords on the piano. Fatova was nearby and she was moved to begin singing, softly, a gypsy air.

If I had remembered that Rachmaninoff was present I should never have dared to think of singing. But at that moment I simply felt like singing, and I sang. When the song ended I was surprised to hear Sergei Vasilyevich's voice. He had moved to the piano where I was standing, and almost in a whisper said, "Please go on singing—don't break this lovely mood. Nowadays one seldom hears a sincere voice. Your song is truly the Russia that we all love and miss so much. Sing, I beg you—sing much—sing long." I could hardly believe my ears; was this really the great Russian composer who spoke so little, wishing to hear one who had lost faith in herself and who thought that there was no one in this foreign country who needed her singing?

The war made a deep and dark impression on Rachmaninoff. Every time the conversation turned to the East European front and the sufferings being endured by his beloved native country, one could easily observe how strongly he suffered himself. The mere thought of the hundreds of thousands of Russian people meeting their death, and of the barbarous destruction of priceless ancient Russian monuments, made him shudder.

Whenever he heard on the radio such recordings as the *Russian Easter Overture* by Rimsky-Korsakov, Stravinsky's *Fire Bird,* excerpts from Musorgsky's *Boris Godunov* in Chaliapin's incomparable interpretation, or any composition with the flavor of Russia, he would become visibly excited. I shall never forget how, when we were listening together to the solemn yet joyous finale of *The Fire Bird,* Rachmaninoff's eyes filled with tears, and he exclaimed, "Lord, how much more than genius this is—it is real Russia!"

Along with mounting anxieties about the war in Europe, his private worry about his daughter Tania's family also increased, for even indirect word of their health was rare. He continued to send them things through the caretaker at Senar, but could never be sure that they reached her safely. He knew that Stravinsky's children were also caught in France, and this gave him the idea of telephoning me to say, "I know that Stravinsky's family is there and I well know how he must feel about it, for I'm in the same position. I'm eager to meet someone whose family, like mine, is over there, and with whom I could discuss ways to send money and other things. As I know how much Igor Fyodorovich has always disliked my compositions, even though he respects me as a pianist, and he must know my attitude to modern music [but Rachmaninoff had always praised both *The Fire Bird* and *Petrushka* as works of genius], I'm not sure whether I could invite him and his wife to my house—which I'd love to do—because I don't know how he would receive my invitation. Would you be so kind as to send out a feeler to gauge his reaction to such an idea?" I called Vera Arturovna, and her immediate response was "delighted" —they would be glad to go to the Rachmaninoffs' for dinner. When I telephoned to Rachmaninoff that he could invite them directly, I was asked to come, too. Before dinner and during it, besides comparing notes on their families in France, they had a very lively discussion of musical matters—but not a word about compositions. They talked about managers, concert bureaus, agents, ASCAP, royalties. It was a cordial meeting; both composers were glad to have the old barrier broken down. The Stravinskys later returned the invitation. At the first dinner Stravinsky mentioned that he was fond of honey, and within a few days Sergei Vasilyevich found a great jar of fine honey, and delivered it personally at the Stravinsky door.

Rachmaninoff played at the Hollywood Bowl on July 17 and 18, in an all-Russian program conducted by Bakaleinikoff, with painful results, as he wrote to Mandrovsky:

Besides the check for these concerts I also received a Lumbago. I can hardly stand up, and when I walk I look like a comma. Serves me right! Don't snatch bread from the mouths of the young and at this age don't push where you don't belong!

At dinner the following night, with the Stravinskys and Rubinsteins, the lumbago continued to torment him.

Played here twice on an open-air stage [he wrote Somov]. Results as follows: received a rather large check and a most violent Lumbago. I can still sit and lie down—but stand up—no, no! Serves me right! Such playfulness doesn't suit my age! While playing I had the unpleasant sensation of a cold little wind blowing right through me.

From your part of the country we hear of terrific and oppressive heat. This is one thing we can brag about: here it is cool and so far (we've been here over two months now) it hasn't rained once. This is a blissful climate.

In half an hour Natasha goes to send the landlady packing and to receive the key for the house. I accept your congratulations! If you can't think up a gift for our housewarming—fifty glass cigarette-holders will be sufficient.

Continuing, for the summer, to live in the Tower Road house, Rachmaninoff could not resist spending most of his daytime freedom in the garden of the smaller house on Elm Drive. There he spaded and raked and planned the trees that he would add to the lovely birches already matured on the lot. When Somova sent him a new issue of *Novyi Zhurnal*, the first words that caught his eye were in a lyric by the poet Prokofiev:

> I love the Russian birch,
> Now shining, now sad ...

His Russian friends living in or near Beverly Hills were delighted that he was to make his home among them, and they all tried to make some contribution to the comfort and beauty of his new home. Nikolai Remisoff designed a workroom to be built over the garage. Rachmaninoff was happy to have found such congenial surroundings and companions, for he was approaching a difficult decision.

His public activity must soon end; he could not endure the idea of continuing to appear on the concert platform when unable to maintain the heights of his achievement, though the idea of life without concerts was appalling. For the past two or three years his complaints of fatigue had increased, and when he told Dr. Golitzin that he intended to make his next tour his last, retiring to composition after one last public appearance in his adopted California, the physician agreed that this was a wise decision; sclerosis and high blood pressure required a halt to the constant nervous tension of a pianist's career.

This was the most social summer he had spent in the United States; he wrote to Somov on August 17:

As before we live on a grand scale and dissipatingly. For example at yesterday's dinner, served on our splendid balcony with powerful electric illumination, there were 22 persons. And enough provisions to feed 122 persons, as always with Natasha. The chief inconvenience of this is that the five of us will be eating this for the next two weeks.

A few days later came the saddening news of another friend's death; the *Symphonic Dances* had lost its choreographer:

Yesterday [he wrote to Mandrovsky] I received a telegram about Fokine's death. . . .
What a great sorrow! Chaliapin, Stanislavsky, Fokine—this was an epoch in art. Now all are gone! And there's no one to take their place. Only trained walruses are left, as Chaliapin used to say.

When Mandrovsky forwarded letters complaining of Rachmaninoff's benefit concerts for Russian war relief, Rachmaninoff wrote him sharply:

Of course I'll play again for Russia. To help Russia now is to help America. But everybody helps the latter and not many are helping Russia. I am still a Russian and therefore it's natural for me to go on struggling for her.

Before leaving California he heard of an exhibition in wartime Moscow to celebrate the fiftieth anniversary of his artistic activity:

A Rachmaninoff exhibit recently opened at the State Conservatory in Moscow has been attracting crowds of visitors. On the walls hang pictures of world-famous Russian musicians of the nineteenth century, including Rachmaninoff's teachers at the Moscow Conservatory—Taneyev, Arensky, Siloti, and Safonov. Rachmaninoff is shown in a group of students of his childhood days, with another of his teachers, Professor N. Zverev. The composer's mature countenance is pictured on a big canvas presented to the Conservatory by his deceased professor, Anna Ornatzkaya. There is an old faded photograph of him with Josef Hofmann. Another, entitled "The Artistic Family," shows him with Fyodor Chaliapin and Sergei Koussevitzky. On one portrait we find his autograph dated 1909, with a musical phrase from his Third Concerto. Below the musical text, the painter has penned "Glory to the People bringing Freedom!" From the same year is an oil portrait by Robert Sterl. In glass cases, in rows and stacks, are Rachmaninoff's compositions, the bulk of which have been published in Russia during the past twenty years.

Rachmaninoff's fiftieth and last season began with a recital in Detroit on October 12, and it evoked comment that may have made his contemplated retirement sound premature:

Although we know the number of opportunities left to hear this Titan of the keyboard are growing fewer—he's 70 years old now—there seems to be no faltering of his fingers, no weakening of his attack, no waning of his powers.

Rather he seems to defy the idea of old age with a vigor and a force which is indeed incredible. The facility with which he can encompass the technical demands of lightning passages in a Liszt bravura piece, for example, is something you can hardly bring your ear to believe.

And in New York Henry Simon's "Musical Diary" in *PM* said:

Saturday, Nov. 7.—Lots of argument during the intermission of Rachmaninoff's piano recital. Everyone said there were ups and downs, but few agreed what was up and what was down. As for me, I didn't like his transcription of the Bach E major Partita for violin. Too many inner voices and harmonies that the organist from Eisenach couldn't have dreamed of. The pianist also hit too many wrong notes.

The Beethoven Sonata Op. 31 No. 2 went much better, especially the Schumannesque last movement, which was a poetic caress as Rachmaninoff played it. The Chopin group hit a high with the F-sharp Nocturne, but was very unconventional Chopin in some other spots.

After the intermission there could not have been much room for argument. Rachmaninoff was in top form with both his own four etudes (op. 39) and a Liszt group. He did the *Venice and Naples* with all the technical virtuosity of a youngster who practises eight hours a day and the variety in tone color and singing melody you get only from a truly great pianist.

All receipts of this November 7 recital were turned over to war charities—part to the Soviet consul-general for the purchase of supplies, and part to the American Red Cross.

In mid-December Rachmaninoff was pleased to hear a radio performance, from New York's WQXR, of his sonata for piano and cello, played by Nadia Reisenberg and Joseph Schuster. He telephoned Miss Reisenberg to praise the interpretation and the tempi of the performance, but also to remind her that the work "is not for cello with piano accompaniment, but for two instruments in equal balance." In favoring the cello the engineers and their microphone had once more confirmed his distrust of the radio for musical purposes.

The arrangements for Mitropoulos to conduct the New York Philharmonic's first performances (on December 17, 18, 20) of the *Symphonic Dances* were assisted by the composer, and he explained his intentions in detail to the conductor by going over the score of the *Dances* with him at the piano. The Philharmonic concerts of December 17 and 18 were as exclusively Rachmaninoff programs as the Philharmonic ever had, for in addition to the *Symphonic Dances,* Mitropoulos conducted the Rhapsody, with the composer at the piano. For him the triumph of the evening was the fresh critical consideration given to the *Dances* in Mr. Mitropoulos' interpretation. This last appearance in New York of Rachmaninoff maintained his dual career of composer and pianist resolved on at his arrival in this country in 1918.

Though he had been happy to hear of the Moscow celebration of his fiftieth jubilee, he forbade his family to mention the anniversary. His chief fear was that the press would begin referring to the jubilee, and that this would snowball into celebrations, banquets, speeches— all of which, during the trials of war, seemed to him an unbearable dissonance. It is possible, too, that he may have been a little hurt that it was so completely forgotten; only one reporter, in Philadelphia, seemed to have counted the years, and Rachmaninoff was certainly happy about the celebration news from his native country, much closer to the war. His friends in New York did remember, after all: following the Mitropoulos concert a small group of friends staged a quiet surprise party. To add to his pleasure Steinway sent a handsome piano to his new home in California.

After the concert of December 18 Rachmaninoff kept his promise to take a six-week interval in his concert schedule. Staying in New York, he rested conscientiously and practiced his usual daily three

hours. He allowed a *Life* photographer, Eric Schall, to take a group
of intimate photographs—his last ones. In the middle of January he
complained of unusual fatigue; a stubborn cough began, and his loss
of weight was evident. He mentioned pains in his left side, and his
complexion took on a disturbingly yellowish tone. But these symptoms did not seem extraordinary in a man approaching his seventieth
birthday through years of an uninterruptedly nervous artistic career.
On February 1, Rachmaninoff and his wife received their final papers
as United States citizens, and made ready for the tour to be resumed
on February 3 at State College, Pennsylvania.

Everything seemed wrong: it had been so long since reliable word
had come from Tatiana in France that Rachmaninoff wrote Somov,
"There's such anguish in my soul that it could be measured in yards";
the news from the Russian front seemed nearly hopeless; and he could
not feel sure of his playing. The second recital of his tour was to be
in Columbus, Ohio. Knowing that the Somovs were sure to go up
there from Yellow Springs, he sent them a pleading post card from
New York, on January 28:

Dear Zhenya, please do *not* come to Columbus. In the first place, we
leave immediately after the concert, and secondly, I shall play badly and
I'll be ashamed that you should have taken such a trip for the sake of
such playing.

But the Somovs did come to Columbus for the February 5 recital.
When they visited him in the intermission they were both horrified
by his appearance. Mrs. Somov wrote of their last meeting:

Sergei Vasilyevich had often said that he was made of 85 per cent
musician and only 15 per cent man. Music, the creation of music, was
the chief thing in his life. He couldn't imagine life without it. I remember
how angry he once became when a doctor prescribed total rest and a halt
to all musical activity. "Does he really think that I could sit in the sun
and feed pigeons! No, such a life is not for me—better death. . . ."

I recalled these words when we saw him in the Columbus dressing
room. My heart contracted when I saw his thin and suffering face. In
answer to my question as to his health, instead of his usual joking shout,
"A-Number One, First Class!" I heard complaints of pains and weakness.
"What's bad," he said, "is that it grows hard for me to play concerts.
What would life be for me without music?" When I mentioned that he

might stop his concerts and devote himself solely to composition, he shook his head sadly. "I am too tired for that, too. Where should I find the strength and the fire?" I reminded him of the fire and inspiration in his *Symphonic Dances*. "Yes," he replied, "I don't know how that happened. That was probably my last flicker."

From Columbus to Chicago, where he was greeted with such ovations on February 11 and 12 that he gave performances that satisfied even him. He played the same two works with which he had said farewell to Switzerland: Beethoven's First Concerto and his own Rhapsody.

The following day he complained of a pain in his side and a Russian doctor was called. The diagnosis was a slight pleurisy and neuralgia, and the doctor advised him to go somewhere soon where he could get lots of sunshine. For the present the tour could continue. It was a totally exhausted Rachmaninoff who played in Louisville on February 15. When the advisability of canceling his next concert, in Knoxville, was suggested, Rachmaninoff recalled that he had recently disappointed the local concert manager there by postponing an announced fall concert till now, on February 17. He could not trouble him again. That evening he played his last program: Bach, Schumann, Liszt, Chopin, Wagner, Rachmaninoff; before the intermission he played his beloved Chopin sonata, in B-flat minor —*Grave, Scherzo, March funèbre, Finale.*

On the way to his next date, in Florida, he felt so ill that he and his wife left the train at Atlanta. From there the Florida concert was canceled, and they went directly to New Orleans, to get two days' rest in the prescribed sun before facing the Texan audiences, next on their schedule. He felt much worse on their arrival in New Orleans, and their plans again changed. Rachmaninoff wrote to Professor Rashevsky on February 22, from the Roosevelt Hotel:

Dear Nikolai Petrovich, yesterday I canceled a concert, and I am canceling three concerts of this week, for tomorrow I leave for "summer quarters" in California. There's little I can brag about—for my health is definitely run down: the pains in my side seem stronger and I feel terrific weakness. It's hard for me to play. I should see a doctor, but on this question I am a narrow-minded nationalist: I recognize only Russian doctors, and there is one I can see in California, but not before. He's from

Moscow University: I'll talk with him about my side, and we can recall old times. It will be good for both body and soul.

It was wartime, and all train schedules were committed to the movement of troops and supplies: and the Rachmaninoffs could not get an immediate reservation. After three agonizing days of waiting, they spent three more days on a slow train to Los Angeles, where an ambulance awaited him. Fedya Chaliapin met him there and went with them to the hospital:

His greatest worry was that he could not do his daily practice. To encourage him I said something about his getting well and playing again.
"Not at my age, Fedya. At my age one can't miss practice. . . ." And he looked at his hands. "My dear hands. Farewell, my poor hands."

The next day, February 27, Rachmaninoff began a letter to Somov from a bed in the Hospital of the Good Samaritan:

My dear Zhenichka, after sitting with me all day Natasha has just left; well, so here I lie in a hospital. . . . I'll try to tell you, briefly, how it happened. Leaving you, I went to Chicago. There a Russian doctor was summoned. He discovered a slight pleurisy, but the severe pain in the side can't be pleurisy—it is a nervous symptom. Some knot in the nerves aches and it would be useless to expect it to pass soon. Only with heat and lots of sun! After three days the doctor found nothing in the lungs, but the side began to ache with more severe pain. We went on and gave two more concerts. It was so hard for me to play! Oh, how hard! We decided to cancel the next concert and to go to New Orleans, from where I was to go on for three concerts in Texas. In New Orleans I noticed that the cough had definitely increased, as well as the pain in the side, and that soon I shouldn't be able to stand, or to sit, or to lie down. We took desperate measures, canceled three concerts, took a terrible train from Texas (60 hours), and moved straight on to Los Angeles. . . . Irinochka left for here last night. Dr. Russell arranged for a doctor friend of his, who wired to us on the train, to meet us at the station with an ambulance. So last night, then, we landed here. Two fellows grabbed me under the arms and brought me here. That was 9 in the evening. A specialist was waiting and at once they began to sound me and listen. And early this morning, an X-ray. Now all grows clear. Here's a report for you. There are only two small spots on the lungs, with a *not* very large inflammation. . . . As you see, much ado about nothing. I scared Irina almost to death, and Sonichka nearly quit her job, and so forth. So now I feel so embarrassed and guilty . . .

For three days Dr. Alexander Golitzin (the trusted doctor from Moscow University) kept Rachmaninoff under observation at the hospital, chiefly for the purpose of regular tests, but at last he had to yield to Rachmaninoff's extreme depression amidst hospital surroundings and to his insistent demands to be taken to his home on Elm Drive, where he believed he should recover as soon as the warm weather returned. A trained Russian nurse, Olga Mordovskaya was engaged for him and she awaited his arrival at home on March 2:

At 1 P.M. an ambulance brought Sergei Vasilyevich home. His face expressed relief that he was in his own home, but fatigue and tension were apparent, too. After being put to bed, he looked about his room attentively and fixed his gaze on an old family ikon of St. Panteleimon, saying, "How nice to be home.". . .

During his first week at home Sergei Vasilyevich showed interest in everything and spent a great deal of his time in reading American newspapers. He was concerned about his garden, asking which flowers were in bloom each day. He inquired after the newly planted trees, asked for seed catalogues, and spoke of working in his beloved garden as soon as he was well. He worried about the furniture overdue from New York. When a radio was installed he asked me to tune in the Moscow station, for he wanted only to hear music from Moscow. Though he complained of an increasing pain in his arm, he continued his wrist and finger exercises for his future piano playing.

Small swellings appeared on his body and his appetite decreased with disturbing rapidity. Even the arrival of his sister-in-law Sophia brought no more than temporary distraction. On several occasions Dr. Golitzin had expressed his private opinion that the illness was far more serious than the patient had assumed. By the middle of March he asked the surgeon Dr. E. C. Moore for a consultation, and a minor operation was decided upon, to test the swellings. With this and successive tests they determined that Rachmaninoff's disease was fatal: a rare and rapid form of cancer—melanoma—had spread throughout his vital organs, attacking the liver, lungs, bones, and muscles, and was now beneath the surface of the skin. Operation was out of the question.

The family was told, but the diagnosis was concealed from Rachmaninoff. The doctors gave him vague and improbable explanations of his condition, and it was the task of the family to keep him cheered with talk of future plans and trips. His chief concern seemed for those around him; he urged his wife to spend more time out in the fresh air of the garden and told his daughter to visit friends and see films. On their part, they found it painful to be away from him any of these last hours. When he could no longer read, his wife read Pushkin to him and answered his daily inquiries as to the situation on the Russian front. Hearing that the Red Army had taken the initiative and had recaptured several towns, he sighed with relief, "Praise the Lord! God grant them strength." Whenever his condition allowed him an interval of peace, close friends were admitted to see him. Fedya Chaliapin came in once, just as Rachmaninoff was waking from a sleep:

"Who is it who keeps playing?" he asked. "Why do they keep on playing?"

When Natalia Alexandrovna assured him that no one was playing, he seemed to understand, "A-a-ah . . . that means it's playing in my head. . . ."

Dr. Golitzin wrote:

These lucid intervals became more rare and more brief. The doses of narcotic, though comparatively small, had to be increased. For a man who had never resorted to narcotics or alcohol, minimum doses of morphine twice a day were sufficient to give him relief. As his weakness increased his morale declined; his words and queries expressed hopelessness. It is possible that he recognized the approach of death, and during pain, before an injection could take effect, he may even have wished for it. Soon his illness was progressing, not by days, but by hours. An arrested pneumonia developed, the pulse weakened, and three days before death came, Rachmaninoff began to lose consciousness for long periods. Natalia Alexandrovna, who never left him at this time, said that in his delirium he often moved his hands, as if conducting an orchestra, or playing a piano.

Each time Dr. Golitzin took Rachmaninoff's hand to check the pulse, he thought, "These beautiful thin hands will never again touch a keyboard, and give the same delight they have given for fifty years."

From Moscow came news of plans for the celebration of his seventieth birthday, centered in a concert of his works, and along with this word a cable arrived, signed by the eleven most distinguished names in Soviet music:

Dear Sergei Vasilyevich!

On the day of your seventieth anniversary the Union of Soviet Composers sends you warm congratulations and hearty wishes for good spirits, strength, and health for many years to come. We greet you as a composer of whom Russian musical culture is proud, the greatest pianist of our time, a brilliant conductor and public man who in these times has shown patriotic feelings that have found a response in the heart of every Russian. We greet you as a creator of musical works penetrating in their depth and expressiveness. Your piano concertos and symphonies, your chamber works, songs, and other compositions are often played in the Soviet Union, and the public here watches with close attention your creative activity and is proud of your triumphs. . . .

He read neither these nor any other words; he was in a coma. Early on March 27 a priest was called who administered the holy sacrament, and at 1:30 the next morning Rachmaninoff died.

The body of Sergei Vasilyevich Rachmaninoff was taken East and buried in Kensico Cemetery, near a little New York town named Valhalla.

NOTES AND APPENDICES

Notes on the Text

Abbreviations
for principal
sources

A   The Rachmaninoff Archive (formerly in New York City, Northamp-
        ton, Massachusetts, and "Senar," Switzerland), now deposited at the
        Library of Congress

AA   A. D. Alexeyev, *S. V. Rakhmaninov*. Moscow, 1954

BA   B. V. Asafiev (pseud: Igor Glebov), *Izbrannye Trudy*. Moscow,
        1954. Vol. II contains his articles on Rachmaninoff.

CH   F. I. Chaliapin, *Stranitzi iz moyei zhizni*, Petrograd, 1918? (trans-
        lation published in New York, 1927: *Pages from My Life*)

DR   Dictated reminiscences: these unpublished fragments are the only
        memoirs dictated by Rachmaninoff in Russian and translated into
        English under his supervision. They were prepared in 1931 for an
        American journalist whose planned biography was not realized.

FM   Frederick H. Martens, *Little Biographies: Rachmaninoff*. New York,
        1922

IG   "Iz arkhiva K. N. Igumnova," *Sovietzkaya Muzyka,* No. 1, 1946

LS   Leonid Sabaneyev, "Moi Vstrechi: Rakhmaninov," *Novoye Russ-
        koye Slovo* (New York), September 28, 1952

M   Papers of Nikolai Medtner, deposited at the Library of Congress

MMC   Rachmaninoff Room in the State Central Museum of Musical Cul-
        ture, Moscow.

MS   Rachmaninoff, "Pisma k Re [Marietta Shaginyan]," *Novyi Mir*
        (Moscow), No. 4, 1943

MT   Rachmaninoff, "Some Critical Moments in My Career," *The Musi-
        cal Times,* June 1930. An interview, possibly given in Germany; a
        French translation appeared in *Candide,* September 4, 1930.

NA   N. K. Avierino, "Iz vospominanii o S. V. Rakhmaninove," *Novyi
        Zhurnal* (New York), XVIII, 1948

PR   *Pamyati Rakhmaninova,* a collection edited by M. V. Dobuzhinsky.
        New York, 1946

RO *S. V. Rakhmaninov i Russkaya Opera,* a collection edited by Igor Belza. Moscow, 1947

RR *Rachmaninoff's Recollections Told to Oskar von Riesemann.* London and New York, 1934

SB Sergei Bertensson, "Rachmaninoff as I Knew Him," *The Etude,* March 1948

SK *Molodye Godi Sergeya Vasilyevicha Rakmaninova* (letters to the sisters Skalon, with a memoir by Ludmila [Skalon] Rostovtzeva). Leningrad and Moscow, 1949

SS Sophia Satina, *Materials for a biography of S. V. Rachmaninoff*: an unpublished manuscript (completed in 1943)

Swan Alfred and Katherine Swan, "Rachmaninoff: Personal Reminiscences," *The Musical Quarterly,* January, April 1944

SZ Rachmaninoff, "Pisma k M. A. Slonovu i A. V. Zatayevichu," *Sovietzkaya Muzyka,* No. 4, 1945

TD *The Diaries of Tchaikovsky,* translated by Wladimir Lakond. New York, 1945

TR Anna Trubnikova, "Sergei Rakhmaninov," *Ogonyok* (Moscow), No. 4, 1946

TT *S. V. Rakhmaninov,* a collection edited by T. E. Tzitovich. Moscow, 1947

VRW "Iz perepiski S. V. Rakhmaninova" (letters to V. R. Wilshaw), *Sovietzkaya Muzyka,* No. 2, 1948

Z M. Pressman, "A Corner of Musical Moscow of the '80s; In Memory of the Moscow Conservatory Professor N. S. Zverev," an unpublished manuscript, extracted in Alexeyev, *Russkiye Pianisti* (Moscow, 1948), and in TT.

ZA *S. V. Rakhmaninov: Pisma,* edited by Zaruya Apetianz. Moscow, 1955. This edition of Rachmaninoff's letters includes all previous Soviet publications of his letters, in addition to newly published letters. The collection arrived in this country too late to revise the following notes, but several letters and considerable information from it have been incorporated into our text.

PROLOGUE [Page numbers are in bold face type.]

1 TR; **2** Varvara Arkadyevna Satina to Sophia Satina (SS); **3** Mme. L. Defert to R., September 5, 1934 (A); **6** Olga Trubnikova to Varvara Satina, 1930 (SS); **7–8** SS.

I. ZVEREV AND HIS CUBS

10 Z; **11** DR; Sabaneyev, *S. I. Taneyev* (Paris, 1936); **12** RR, pp. 49–50; p. 51; **13** TD, February 3, and July 27, 1886; Z; **14** TD, September 1, 1886; MT; TD, December 8, and December 6, 1886; **15** FM; Z; **16** NA; **17** Natalia Rachmaninoff to Sophia Satina, 1948 (Satina); **18** RR, pp. 60–61; Tchaikovsky to Mme. von Meck, June 1, 1888, in *Dni i Godi Chaikovskovo* (Moscow, 1940); **19** Mme. Anatol Tchaikovsky, "Recollections of Tchaikovsky," *Music and Letters*, April 1940; Swan, p. 18; TD, May 7, May 9, May 28, 1889; **20** Somov (PR); **21–22** SS.

II. A NEW FAMILY

23 Swan, pp. 14, 13; **24** Introduction, SK; **25** DR; **26** R. to Natalia Skalon, September 1, 1890 (SK); **27** R. to N. Skalon, September 8, 1890 (SK); NA; Bukinik (PR) [translated as "Reminiscences of Young Rachmaninoff," in *Local 802*, May 1943]; **29** R. to N. Skalon, October 2, 1890 (SK); R. to N. Skalon, October 10, 1890 (SK); **30** R. to Skalon sisters, October 21, 1890 (SK); R. to N. Skalon, November 1, 1890 (SK); R. to N. Skalon, December 10, 1890 (SK); Introduction, SK; R. to N. Skalon, January 6, 1891 (SK); **31** R. to N. Skalon, January 10, 1891 (SK); Wilshaw to R., June 5, 1934 (A); **32** R. to Skalon sisters, February 5, 1891 (SK); R. to N. Skalon, March 26, 1891 (SK); **33** SS; **34** R. to Skalon sisters, May 31, 1891 (SK); R. to N. Skalon, June 11, 1891 (SK); **35** R. to Slonov, June 18, 1891 (ZA); Tchaikovsky to Jürgenson, June 14, 1891 (ZA); Tchaikovsky to Siloti, June 14, July 7, 1891 (ZA); **36** R. and Siloti to N. Skalon, July 11, 1891 (SK); n., Tchaikovsky to Mme. Hubert, February 4, 1892, in *Proshloye Russkoi Muzyki*, Vol. I: *P. I. Chaikovski* (Petrograd, 1920); R. to Slonov, July 20, 1891 (SZ); **37** R. to Slonov, July 24, 1891 (SZ); SS; **38** Slonov to N. Skalon, September 22, 1891 (SK).

III. ALEKO AND "FREE ARTIST"

39 R. to N. Skalon, October 31, 1891 (SK); R. to N. Skalon, December 7, 1891 (SK); **40** RR, pp. 77–78; **41** Goldenweiser reminiscences (TT);

42 R. to N. Skalon, February 18, 1892 (SK); **43** Bukinik (PR); **44** A.N.S., *Dnevnik Artista,* April 1892 (TT); SS and RR, p. 79; R. to N. Skalon, March 23, 1892 (SK); **45** RR, p. 80; R. to N. Skalon, April 30, 1892 (SK); **46** SS; *Dnevnik Artista,* July 1892; **47** NA; R. to Slonov, June 7, 1892 (SZ); R. to N. Skalon, June 10, 1892 (SK); **48** R. to N. Skalon, August 2, 1892 (SK); **49** S., *Artiste,* November 1892; interview by Basanta Koomar Roy, in *Musical Observer,* May 1927; LS; MT; R. to N. Skalon, October 13, 1892 (SK); **50** R. to Ludmila Skalon, October 15, 1892 (SK); R. to Slonov, December 14, 1892 (SZ); **52** R. to N. Skalon, February 7, 1893 (SK); **53** Taneyev to Tchaikovsky, March 20, 1893, in *P.I. Chaikovski-S.I. Taneyev, Pisma* (Moscow, 1951); n., Tchaikovsky to Siloti, May 3, 1893 (ZA); P. Tchaikovsky to M. Tchaikovsky, April 17, 1893, in M. Tchaikovsky, *Zhizn Pyotra Ilyicha Chaikovskovo,* Vol. III (Moscow, 1902); MT; RR, pp. 86–87; **54** Poplavsky, in *Russkoye Vremya* (Paris), November 1928?; n., P. Tchaikovsky to Slatin, May 3, 1893, in *Dni i Godi Chaikovskovo,* Kruglikov, in *Artiste,* May 1893; **55** FM.

IV. DEATHS AND FAILURE

56 R. to M. Tchaikovsky, May 13, 1893 (TT); **57** R. to N. Skalon, June 5, 1893 (SK); R. to L. Skalon, June 29, 1893 (SK); **58** R. to N. Skalon, August 25, 1893 (SK); **59** S. Balukhatyi, "Biblioteka Chekhova," in *Chekhov i yevo sreda,* ed. N. F. Belchikov (Leningrad, 1930); **60** BA (this meeting is dated by a letter of September 27, 1893, from Taneyev to Tchaikovsky); Ippolitov-Ivanov, *50 Let Russkoi Muzyki v Moikh Vospominaniyakh* (Moscow, 1934); **61** Swan, p. 177; R. to Skalon sisters, October 3, 1893 (SK); **62** R. to M. Tchaikovsky, October 14, 1893 (TT); SS; **63** R. to N. Skalon, December 17, 1893 (SK); N.V.S., in *Artiste,* February? 1894 (TT); **64** SS; R. to Slonov, July 24, 1894 (TT); R. to Slonov, August 2, 1894 (AA); **65** Introduction, SK; R. to Slonov, September 3, 1894 (TT); **66** R. to Liventzova, 1894 (ZA); S. Satina to authors, April 4, 1955; **67** R. to Slonov, November 9, 1895 (AA); R. to Slonov, September 2, 1895 (SZ); **68** Glazunov to Taneyev, November 23, 1895, in *P.I. Chaikovski-S.I. Taneyev, Pisma;* Cui, in *Novosti,* January 22, 1896; **69** Taneyev diary (TT); LS; R. to Zatayevich, December 7, 1896 (SZ); **70** n., R. to Kerzin, April 15/28, 1906 (ZA); LS; Taneyev to Belayev, October 26, 1896 (ZA); **71** R. to Taneyev, November 9, 1896 (ZA); n., Yasser, in *The New York Times,* December 21, 1947; SS; Cui, in *Novosti,* March 17, 1897; **72** n., Cui to Kerzina, December 19, 1904, in *Sovietskaya Muzyka,* #7, 1948; Findeisen, in *Russkaya Muzykalnaya*

Gazeta, April 1897; R. to N. Skalon, March 18, 1897 (SK); **73** R. to Zatayevich, May 6, 1897 (SZ); **74** R. to Asafiev, April 13, 1917 (BA).

V. SECOND CONCERTO

75 MT; Swan, p. 185; **76** DR; **77** SS; **78** *Moskovskiye Vedomosti,* October 14, 1897; *Russkoye Slovo,* October 14, 1897; R. to N. Skalon, October 19, 1897 (SK); Chaliapin, *Maska i Dusha* (Paris, 1932) [translated as *Man and Mask* (New York, 1932)]; **79** R. to Zatayevich, November 4, 1897 (SZ); Lipayev, in *Russkaya Muzykalnaya Gazeta,* January 1898; **80** DR; **81** R. to L. Skalon, November 22, 1897 (SK); **82** R. to Zatayevich, April 18, 1898 (SZ); CH; R. to M. Tchaikovsky, July 28, 1898 (TT); **83** R. to M. Tchaikovsky, August 28, 1898 (TT); CH; Somova (PR); R. to Zatayevich, October 26, 1898 (SZ); **84** R. to Zatayevich, March 3, 1899 (SZ); **85** CH; *Musical Opinion,* May 1899; **86** *Monthly Musical Record,* May 1899; *Musical Times,* May 1899; *Times,* April 21, 1899; **87** R. to Natalia Satina, May 17, 1899 (MMC); Ivanov, in *Teatr i Iskusstvo,* 1899; R. to Slonov, July 18, 1899 (SZ); R. to N. Skalon, July 18, 1899 (SK); **88** Chaliapin, *Maska i Dusha;* **89** Swan, p. 185; SS; **90** RR, p. 112; Yulia Koutirina, in *Ogonyok* (Paris), May 1933; **91** Kalinnikov to Kruglikov, May 2; May 19; June 20, 1900 (ZA); **92** CH; **93** R. to Morozov, June 14/27, 1900 (TT); R. to Morozov, June 22/July 5, 1900 (TT); CH; R. to N. Skalon, July 9/22, 1900 (SK); **94** R. to Morozov, July 18, 1900 (TT); SS; Lipayev, in *Russkaya Muzykalnaya Gazeta,* #55, 1900; **95** SS; R. to Morozov, October 22, 1901 (TT); **96** n., information from Arcadie Kougell.

VI. IMPERIAL THEATER

97 TR; R. to N. Skalon, April 1, 1901 (SK); **98** TR; R. to Morozov, June 17, 1902 (TT); **99** R. to Morozov, September 11, 1902 (TT); **100** Engel, in *Russkiye Vedomosti,* February 12, 1903; R. to Taneyev, November 27, 1902 (ZA); Taneyev diary (ZA); Schor to R., July 29, 1929 (A); **101** R. to Morozov, August 18, 1903 (TT); **102** R. to M. Tchaikovsky, March 26, 1904 (RO); **103** R. to M. Tchaikovsky, June 8, 1904 (RO); R. to Morozov, July 2, 1904 (TT); **104** R. to Morozov, July 21, 1904 (TT); R. to M. Tchaikovsky, August 3, 1904 (RO); R. to Morozov, August 4, 1904 (TT); **105** F. F. Chaliapin (PR); **106** R. to M. Tchaikovsky, September 10, 1904 (RO); Salina, *Zhizn i Stzena* (Leningrad, 1941); **107** DR; Engel, in *Russkiye Vedomosti,* September 22, 1904; **108**

Teleshov, *A Writer Remembers,* translated by Lionel Britton (London, 1946); n., BA; **109** Kashkin, in *Moskovskiye Vedomosti,* October 28, 1904; *Russkaya Muzykalnaya Gazeta,* January 8/21, 1905 (translated by N. Slonimsky); Medtner, in *Rossiya i Slavyanstvo* (Paris), May 1, 1933; **110** Engel, in *Russkiye Vedomosti,* March 20?, 1905; FM; *Nashi Dni,* February 2/15, 1905; reprinted in *Russkaya Muzykalnaya Gazeta,* #7, 1905 (translated by N. Slonimsky).

VII. OPERAS AND PROJECTS

112 R. to Morozov, July 6, 1905 (TT); **113** Swan, pp. 177–78; R. to Rimsky-Korsakov, September 17, 1905 (ZA); Rimsky-Korsakov, *Chronicle of My Musical Life;* **114** RR, pp. 127–28; **115** Engel, in *Russkiye Vedomosti,* January 14, 1906; Telyakovsky, *Imperatorsky teatri v 1905 godu* (Leningrad, 1926); **117** R. to Morozov, March 19/April 1, 1906 (TT); **120** R. to Morozov, March 28/April 10, 1906 (TT); **121** R. to Morozov, April 27, 1906 (TT); **123** R. to Morozov, May 4/17, 1906 (TT); R. to Slonov, May 8/21, 1906 (SZ); **124** R. to Slonov, May 16/29, 1906 (SZ); **125** R. to Slonov, May 24/June 6, 1906 (SZ); TR; R. to Morozov, June 18, 1906 (TT); **126** R. to Morozov, July 3, 1906 (TT); **127** R. to Morozov, July 23, 1906 (TT); R. to Kerzina, August 2, 1906 (ZA); R. to Morozov, August 21, 1906 (TT); R. to Morozov, August 29, 1906 (TT).

VIII. DRESDEN

130 R. to Morozov, November 9, 1906 (TT); **131** R. to Slonov, November 3, 1906 (SZ); R. to Slonov, November 21, 1906 (SZ); R. to Morozov, December 5 (N.S.), 1906 (TT); **132** R. to Kerzina, December 7, 1906 (AA); R. to Morozov, December 10, 1906 (TT); **133** R. to Morozov, December 21, 1906 (TT); **134** R. to Slonov, January 4, 1907 (SZ); R. to Morozov, February 11, 1907 (TT); n., R. to Morozov, February 27, 1907 (TT); **136** R. to Morozov, April 13, 1907 (TT); **137** R. to Morozov, May 8, 1907 (TT); **138** n., *Monna Vanna* (A); Haskell, *Diaghileff* (London, 1935), note, p. 174; Swan, p. 178; **139** IG; R. to Igumnov, June 15, 1907 (IG); **140** R. to Morozov, June 16, 1907 (TT); R. to Morozov, June 24, 1907 (TT); R. to Slonov, July 27, 1907 (SZ); **141** R. to Morozov, August 2, 1907 (TT); Stanislavsky to Maeterlinck, 1908 (ZA); Maeterlinck to Stanislavsky, December 9/22, 1908 (ZA).

IX. EUROPE

143 IG; R. to Morozov, November 20, 1907 (TT); R. to Morozov, December 31, 1907 (TT); **144** Engel, in *Russkiye Vedomosti* (TT); R. to Morozov, April 12, 1908 (TT); **145** R. to Igumnov, April 12, 1908 (IG); **146** *Times*, May 28, 1908; R. to Morozov, June 21, 1908 (TT); R. to Morozov, June 29, 1908 (TT); **147** R. to Stanislavsky, October 14, 1908; score in *Sovietskaya Muzyka*, October 1948; **152** IG; Engel, in *Russkiye Vedomosti*, October 19, 1908; **153** IG; R. to Morozov, November 6, 1908 (TT); **154** R. to Morozov, December 2 (N.S.), 1908 (TT); R. to Morozov, December 11 (N.S.), 1908 (TT); **155** R. to Goedicke, December 19, 1908 (ZA); R. to Slonov, January 1, 1909 (SZ); **156** interview by B. K. Roy, in *Musical Observer*, May 1927; interview in *The Etude*, December 1941; FM; interview quoted by Kolodin, in *The International Cyclopedia of Music and Musicians*, ed. by Oscar Thompson (New York, 1939), note, p. 1484; **157** R. to Morozov, March 21 (N.S.), 1909 (TT); **158** R. to Morozov, June 6, 1909 (TT); R. to Yasser, April 30, 1935 (Yasser, copy in A); **159** R. to Morozov, July 15, 1909 (TT).

X. FIRST AMERICAN TOUR

161 [Aldrich] in *The New York Times*, November 14, 1909; **162** *The Delineator*, February 1910; **163** [Aldrich?] in *The New York Times*, November 21, 1909; *Sun*, December 1, 1909; R. to Pribitkova, December 12, 1909 (ZA); **164** RR; pp. 159–60; Aldrich, in *The New York Times*, January 28, 1910; **165** interview in *Muzykalni Truzhenik* (ZA); Tolstaya, *The Final Struggle*; **166** G. Prokofiev, in *Russkiye Vedomosti*, April 6?, 1910; R. to E. F. Goldman, December 27, 1937 (University of Michigan); SS and Satina to authors, January 23, 1950; **167** DR; SS; R. to Morozov, June 4, 1910 (TT); **168** R. to Morozov, July 31, 1910 (TT); **169** *Utro Rossii*, November 3, 1910; reprinted in Telyakovsky, *Vospominaniya 1898–1917*; R. to *Russkiye Vedomosti*, November 8/21, 1910, published November 14, 1910; **171** DR; **172** NA; **173** *Russkaya Muzykalnaya Gazeta*, April 3, 1911; n., BA; *Times*, October 14, 1911; **174** Drozdov, in *Novoye Russkoye Slovo* (New York), December 18, 1932; **175** Engel, in *Russkiye Vedomosti*, December 15?, 1911.

XI. "RE" AND THE BELLS

176 MS; R. to Shaginyan, February 14, 1912 (MS); **177** R. to Shaginyan, March 15, 1912 (MS); R. to Shaginyan, March 29, 1912 (MS); **178** R.

to Shaginyan, April 28, 1912 (MS); **179** R. to Shaginyan, May 8, 1912 (MS); **181** R. to Shaginyan, June 19, 1912 (MS); **182** Engel, in *Russkiye Vedomosti,* October 24?, 1912; R. to Shaginyan, November 12, 1912 (MS); **183** Busoni to his wife, November 19, 1912, *Briefe an seine Frau* (Zurich, 1935); Harold Bauer, *His Book* (New York, 1948), p. 213; RR, pp. 170–71; **184** DR; **185** R. to Shaginyan, March 23, 1913 (MS); R. to Shaginyan, July 29, 1913 (MS); **186** Warsaw correspondence by Linitzki, in *Russkaya Muzykalnaya Gazeta,* January 1914; Karatygin, in *Rech,* November 24?, 1913; reprinted in *V. G. Karatygin* (Leningrad, 1927); **187** Bukinik (PR); Tyuneyev, in *Russkaya Muzykalnaya Gazeta,* December 8, 1913; **188** R. to Shaginyan, April 30, 1914 (MS).

XII. WAR AND NIGHT VIGIL

189 DR; **190** R. to Siloti, November 1, 1914 (ZA); **191** R. to Yasser, April 30, 1935 (Yasser, copy in A); RR, p. 177; Kastalsky, in *Russkoye Slovo,* March 7, 1915; **192** R. to the Editor of *Russkiye Vedomosti,* June 9, 1915 and June 16, 1915; **194** R. to Goldenweiser, August 9, 1915 (ZA); **195** MS; **196** S. Prokofiev [Autobiography], *Sovietskaya Muzyka,* April 1941; n., *The Nation,* April 4, 1953; G. Prokofiev, in *Russkaya Muzykalnaya Gazeta,* December 6, 1915; **197** Glinsky, in *Russkaya Muzykalnaya Gazeta,* December 6, 1915; Yasser, in *Novoye Russkoye Slovo* (New York), February 22, 1931; **198** NA; **199** MS; SS; R. to Koshetz, July, 1916 (Koshetz); **200** R. to Koshetz, September 1, 1916 (Koshetz); R. to Shaginyan, September 20, 1916 (MS); **201** Engel, in *Russkiye Vedomosti,* October 25, 1916; Tyuneyev, in *Russkaya Muzykalnaya Gazeta,* December 11, 1916; Engel, in *Russkiye Vedomosti,* December 5, 1916; **202** Sabaneyev, in *Muzykalni Sovremennik,* December 23, 1916; **203** R. to Koshetz, December 22, 1916 (Koshetz); R. to Shaginyan, January 26, 1917 (MS); **204** S. Prokofiev [Autobiography], *Sovietskaya Muzyka,* April 1941; **205** R. to Siloti, June 1, 1917 (ZA); **206–207** SS; **208–209** facsimiles (A).

XIII. VIRTUOSO

210–211 SS; **212** Gabrilowitsch to Ellis, April 23, 1918, in Clara Clemens, *My Husband Gabrilowitsch* (New York, 1938), pp. 100–1; **213** SS; **214** *New York Times,* November 13, 1918; Rybner-Barclay (PR); **215** SS; Hale, in *Boston Herald,* December 16, 1918; **216** Parker, in *Boston Evening Transcript,* December 16, 1918; **217** Huneker, in *New York Times,* December 22, 1918 (mistakenly reprinted as by Aldrich in *Con-*

cert *Life in New York* [New York, 1941], pp. 584–86); de Koven, *New York Herald,* January 13, 1919, **218** Huneker, *World,* January 30, 1919; *Boston Herald,* February 23, 1919; Rosenfeld, in *The New Republic,* March 15, 1919; reprinted in his *Musical Portraits* (New York, 1920); **219** Sackville West, in *The Spectator,* September 20, 1924; R. to Rybner, June 15, 1919 (Rybner-Barclay, copy in A); Cowell to authors, February 23, 1954 (A); **220** *The Etude,* October 1919 ("Fragments" reprinted in *The Etude,* September 1941); Downes, in *New York Times,* November 26, 1939; **221** Sanborn, in *Telegram,* February 11, 1920; **222** R. to Avierino, November 1, 1920 (A); **223** R. to Medtner, October 29, 1921 (M); **224** Parker, in *Boston Evening Transcript,* December 8, 1921; Hale, in *Boston Herald,* December 8, 1921; R. to Medtner, December 29, 1921 (M); **225** *Lincoln State Journal,* January 24, 1922; Parker, in *Boston Evening Transcript,* February 20, 1922; n., *New York Tribune,* April 3, 1922; **226** *Observer,* May 7, 1922; *Musical Times,* June 1, 1922; RR, p. 198; R. to Rybner, May, 1922 (Rybner-Barclay, copy in A); **227** R. to Medtner, August 4, 1922 (M); R. to Wilshaw, September 9, 1922 (VRW).

XIV. TIES WITH RUSSIA

228 R. to Morozov, November 13, 1922 (TT); Marinsky Chorus to R., July 15, 1922 (A); Kiev Conservatory to R., June 20, 1922 (A); Stanislavsky to R., May 26, 1922 (A); R. in *Musical America,* October 7, 1922; **229** Blumenfeld to R., January 1, 1922 (A); SB; **230** R. to Somov, January 27, 1923 (Somov); **231** R. to Morozov, April 15, 1923 (TT); "New Lights on the Art of the Piano," an interview in *The Etude,* April–May 1923; **232** Gliere-Wilshaw cantata (A); R. to Wilshaw, May 1, 1923 (VRW); R. to M. Rimsky-Korsakov, May 5, 1923 (copy in A); **233** Somova (PR); Ostromislensky, in *Novoye Russkoye Slovo* (New York), December 18, 1932; R. to Morozov, November 18, 1923 (TT); **234** K.P., in *Boston Herald,* November 26, 1923; R. to Morozov, December 25, 1923 (TT); **235** R. to Rybner, April 6, 1924 (Rybner-Barclay, copy in A); R. to the Somovs, May 12, 1924 (Somov); Culshaw, *Sergei Rachmaninov* (London, 1949), p. 161; R. to Medtner, June 20, 1924 (M); **236** SS; R. to Wilshaw, August 21, 1924 (VRW); F. I. Chaliapin to R., September 19, 1924 (A); **237** *New Orleans Item,* January 21, 1925; R. to Morozov, January 15–19, 1925 (TT); **238** R. to Somov, January 24, 1925 (Somov); Elsie Flower, in *Stockton Evening Record,* February 13, 1925; **239** R. to Wilshaw, May 16, 1925 (VRW); R. to Wilshaw, July 2, 1925 (VRW); **240**

R. to Mrs. Cornelius Rybner, September 8, 1925 (Rybner-Barclay, copy in A); **241** A.H.M., in *Boston Evening Transcript*, November 9, 1925; Fatova (PR); **242** R. to Medtner, January 14, 1926 (M).

XV. THE COMPOSER RESUMES

244 Hofmann to R., March 26, 1926 (A); R. to Wilshaw, April 19, 1926 (VRW); **245** R. to the Somovs, August 28, 1926 (Somov); R. to the Somovs, September 8, 1926 (Somov); **246** R. to Medtner, September 9, 1926 (M); Medtner to R., September 13, 1926 (A); **247** R. to Medtner, September 22, 1926 (M); R. to Medtner, October 9, 1926 (M); Samaroff, in *New York Evening Post*, February 20, 1927; **248** Hofmann to R., February 20, 1927 (A); Gilman, in *New York Herald-Tribune*, March 23, 1927; **249** Chotzinoff, in *World*, March 23, 1927; Sanborn, in *Evening Telegram*, March 23, 1927; **250** Stokes, in *Evening World*, March 23, 1927; R. to Medtner, June 25, 1927 (M); **251** R. to Medtner, September 27, 1927 (M); R. to the Somovs, August 7, 1927 (Somov); **252** "The Artist and the Gramophone," an interview in *The Gramophone*, April 1931 (R's correction printed June 1931); R. to *New York Times*, published April 29, 1928; **253** *Times*, May 27, 1928; R. to the Somovs, May 24, 1928 (Somov); R. to the Somovs, June 17, 1928 (Somov); **254** R. to Somov, August 12, 1928 (Somov); Swan, pp. 2–3; p. 12; **255** R. P.–B., *8 Uhr Abendblatt*, November 10, 1928; Paul Zschorlich, in *Deutsche Zeitung*, November 23, 1928; AP dispatch, December 22, 1928; **256** *New York Times*, December 23, 1928; *New York Times*, January 6, 1929; R. to Somov, February 7, 1929 (Somov); **257** n., Holmes, in *Detroit Evening Times*, February 6, 1929; memorandum of A. Greiner, March 29, 1929 (Greiner); R. to the Somovs, May 30, 1929 (Somov); **258** Swan, p. 4; R. to the Somovs, July 14, 1929 (Somov); **259** R. to Somov, September 29, 1929 (Somov); R. to the Somovs, November 3, 1929 (Somov); **260** Newman, in *Sunday Times*, November 10, 1929; N.C., in *Manchester Guardian*, November 25, 1929.

XVI. WORK AND REST

262 R. to Paichadze, January 2, 1930 (carbon in A); R. to Respighi, January 2, 1930 (carbon in A); **263** Respighi to R., March 20, 1930 (A); R. to Hofmann, January 14, 1930 (carbon in A); **264** Hofmann to R., April 4, 1930 (A); Swan, pp. 12–13; Henderson, in *Sun*, February 16, 1930; **265** Swan, pp. 11–12; R. to Somov, March 24, 1930 (Somov); **266**

Swan, pp. 17–18; **267** Hofmann to R., April 4, 1930 (A); R. to Somov, April 25, 1930 (Somov); R. to Swan, May 12, 1930 (Swan); **268** R. to Somov, June 13, 1930 (Somov); Swan, pp. 4–7; **270** MT; Aldanov to R., September 12 and 16, 1930 (A); SS.

XVII. EXILE REINFORCED

271 Gabrilowitsch to R., December 28, 1930 (A); R. to Gabrilowitsch, January 2, 1931 (copy in A); *New York Times,* January 15, 1931; **272** Hofmann to R., January 15, 1931 (A); R. to Hofmann, January 19, 1931 (carbon in A); R. to Somov, February 2, 1931 (Somov); **273** R. to Somov, February 20, 1931 (Somov); *Pravda,* March [?], 1931, translated in RR, pp. 200–3; *Vechernaya Moskva,* March 9, 1931; **274** E. Cushing, in *Brooklyn Daily Eagle,* March 29, 1931; R. to Somov, n.d. (Somov); R. to Somov, May 3, 1931 (Somov); **275** R. to Somov, July 16, 1931 (Somov); M. Chekhov (PR); R. to S. Satina, August 8, 1931 (A); **276** R. to Somov, August 25, 1931 (Somov); Swan, pp. 8–9; **278** Yasser, in *Novoye Russkoye Slovo* (New York), November 10, 1931; Yasser (PR); **279** "Interpretation Depends on Talent and Personality," an interview with Florence Leonard, *The Etude,* April 1932; Swan, pp. 175–76; **280** R. R. Bennett to the authors, October 29, 1949; R. to Koussevitzky, December 8, 1931 (copy in A); Koussevitzky to R., December 16, 1931 (A); R. to Medtner, December 21, 1931 (M); **281** n., R. Howell, in *Washington Daily News,* November 6, 1931; Yasser (PR); **283** Gunn, in *Chicago Herald and Examiner,* January 15, 1932.

XVIII. SENAR AND RAPSODIE

284 *New York Times,* February 25, 1932; **285** Newman, in *Sunday Times,* March 13, 1932; R. to the Somovs, March 20, 1932 (Somov); R. to Satina, March 30, 1932 (A); **286** R. to Somov, April 5, 1932 (Somov); R. to Rybner-Barclay, April 19, 1932 (Rybner-Barclay, copy in A); **287** R. to the Swans, July 1932 (Swan, p. 176); Swan, pp. 179–80; **288** R. to the Somovs, August 15, 1932 (Somov); *New York Times,* October 10, 1932, **289** *London Star,* May 1, 1933; R. to Schor, October 13, 1932 (copy in A); **290** Gunn, in *Chicago Herald and Examiner,* October 31, 1932; R. to Somov, November 15, 1932 (Somov); *New York Times,* December 11, 1932; **291** Thompson, in *New York Evening Post,* December 23, 1932; R. to Walter E. Koons (draft in A); Glazunov to R., December 19, 1932 (A); **292** R. to Satina, January 29, 1933 (A); Stokowski to R., March 18, 1933 (A); **293** Swan, pp. 184, 186–87; **294** Andrei Sedikh (pseud. of Zwieback), in *Posledni Novosti* (Paris), May 1933; **295** Wortham, in *Daily Telegraph*, April 29, 1933; H.S.G., in *News Chronicle*, May 1, 1933; **296** *Star*, May 1, 1933; Moiseiwitsch, "Sergei Rachmaninoff, 1873–1943," *The Gramophone*, May 1943; **297** "Ludo Patris," in a Brussels weekly, May 12?, 1933; de Geynst, in *La Nation Belge*, May 6, 1933; R. to Somov, May 9, 1933 (Somov); Medtner, in *Rossiya i Slavyanstvo* (Paris), May 1, 1933; **299** R. to the Somovs, June 25, 1933 (Somov); SS; **300** R. to M. Trubnikova, October 11, 1933 (ZA); Henry Beckett, in *New York Evening Post*, December 26, 1933; **301** *New York Times*, March 1, 1934; R. to the Somovs, March 14, 1934 (Somov); "The Composer as Interpreter," an interview with Norman Cameron (pseud. of Norah Barr Adams), in *The Monthly Musical Record*, November 1934; R to Wilshaw, April 6, 1934 (VRW); **302** R. to the Somovs, April 11, 1934 (Somov); R. to Greiner, April 12, 1934 (Greiner, copy in A); **303** SB; Wilshaw to R., May 8, 1934 (A); **304** R. to Satina, August 19, 1934 (A); **305** R. to the Somovs, August 31, 1934 (Somov); R. to Wilshaw, September 8, 1934 (VRW).

XIX. THE "RUSSIAN" SYMPHONY

306 Chotzinoff, in *New York Post*, November 5, 1934; Henderson, in *Sun*, November 5, 1934; **307** Liebling to R., November 3, 1934 (A); Gilman, in *New York Herald-Tribune*, November 4, 1934; **308** G. K., in *Musical Courier*, November 17, 1934; Somova (PR); R. to Somov, November 14, 1934 (Somov); R. to Medtner, December 8, 1934 (M); **309** R. to Medtner, December 17, 1934 (M); *Musical America*, January 10, 1935; Simon, in *The New Yorker*, January 12, 1935; **310** Chasins to R., December 28, 1934 (A); R. to Chasins, December 29, 1934 (Chasins); R. to the Somovs, February 10, 1935 (Somov); **311** R. to the Somovs, March 9, 1935 (Somov); n., Tatiana Conus to Somov, January 30, 1935 (Somov); R. to Yasser, April 30, 1935 (Yasser, copy in A); PR includes a quotation of the church chant referred to by Yasser as an "unconscious" source for the opening theme of the Third Concerto; **313** R. to Rybner-Barclay, May 4, 1935 (Rybner-Barclay, copy in A); R. to Somov, July 3, 1935 (Somov); R. to Somov, August 22, 1935 (Somov); R. to Somov, September 1, 1935 (Somov); manuscript, LC; R. to Wilshaw, September 26, 1935 (VRW); **314** n., R. to Amram Scheinfeld, December 1937 (draft in A; published in Scheinfeld, *You and Heredity* [New York, 1939]); Wilshaw to R., April 10, 1936 (A); Downes, in *New York Times*, November 3, 1935; **315** Ilf and Petrov, *Odnoetazhnaya Amerika*, first published serially in *Krasnaya Nov;* translated by C. Malamuth, *Little Golden America* (New York, 1937); Sherman, in *Minneapolis Star,* November 30, 1935; **316** Swan, pp. 187–88; **317** *Times,* March 31, 1936; R. to Wilshaw, April 15, 1936 (VRW); **318** Ormandy to R., May 3, 1936 (A); R. to Ormandy, May 11, 1936 (copy in A); **319** Stokowski to R., May 20, 1936 (A); n., radio transcript, November 8, 1935, (A); **320** Swan, pp. 189–90; R. to Satina, June 30, 1936 (A); **321** R. to the Somovs, July 5, 1936 (Somov); R. to Wilshaw, July 18, 1936 (VRW).

XX. THE COMPOSER REBUFFED

322 R. to Somov, September 7, 1936 (Somov); note by Wood, in *Sheffield Festival Program,* 1936; **323** *Times,* October 22, 1936; *New York Times,* November 8, 1936; Schloss, in *Philadelphia Record,* November 7, 1936; **324** Laciar, in *Public Ledger,* November 7, 1936; Haggin, in *Brooklyn Daily Eagle,* November 11, 1936; Henderson, in *Sun,* November 11, 1936; Downes, in *New York Times,* November 11, 1936; **325** R. to Aslanov, November 13, 1936 (Aslanov, photostat in A); **326** N. Weinberg, in *Washington Herald,* December 2, 1936; A. Williams, in *Boston Herald,* December 7, 1936; R. to Somov, January 20, 1937 (Somov); **327** R. to Slonimsky, January 20, 1937 (Slonimsky, copy in A); D. W. Hazen, in *Morning Oregonian,* January 23, 1937; Frankenstein, in *San Francisco Chronicle,* February 6, 1937; **328** M. H. Davidson, in *San Francisco Call-Bulletin,* February 6, 1937; *Detroit Free Press,* February 26, 1937; **329** R. to Somov, March 24, 1937 (Somov); R. to the Somovs, April 24, 1937 (Somov); R. to Somov, May 4 and 11, 1937 (Somov); **330** Mrs. A. M. Henderson, "Rachmaninoff at Home," *Musical Opinion,* April 1938; R. to Wilshaw, June 7, 1937 (VRW); **331** Wilshaw to R., June 18, 1937 (A); R. to Somov, June 17, 1937 (Somov); **332** Fokine to R., August 23, 1937 (A); **333** R. to Fokine, August 29, 1937 (Fokina, draft in A); **334** Fokine to R., September 9, 1937 (A).

XXI. RETREAT FROM EUROPE

335 W. G. King, in *Sun,* October 13, 1937; R. Hynds, in *St. Louis Star-Times,* November 15, 1937, **336** A.B., in *Philadelphia Record,* November 21, 1937; Simon, in *The New Yorker,* December 4, 1937; F. Bonavia, in *New York Times,* December 5, 1937; Wood to R., November 26, 1937 (A); **337** R. to Wood, December 15, 1937 (copy in A); Chasins to R., December 2, 1937 (A); **338** Chasins to Satina, October 27, 1948 (Satina); R. to Chasins, January 10, 1938 (Chasins, copy in A); **339**

Gray-Fiske, in *Hampstead News and Advertiser*, March 12, 1938; **340** *Cavalcade*, March 19, 1938; **341** *Dublin Evening Mail*, March 26, 1938; R. to the Somovs, March 27, 1938 (Somov); n., Wood, *About Conducting* (London, 1945); **342** R. to Satina, April 20, 1938 (A); draft (Verkholantzeff), published in *Posledniye Novosti* (Paris), April 17, 1938; **343** R. to Somov, April 29, 1938 (Somov); Ormandy to R., July 8, 1938 (A); R. to Ormandy, July 1938 (draft in A); R. to the Somovs, July 19, 1938 (Somov); **344** R. to Mrs. Barclay, July 19, 1938 (Rybner-Barclay, copy in A); R. to Somov, July 31, 1938 (Somov); *Time*, October 31, 1938; **345** J. F. Lissfelt, in *Pittsburgh Sun Telegraph*, October 25, 1938; Frankenstein, in *San Francisco Chronicle*, November 19, 1938; R. to Somov, November 30, 1938 (Somov); R. to Somov, December 8, 1938 (Somov); **346** R. to Medtner, January 12, 1939 (M); Fokine to R., February 15, 1939 (A); *Glasgow Herald*, February 20, 1939; **347** *The Northern Echo*, March 1, 1939; *Evening News*, March 13, 1939; R. to the Somovs, April 2, 1939 (Somov); **348** R. to Fokine, April 3, 1939 (Fokina, copy in A); R. to Somov, May 20, 1939 (Somov); **349** R. to Fokine, June 22, 1939 (Fokina, copy in A); Mme. R. to Satina, June 25, 1939 (Satina); Fokine to R., June 24, 1939 (A); **350** *Times*, July 1, 1939; Fokine to R., June 30, 1939 (A); **351** R. to Fokine, July 1939 (Fokina, copy in A); R. to the Somovs, July 5, 1939 (Somov); R. to Liebling (published in *Musical Courier*, April 5, 1943); **352** Wilshaw to R., June? 1939 (A); R. to Wilshaw, July 26, 1939 (VRW); **353** R. to Somov, August 3, 1939 (Somov); SS.

XXII. SYMPHONIC DANCES

356 Downes, in *New York Times*, November 27, 1939; J. F. Williamson to R., December 20, 1939 (A); **357** R. to Hirst, December 21, 1939 (copy in A); Mme. R. to the Somovs, January 31, 1940 (Somov); **358** *Providence Sunday Journal*, February 11, 1940; **359** R. to Ormandy, August 21, 1940 (copy in A); R. to Ormandy, August 28, 1940 (copy in A); **360** Fokine to R., September 23, 1940 (A); **361** R. to Glantz, October 8, 1940 (Glantz, copy in A); R. R. Bennett to authors, October 29, 1949 (A); E. Arnold, in *New York World-Telegram*, October 17, 1940; **362** R. McLauchlin, in *Detroit News*, October 15, 1940; V. Spence, in *Havana PM*, January 8, 1941; **363** L. Biancolli, in *New York World-Telegram*, January 8, 1941; **364** Downes, in *New York Times*, January 8, 1941; Ormandy to R; January 10, 1941; **365** K. Pate, in *Corpus Christi Caller-Times*, January 26, 1941; Pollak, *Chicago Daily Times*, March 14, 1941;

366 O'Connell, *The Other Side of the Record* (New York, 1947); **367** Schloss, in *Philadelphia Record*, October 18, 1941; **368** n., *New York Herald-Tribune,* December 7, 1941; "Music Should Speak from the Heart," an interview with David Ewen in *The Etude,* December 1941 (a part of this, approved by R., is in A); **370** Pollak, in *Chicago Daily Times,* November 7, 1941; H. R. Burke, in *St. Louis Daily Globe-Democrat,* December 10, 1941.

XXIII. CALIFORNIA

371 SB; **372** *Musical Courier,* July 1942; R. to Mandrovsky, June 29, 1942 (A); **373** Fatova (PR); SB; **374** R. to Mandrovsky, July 21, 1942 (A); **375** R. to Somov, July 24, 1942 (Somov); **376** R. to Somov, August 17, 1942 (Somov); R. to Mandrovsky, August 23, 1942 (A); R. to Mandrovsky, August 31, 1942 (A); Chernukhin, in *The Musician,* October 1942; **377** C. Gentry, in *Detroit Evening Times,* October 13, 1942; Simon, in *PM,* November 10, 1942; **378** Reisenberg to Satina, October 31, 1949 (Satina); **379** photographs by Eric Schall published in *Life,* April 12, 1943; reprinted in Seroff, *Rachmaninoff* (New York, 1950); R. to Somov, January 21, 1943 (Somov); R. to Somov, January 28, 1943 (Somov); Somova (PR); **380** R. to Rashevsky, February 22, 1943 (A); **381** F. F. Chaliapin (PR); R. to Somov [February 27, 1943] (Somov); **382** Mordovskaya (PR); **383** F. F. Chaliapin (PR); Golitzin, "Illness and Death of S. V. Rachmaninoff," *Russkaya Zhizn* (San Francisco), April 14, 1943; **384** Union of Soviet Composers (Moscow) to R., March 22, 1943 (A).

Appendix 1

Works

An asterisk indicates a composition left in manuscript and/or post-humously published. The composer's sketchbooks, in the Library of Congress, are not fully itemized in this list. There also may be uncatalogued sketchbooks in the other large collection of Rachmaninoff manuscripts in the Rachmaninoff Room, State Central Museum of Musical Culture, Moscow.

SCHOOL YEARS, 1887–1891

*Scherzo for orchestra, F major; dated February 5–21, 1887. First performed November 2, 1945, Moscow, N. Anosov conductor. Score published by Muzgiz, 1947, P. Lamm editor. MS. in State Central Museum of Musical Culture, Moscow (MMC).

*Three Nocturnes for piano; dated (1) November 14–21, 1887; (2) November 22–25, 1887; (3) December 3, 1887–January 12, 1888. Published by Muzgiz, 1949, I. Belza editor. MSS., MMC.

*Four pieces for piano [originally intended for publication, with two songs, as Op. 1]: (1) Romance, F-sharp minor; (2) Prélude, E-flat minor; (3) Melody, E major; (4) Gavotte, D major. Dated, in the writing of Goldenweiser, 1887. Published by Muzgiz, 1948. MSS. MMC.

Piano piece in binary song form (composed for an examination in harmony). Written from memory by the composer for publication (in facsimile) in Riesemann's biography (1934; p. 253); this MS. in possession of Basil Verkholantzeff, Zurich.

*Esmeralda, fragments of an opera based on Victor Hugo's Notre Dame de Paris: piano score of Introduction to Act I, an entr'acte, and portions of Act III, dated October 17, 1888. MSS., MMC.

*Concerto for piano and orchestra. Sketches dated November 1889. MS., MMC.

*Two movements for string quartet: a. Romance, Andante espressivo, G minor; b. Scherzo, Allegro, D major. Dated, in unidentified hand, 1889, and inscribed by the composer to "Sasha." First performed October 1945, Moscow, by the Beethoven Quartet. Published by Muzgiz, 1947. MSS., MMC. [These were arranged for orchestra in 1890 and performed February 24, 1891 at a student concert conducted by Safonov.]

*Deus Meus, motet for mixed chorus in six parts. Composed in spring 1890 as an entrance examination to enter class in the Fugue. First performed February 1891 by the Conservatory chorus, conducted by the composer. MS., Moscow Conservatory.

*"At the Gate of the Holy Abode," dated April 29, 1890; text by Mikhail Lermontov; dedicated to Mikhail Slonov. Published by Muzgiz, 1947, P. Lamm editor. MS., MMC.

*"I'll tell you nothing," dated May 1, 1890; text by Afanasy Fet. Published by Muzgiz, 1947, P. Lamm editor. MS., MMC.

*Romance for cello and piano, dated August 1890, Ivanovka; dedicated to Vera Skalon. Published by Muzgiz, 1948. MS., MMC.

*Manfred, an unfinished (?) symphonic work, mentioned in letters to Natalia Skalon, October 2 and 10, 1890. MS. lost.

*Sketches for a fugal development by Arensky. MSS., MMC.

*Russian Rhapsody, in E minor, for two pianos, dated January 12–14, 1891. First performed November 17, 1891 at a student concert, by the composer and Joseph Lhévinne. Published by Muzgiz, 1948. MS., MMC.

*C'était en avril," dated April 1, 1891; text by E. Pailleron. Published by Muzgiz, 1947, P. Lamm editor. MS., MMC.

*"Dusk has fallen," dated April 22, 1891; text by Alexei Tolstoy. Published by Muzgiz, 1947, P. Lamm editor. MS., MMC. [These two songs were intended for publication as part of the planned Op. 1; see "Four pieces for piano," above.]

Op. 1. First Concerto, for piano and orchestra, F-sharp minor; first movement composed in 1890, completed July 6, 1891, at Ivanovka; dedicated to Alexander Siloti. First performed (first movement only) at a student concert, March 17, 1892, played by the composer, conducted by Safonov. Full score and composer's arrangement for two pianos published by Gutheil. New revised edition, dated November 10, 1917, published by Russian State Music Editions, March 1920.

*Prélude, for piano, F major, dated July 20, 1891, Ivanovka. Published by Muzgiz, 1948. MS., MMC.

*Valse and Romance, for piano trio. Valse dated August 15, 1890; Romance dated September 20, 1891. Dedicated to Natalia, Ludmila, and Vera Skalon. Published by Muzgiz, 1948, P. Lamm editor. MSS., MMC.

*[Youthful Symphony], first movement only, D minor, dated September 28, 1891. Score published by Muzgiz, 1947, P. Lamm editor. MS., MMC.

*_Prince Rostislav_, poem for orchestra, from a ballade by Alexei Tolstoy. Dated December 9-15, 1891, dedicated to Anton Arensky. First performed November 2, 1945, Moscow, N. Anosov conductor. Score published by Muzgiz, 1947, P. Lamm editor. MS., MMC.

*_Boris Godunov_, two fragments based on the play by Pushkin: (1) Arioso by Boris (in three variants); (2) Pimen's Monologue (in two variants). Selected variants published by Muzgiz, 1947, P. Lamm editor. MSS., MMC.

*_Masquerade_, fragment in two variants ("Arbenin's Monologue") for bass and piano; text by Mikhail Lermontov. Second variant published by Muzgiz, 1947, P. Lamm editor. MSS., MMC.

*_Mazeppa_, fragment (vocal quartet), text from the poem, _Poltava_, by Pushkin. MS., MMC.

String quintet, mentioned in the Belayev list.

*"Again you leapt, my heart," text by Grekov. Published by Muzgiz, 1947, P. Lamm editor. MS., MMC.

*"You recall that evening?" text by Alexei Tolstoy. Published by Muzgiz, 1947, P. Lamm editor. MS. lost; published from copy.

*"Grianem-ukhnem," a Russian boatmen's song arranged for voice and piano. Dedicated to Adolf Yaroshevsky. Published by Muzgiz, 1944. MS. in possession of Shishov, Moscow.

  * In 1924 Victor Belayev published a list of Rachmaninoff's works, evidently on the basis of manuscripts found among Rachmaninoff's papers in Moscow. Most of these works are now published.

*Romance, for piano and violin. Published by Leeds, 1951, edited by Louis Persinger, from MS. found in Moscow.

*Piece for cello and piano. Published by Composers Press, 1947, edited by Modeste Altschuler from MS. given him by composer as student.

See also, in 1893, Op. 4, Nos. 1, 2, 3.

1892

Trio élégiaque, for piano, violin, and cello, G minor, dated January 18–21, 1892, Moscow. First performed January 30, 1892, Moscow, by the composer, David Krein, and Anatoli Brandukov. Published (revised by Dobrokhotov) by Muzgiz, 1947. MS., MMC.

Op. 2. Two pieces, for cello and piano: Prélude, F major, and Oriental Dance; dedicated to Anatoli Brandukov. First performed January 30, 1892, Moscow, by Brandukov and the composer. Published by Gutheil.

Aleko, opera in one act, libretto by Vladimir Nemirovich-Danchenko, from the poem *Gypsies,* by Pushkin. Composed in spring 1892 (completed April 13, 1892) for final examination, Moscow Conservatory. First performed April 27, 1893 at the Bolshoi Theater, Moscow, under the direction of Ippolit Altani. Vocal score, arranged for piano by the composer, published by Gutheil, 1892. Full score published by Muzgiz, 1953.

Op. 3. Five pieces, for piano: (1) Elegy, E-flat minor; (2) Prélude, C-sharp minor; (3) Melody, E major; (4) Polichinelle, F-sharp minor; (5) Serenade, B-flat minor. Composed fall 1892; dedicated to Anton Arensky. No. 2 first performed September 26, 1892, Moscow, by the composer; whole opus first performed December 1892, Kharkov. Published by Gutheil, 1893, as "Morceaux de Fantaisie." (No. 2, arranged for two pianos by composer, published by Tair, Paris, and Charles Foley, New York, 1938. No. 3, revised by composer February 26, 1940, published by Charles Foley, 1940. No. 5, revised by composer, published by Charles Foley, 1940. MSS., Library of Congress.)

1893

Op. 4. Six songs.* Published by Gutheil. (1) "Oh, no! I beg you, don't forsake me," for soprano or baritone (February 26, 1892), text by Dmitri

---

* As above, song titles are translations of the original Russian titles, rather than those given the songs by various English adapters; these latter, sometimes more familiar, English variants are here given in brackets.

Merezhkovsky; dedicated to Anna Lodyzhenskaya. (2) "Morning," for contralto or bass (1891), text by M. Yanov; dedicated to Yuri Sakhnovsky. (3) "In the silence of the secret night," for soprano or baritone (October 17, 1890), text by Afanasy Fet; dedicated to Vera Skalon. (4) "Sing not, beauty, in my presence," for soprano or tenor (summer 1893), text by Alexander Pushkin; dedicated to Natalia Satina. (5) "O thou, my field" ["The Harvest of Sorrow"], for soprano or tenor (summer 1893), text by Alexei Tolstoy; dedicated to Ye. Lysikova. (6) "How long, my friend?" for soprano or tenor (summer 1893), text by Arseni Golenishchev-Kutuzov; dedicated to the Countess Olga Golenishcheva-Kutuzova. Nos. 4–6 composed at the Lysikov Estate, Lebedin. Nos. 3 and 4 revised for voice, violin, and piano by the composer (violin obbligato by Fritz Kreisler), published by Fischer, 1922.

*"O Mother of God, perpetually praying," sacred concert for mixed choir, in three parts. Composed summer 1893, in Lebedin. First performed December 12, 1893 by the Synodical Choir, Moscow. MS. formerly in possession of the Synodical School, Moscow; copy in Library of Congress.

Op. 5. Fantasia for two pianos (First Suite): a. Barcarole; b. O night, O love; c. Tears; d. Holy Night. Composed summer 1893, in Lebedin; dedicated to Pyotr Tchaikovsky. First performed November 30, 1893, Moscow, by the composer and Paul Pabst. Published by Gutheil.

Op. 6. Two pieces, for violin and piano: Romance, D minor; Hungarian Dance. Composed summer 1893, in Lebedin; dedicated to Julius Conus. Published by Gutheil.

Op. 7. *The Crag* [*The Rock*], fantasia for orchestra. Composed summer 1893, in Lebedin; dedicated to Nikolai Rimsky-Korsakov. First performed March 20, 1894, Moscow, conducted by Vasili Safonov. Score and composer's arrangement for piano duet published by Jürgenson.

Op. 8. Six songs, from translations by Alexei Pleshcheyev. Composed fall 1893, in Lebedin. Published by Gutheil, 1894. (1) "The Water Lily," for mezzo-soprano, text by Heinrich Heine; dedicated to Adolf Yaroshevsky. (2) "Child, thou art as beautiful as a flower," for mezzo-soprano or baritone, text by Taras Shevchenko; dedicated to Leonid Yakovlev. (4) "My love has brought me sorrow" ["The Soldier's Wife"], for mezzo-soprano, text by Heine; dedicated to Mikhail Slonov. (3) "Meditation," for mezzo-soprano or baritone, text by Taras Shevchenko;

dedicated to Maria Olferyeva. (5) "A Dream," for soprano or tenor, text by Heine; dedicated to Natalia Skalon. (6) "A Prayer," for soprano, text by Goethe; dedicated to Maria Deisha-Sionitzkaya.

Op. 9. *Trio élégiaque,* for piano, violin, and cello, in D minor, dated October 25–December 15, 1893; inscribed "In Memory of a Great Artist" [Pyotr Tchaikovsky]. First performed January 31, 1894, Moscow, by the composer, Julius Conus, and Anatoli Brandukov. First and revised editions published by Gutheil, 1894 and 1907. Final revisions edited by Goldenweiser, published by Muzgiz, 1950.

[The following works can be dated 1893 or earlier:]

*Romance, for piano duet, G major. Published by Muzgiz, 1950. MS., MMC.

*"Song of the Disillusioned," text by Dmitri Rathaus. Published by Muzgiz, 1947, P. Lamm editor. MS., MMC.

*"The flower had faded," text by Dmitri Rathaus. Published by Muzgiz, 1947, P. Lamm editor. MS., MMC.

1894

Op. 10. Seven piano pieces: (1) Nocturne, A minor; (2) Valse, A major; (3) Barcarole, G minor; (4) Melody, E minor; (5) Humoresque, G major; (6) Romance, F minor; (7) Mazurka, D-flat major. Composed December 1893–January 1894; dedicated to Paul Pabst. First performance, January 31, 1894. Published by Gutheil, 1894, as "Morceaux de Salon." (No. 5 revised by composer March 3, 1940, published by Charles Foley, 1940. MS., LC.)

Op. 11. Six piano duets: (1) Barcarole, G minor; (2) Scherzo, D major; (3) Russian song, B minor; (4) Valse, A major; (5) Romance, C minor; (6) "Slava!" (Glory!), C major. Composed April 1894. Published by Gutheil.

Op. 12. Capriccio on Gypsy Themes, for orchestra. Composed summer 1894; dedicated to Pyotr Lodyzhensky. First performed November 22, 1895. Score and composer's arrangement for piano duet published by Gutheil.

*Two episodes à la Liszt: (1) Don Juan; (2) Juan and Haidée; Lambro and Haidée. A work begun in the summer of 1894, left unfinished. MS.

presumably destroyed. There is, however, one extant MS. related to this project:

*Chorus of Spirits, from the poem *Don Juan;* for mixed chorus *a cappella.* MS., MMC.

1895

*Op. 13. First Symphony, D minor: a. Grave, Allegro ma non troppo; b. Allegro animato; c. Larghetto; d. Allegro con fuoco. Composed January–August 1895; dedicated to A.L. [Anna Lodyzhenskaya]. First performed March 15, 1897, St. Petersburg, conducted by Alexander Glazunov. (The composer made a piano arrangement for four hands in 1896, Ivanovka; published by Muzgiz, 1950. MS., MMC.) MS. of orchestral score lost in Moscow, reconstructed by B. Shalman from the orchestra parts in Leningrad Conservatory and from the composer's piano arrangement; published by Muzgiz, 1947.

Op. 15. Six choruses for women's or children's voices, with piano: (1) "Slavsya!" (Be praised!), text by Nikolai Nekrasov; (2) "The Night," text by Vladimir Ladyzhensky; (3) "The Pine Tree," text by Mikhail Lermontov; (4) "The Waves Slumbered" ["Dreaming Waves"], text by K[onstantin] R[omanov]; (5) "Bondage" ["Captivity"], text by N. Tziganov; (6) "The Angel," text by Mikhail Lermontov. First published 1895 in a magazine (probably *Pedagogichesky Listok*); by Jürgenson, 1896.

1896

*Two movements for string quartet: a. G minor; b. C minor. (Golden-weiser suggests 1910–13 for these.) First performed October 1945, Moscow, by the Beethoven Quartet. Published by Muzgiz, 1948, G. Kirkov and B. Dobrokhotov editors. MS., MMC.

Op. 14. Twelve songs. Composed September 1896. Published by Gutheil, 1896. (1) "I wait for thee," for soprano, text by M. Davidova; dedicated to Ludmila Skalon. (2) "The Isle," for soprano or tenor, text by Percy Bysshe Shelley, in translation by Konstantin Balmont; dedicated to Sophia Satina; (3) "For long love has brought little consolation" ["How few the joys"], for contralto or bass, text by Afanasy Fet; dedicated to Zoya Pribitkova; (4) "I came to her," for mezzo-soprano or baritone, text by Alexei Koltzov; dedicated to Yuri Sakhnovsky; (5) "These summer nights" ["Midsummer Nights"], text by Dmitri Rathaus; dedicated to Maria Gutheil; (6) "How everyone loves thee!" for mezzo-soprano or baritone, text by Alexei Tolstoy; dedicated to A. Ivanovsky; (7) "Believe me not, friend!" for soprano or tenor, text by Alexei Tolstoy; dedicated to Anna Klokacheva; (8) "Oh, do not grieve!" for mezzo-soprano or baritone, text by Alexei Apukhtin; dedicated to Nadezhda Alexandrova; (9) "She is lovely as the noon," for mezzo-soprano or baritone, text by Nikolai Minsky; dedicated to Yelizaveta Lavrovskaya; (10) "In my soul" ["Love's flame"], for contralto or bass, text by Nikolai Minsky; dedicated to Yelizaveta Lavrovskaya; (11) "Floods of Spring" ["Spring Waters"], for soprano or tenor, text by Fyodor Tiutchev; dedicated to Anna Ornatz-kaya; (12) " 'Tis time!" for contralto or bass, text by Semyon Nadson.

Op. 16. Six moments musicaux for piano: (1) Andantino, B-flat minor; (2) Allegretto, E-flat minor; (3) Andante cantabile, B minor; (4) Presto, E minor; (5) Adagio sostenuto, D-flat major; (6) Maestoso, C major. Composed October–December 1896; dedicated to Alexander Zatayevich. Published by Jürgenson. (No. 2 revised by composer February 5, 1940 [marked "Allegro"], published by Charles Foley, 1940.)

*Improvisation for piano, in "Four Improvisations," by Arensky, Glazunov, Rachmaninoff, and Taneyev. Themes and variations published in *Sergei Taneyev*, edited by K. Kuznetzov, Moscow, 1925–26.

1897

*Symphony. Discarded sketches dated April 5, 1897. MS., MMC.

1899

*Fantasy-pieces for piano: (1) Morceau de Fantaisie, C minor, dated January 11, 1899; (2) D minor (untitled, undated, possibly an earlier work). Published by Muzgiz, 1950. MSS., MMC.

*Fughetta, for piano, F major, dated February 4, 1899, Moscow. Published by Muzgiz, 1950. MS., MMC.

*Two Russian and Ukrainian songs, arranged for chorus: (1) "At the Gate" (MS. lost.); (2) "Shoes." Published by Muzgiz.

*"Were you hiccuping?" a song-jest, text by P. Viazemsky adapted by the composer. Dated May 17, 1899, sent to Natalia Satina. Published by Muzgiz, 1947, P. Lamm editor. MS., MMC.

1900

Pantelei, the Healer, for mixed chorus *a cappella*, text by Alexei Tolstoy. Composed June–July 1900. First performed by the Synodical Choir, Moscow, in 1901(?). Published by Gutheil(?).

See also Op. 18, Op. 21, No. 1 ("Fate"), and Op. 25 (2nd scene).

1901

Op. 17. Second Suite for two pianos: Introduction, Valse, Romance, Tarantella. Composed December 1900–April 1901; dedicated to Alexander Goldenweiser. First performed November 24, 1901, Moscow, by the composer and Alexander Siloti. Published by Gutheil, October 1901.

Op. 18. Second Concerto for piano and orchestra, C minor. Composed autumn 1900 (2nd and 3rd movements), completed April 21, 1901; dedicated to Dr. Nikolai Dahl. First performed (last two movements only) by the composer, with Alexander Siloti conducting, December 2, 1900, Moscow; completed work first performed by the same artists October 27, 1901, Moscow. Score and composer's arrangement for two pianos published by Gutheil, October 1901.

Op. 19. Sonata for piano and cello, G minor. Composed summer 1901, and dated December 12, 1901; dedicated to Anatoli Brandukov. First performed by the composer and Brandukov, December 2, 1901, Moscow. Published by Gutheil, March 1902.

See also Op. 23, No. 5.

1902

Op. 20. *Spring,* cantata for baritone solo, mixed chorus, and orchestra, text by Nikolai Nekrasov. Composed January–February 1902; dedicated to Nikita Morozov. First performed March 11, 1902, Moscow. Score and composer's piano reduction published by Gutheil, March 1903. MS., MMC.

Op. 21. Twelve songs. Composed April 1902, in Ivanovka (with the exception of No. 1). Published by Gutheil, December 1902. (1) "Fate," for baritone or mezzo-soprano, on the opening notes of Beethoven's Fifth Symphony, text by Alexei Apukhtin. Dated February 18, 1900; dedicated to Fyodor Chaliapin. (2) "By the New Grave," for contralto, text by Semyon Nadson. (3) "Twilight," for soprano or tenor, text by M. Guyot, translated by Korneli Tkhorzhevsky; dedicated to Nadezhda Zabela-Vrubel. (4) "They answered" ["The Answer"], for soprano or tenor, text by Victor Hugo, translated by Lev Mey; dedicated to Yelena Kreutzer. (5) "Lilacs," for soprano, text by Ekaterina Beketova. (6) "Fragment from Musset" ["Loneliness"], for soprano, translated by Apukhtin (from *Nuit de Mai*); dedicated to the Princess Alexandra Lieven. (7) "How nice it is here" ["How fair this spot"], for soprano, text by Glafira Galina. (8) "On the Death of a Linnet," for mezzo-soprano or baritone, text by

Vasili Zhukovsky; dedicated to Olga Trubnikova. (9) "Melody," for soprano or tenor, text by Semyon Nadson; dedicated to Natalia Lanting. (10) "Before the Ikon," for mezzo-soprano, text by Arseni Golenishchev-Kutuzov; dedicated to Maria Ivanova. (11) "No prophet I!" for soprano, text by Alexander Kruglov. (12) "How painful for me" ["Sorrow in Springtime"], for soprano, text by Glafira Galina; dedicated to Vladimir Satin. No. 5 transcribed for piano solo by the composer, 1913, published by Gutheil, March 1919.

1903

Op. 22. Variations for piano on a theme by Chopin [Prélude No. 20, in C minor]. Composed August 1902–February 1903; dedicated to Theodore Leschetizky. First performed February 10, 1903, Moscow, by the composer. Published by Gutheil, February 1904.

Op. 23. Ten préludes for piano: (1) Largo, F-sharp minor; (2) Maestoso, B-flat major; (3) Tempo di menuetto, D minor; (4) Andante cantabile, D major; (5) Alla marcia, G minor; (6) Andante, E-flat major; (7) Allegro, C minor; (8) Allegro vivace, A-flat major; (9) Presto, E-flat minor; (10) Largo, G-flat major. Composed in 1903, except for No. 5, in 1901; dedicated to Alexander Siloti. First performed February 10, 1903, Moscow, by the composer. Published by Gutheil, February 1904.

1903–5

"Night," for voice and piano, text by Dmitri Rathaus. Published by Jürgenson, in *Works by Contemporary Russian Composers*, Vol. 2, 1904.

Op. 24. *The Miserly Knight*, opera in three scenes, from a play by Pushkin. Composition begun August 1903, completed February 28, 1904. (Score dated 1905: Scene 1, May 19; Scene 2, May 30; Scene 3, June 7.) First performed January 11, 1906 at the Bolshoi Theater, Moscow, conducted by the composer. Score and composer's arrangement for voices and piano published by Gutheil, 1905.

Op. 25. *Francesca da Rimini*, opera in two scenes with prologue and epilogue, libretto by Modeste Tchaikovsky, based on an episode in Dante's *Inferno* (Canto V). Composed summer 1904 (piano score dated July 30, 1904), except for the duet of Paolo and Francesca (Scene 2), composed July 1900. Orchestration completed July 22, 1905. First performed, along with *The Miserly Knight*, on January 11, 1906 at the Bolshoi Theater,

Moscow, conducted by the composer. Score and composer's arrangement for voices and piano published by Gutheil, 1905.

1906

Op. 26. Fifteen songs, dedicated to Maria and Arkadi Kerzin. (1) "There are many sounds" ["The Heart's Secret"], for mezzo-soprano (August 14), text by Alexei Tolstoy; (2) "He took all from me" ["All once I gladly owned"], for mezzo-soprano (August 15), text by Fyodor Tiutchev; (3) "Let us rest," for contralto or bass (August 14), text by Anton Chekhov (from Act IV of *Uncle Vanya*); (4) "Two Partings, A Dialogue," for baritone and soprano (August 22), text by Alexei Koltzov; (5) "Let us leave, my dear" ["Beloved, let us fly"], for tenor (August 22), text by Arseni Golenishchev-Kutuzov; (6) "Christ is risen," for mezzo-soprano (August 23), text by Dmitri Merezhkovsky; (7) "To the Children," for mezzo-soprano (September 9), text by A. Khomyakov; (8) "I implore pity!" for tenor (August 25), text by Dmitri Merezhkovsky; (9) "Again I am alone" ["Let me rest here alone"], for tenor (September 4), text by Taras Shevchenko, translated by Ivan Bunin; (10) "Before my window," for soprano (September 17), text by Glafira Galina; (11) "The Fountain," for tenor (September 6), text by Fyodor Tiutchev; (12) "The night is mournful," for tenor (September 3), text by Ivan Bunin; (13) "When yesterday we met," for mezzo-soprano (September 3), text by Yakov Polonsky; (14) "The Ring," for mezzo-soprano (September 10), text by Alexei Koltzov; (15) "All things pass," for bass (September 5), text by Dmitri Rathaus. Entire opus first performed February 12, 1907 at the Kerzin Concerts, Moscow. Published by Gutheil, March 1907. No. 12 arranged by the composer for cello and piano.

"Polka Italienne," for piano duet, based on a theme heard in Italy in 1906. Composed in 1906 or later; dedicated to Sergei Siloti. Published by Charles Foley, 1938. MS., LC. (An arrangement for band, made by the leader of the Imperial Navy Band, was embellished by the composer with fanfares.)

1907

Op. 27. Second Symphony, E minor. a. Largo, Allegro moderato. b. Allegro molto. c. Adagio. d. Allegro vivace. Composed October 1906–April 1907, Dresden; dedicated to Sergei Taneyev. First performed January 26, 1908, St. Petersburg, conducted by the composer. Score and Vladimir Wilshaw's arrangement for piano duet published by Gutheil, August 1908 and April 1910.

Op. 28. First Sonata for piano, D minor. Composed January–February 1907; completed May 14, 1907, Dresden. First performed October 17, 1908, Moscow, by Konstantin Igumnov. Published by Gutheil, June 1908.

*Monna Vanna, an unfinished opera based on the play by Maeterlinck, libretto by Mikhail Slonov. MSS. of Act I in piano score (dated April 15, 1907, Dresden) and fragments of Act II in LC. (See facsimile, page 208.)

1908

"Letter to K. S. Stanislavsky," for voice and piano. Composed October 1908, Dresden. First performed by Fyodor Chaliapin October 14, 1908, at the Moscow Art Theater. Published by Gutheil.

1909

Op. 29. *The Isle of the Dead,* symphonic poem for orchestra, on a painting by Böcklin. Dated April 17, 1909; dedicated to Nikolai Struve. First performed [O.S.] April 18, 1909, Moscow, at a Philharmonic Society Concert, conducted by the composer. Score and Otto Taubmann's arrangement for piano duet published by Gutheil, October 1909 and May 1910.

Op. 30. Third Concerto for piano and orchestra, D minor. Composed summer 1909, Ivanovka; dedicated to Josef Hofmann. First performed November 28, 1909, New York, with the composer and conducted by Walter Damrosch. Score and composer's arrangement for two pianos published by Gutheil, October 1910.

1910

See Op. 34, No. 7 ("It cannot be").

Op. 31. *Liturgy of Saint John Chrysostom* (in twenty numbers) for mixed choir. Completed July 30, 1910, Ivanovka. First performed November 25, 1910, Moscow, by the Synodical Choir, under the direction of Nikolai Danilin. Published by Gutheil.

Op. 32. Thirteen préludes for piano: (1) Allegro vivace, C major (August 30); (2) Allegretto, B-flat minor (September 2); (3) Allegro vivace, E major (September 3); (4) Allegro con brio, E minor (August 28); (5) Moderato, G major (August 23); (6) Allegro appassionato, F minor (August 25); (7) Moderato, F major (August 24); (8) Vivo, A minor

(August 24); (9) Allegro moderato, A major (August 26); (10) Lento, B minor (September 6); (11) Allegretto, B major (August 23); (12) Allegro, G-sharp minor (August 23); (13) Grave, D-flat major (September 10). Published by Gutheil, September 1911.

1911

"Polka V. R.," for piano, based on a theme by Vasili Rachmaninoff. Composed March 11, 1911; dedicated to Leopold Godowsky. Published by Russian Music Editions, June 6, 1911, in *Nouvelle Collection de Musique*.

Op. 33. *Etudes-Tableaux* for piano: (1) Allegro non troppo, F minor (August 11); (2) Allegro, C major (August 16); (3) Non allegro, presto, E-flat minor (August 23); (4) Allegro con fuoco, E-flat major (August 17); (5) Moderato, G minor (August 15); (6) Grave, C-sharp minor (August 13). Published by Gutheil, April 1914.

*[*Etudes* composed for this opus were omitted by the composer before publication: Grave, C minor (numbered 3, dated August 18); Allegro, A minor (numbered 4, dated September 8); Moderato, D minor (numbered 5, dated September 11). Nos. 3 and 5 published by Muzgiz, 1948. MS., MMC.]

See also Op. 39, No. 6.

1912

Op. 34. Fourteen songs. Composed June 1912 (except Nos. 7 and 14). (1) "The Muse," for soprano or tenor (June 6), text by Alexander Pushkin; dedicated to "Re" [Marietta Shaginyan]; (2) "In the soul of each of us" ["The soul's concealment"], for contralto or bass (June 5), text by Apollon Korinfsky; dedicated to Fyodor Chaliapin; (3) "The Storm," for tenor or soprano (June 7), text by Pushkin; dedicated to Leonid Sobinov; (4) "The Migrant Wind," for tenor or soprano (June 9), text by Konstantin Balmont; dedicated to Leonid Sobinov; (5) "Arion," for tenor or soprano (June 8), text by Pushkin; dedicated to Leonid Sobinov; (6) "The Raising of Lazarus," for bass or contralto (June 4), text by A. Khomyakov; dedicated to Fyodor Chaliapin; (7) "It cannot be" ["So dread a fate I'll never believe"], for mezzo-soprano (March 7, 1910, revised June 13, 1912), text by Apollon Maikov; dedicated to the memory of Vera Komissarzhevskaya; (8) "Music," for mezzo-soprano (June 12), text by Yakov Polonsky; dedicated to P. Ch. [Pyotr Tchaikovsky?]; (9)

"You knew him well" ["The Poet"], for baritone or mezzo-soprano (June 12), text by Fyodor Tiutchev; dedicated to Fyodor Chaliapin; (10) "I remember that day" ["The morn of life"], for tenor or soprano (June 10), text by Fyodor Tiutchev; dedicated to Leonid Sobinov; (11) "With holy banner firmly held," for bass or contralto (June 11), text by Afanasy Fet; dedicated to Fyodor Chaliapin; (12) "What happiness" ["What wealth of rapture"], for tenor or soprano (June 19), text by Afanasy Fet; dedicated to Leonid Sobinov; (13) "Dissonance" ["Discord"], for soprano (June 17), text by Yakov Polonsky; dedicated to Felia Litvin; (14) "Vocalise," for soprano or tenor (April 1912, revised September 21, 1915), without text; dedicated to Antonina Nezhdanova. Published by Gutheil, January 1913. No. 14 arranged by the composer for violin, for cello, and for orchestra.

1913

Op. 35. *The Bells,* poem for orchestra, chorus and solo voices; text by Edgar Allan Poe, translated by Konstantin Balmont. Composed January–April 1913 in Rome, completed July 27, 1913 at Ivanovka; dedicated "To my friend Willem Mengelberg and his Concertgebouw Orchestra in Amsterdam." First performed November 30, 1913, St. Petersburg, conducted by the composer. Score and Alexander Goldenweiser's arrangement for piano published by Gutheil. (Partial revision of vocal parts by the composer, 1936.) MS., MMC.

Op. 36. Second Sonata for piano, B-flat minor. Composed January–August 1913, completed September 13, 1913, Ivanovka; dedicated to Matvei Pressman. Published by Gutheil, June 1914. (Revision, summer 1931, published by Tair, November 21, 1931.)

1914

"From the Gospel of St. John," for voice and piano [text: 15:13]. Composed autumn 1914. Published by Jürgenson in a collection *Klich* (Appeal), 1915.

1915

Op. 37. *Night Vigil* [*Vesper Service*], in 15 numbers, for mixed choir. Composed January–February 1915, Moscow; dedicated to the memory of Stepan Smolensky. First performed March 10, 1915, Moscow, by the Synodical Choir, under the direction of Nikolai Danilin. Published by

Russian Music Editions. (An English edition appeared in 1920, as "Songs of the Church.")

The Scythians. Ballet begun with the choreographers Gorsky and Goleizovsky. MS. lost.

1916

Op. 38. Six songs, for soprano, dedicated to Nina Koshetz. (1) "In my garden at night" (September 12), text by Isaakian, translated by Alexander Blok; (2) "To her" (September 12), text by Andrei Belyi; (3) "Daisies," text by Igor Severyanin; (4) "The Rat-Catcher" (September 12), text by Valeri Briusov; (5) "The Dream" (November 2), text by Fyodor Sologub; (6) "A-oo" (September 14), text by Konstantin Balmont. First performed in Moscow, October 24, 1916, by the composer and Mme. Koshetz. Published by Russian Music Editions, 1916. (No. 3 transcribed by the composer for piano solo, published by Tair, 1924. MS., LC.) MSS., Koshetz.

*Two songs, left in sketch: (1) "Prayer," text by K[onstantin] R[omanov]; (2) "All Wish to Sing" ("Glory to God"), text by Fyodor Sologub. MSS., Koshetz.

1917

Op. 39. Nine *études-tableaux* for piano: (1) Allegro agitato, C minor (October 5, 1916); (2) Lento assai, A minor; (3) Allegro molto, F-sharp minor (October 14, 1916); (4) Allegro assai, B minor (September 24, 1916); (5) Appassionato, E-flat minor (February 17, 1917); (6) Allegro, A minor (September 18, 1911, revised September 27, 1916); (7) Lento lugubre, C minor; (8) Allegro moderato, D minor; (9) Allegro moderato, Tempo di marcia, D major (February 2, 1917). Composed autumn 1916 and February 1917; first performed November 29, 1916, Petrograd. Published by Russian Music Editions, October 9, 1920.

"Oriental Sketch," for piano. Dated November 14, 1917, Moscow. First performed November 12, 1931, at the Juilliard School, New York. Published by Charles Foley, 1938. MS., LC.

*An untitled, unpublished piano work, in D minor, dated November 14, 1917. MS., LC. (See facsimile, page 209.)

"Fragments," for piano, dated November 15, 1917, Moscow. Published by Presser, Philadelphia, 1919 (in *The Etude*, October 1919). MS., LC.

1920

*"Luchinushka" ("The Splinter"), a Russian song arranged [for John McCormack] for tenor voice and piano, dated July 3, 1920, Goshen, New York. Copy of MS., LC.

"Apple Tree, O Apple Tree," a Russian song harmonized for a collection by Alfred J. Swan, published as *Songs from Many Lands* (London, Enoch & Sons, 1921). MS. in possession of Alfred Swan, Philadelphia (facsimile in *Musical Quarterly*, January 1944).

*"Along the Street," a sketched arrangement of a Russian song. MS., LC.

1925

*"Quickly, quickly, from my cheeks," a Russian song arranged [for Nadezhda Plevitzkaya] for voice and piano. MS., MMC (gift of Yevgeni Somov); photostat, LC.

1926

Op. 40. Fourth Concerto for piano and orchestra, G minor. Dated January–August 25 [1926], New York-Dresden; dedicated to Nikolai Medtner. First performed March 18, 1927, Philadelphia, played by the composer, and conducted by Leopold Stokowski. Score and composer's arrangement for piano duet published by Tair, 1928. Revised edition (1941) published in score and arrangement (by the composer and Robert Russell Bennett) for two pianos, by Charles Foley, 1944–46. MSS. (including sketches), LC.

Op. 41. Three Russian Songs, for orchestra and chorus: (1) "Over the little river" ("See! a wooden bridge"); (2) "Oh, Vanka, you bold fellow" ("Oh! my Johnny!"), dated November 16, 1926; (3) "Quickly, quickly, from my cheeks." Dedicated to Leopold Stokowski. First performed March 18, 1927, Philadelphia, conducted by Leopold Stokowski. Score and composer's arrangement for piano and voices published by Tair, 1927. MSS., LC.

1931

Op. 42. Variations for piano on a theme by Corelli [Sonata 12, based on the *Folia*]. Completed at "Le Pavillon" June 19, 1931; dedicated to Fritz Kreisler. First performed by the composer in Montreal, Canada, October 12, 1931. Published by Tair. MSS. (including sketches), LC.

1933

*Settings for verses by the composer's granddaughter. MSS., lost.

1934

Op. 43. *Rhapsody on a Theme by Paganini,* for piano and orchestra. Composed July 3–August 18, 1934, Senar. First performed November 7, 1934, Baltimore, by the composer with the Philadelphia Orchestra, conducted by Leopold Stokowski. Score and composer's arrangement for two pianos published by Charles Foley, 1934. MSS. (including sketches), LC.

1936

Op. 44. Third Symphony, A minor: a. Lento, Allegro moderato; b. Adagio ma non troppo; c. Allegro. Dated, a. June 18–August 22, 1935 (corrected May 18–June 1, 1936); b. August 26–September 18, 1935, Senar; c. June 6–30, 1936, Senar. First performed November 6, 1936, Philadelphia, by the Philadelphia Orchestra, conducted by Leopold Stokowski. Score published by Charles Foley. MS., LC.

1940

Op. 45. *Symphonic Dances,* for orchestra: (1) Non allegro; (2) Andante con moto (Tempo di Valse); (3) Lento assai, Allegro vivace. Dated, (1) September 22–October 8, 1940; (2) September 27, 1940; (3) October 29, 1940, New York. I thank Thee, Lord. Dedicated to Eugene Ormandy and the Philadelphia Orchestra. First performed January 3, 1941 by the Philadelphia Orchestra, conducted by Eugene Ormandy, Philadelphia. Score and composer's arrangement for two pianos (dated August 10, 1940, Long Island) published by Charles Foley. MSS., LC.

TRANSCRIPTIONS FOR PIANO SOLO

Bach. Prélude, Gavotte, and Gigue, from the Violin Partita in E major (dated September 9, 1933). Prélude first performed February 20, 1933, Portland, Oregon; Suite first performed November 9, 1933, Harrisburg, Penn. Prélude published by Tair and Charles Foley, 1933; Suite published by Charles Foley, 1941. MSS. (including sketches), LC.

Bizet. Minuetto, from *L'Arlésienne,* Suite No. 1. First performed Tulsa, Okla. January 19, 1922. Published by Charles Foley, 1923. MSS., MMC (September 13, 1903), LC.

Kreisler. *Liebesfreud*. First performed October 29, 1925, Stamford, Conn. Published by Charles Foley, 1926.

  Liebesleid. First performed November 20, 1921, Chicago, Ill. Published by Charles Foley, 1923. MS., LC.

Liszt. *Cadenza for Hungarian Rhapsody No. 2. First performed January 10, 1919, Boston.

Mendelssohn. Scherzo, from *A Midsummer Night's Dream* (dated March 6, 1933). First performed January 23, 1933, San Antonio, Texas. Published by Tair and Charles Foley, 1933. MSS. (including sketches), LC.

Musorgsky. Gopak, from *Fair at Sorochintzi* (dated January 1, 1924). First performed November 13, 1923, Scranton, Penn. Published by Charles Foley, 1924. MS., LC.

Rimsky-Korsakov. Flight of the Bumble Bee, from *The Tale of Tzar Saltan*. Published by Charles Foley, 1931.

Schubert. The Brooklet ("Wohin?" from *Die Schöne Müllerin*). First performed October 29, 1925, Stamford, Conn. Published by Charles Foley, 1926.

Smith. *The Star-Spangled Banner. First performed December 15, 1918, Boston.

Tchaikovsky. Lullaby, Op. 16, No. 1 (dated August 12, 1941). First performed October 14, 1941, Syracuse, New York. Published by Charles Foley, 1941. MS., LC.

TRANSCRIPTIONS FOR PIANO DUET

Glazunov. Symphony No. 6, Op. 58. Published by Belayev, 1897.

Tchaikovsky. *Manfred*. Transcription (1886) unpublished. MS., lost.
  The Sleeping Beauty, score for ballet. Published by Jürgenson, 1892.
  Suite from *The Sleeping Beauty*. Published by Jürgenson, 1892.

TRANSCRIPTION FOR PIANO AND VIOLIN

Musorgsky. Gopak, from *Fair at Sorochintzi*. Published by Tair and Charles Foley, 1926.

Rachmaninoff's Work on Records

Compiled by Philip L. Miller

PERFORMANCES of the composer, whether as pianist or conductor, are regarded as authoritative; works recorded by other artists are listed here only when the composer left no electrical record of his performance. Wherever a recording is available in long-playing form, the LP number is given first. (LCT is the symbol for RCA Victor's "Treasury" series of reissues; M represents the old 78 r.p.m. album sets; DB and DA are the code letters for 12-inch and 10-inch European His Master's Voice issues, 78 r.p.m.) Because of Rachmaninoff's intimate association with the Philadelphia Orchestra, records of that organization are considered more or less "official"; where the choice lies between other organizations or solo artists, listings have been more or less arbitrary. Naturally, high-fidelity reproduction has not been a consideration in compiling this list. In general, arrangements are listed only when, so far as can be ascertained, they are the composer's own.

The list does not take into account the current availability of the recordings. It is reasonably safe to assume, however, that long-playing records are to be had, whereas those playing at 78 r.p.m. will be found only in collectors' shops. The first recordings that Rachmaninoff made were for the Edison company; these could be played only on Edison machines, as that company used the "hill-and-dale" method of recording. Although they have been included in the list because of their historic interest, they have not been on the market for some years. The same is true of the Ampico player rolls listed after the phonograph records.

As this book goes to press the Victor Company announces that it is reissuing, in a long-playing album (LM–6123), Rachmaninoff's performances with the Philadelphia Orchestra under Stokowski and Ormandy of all four piano concertos and the Rhapsody.

KEY TO RECORD LABELS

An	Angel	Parl	Parlophone (78 r.p.m.)
C	Columbia	RS	Rachmaninoff Society
Cap	Capitol	RVW	Rimington Van Wyck
CHS	Concert Hall Society		(78 r.p.m.)
DX	English Columbia (78 r.p.m.)	Sch	Schirmer (78 r.p.m.)
HMV	His Master's Voice (Gramo-	Sup	Supraphone (78 r.p.m.)
	phone Company, European	U	Urania
	affiliate of RCA Victor) (78	USSR	Recording made in the
	r.p.m.)		Soviet Union (78 r.p.m.)
LLP	London (LD for 10–inch)	V	RCA Victor
MG	Mercury	VRS	Vanguard
NRLP	New Records	WL	Westminster

WORKS FOR ORCHESTRA
(including those with solo instrument and with chorus)

Youthful Symphony. State Radio Orchestra; Alexei Kovalev conductor (to be released, through Leeds, in 1956).

Op. 1 *Piano Concerto No. 1, F-sharp minor.* Rachmaninoff and Philadelphia Orchestra; Eugene Ormandy conductor. V LCT 1118; M–865 (18374–76); DB 3706–8. (Recorded 1939)

Op. 7 *The Crag (The Rock),* fantasia for orchestra. Rome Symphony Orchestra; Jacques Rachmilovich conductor. RS 9 (projected).

Op. 13 *Symphony No. 1, D minor.* Dresden Philharmonic Orchestra; Heinz Bongartz conductor. U 7131. Stockholm Radio Orchestra: Jacques Rachmilovich conductor. MG 10111.

Op. 18 *Piano Concerto No. 2, C minor.* Rachmaninoff and Philadelphia Orchestra; Leopold Stokowski conductor. V LCT 1014; M–58 (8148–52); HMV set 84 (DB 1333–37). (Recorded 1929)

Op. 27 *Symphony No. 2, E minor.* Philadelphia Orchestra; Eugene Ormandy conductor. C ML 4433.

Op. 29 *The Isle of the Dead,* symphonic poem. Philadelphia Orchestra; Rachmaninoff conductor. V M–75 (7219–21); DB 2011–13. (Recorded 1929)

Op. 30 *Piano Concerto No. 3, D minor.* Rachmaninoff and Philadelphia Orchestra; Eugene Ormandy conductor. V M–710 (17491–95); DB 5709–13. (Recorded 1939)

Op. 34　No. 14, *Vocalise* (orchestration by the composer). Philadelphia Orchestra; Rachmaninoff conductor. V 7221 (M–75); DB 2013; or V 17440–B (M–712); DB 5784. (Recorded 1929)

Op. 35　*The Bells,* poem for orchestra, chorus, and solo voices. (In English.) Orietta Moscucci, soprano; Charles Anthony, tenor; Lorenzo Malfatti, baritone; Rachmaninoff Society Chorus and Orchestra; Jacques Rachmilovich conductor. RS 8.

Op. 40　*Piano Concerto No. 4, G minor.* Rachmaninoff and Philadelphia Orchestra; Eugene Ormandy conductor. LCT 1019; M–972 (11–8611–14); DB 6284–87.

Op. 41　*Three Russian Songs,* for orchestra and chorus (*Over the Little River; Oh Vanka, you bold fellow; Quickly, quickly, from my cheeks*). Rome Symphony Orchestra and Chorus; Jacques Rachmilovich conductor. RS 9 (to be released in 1956).

Op. 43　*Rhapsody on a Theme by Paganini,* for piano and orchestra. Rachmaninoff and Philadelphia Orchestra; Leopold Stokowski conductor. V LCT 1118; M–250 (16644–46); DB 2426–28. (Recorded 1934)

Op. 44　*Symphony No. 3, A minor.* Philadelphia Orchestra; Rachmaninoff conductor. V M–712 (17436–40); DB 5780–84. (Recorded 1939)

Op. 45　*Symphonic Dances.* Rochester Philharmonic Orchestra; Erich Leinsdorf conductor. C ML 4621.

　　　　　Five Études-Tableaux (orchestration by Respighi). Rome Symphony Orchestra; Jacques Rachmilovich conductor. RS 9 (projected).

OPERAS

Aleko. Nina Pokrovskaya, soprano; Biela Zlatogorova, contralto; Anatole Orfenov, tenor; Ivan Petrov, baritone; Alexander Ognivtzev, basso; Bolshoi Theater Chorus and Orchestra; Nicolai Golovanov conductor. CHS 1309. (There is also a film of *Aleko,* sung by a slightly different cast; produced by Lenfilm in 1953 and distributed abroad.)

　　　　　The moon is high in the sky. Fyodor Chaliapin, basso, with orchestra; Lawrence Collingwood conductor. V 14902; DB 2145. Boris Gmirya, basso. USSR 17418–19.

Romance of the Young Gypsy. Dmitri Smirnoff, tenor, with piano. DB 566 (acoustic recording). Solomon Khromchenko, tenor. Compass 4598/5746.

Op. 24 *The Miserly Knight: Act 2*. Cesare Siepi, basso; Little Orchestra Society; Thomas Scherman conductor. (Sung in English.) C ML 4526.

Op. 25 *Francesca da Rimini: Arioso* from *Act I*. Alexander Pirogov, basso. USSR 20104.

SONGS

The following list is fairly comprehensive, though only the outstanding interpreters of the most popular songs could be included. There are several noteworthy collections: Maria Kurenko, a fine artist and perhaps the most authoritative singer of the songs today, has given us fourteen songs from Op. 21, 26, 34, and 38 (RS 2) and thirteen from Op. 21, 26, and 34 (RS 5), as well as a miscellaneous collection on Cap P 8265. Jennie Tourel offers an LP recital on C ML 4357, and the Soviet artists Nadezhda Oboukhova, Sergei Lemeshev, and Boris Gmirya can be heard in a Rachmaninoff program on VRS 6023. A prewar album made by Nina Koshetz, the work of a great artist past her prime, has not been transferred to LP (Sch 5508–11).

At the Gate of the Holy Abode. Alexander Pirogov, basso. USSR 15631.

I'll tell you nothing. S. Shaposhnikov. USSR 20063.

Masquerade: Arbenin's Monologue. Alexander Pirogov, basso. USSR 15632.

Daydreams swiftly passed. Nadezhda Oboukhova, mezzo-soprano, with piano. VRS 6023.

Grianem-ukhnem, a Russian boatsmen's song (arr. Rachmaninoff). Pyotr Kirichek. USSR 13527.

Op. 4 No. 1, *Oh, no! I beg you, don't forsake me*. Boris Gmirya, basso, with piano. VRS 6023. (In English) Vladimir Rosing, tenor; Ivor Newton, piano, Parl E 11251.

No. 2, *Morning*. Zaria Dolukhanova, contralto. USSR 18581. Alexander Pirogov, basso. USSR 14245/4.

No. 3, *In the silence of the secret night,* Maria Kurenko, soprano; Vsevolod Pastukhoff, piano. Cap P 8265. Jennie Tourel, mezzo-soprano; Erich Itor Kahn, piano. C ML 4357. Nina Koshetz, soprano; Celius Dougherty, piano. Sch 5510. (In English) John McCormack, tenor; Fritz Kreisler, violin; Edwin Schneider, piano. V 3020 (87571); DA 457 (acoustic recording).

No. 4, *Sing not, beauty, in my presence.* Maria Kurenko, soprano; Vsevolod Pastukhoff, piano. Cap P 8265. Jennie Tourel, mezzo-soprano; Erich Itor Kahn, piano. C ML 4357. Vladimir Rosing, tenor; Hans Gellhorn, piano. Parl R 20378. Nina Koshetz, soprano; Celius Dougherty, piano. Sch 5508. Boris Gmirya, basso, with piano. VRS 6023. (In English) John McCormack, tenor; Fritz Kreisler, violin; Edwin Schneider, piano. V 3020 (87574); DA 457 (acoustic recording).

No. 5, *O thou, my field.* Jennie Tourel, mezzo-soprano; Erich Itor Kahn, piano. C ML 4357. Nadezhda Oboukhova, mezzo-soprano, with piano. VRS 6023. Alexander Kipnis, basso; Celius Dougherty, piano. V 11–8595.

No. 6, *How long, my friend?* N. Shpiller, soprano; Semyon Stuchevsky, piano. USSR 11577.

Op. 8 No. 1, *The Water Lily.* Zaria Dolukhanova, contralto; B. Kozel, piano. USSR 20391.

No. 4, *My love has brought me sorrow.* Maria Kurenko, soprano; Vsevolod Pastukhoff, piano. Cap P 8265. Jennie Tourel, mezzo-soprano; Erich Itor Kahn, piano. C ML 4357. Nadezhda Oboukhova, mezzo-soprano, with piano. VRS 6023. Ada Sari, soprano; Otto Schulhof, piano. HMV ER 289; AM 2832.

No. 5, *A Dream.* Sergei Lemeshev, tenor. USSR 16272.

no op. *The flower had faded.* T. Lavrova. USSR 19587.

Op. 14 No. 1, *I wait for thee.* Boris Gmirya, basso. USSR 18497a.

No. 2, *The Isle.* Nina Koshetz, soprano; Celius Dougherty, piano. Sch 5509. Vladimir Rosing, tenor; Hans Gellhorn, piano. Parl R 20378. Sergei Lemeshev, tenor. USSR 21306.

No. 3, *For long love has brought little consolation.* Veronica Borisenko, mezzo-soprano. USSR 16200.

No. 4, *I came to her.* Sergei Lemeshev, tenor, with piano. VRS 6023.

No. 5, *Those summer nights.* Maria Kurenko, soprano; Vsevolod Pastukhoff, piano. Cap P 8265. Zaria Dolukhanova, contralto. USSR 20392.

No. 7, *Believe me not, friend!* V. Victorova, soprano; Alexander Goldenweiser, piano, USSR 13071.

No. 9, *She is lovely as the noon.* Boris Gmirya, basso. USSR 18496.

No. 11, *Floods of Spring.* Jennie Tourel, mezzo-soprano; Erich Itor Kahn, piano. C ML 4357. Sergei Lemeshev, tenor, with piano. VRS 6023. Vladimir Rosing, tenor; Hans Gellhorn, piano. Parl R 20378. Ada Sari, soprano; Otto Schulhof, piano. HMV ER 289; AM 2832.

Op. 21 No. 1, *Fate.* Raphael Arie, basso; Wilfred Perry, piano. LD 9101.

No. 3, *Twilight.* E. Katulskaya, soprano. USSR 15775.

No. 4, *They answered.* Jennie Tourel, mezzo-soprano; Erich Itor Kahn, piano. C ML 4357. Sergei Lemeshev, tenor. USSR 16272. Zaria Dolukhanova, contralto. USSR 18582.

No. 5, *Lilacs.* Maria Kurenko, soprano; Vsevolod Pastukhoff, piano. Cap P 8265. Jennie Tourel, mezzo-soprano; Erich Itor Kahn, piano. C ML 4357. Oda Slobodskaya, soprano; Ivor Newton, piano. RVW 106. Nina Koshetz, soprano; Celius Dougherty, piano. Sch 5510. Sergei Lemeshev, tenor. USSR 17268. Dmitri Smirnoff, tenor; Gerald Moore, piano. DA 752 (acoustic recording).

No. 6, *Fragment from Musset.* Maria Kurenko, soprano; Laurence Rosenthal, piano. RS 5. Nina Koshetz, soprano; Celius Dougherty, piano. Sch 5508.

No. 7, *How nice it is here.* Maria Kurenko, soprano; Laurence Rosenthal, piano. RS 5. Oda Slobodskaya, soprano; Ivor Newton, piano. RVW 106. Nina Koshetz, soprano; Celius Dougherty, piano. Sch 5509. (In English) John McCormack, tenor; Fritz Kreisler, violin; Edwin Schneider, piano. DA 680 (acoustic recording).

No. 8, *On the death of a linnet*. Maria Kurenko, soprano; Vsevolod Pastukhoff, piano. RS 2.

No. 9, *Melody*. Maria Kurenko, soprano; Vsevolod Pastukhoff, piano. RS 2.

No. 12, *How painful for me*. Maria Kurenko, soprano; Vsevolod Pastukhoff, piano. Cap P 8265. Jennie Tourel, mezzo-soprano; Erich Itor Kahn, piano. C ML 4357. Sergei Lemeshev, tenor. USSR 19454.

Op. 26   No. 1, *There are many sounds*. (In English.) Eric Marshall, baritone, with piano. HMV E 455.

No. 2, *He took all from me*. Maria Kurenko, soprano; Laurence Rosenthal, piano. RS 5.

No. 3, *Let us rest*. Maria Kurenko, soprano; Laurence Rosenthal, piano, RS 5.

No 4, *Two Partings, A Dialogue*. Maria Kurenko, soprano; Vadim Gontzoff, baritone; Laurence Rosenthal, piano. RS 5.

No. 5, *Let us leave, my dear*. Georgi Vínogradov, baritone. USSR 12981.

No. 6, *Christ is risen*. Nina Koshetz, soprano; Celius Dougherty, piano. Sch 5511. G. M. Yourenev, baritone, with piano. HMV EK 136.

No. 7, *To the Children*. Nina Koshetz, soprano; Celius Dougherty, piano. Sch 5511. (In English) John McCormack tenor; Edwin Schneider, piano. V 1288; DA 1112.

No. 8, *I implore pity!* Maria Kurenko, soprano; Vsevolod Pastukhoff, piano. RS 2.

No. 9, *Again I am alone*. Maria Kurenko, soprano; Laurence Rosenthal, piano. RS 5.

No. 10, *Before my window*. Maria Kurenko, soprano; Vsevolod Pastukhoff, piano. Cap P 8265. Jennie Tourel, mezzo-soprano;

Erich Itor Kahn, piano. C ML 4357. Dmitri Smirnoff, tenor. DA 476 (acoustic recording). (In English) John McCormack, tenor; Fritz Kreisler, violin; Edwin Schneider, piano. DA 644 (acoustic recording).

No. 11, *The Fountain.* Maria Kurenko, soprano; Laurence Rosenthal, piano. RS 5.

No. 12, *The night is mournful.* Maria Kurenko, soprano; Vsevolod Pastukhoff, piano. RS 2. Alexander Pirogov, basso. USSR 14245/4.

No. 13, *When yesterday we met.* Maria Kurenko, soprano; Laurence Rosenthal, piano. RS 5. Nina Koshetz, soprano; Celius Dougherty, piano. Sch 5510.

No. 14, *The Ring.* Maria Kurenko, soprano; Laurence Rosenthal, piano. RS 5.

No. 15, *All things pass.* Jennie Tourel, mezzo-soprano; Erich Itor Kahn, piano. C ML 4357. Nina Koshetz, soprano; Celius Dougherty, piano. Sch 5508.

Op. 31 *Liturgy of Saint John Chrysostom.*

We sing Thy praise. Don Cossack Choir; Serge Jaroff conductor. C 7360M. (In English) All Saints Choir, Worcester, Massachusetts; William Self conductor. Classic Editions 1022.

Op. 34 No. 1, *The Muse.* Maria Kurenko, soprano; Laurence Rosenthal, piano. RS 5.

No. 4, *The Migrant Wind.* Maria Kurenko, soprano; Laurence Rosenthal, piano. RS 5.

No. 5, *Arion.* Maria Kurenko, soprano; Vsevolod Pastukhoff, piano. RS 2. V. Kilchevsky, tenor. USSR 17700.

No. 8, *Music.* Maria Kurenko, soprano; Vsevolod Pastukhoff, piano. RS 2.

No. 10, *I remember that day.* Maria Kurenko, soprano; Vsevolod Pastukhoff, piano. RS 2.

No. 12, *What happiness.* Maria Kurenko, soprano; Laurence Rosenthal, piano. RS 5.

No. 13, *Dissonance*. Maria Kurenko, soprano; Laurence Rosenthal, piano. RS 5.

No. 14, *Vocalise*. Maria Kurenko, soprano; Vsevolod Pastukhoff, piano. Cap P 8265; RS 2.

Op. 37 *Night Vigil (Vesper Service): Anthems*. Collegium Musicum of Rome; Butkevich conductor. RS 10 (projected).

No. 6, *Mother of God*. Don Cossack Choir; Serge Jaroff conductor. C ML 2163.

No. 7, *Glorification*. Russian Church Choir. V 46151. (In English) Yale Divinity School Choir; James Borden conductor. Overtone LP 2.

No. 10, *Veneration of the Cross*. (In English) Westminster Abbey Choir. HMV B 3763.

Op. 38 No. 1, *In my garden at night*. Maria Kurenko, soprano; Vsevolod Pastukhoff, piano. RS 2.

No. 2, *To her*. Maria Kurenko, soprano; Vsevolod Pastukhoff, piano. RS 2.

No. 3, *Daisies*. Maria Kurenko, soprano; Vsevolod Pastukhoff, piano. RS 2. Nina Koshetz, soprano; Celius Dougherty, piano. Sch 5510.

No. 4, *The Rat-Catcher*. Maria Kurenko, soprano; Vsevolod Pastukhoff, piano. RS 2. Sergei Lemeshev, tenor; with piano. VRS 6023.

No. 5, *The Dream*. Maria Kurenko, soprano; Vsevolod Pastukhoff, piano. RS 2. Sergei Lemeshev, tenor. USSR 16272.

no op. *Quickly, quickly, from my cheeks* (arr. Rachmaninoff). Nadezhda Plevitzkaya, mezzo-soprano; Rachmaninoff, piano. RS 6 (recorded February 22, 1926).

PIANO AND CHAMBER MUSIC

The most important of the recorded collections is the composer's own program, Victor LCT 1136, comprising fourteen of his pieces, along with works of Mendelssohn, Chopin, and Schubert-Liszt and Rachmaninoff's transcription of Kreisler's *Liebesfreud*. Most of the original works formerly appeared in album M–722, but the *Étude*, Op. 33, No. 2, included in that set is omitted from the LP. The twenty-four *Préludes* are available on two disks performed by Moura Lympany (LLP 328–29), and Nadia Reisenberg has made a Rachmaninoff program (WL 5344).

> *String quartet: Romance and Scherzo*. Beethoven Quartet. USSR 16230/1, 16314/5. Guilet Quartet. MGM E/3133.
>
> *Russian Rhapsody, for two pianos*. Adolf and Mikhail Gottlieb (to be released, through Leeds, in 1956). Menahem Pressler and William Masselos (to be released by MGM in 1956).
>
> *Trio élégiaque, G minor*. Alexander Goldenweiser, piano; Dmitri Tziganov, violin; Sergei Shirinsky, cello. USSR 15960–63.

Op. 2　No. 2, *Oriental Dance*. Mstislav Rostropovich, cello; Alexander Dedyukhin, piano. USSR 021124/5. Edmund Kurtz, cello; Emanuel Bay, piano. V 11–9024; DB 21068.

Op. 3　*Five pieces for piano*. Nadia Reisenberg, piano. WL 5344.

> No. 1, *Elegy, E-flat minor*. Anatole Kitain, piano. C 69272D; DX 853.
>
> No. 2, *Prélude, C-sharp minor*. Rachmaninoff, piano. LCT 1000; LCT 1136; V 1326; DA 996 (1928); or V 814 (66016) (acoustic recording, 1921); or Edison 82187.
>
> No. 3, *Mélodie, E major*. Rachmaninoff, piano. LCT 1136; 2123 (M–722); DA 1787 (1940).
>
> No. 4, *Polichinelle, F-sharp minor*. Rachmaninoff, piano. V 6452 (74807) (acoustic recording, 1923). Leff Pouishnoff, piano. C 5078M (9368).
>
> No. 5, *Serenade, B-flat minor*. Rachmaninoff, piano. V 1762; DA 1522 (1936); also V 816 (66129) (acoustic recording, 1923).

Op. 5　*Fantasia (First Suite for two pianos)*. Vitya Vronsky and Victor Babin, piano duo. C ML 4379. Alexander Goldenweiser and Gregori Ginzburg, piano duo (to be released, through Leeds, in 1956).

Op. 6 *Romance, for violin and piano*. David Oistrakh, violin. USSR 17367.

Op. 9 *Trio élégiaque, D minor, for piano, violin, and cello*. Compinsky Trio. Alco 1008.

Op. 10 *Seven piano pieces*. Nadia Reisenberg, piano. WL 5344.

No. 1, *Nocturne, A minor*. Alexander Goldenweiser, piano. USSR 015655.

No. 2, *Valse, A major*. Nina Yemelyanova, piano. USSR 16015.

No. 3, *Barcarole, G minor*. Rachmaninoff, piano. Edison 82202 (acoustic recording). Madeleine de Valmalète, piano. Polydor 95175.

No. 5, *Humoresque, G major*. Rachmaninoff, piano. LCT 1136; 2123 (M–722); DA 1771 (1940).

Op. 16 No. 2, *Moment musical, E-flat minor*. Rachmaninoff, piano. LCT 1136; 2124 (M–722); DA 1771 (1940).

No. 3, *Moment musical, B minor*. V. Sofronitsky, piano. USSR 15000.

No. 4, *Moment musical, E minor*. Benno Moiseiwitsch, piano. HMV C 3370.

Op. 17 *Second Suite for two pianos*. Vitya Vronsky and Victor Babin, piano duo. C ML 54379.

Op. 19 *Sonata, cello and piano, G minor*. Edmund Kurtz, cello; William Kapell, piano. V LM 1074. Joseph Schuster, cello; Leonard Pennario, piano. Cap P 8248. Sviatoslav Knushevitsky, cello; Alexander Goldenweiser, piano. USSR 015646–54.

Op. 21 No. 5, *Lilacs* (transcribed by the composer). Rachmaninoff, piano. V 1051 (64906) (acoustic recording, 1920). (There is also an unreleased master, PCS 072132–1; recorded Hollywood, February 26, 1942.)

Op. 22 *Variations on a Theme by Chopin*. Robert Goldsand, piano. CHS 1149. Bernhard Weiser, piano. RS 4.

Op. 23 *Ten Préludes for piano.* Moura Lympany, piano. LLP 328–29.

No. 1, *F-sharp minor.* Yakov Zak, piano. Ultraphon H 23969.

No. 2, *B-flat major.* Pavel Serebriakov, piano. USSR 16398.

No. 4, *D major.* Constance Keene, piano. MG 10113.

No. 5, *G minor.* Rachmaninoff, piano. V 6261 (74628); DB 410 (acoustic recording, 1920). Josef Hofmann, piano. C ML 4929.

No. 6, *E-flat major.* Eileen Joyce, piano. DL 9528; Parl E 11351. Constance Keene, piano. MG 10113.

No. 7, *C minor.* Eileen Joyce, piano. DL 9528; Parl E 11351.

No. 8, *A-flat major.* Eileen Joyce, piano. Parl E 11377.

No. 9, *E-flat minor.* Constance Keene, piano. MG 10113.

No. 10, *G-flat major.* Rachmaninoff, piano. V LCT 1136; 2124 (M–722); DA 1772 (1940).

Op. 28 *Sonata No. 1, for piano, D minor.* Warren Perry Thew, piano. RS 6.

Op. 32 *Thirteen Préludes for piano.* Moura Lympany, piano. LLP 328–29.

No. 3, *E major.* Rachmaninoff, piano. LCT 1136; 2125 (M–722); DA 1772 (1940).

No. 5, *G major.* Rachmaninoff, piano. V 6261 (74645); DB 410 (acoustic recording, 1920). Geza Anda, piano. An 35093.

No. 6, *F minor.* Rachmaninoff, piano. LCT 1136; 2125 (M–722); DA 1787 (1940).

No. 7, *F major.* Rachmaninoff, piano. LCT 1136; 2125 (M–722); DA 1787 (1940).

No. 8, *A minor.* Eileen Joyce, piano. Parl E 11377. Tatiana Nikolayeva, piano. USSR 15804/5.

No. 10, *B minor.* Benno Moiseiwitsch, piano. V 18295; HMV C 3209.

No. 12, *G-sharp minor.* Rachmaninoff, piano. V 812 (64693); DA 368 (acoustic recording, 1921). Lev Oborin, piano (to be released, through Leeds, in 1956).

No. 13, *D-flat major.* Eileen Joyce, piano. Parl E 11377.

no op. *Polka V. R.* Rachmaninoff, piano. LCT 1136; 6857; DB 1279 (1928). V 6260 (74728) (acoustic recording, 1922); Edison 82187. Nadia Reisenberg, piano. WL 5344.

Op. 33 *Eight Études-Tableaux.* Bernhard Weiser, piano. RS 1.

No. 1, *F minor.* Anatole Kitain, piano. C 69569D; DX 905.

No. 2, *C major.* Rachmaninoff, piano. LCT 1136; 2126 (M–722); DA 1788 (1940).

No. 4, E-flat major. Lev Oborin, piano (to be released, through Leeds, in 1956).

No. 7, *E-flat major.* Rachmaninoff, piano. LCT 1136; 2126 (M–722); DA 1788 (1940).

No. 8, *G minor.* Rachmaninoff, piano. (Unreleased master B–24652–1, Camden, October 21, 1920) (acoustic recording). Lev Oborin, piano (to be released, through Leeds, in 1956).

Op. 36 *Sonata No. 2, for piano, B-flat minor.* Bernhard Weiser, piano. RS 1.

Op. 38 No. 3, *Daisies* (transcribed by the composer). Rachmaninoff, piano. LCT 1136; 2127 (M–722).

Op. 39 *Nine Études-Tableaux.* Warren Perry Thew, piano. RS 3.

No. 1, *C minor.* Emil Gilels, piano. Sup 40045; USSR 10607.

No. 6, *A minor.* Rachmaninoff, piano. LCT 1136; LCT 1000; 1184; DA 4437; DA 827 (1925).

no op. *Oriental Sketch.* Rachmaninoff, piano. LCT 1136; 2127 (M–722) (1940).

Op. 42 *Variations on a Theme by Corelli.* Bernardo Segall, piano. NRLP 404. Bernhard Weiser, piano. RS 4.

PIANO TRANSCRIPTIONS BY RACHMANINOFF

Bach: *Violin partita No. 3, E major—Prélude, Gavotte; Gigue.* Rachmaninoff, piano. V 11–8607 (1942).

Bizet: *L'Arlésienne—Minuet.* Rachmaninoff, piano. V 816 (66085) (acoustic recording, 1922).

Kreisler: *Liebesfreud.* Rachmaninoff, piano. LCT 1136; V 11–8728 (1946); or 1142; DA 786 (1926).

Kreisler: *Liebesleid.* Rachmaninoff, piano. V 6259 (74723) (acoustic recording, 1920).

Mendelssohn: *A Midsummer Night's Dream—Scherzo.* Rachmaninoff, piano. DB 3146 (1935).

Musorgsky: *Fair at Sorochintzi—Gopak.* Rachmaninoff, piano. V 1161 (1925).

Rimsky-Korsakov: *The Tale of Tzar Saltan—Flight of the Bumble Bee.* Rachmaninoff, piano. (Unreleased masters BVE 51805–1, 51805–2, 51805–3, 51805–4, 51805–5, Camden, April 16, 1929.)

Schubert: *The Brooklet (Wohin?).* Rachmaninoff, piano. V 1196 (1925).

Tchaikovsky: *Lullaby, Op. 16, No. 1.* Rachmaninoff, piano (Unreleased master PCS c72131–1; recorded Hollywood, February 26, 1942).

OTHER COMPOSERS' WORKS RECORDED BY RACHMANINOFF

Bach: *Sarabande.* V 6621; DB 1016 (1927)

Beethoven: *Sonata, Op. 10, No. 2—Presto.* (Unreleased masters B–23961–1, Camden, April 26, 1920; B–23961–4, Camden, May 4, 1920; B–23961–5, Camden, May 17, 1920, acoustic recording)

Sonata, Op. 30, No. 3, for violin and piano, G major (with Fritz Kreisler). V 8163–4; DB 1463–4 (1929).

The Ruins of Athens—Turkish March (arr. Anton Rubinstein). V 1196 (1926).

32 Variations, C minor. V 6544 (1925).

Borodin: *Scherzo, A-flat major.* V 1762; DA 1522 (1936).

Chopin: *Ballade, Op. 47, A-flat major.* (Unreleased masters CVE 32510–1, 32510–2, 32511–1, 32511–2, Camden, April 13, 1925).

Études—Op. 10, No. 5, G-flat ("Black Keys"); Op. 25, No. 9, G-flat ("Butterfly"). (Unreleased master B–23964–1, Camden, May 3, 1920, acoustic recording).

Études—F minor; F major (unspecified). (Unreleased masters B–24116–1, 24116–2, Camden, May 17, 1920, acoustic recording).

Mazurka, Op. 63, No. 3, C-sharp minor. V 1008 (66248) (acoustic recording, 1924).

Mazurka, Op. posth., A minor. (Unreleased master BS 98395–1, New York, December 23, 1925.)

Nocturne, Op. 9, No. 2, E-flat major. LCT 1136; V 6731 (1927).

Nocturne, Op. 15, No. 1, F major. An unidentified recording.

Nocturne, Op. 15, No. 2, C-sharp minor. V 6452 (74885) (acoustic recording, 1924).

Polish Songs (arr. Liszt): *No. 1, The Maiden's Wish; No. 6, The Return Home.* V 11–8593 (1942).

Prélude, Op. 28, No. 19, E-flat major. (Unreleased masters B–29223–1, 29223–2, Camden, December 27, 1923) (acoustic recording).

Scherzo, Op. 39, C-sharp minor. (Unreleased masters C–29671–1, 29671–2; C–29678–1, 29678–2, Camden, March 18, 1924) (acoustic recording).

Sonata No. 2, B-flat minor, Op. 35. V M–95; HMV album 151 (recorded February 18, 1930, Camden).

Valse, Op. 18, E-flat major. V 6259 (acoustic recording, 1921).

Valse, Op. 34, No. 3, F major. (Unreleased masters B–24639–1, Camden, October 20, 1920; B–24639–2, Camden, October 21, 1920; B–24639–5, Camden, November 20, 1922) (acoustic recording).

Valse, Op. 42, A-flat major. Edison 82197–LO.

Valse, Op. 64, No. 1, D-flat major. V 815 (64971) (acoustic recording, 1921).

Valse, Op. 64, No. 2, C-sharp minor. V 1245 (1927).

Valse, Op. 64, No. 3, A-flat major. V 1245 (1927). Edison 82202.

Valse, Op. 69, No. 2, B minor. V 972 (66202) (acoustic recording, 1923).

Valse, Op. 70, No. 1, G-flat major. V 6607 (1927).

Valse, Op. 70, No. 2, F minor. (Unreleased master BVE–59415, recorded February 18, 1930, Camden).

Valse, Posthumous, E minor. DA 1189.

Daquin: *Le Coucou.* V 812 (64919) (acoustic recording, 1920).

Debussy: *The Children's Corner—No. 1, Doctor Gradus ad Parnassum; No. 6, Golliwog's Cake Walk.* V 813 (64935, 64980) (acoustic recording, 1921).

The Children's Corner—No. 3, Serenade for the Doll. (Unreleased master B–24902–1, New York, January 21, 1921) (acoustic recording).

Dohnányi: *Étude-Caprice, Op. 28, F minor.* V 943 (66059) (acoustic recording, 1922).

Gluck: *Mélodie* (arr. Sgambati). V 1125; DA 719 (1925).

Grieg: *Lyric Pieces, Book 1, Op. 12—No. 2, Valse; No. 3, Elfin Dance.* V 815 (66105) (acoustic recording, 1922).

Sonata, Op. 45, for piano and violin, C minor (with Fritz Kreisler). LCT 1128; M–45; DB 1259–61 (1928).

Handel: *Harpsichord suite No. 5—Air and Variations ("The Harmonious Blacksmith").* DB 3146 (1936).

Henselt: *Étude, Op. 2, No. 6, F-sharp minor ("Were I a bird").* V 1008 (66249) (acoustic recording, 1924).

Liszt: *Au bord d'une source.* (Unreleased master B–24649–1, Camden, October 21, 1920) (acoustic recording).

La Campanella (Paganini-Liszt). (Unreleased master C–23986–1, Camden, May 3, 1920) (acoustic recording).

Gnomenreigen (Concert Étude No. 2). V 1184; DA 827 (1926).

Hungarian Rhapsody No. 2, C-sharp minor (with cadenza by Rachmaninoff). Edison 82169–70.

Liebestraum. (Unreleased masters C–29670–1, 29670–2, 29670–3, Camden, March 18, 1924) (acoustic recording).

Polonaise No. 2, E major. V 6504 (1925).

Spanish Rhapsody. (Unreleased masters B–29224–1, 29224–2, 29224–3, Camden, December 27, 1923; B–29224–4, 29224–5, 29224–6, Camden, March 18, 1924) (acoustic recording).

Mendelssohn: *Études, Op. 104—No. 2, F major; No. 3, A minor.* V 1266 (1927).

Rondo capriccio. (Unreleased masters B–24117–1, 24117–2, Camden, May 17, 1920) (acoustic recording).

Song without words—No. 34, Spinning Song. LCT 1136; V 1326 (64921); DA 996 (1938).

Song without words (unspecified). (Unreleased master B–24636–1, Camden, October 20, 1920) (acoustic recording).

Moszkowski: *La Jongleuse, Op. 52, No. 4.* V. 943 (66154) (acoustic recording, 1923).

Mozart: *Sonata No. 11, A major, K.331—Theme and Variations.* Edison 82197. *Rondo alla Turca.* V 1124; DA 719 (1925).

Variations (unspecified). (Unreleased master PCS 072124–1, Hollywood, February 25, 1942.)

Paderewski: *Minuet, Op. 14, No. 1, G major.* V 6731 (1927).

Scarlatti: *Pastorale (Sonata, L.413, D minor)* (arr. Tausig). Edison 82170.

Schubert: *Duo for piano and violin, Op. 162, A major* (with Fritz Kreisler). LCT 1128; M–107; DB 1465–67 (December 21, 1928).

Impromptu, Op. 90, No. 4, A-flat major. V 6621; DB 1016 (1927).

Moment musical. An unidentified recording.

Ständchen (Serenade) (arr. Liszt). LCT 1136; 11–8728 (1945).

Das Wandern (Wandering) (arr. Liszt). V 1161 (1926).

Schumann: *Carñaval, Op. 9.* LCT 12; V M–70; DB 1413–15.

Der Contrabandiste (The Smuggler) (arr. Tausig). V 11–8593 (1942).

Novelette in F-sharp minor. (Unreleased masters PCS 072125–1, 072126–1, Hollywood, February 25, 1942.)

Scriabin: *Prélude, Op. 12.* (Unreleased masters BVE 51806–1, 51806–2, Camden, April 16, 1929.)

Strauss, J.: *Blue Danube Waltz.* (Unreleased masters C–27732–1, 27732–2), Camden, April 5, 1923) (acoustic recording).

Man lebt nur einmal (One Lives but Once) (arr. Tausig). V 6636; DB 1140 (1927).

Tchaikovsky: *The Months, Op. 37—No. 11, Troika (November).* V 6857; DB 1279 (1928); also 6260 (74630) (acoustic recording, 1920).

Humoresque, Op. 10, No. 2. V 1051 (acoustic recording, 1924).

Valse, Op. 40, No. 8, A-flat major. V 972 (66138) (acoustic recording, 1923).

Weber: *Momento Capriccio in B-flat, Op. 12.* (Unreleased masters C–24637–1, B–24637–1, Camden, October 20, 1920; B–24637–2, Camden, October 21, 1920) (acoustic recording).

AMPICO PLAYER ROLLS BY RACHMANINOFF

Bizet: **L'Arlésienne—Minuet* (arr. Rachmaninoff). 61601 H.

Chopin: *Valse, Op. 18, E-flat major.* 59743 H.

Valse, Op. 34, No. 3, F major. 63311 H.

Polish Song No. 1, The Maiden's Wish (arr. Liszt). 62803 H.

Henselt: *Étude, Op. 2, No. 6 ("Were I a bird").* 62803 H.

Kreisler: *Liebesleid No. 2 ("Alt Wiener Tanzweisen")* (arr. Rachmaninoff). 62103 H.

Mendelssohn: *Songs without words, No. 34 ("Spinning Song").* 59661 H.

Musorgsky: *Fair at Sorochintzi—Gopak* (arr. Rachmaninoff). 60641 H.

The Star-Spangled Banner (arr. Rachmaninoff). 57282 F.

Tchaikovsky: *The Months, Op. 37–No. 11, Troika (November)*. 57914 H.

Valse, Op. 40, No. 8, A-flat major. 62531 H.

Rachmaninoff: **Op. 3, No. 2, Prélude, C-sharp minor*. 57504 H.

*Op. 3, No. 3, Mélodie, E major. 57545 H.

*Op. 3, No. 4, Polichinelle, F-sharp minor. 57905 H.

Op. 3, No. 5, Serenade, B-flat minor. 62441 H.

*Op. 10, No. 3, Barcarole, G minor. 57504 H.

Op. 10, No. 5, Humoresque, G major. 57965 H.

Op. 21, No. 5, Lilacs (transcribed by the composer). 61761 H.

*Op. 23, No. 5, Prélude, G minor. 57525 H.

*Polka V. R. 57275 H.

Op. 39, No. 6, Étude-Tableau, A minor. 60891 H.

Unauthorized "Rachmaninoff recordings" have recently appeared on the market. These are actually disks made abroad from the above-listed player piano rolls. The long-playing record issued by Allegro-Royale includes the titles starred on the list and also the following, which we have not found listed in the Ampico catalogues:

Chopin: *Nocturne*
Valse No. 8
Scherzo, Op. 31

Rachmaninoff: *Élégie, Op. 3, No. 1*

Index